THE EPISCOPAL CHURCH
IN TEXAS,
1838-1874

THE EPISCOPAL CHURCH
IN TEXAS,
1838-1874

*From Its Foundation to the Division
of the Diocese*

★

LAWRENCE L. BROWN

★

THE CHURCH HISTORICAL SOCIETY
AUSTIN : TEXAS : 1963

Library of Congress Catalogue Card Number 63-19457

Printed in the United States of America
By Von Boeckmann-Jones, Austin, Texas

ACKNOWLEDGMENTS

The encouragement to write this book I owe to the Right Reverend John E. Hines, Bishop of Texas. His desire for such a work to be written has been followed by his full cooperation and support. I owe a great debt of gratitude to two former clergy-historians of this Diocese, both gone to their reward, the Reverend George F. Crocket, whose painstaking care for the records of the Diocese during the many years he served as Registrar account for the plenitude and good order of the material, and the Reverend DuBose Murphy, through whose kindness I have made full use of his work in *A Short History of the Episcopal Church in Texas* (Dallas, 1935). I am further indebted to Mr. Herbert Fletcher and the Anson Jones Press for permission to quote and reproduce pictures from the late William M. Morgan's *Trinity Protestant Episcopal Church, Galveston* (Houston, 1954). For information about the University of the South I gratefully acknowledge my dependence upon Arthur Benjamin Chitty's *Reconstruction at Sewanee* (Sewanee, Tenn., 1954).

For long and tedious hours spent in typing or proofreading I owe much thanks to my wife, to Mrs. Sherman Kennedy, Mrs. Royal Embree and Mrs. R. G. Cunningham of the Seminary Staff, to my Colleagues, the Very Reverend Gray M. Blandy and the Reverend William A. Clebsch, to Mrs. Julian Wright of the Church Historical Society, and to Mrs. Bretch Taulbee.

LAWRENCE L. BROWN

Episcopal Theological Seminary
of the Southwest, Austin,
September, 1963.

CONTENTS

LIST OF ILLUSTRATIONS

PART ONE

THE PRE-DIOCESAN DECADE

I. Prelude to the Mission

THE YEAR 1835 was a decisive one, both for Texas and for the missionary activity of the Protestant Episcopal Church. In that year the predominantly Anglo-American citizens of Texas despaired of receiving justice from the Dictator Santa Anna and revolted. It was generally understood in the United States that either their struggle would fail and they would be expelled, or it would establish the independence of Texas. This opinion prevailed despite the fact that the revolt was raised in defense of the Constitution of 1824 and not, at first, for independence. Protestant worship had been technically illegal in Texas, although in practice it was usually tolerated. The Episcopal Church had never sent a mission to a land where the Roman Catholic Church was established by law, as had been the case so long as Texas was a part of Mexico.

In the same year, 1835, the General Convention of the Episcopal Church took two decisive steps toward meeting more adequately its missionary responsibilities at home and abroad. It amended the constitution of its missionary society, and it passed a canon providing for the election by General Convention of Missionary Bishops to exercise episcopal functions in states and territories or in foreign lands where the Protestant Episcopal Church was not organized.

The Domestic and Foreign Missionary Society of the Protestant Episcopal Church had been organized in 1820 as a voluntary society consisting of annual and life contributors and patrons. The second article of its new constitution declared that every member of the Church was by that fact also a member of the Society. The third article provided that the Board of Missions, by which the Society's work was to be directed, should consist of all the Bishops of the Church, thirty members elected by each General Convention, and the patrons who had contributed before 1829. Thus the direction of the Society was placed in the hands of General Convention as the official governing body of the Church, and the Society became the organ that prosecuted the Church's missionary work. This action made it possible for the Society to support Missionary Bishops elected by General Convention. Thus the Convention of 1835 provided for episcopal ministrations to members of the Church in states and territories in which there were too few clergy and congregations to constitute a diocese and to elect a diocesan bishop. The Church could now send out bishops to build dioceses by ministering to feeble congregations, by founding new parishes, and by directing missionaries sent out by the Society.[1]

By this new canonical authority the House of Bishops nominated and the House of Deputies elected two Missionary Bishops: the Reverend Jackson Kemper, D.D., to work in Missouri and Indiana, and the Reverend Francis L. Hawks, D.D., to work in the State of Louisiana and the Territories of Arkansas and Florida. Kemper

---

[1] *Journal of the Proceedings of the General Convention of the Protestant Episcopal Church in the United States of America Held in the City of Philadelphia,* August 19 to September 1, 1835, pp. 19, 20, 56, 58, 62, 65, 68, 79, 81, 82, 99, 107, 109, 110. The Journals of the General Conventions will hereafter be cited as *General Convention Journal* (with year given).

It is interesting that the Reverend Caleb S. Ives, future missionary to Matagorda, Texas, was the lone Clerical Deputy for Alabama at the 1835 General Convention. He served as chairman of the special committee in the House of Deputies appointed to consider the proposal to allow General Convention to elect Missionary Bishops for areas in which the Church was not organized. On the committee with him were the Reverend Leonidas Polk of Tennessee, who four years thereafter would be the first bishop of the Episcopal communion to visit Texas, and the Reverend Nicholas Hamner Cobbs of Virginia, who would one day be nominated Foreign Missionary Bishop to the Republic of Texas, but would fail of election and become the first Bishop of Alabama.

Ives presented a strong report giving the unanimous endorsement of the committee to the proposal. Polk warmly supported the measure upon debate. The canon proposed had two sections, one providing for Domestic, and the other for Foreign, Missionary Bishops, and specifying the manner of election still used, i.e., nomination by the House of Bishops, who specify the area in which jurisdiction will be exercised, and election by the House of Deputies.

We cannot think that the provision for Missionary Bishops for foreign lands was framed with Texas in mind, for the canon, as the committee introduced it, specified "foreign heathen lands." It was amended on the floor on the motion of the Reverend Dr. James Milnor. *General Convention Journal,* 1835, pp. 6, 20, 56, 65-7, 72-3; *Episcopal Recorder* (Philadelphia [published weekly every Saturday during the Convention]).

accepted his election and was consecrated on September 25, 1835. To the House of Deputies Hawks stated that he was willing to accept election should he be satisfied that his family would be properly supported.[2] Probably on the expectation that Hawks would be working as a bishop in the Southwest, the new Foreign Committee of the board of Missions, meeting on September 9, approved a motion introduced by the Right Reverend George Washington Doane of New Jersey:

> Resolved: That the Committee establish a Mission Station at Texas.[3]

On September 23 a resolution was introduced proposing that the Reverend Richard S. Salmon be appointed missionary to Texas; the substitute introduced by the Reverend Henry W. Ducachet, M.D., was adopted, declaring that Salmon's "intimate and direct connection with a land company" made his appointment inappropriate. The Committee nevertheless resolved that:

> it would be happy to be notified of his [Salmon's] arrival and settlement in Texas, with a view to such measures as it may then be thought fit to adopt.[4]

Salmon was interested in a land company holding a grant for a colony in Texas, and he had recruited a Church colony to take to Texas with him. This man, born in Connecticut in 1797, a Master of Arts from Hobart College and a student of the General Seminary, was ordained Deacon in 1823 and Priest in 1826 by the Right Reverend John Henry Hobart. He had served as a missionary in upstate New York for some years when be became consumed by the desire to go to Texas. While he was missionary at Geddes, New York, he secured an interest in a land grant in the Austin Colony and conceived the idea of forming a group of Episcopalians into a colony of his own. He appeared before the General Convention of 1835 in Philadelphia seeking support. In spite of his failure to receive appointment as a missionary of the Society, Salmon set out for Texas in 1836 with fifteen families. The party arrived in New Orleans after the fall of the Alamo and before the battle of San Jacinto. The Texas Revolution appeared to be collapsing. Unable to proceed, and vexed by the expense incurred by his people while they waited to get into Texas, Salmon at his own expense equipped some volunteers

[2]*General Convention Journal,* 1835, pp. 82, 111, 171.
[3]"Minutes of the Foreign Committee," II, 11. These manuscript minute books are in the Archives of General Convention, Church Historical Society, Austin, Texas.
[4]*Ibid.,* pp. 12, 48, 57, 129, 139.

for the Texas forces and sent them forward. On the news of the victory of San Jacinto, the party arranged to journey to their new homes. Arriving in October, Salmon found his land grant to be worthless.

Salmon was not, however, the first priest of our Church to reach Texas. The Reverend John Wurts Cloud of Brazoria, who then was listed among the clergy of the Diocese of Mississippi, had been in Texas since about 1831. Cloud had conducted a school at Brazoria for a time, but was a planter. If he exercised his ministry publicly in Texas, he left no record of it. He was followed to Texas by his father, Adam Cloud, a superannuated clergyman of Mississippi.[5]

Upon his arrival in Texas Salmon entered energetically into the life of the new Republic. He shared the chaplaincy of the Senate with a Presbyterian minister while the government was at Columbia, where he held public services and preached. He moved to Brazoria, where he attempted to open a school and was stricken with tuberculosis. He wrote the Missionary Society in July 1838, pleading for missionaries to be sent, but no longer asking an appointment for himself. In 1840 he was in Houston as principal of the City School, but mysteriously his name does not appear in the records of the struggling congregation there.

Salmon left Texas in 1840, and resided in New York City without parochial cure until 1849. In that year he embarked for Texas again, but died on the voyage. He founded no congregations in Texas, and ministered in no organized ones. Nevertheless his presence and service must have been a comfort to members and friends of the Texas Church who waited for better days. Among his occasional services was the burial of Stephen F. Austin, the Father of Texas.[6]

The Reverend Chester Newell, a Deacon, operated a school at Velasco in 1837. Upon returning to the United States, he published a history of the Texas Revolution in 1838. This book gave the Foreign Committee of the Missionary Society a basis for an article

[5]I am dependent upon the excellent articles of Dr. Andrew Forest Muir for most of the materials on Salmon and the Clouds. The controversial question of the possible ordination of the elder Cloud in the Episcopal Church is irrelevant to the Texas story. See his: "Early Missionaries in Texas, with Documents Illustrative of Richard Salmon's Church Colony," *Historical Magazine of the Protestant Episcopal Church* (cited hereafter as *Historical Magazine*), X (1941), 219-241; "New Light on Adam Cloud," XXV (1956), pp. 201-207; "John Wurts Cloud, Priest and Planter," XXV (1956), pp. 231-254; and Nash K. Burger, "Adam Cloud, Mississippi's First Episcopal Clergyman," *ibid.*, XVII (1948), pp. 165-173.

Mrs. Frank Smith of Angleton, Texas, believes that Salmon was related to her grandfather, John Adriance of Columbia, who had come into the Austin Colony from upstate New York.

[6]A. F. Muir, "Early Missionaries in Texas," *Historical Magazine*, X (1941), pp. 219-241, and "William Fairfax Gray," *ibid.*, XXVIII (1959), pp. 341-373.

in its missionary magazine, *The Spirit of Missions.* The article sought to stimulate interest in the Texas field, to which two missionaries had at last been appointed.[7]

In 1837 a group of citizens of Matagorda had applied to the Congress of the Republic for a charter incorporating an Episcopal Parish under the name "Christ Church." The charter passed the Senate, but was voted down in the House of Representatives. Albert Clinton Horton, Senator from Matagorda, introduced the petition in the Senate, but it is not known with whom it originated. Possibly the persons interested in this action were at the same time seeking a clergyman from the United States.[8] But the Foreign Committee took no action between 1835 and the summer of 1837 to activate the Texas Mission. Then a letter was received from the Reverend Dr. Cox of Richmond, Virginia, forwarding another letter from a Dr. Beverly Smith of Texas urging that Missionaries be sent. The correspondence was referred to the Committee on Texas.[9]

In August 1838, the Reverend E. A. McGuire of Fredericksburg, Virginia, transmitted a letter from his former parishioner, Colonel William Fairfax Gray of Houston, Texas, who urged that the Church should discharge its responsibility to Texas by sending out a bishop and several clergy. Gray indicated several places where missionaries would be welcome and soon might establish flourishing congregations. At the meeting at which Gray's letter was read, an application for appointment as missionary to Texas was received from the Reverend A. A. Willis; he was recommended by the Right Reverend B. B. Smith, Bishop of Kentucky. These matters were laid on the table.[10]

At the General Convention in Philadelphia in September 1838 pressure built up for the Church to make a beginning in Texas. The meeting of the Foreign Committee in New York finally acted. Hailing the election of the Reverend Leonidas Polk of Tennessee as Missionary Bishop of the Southwest, the Committee expressed

[7]Newell's book, *History of the Revolution in Texas, Particularly of the War of 1835 & 1836; Together with the Latest Geographical, Topographical and Statistical Account of the Country, from the Most Authentic Sources, Also an Appendix* (New York: Wiley & Putnam, 1838), is available in the Library of the University of Texas, Austin. The article in the *Spirit of Missions* appeared in November, 1838, pp. 372-3, and is a close paraphrase of some of Newell's descriptions of Texas, its people and institutions. A. F. Muir, "William Fairfax Gray," *loc. cit.*, is my authority for Newell's activity in Texas.

[8]A. F. Muir, "Caleb Smith Ives, Priest, and the Beginnings of Christ Church, Matagorda, Texas," *Historical Magazine*, XXVIII (1959), pp. 327, 337-8.

[9]"Minutes of the Foreign Committee," II, 64. The lists of the Clergy of Virginia between 1832 and 1838 do not include Dr. Cox's name (*General Convention Journals*, 1832, 1835, and 1838, Appendices). It is possible that Dr. Cox was not an Episcopalian, but eager for missionaries of any denomination to go out to Texas.

[10]"Minutes of the Foreign Committee," III, p. 191.

confidence that they could ask him to supervise the mission in the Republic of Texas. Despite the absence of the Chairman of the Texas Committee. Dr. Milnor, the Foreign Committee as a whole considered the letters which lay before them. They made only such decisions as they felt appropriate until Polk could be consecrated and requested to survey opportunities in Texas. Houston and Matagorda were designated as stations. The Reverend Caleb S. Ives of Alabama was appointed missionary, to serve without salary, since he was to establish a school in response to an invitation from Matagorda citizens. Another applicant, the Reverend D. E. Brown recommended by Bishop Kemper, was appointed, but his field was not designated. Willis' application was postponed until recommendations stemming from Polk's visitation could be considered. The Reverend Chester Newell's application was indefinitely postponed. A letter received from Salmon, written from Brazoria, was heard at the meeting. Salmon did not ask appointment for himself but strongly urged that missionaries be sent.[11]

At the next meeting of the Committee another letter from Chester Newell sought to justify his "apparent neglect of ministerial duties while in Texas." Evidently the young Deacon had devoted so much of his out-of-school time to gather materials for his book that none remained for conduct of services. Complaints from Texas had reached the Committee. His application was not approved. But the Reverend R. M. Chapman of the Eastern Diocese (New England) was recommended by Dr. Milnor and endorsed by his Bishop; he was appointed to Texas without a fixed station. The Committee wished to reserve the right to make another appointment to Houston, although Chapman seemed to have prospects for self-support by teaching in Houston.[12]

The attitude of the Foreign Committee becomes understandable when its financial situation is taken into account. At its meeting on December 12, 1837, the fact was brought forth that expenditures for the last six months had exceeded receipts by $7,732. The work of the Committee had enormously expanded since the reorganization of 1835, and projected program for 1838, apart from new work in Texas, would cost $26,000. The ordinary sources of income—offerings taken for Foreign Missions once a year—would not suffice, especially since the Domestic Committee was appealing to the same congrega-

11*Ibid.*, III, pp. 195, 198-200. Salmon's letter and that of Colonel Gray are printed in part in *Spirit of Missions*, 1838, pp. 328-331. Ives, on reaching his station, found he must apply for a salary, and the Committee granted him one of five hundred dollars per year. ("Minutes of the Foreign Committee," III, pp. 235, 237.)

12*Ibid.*, III, pp. 202-204.

tions to support their swiftly growing work.[13] General Convention
had decreed that every member of the Church was by virtue of his
baptism a member of the Missionary Society, and obligated thereby
to spread the Gospel by contributions as well as by personal efforts;
but unless the parochial clergy urged the duty or allowed visiting
preachers to do so, offerings were not made. Hard times had made
the situation even more grave.[14] Had not two clergy received offers
to go out to teach school and volunteered their services as missionaries, it is doubtful that any appointments could have been made
to Texas.

Caleb Smith Ives was well known to the readers of the Missionary Society's publications, for he had served ably on the Alabama
frontier and had written at length about his work. A native of Tinmouth, Vermont, he had come into the Episcopal Church and had
felt called to its ministry some years after he should have begun his
schooling for the purpose. He enrolled at the age of 29 in Trinity
College, Hartford, in 1826, graduated in 1830, and then enrolled at
the General Seminary. He completed the three-year course and was
ordained Deacon and Priest in 1833 by the Right Reverend Thomas
Church Brownell of Connecticut. Brownell was then in charge of
the work being done in Alabama by the Domestic Committee of
the Missionary Society. No doubt it was at his suggestion that Ives
sought and received appointment as missionary to that field. In spite
of great difficulties of travel and quite primitive living conditions,
Ives founded three Churches within five years, and gained experience
in frontier missionary work that was to stand him in good stead in
Texas. Ives married Miss Katherina Duncan Morison in Mobile in
1834, and the following year moved to that city to become a member
of the faculty of Mobile Institute. He also assisted his brother-in-law,
the Reverend Samuel S. Lewis, Rector of Christ Church, Mobile, and
of the Church at Spring Hill.

Probably one or more of the friends Ives made in Mobile had
moved to Texas and initiated the invitation for him to remove there.
But he had a brother in Texas, too; David Ives had settled at Victoria before the Texas Revolution. Possibly he recommended Caleb
to his Matagorda friends.[15]

---

[13]*Ibid.*, III, pp. 124-5.

[14]*The Churchman* (New York), March 3, 1839, p. 12, and December 14, 1839,
p. 159. In the latter account the distress of the normally well-financed diocesan
Missionary Society of New York is pictured as desperate. For increase in foreign
missionary force, see: *Proceedings of the Board of Missions*, 1838, pp. 397-8; *Spirit
of Missions*, 1838, p. 347.

[15]A. F. Muir, "Caleb Smith Ives," *Historical Magazine*, XXVIII (1959). For
Ives' repute with the Missionary Society, see *Spirit of Missions*, 1838, p. 373.

Thus three years after the motion to adopt Texas as a Foreign Mission of the Episcopal Church, two missionaries—for whom the Society did not appropriate salaries—were appointed and sent out.

The failure to do more is understandable, in view of two unforeseen difficulties. The first was the refusal of the Missionary Episcopate by Hawks,[16] which left the old Southwest without the anticipated leadership. Certainly if Louisiana, Florida and Arkansas could not be cared for, little could be done for the struggling young Texas Republic. Applicants for missionary appointment like Salmon and Newell, about whom the Committee had doubts, would hardly be appointed with no supervision. Secondly, a financial panic engulfed the United States, creating problems for the support of the Church's missionary program; naturally Churchmen would hesitate to increase their obligations by new appointments. Episcopalians already in Texas did little to meet the great need, and they did not receive the help they deserved in those early years. Yet the day of better things was at hand.

II.   The Foreign Mission 1838-1844

THE FOREIGN MISSION to the Republic of Texas finally got underway in the fall of 1838 when the first missionaries arrived. Ives, the first to be appointed, was delayed because he had to arrange for moving his family; Brown never went out. Chapman, a Deacon and a bachelor, made the earliest start, and arrived first in the field. But since Ives formed the first parish in the new nation, the story properly begins with his efforts.

THE FIRST MISSIONARIES

Ives arrived in Matagorda on December 12, 1838, and went promptly to work. He reported to the Foreign Committee on February 18, 1839, that he was officiating regularly every Sunday, conducting a Sunday School, and teaching five days a week. The Holy Communion on Christmas he believed to be the first Prayer Book celebration in Texas; but Salmon must have celebrated while at Columbia or Brazoria, where he certainly had communicants, at least the Clouds

---

[16]Not until October 16, 1835, was Presiding Bishop William White notified by Hawks that he was declining the election (*Episcopal Recorder*, October 24, 1835, p. 118). For Hawks' previous election to the episcopate of the abortive "Southwestern Diocese" see E. Clowes Chorley, "The Missionary March of the American Episcopal Church, Part II," *Historical Magazine*, XVII (1948), pp. 27-8.

The Reverend Caleb S. Ives, First Foreign Missionary appointed to the Republic of Texas, First Rector, Christ Church, Matagorda, Texas.

The Right Reverend Leonidas Polk, First Missionary Bishop of the Southwest.

To the Foreign Committee
of the Board of Missions
of the Protestant Episcopal Church
in the United States.

The undersigned, feeling interested in the advancement of the Protestant Episcopal Church within this Republic, and believing that the promotion of the Rev'd Benj'n Eaton, Rector of Trinity Church, Galveston, to the Episcopate would contribute much towards the extension and welfare of the church; do hereby strongly recommend that your committee take the proper steps to bring the matter in form under the consideration of the next general Convention of the Protestant Episcopal church in the United States, and that you be respectfully solicited to use your influence in having the said Rev'd Mr Eaton appointed and consecrated a Bishop of Texas.

Republic of Texas,
July 1841.

Mirabeau B. Lamar,
President of Texas

J A Morris
Atty. Genl.

Sam'l A. Roberts
Secretary of State

John G Chalmers
Sec'y Treasury

B T Archer
Sec'y War & Navy

James Webb
Late Minister to Mex.

The letter of President Lamar.

and his own wife. Ives had great hopes for the town of Matagorda;
its protected harbor in Matagorda Bay promised to become the port
from which the commerce of the rich Colorado River Valley would
be transferred to ocean-going ships. He wrote:

> This town is growing rapidly, and must, it is thought by many,
> eventually become the most important place in this Republic.
> That this, or some other one on Matagorda bay, must become
> a place of great commercial importance, no one can doubt, who
> is acquainted with the country.[1]

On January 27, 1839, Christ Church, Matagorda, was organized. Ives reported his great expectations:

> It will, no doubt, be pleasing to the Missionary Society to learn,
> that almost all the respectable families and individuals here
> are interested in, and gratified with, this step. I believe this is
> the first and only Church yet organized in the Republic.[2]

The Episcopal Church at this time held services in the Masonic
hall.[3] No other denomination was active there, though two Presbyterian ministers had visited the place and each conducted three Sunday services before Ives' coming. All the religious population except
the Baptist had attached themselves to the new congregation as attendants at least, and almost all the children in town enrolled in
the Sunday School.[4] Thus the Mother Church of the Diocese of
Texas began with bright prospects in a community which seemed to
promise future greatness.

Chapman, who reached Texas a month before Ives did, and
divided his time between Houston and Galveston, found his labor
more difficult. The town of Houston was scarcely two years old.
Harrisburg, lower down on Buffalo Bayou, had been burned by
Santa Anna, and Houston, promoted by the Allen brothers, was the
raw, bustling new capital of the Republic.[5] The April, 1839, issue
of *The Spirit of Missions* copied the letter which had been printed
in *The Christian Advocate,* in which a Methodist missionary said
of Houston:

> Two theatres are open every night, but not a church yet marks
> the site, and no denomination of Christians has yet organized

[1]*Spirit of Missions,* 1839, pp. 88-9.

[2]*Ibid.,* pp. 147-8.

[3]A. F. Muir, "Caleb Smith Ives," *Historical Magazine,* XXVIII (1959), p. 329.

[4]*Spirit of Missions,* 1839, pp. 147-8.

[5]William Ransom Hogan, *The Texas Republic: A Social and Economic History*
(Norman, Okla., 1946), p. 92.

a society, though there are numerous individuals of the leading sects residing here. I have preached in the Senate chamber to large and attentive audiences, and there is an apparent interest for the means of religious instruction; but such is the pressure of business, and the excitement of speculation, and the want of money, that no successful effort for the erection of a church has yet been made. Building materials are extremely expensive. Houses are going up in every street. Carpenters are receiving five dollars a day, and are all employed.[6]

When Chapman arrived in Houston, the leading layman, William Fairfax Gray, was out of the country bringing his family to Texas. In spite of this disappointment, the young Deacon began conducting services in the capitol.[7] When the Gray family returned, events moved on toward the organization of a Church on April 1, 1839.[8]

If the capital city was rude and new, Chapman's other scene of labor was even newer. The east end of Galveston Island had been inhabited earlier by Jean Lafitte and his buccaneers, but in Mexican days had been abandoned. In 1837 there was but one dwelling there, but the influx of settlers, the revival of commerce following the Revolution, the natural advantages of the harbor, and the trade routes of the Trinity and San Jacinto rivers, made Galveston grow rapidly toward its long-time status as Texas' greatest city. By mid-1839 the harbor usually held fifty or more ships and boats,[9] and the town's rapid growth apparently made it profitable to ship in houses from New York. Chapman occasionally officiated, but seems not to have met his best response, amongst Galvestonians, for he spent most of his time in Houston, where he boarded with the family of Colonel Gray and tutored the children.[10]

During his short stay in the Houston-Galveston field, Chapman also visited and officiated at Velasco and Quintana at the mouth of the Brazos River.[11] Perhaps his invitation to preach there came from people he had met from those communities at Houston or Galveston; perhaps either Salmon or Newell had held services there and aroused the hope of permanent provision for the ministrations of our Church.

[6]*Spirit of Missions*, 1839, pp. 121-2.

[7]A. F. Muir, "William Fairfax Gray," *Historical Magazine*, XXVIII (1959), pp. 357-8.

[8]*Spirit of Missions*, 1839, p. 367. See additional note, p. 38.

[9]Hogan, *op. cit.*, pp. 91-2.

[10]A. F. Muir, "William Fairfax Gray," *loc. cit.*

[11]*Spirit of Missions*, 1839, p. 367.

BISHOP POLK'S VISITATION

Leonidas Polk was consecrated Missionary Bishop of the South-west in a service held at Cincinnati on December 9, 1838.[12] Upon returning home to Columbia, Tennessee, Polk found awaiting him the invitation of the Foreign Committee to visit Texas, and on January 10 he replied that he would accept.[13] He included Texas in his first missionary tour; remarkably, in the light of the previous history of the missions of the Protestant Episcopal Church, the Texas Mission received an episcopal visitation in the first year of its life.

After an exhausting journey through Alabama, Mississippi and Arkansas, Polk visited some planters in the "disputed territory" be-tween the United States and Texas, across the Red River from Arkansas. Going on to Shreveport, Louisiana, by the Red River— a voyage made notable by the Bishop's devising a scheme to raise the steamboat after it had struck a snag and sunk—Polk then visited Natchitoches and Fort Jessup, and from there crossed the Sabine to visit Sabinetown, Texas, about midway between Fort Jessup and San Augustine, Texas. He reported that most of the inhabitants of Sabinetown were Episcopalians, and proposed that the Domestic and Foreign Committees share the salary of a missionary who could divide his time between the Fort and Sabinetown.[14]

Having completed his visitation of Louisiana at New Orleans, the Bishop, accompanied by the Reverend David C. Page of Natchez, Mississippi, took ship for Galveston on May 10. After a two-day voyage they arrived in Galveston on a Sunday afternoon to find that the Reverend Rodrick H. Ranney of Louisiana was conducting serv-ices there. They joined in the afternoon service, and the Bishop preached that night.

Polk was favorably impressed with Galveston, about which he seems to have learned a lot on a busy Sunday and Monday. He made contact with many of the friends of the Church, selected a church site, negotiated with the real estate people for its donation, and expressed the hope that a building would be erected in the course of one or two years. He rightly discerned the importance of the place, predicting that its population of around two thousand would rapidly increase because of business opportunities and comfortable climate.

Taking a steamboat in the late afternoon, the Bishop reached Houston at seven o'clock the next morning. He found the city a little larger than two thousand in population, and thought its importance

[12]*Ibid.*, p. 28.   [13]*Ibid.*, pp. 80, 88.   [14]*Ibid.*, pp. 306-12.

would continue even though President Lamar secured legislation that soon would move the Capitol of the Republic to the new town of Austin. The congregation at Houston had raised subscriptions amounting to between four and five thousand dollars for the erection of a building, and had high (and as the event proved, illusory) hopes for an early beginning on it.

The Bishop reported to the Foreign Committee by letter before leaving Houston. He wrote urgently, sensing some peril to the Church:

> You suggest the appointment of something like a standing committee within this republic, which shall constitute, not only a medium of communication with the Foreign Committee, but also, the Ecclesiastical authority of the State, until its organization can be made complete. The suggestion I like exceedingly; it just meets the wants of the country, and is the best arrangement that could be made, until they can have a bishop. Indeed, I am satisfied from what I have seen since here, that the safety of the Church and the purity of religion, demand the immediate presence of some such authorized organization. *There is work for it to perform if it were here now.* And you will see that, should your Board think it advisable to establish one, you should select men of experience and character to compose it. A bishop, however is wanted here, and he should be sent as soon as the competent authorities can convene. His influence would be immense, and no substitute can adequately take his place.[15]

His references to threats to the Church, and to work for an authoritative committee to perform, are mysterious, and extant evidence supports only surmises about them. The Bishop doubtless heard in Houston, if he did not already know, of the presence of the Clouds, Salmon and Newell in Texas. He was to visit the Clouds in Brazoria County shortly and baptize the John Clouds' baby.[16] The other two he did not mention. Perhaps Chapman had taken unkindly to Ranney's visit to Galveston, though we do not know that he was not invited by the young Deacon. Somewhat later the clergy of Texas were to warn that genuine communicants of the Church coming to Texas should bring credentials with them, to protect the good name of the Church.[17]

From Houston the Bishop and Page proceeded on horseback to Cloud's residence in Brazoria County, near the present village of Anchor, where he baptized the new baby. Thence they went to Columbia, where public services were held, then through Brazoria

---

[15]*Ibid.*, pp. 198-200. Italics in quotation are mine.
[16]*General Convention Journal*, 1841, p. 161.
[17]*Spirit of Missions*, 1843, p. 201; see below pp. 23-4.

to Velasco, where services were held again and several men friendly to the Church made themselves known.[18] An unknown person at Velasco gave the Bishop a church lot and a pledge for $1000 toward a building, to which another added his $1000 pledge.[19] Polk was impressed with the fertility of the Brazos Valley and thought the Church should do well in that region. From Velasco the travellers pressed on to McNeil's Prairie, where they visited with a Church family, one of whom had been confirmed many years before by Bishop White in Philadelphia. The route thence took the Bishop and his companion through dense thickets and swamps that lay between the San Bernard and Colorado rivers; they did well to negotiate this trip in two days. Upon reaching Matagorda they were disappointed to find that the Rector, Ives, had departed for the East to seek money to build a church.[20]

Things had gone well for the little congregation of Christ Church, Matagorda, in the first five months. On May 6 Ives had written the Foreign Committee, relating the good success of the efforts of the congregation. Church services were very well attended and the Sunday School had five teachers and thirty-one pupils. They lacked only a suitable place to hold services. A fine church lot was donated by Albert Clinton Horton and Abner Lee Clements, and a subscription for building funds had realized $3000; but this sum was in the severely depreciated currency of the Republic, and, in view of the high cost of lumber and labor, would not go far toward erecting a church of the size needed. No other church structure stood in Matagorda, nor, so far as Ives knew, in Texas. Residents of the town met, and urged Ives to make a tour of the United States to solicit building funds. He complied almost immediately, sailing on May 8.[21]

In the interval between Ives' departure and the arrival of Polk and Page, no services had been held for Christ Church. The two visitors were welcomed most warmly and they remained to conduct services on Sunday, May 26. Leaving the next day with the purpose of visiting Bastrop and Austin, Polk and Page discovered the power of the Texas sun on the prairie. Both were threatened with sunstroke, and when the Bishop became ill they returned to Matagorda by night and made their way along the coast through Velasco to Galveston, whence they returned by steamer to New Orleans. Thus

[18]*General Convention Journal*, 1841, p. 161.

[19]*Spirit of Missions*, 1839, p. 350.

[20]*General Convention Journal*, 1841, p. 161.

[21]*Spirit of Missions*, 1839, p. 200; A. F. Muir, "Caleb Smith Ives," *Historical Magazine*, XXVIII (1959), pp. 330-1.

Polk was unable to see for himself some of the points for which he recommended missionaries.[22]

Writing after his return to his home in Columbia, Tennessee, the Bishop expressed his conviction that the Church could flourish in Texas if the means and men could be secured. The population consisted of people generally from the southwestern part of the United States, in which the Church was making such rapid strides at that time; the Texas government had secured human rights and civil liberties like those in the States. Four things the Church in the States should do at once: first, send a missionary bishop with six clergy; second, buy church lots while good ones in convenient locations in the towns were available at low costs (he himself had procured several lots and a tract for a college or theological school in Texas); third, secure the money needed to finance this program, since financial troubles were hampering every endeavor in Texas; fourth, enlist clergy to work the field. At the time of this report, Houston and Galveston were vacant—Chapman had returned to the East after only seven months of ministry—and Polk recommended a missionary for each of these cities. Matagorda he thought very ably cared for by Ives. Bastrop and Austin could be tended by one man, at least until Austin should grow enough to demand the full time of a minister. The towns of Nacogdoches and San Angustine, only twenty-five miles apart, should have a missionary. Sabinetown, which the Bishop had visited on his way to New Orleans, being composed of Church people, should certainly be manned, in combination with Fort Jessup in Louisiana, as he had recommended previously to the Foreign and Domestic Committees. The Bishop was informed that a new town of some promise was developing at the mouth of the Sabine River, and he thought a clergyman should be sent there. The Church ought to anticipate rapid development in the fertile Brazos Valley; Velasco and Quintana could be combined with Brazoria and Columbia, only a few miles upstream, into a field for a missionary, until population increase should call for another man. There might also be a field much farther up the river at Washington and Nashville, where there was some promise for the support of a minister.[23]

Bishop Polk's recommendations and observations after just a month's visitation in Texas were remarkably prophetic. Although it would take too long to implement his plans, he foresaw what should be done. Houston and Galveston certainly fulfilled the promise he

22*Spirit of Missions*, 1839, p. 333.
23*Ibid.*, pp. 334-5.

sensed, and though the congregations shared the next missionary for a time, each soon engaged the full time of a clergyman. Matagorda never became the great metropolis its enthusiastic backers predicted, but the influence of Ives' labors in church and school spread up the entire valley and beyond. The two fields in the Brazos Valley materialized, as did churches in Austin and Bastrop. San Augustine and Nacogdoches long awaited attention, but it came. Only in the Sabine Valley was nothing to be done.

STRUGGLE FOR SURVIVAL

Caleb Ives reached New York, and in spite of the financial distress which was discouraging all activity, secured considerable support.[24] He was encouraged by Polk's endorsement.[25] He preached many times in the East, and he and Polk appeared together before the Board of Missions and impressed upon that body the great importance of work in the new Republic. When he had enough money to justify the risk, Ives contracted for a church building to be pre-cut in New York and arranged to have it shipped to Matagorda.[26] Reaching home by mid-January, he resumed his duties in school and the Church, but his concern over the cost of the building continued; he thought he would need another one hundred dollars, and wrote asking the Committee to help; All Saints' Church, New York City, was thanked for its gift of books for the Sunday School, but more were needed, as well as books for the library; the congregation was awaiting the arrival of their church building.[27]

In the January number of *The Spirit of Missions* there appeared a long letter from Colonel Gray of Houston, pleading for a clergyman to replace Chapman. No minister of any denomination served Houston, since the Presbyterian who had ministered there for a year and a half had followed the government offices to Austin. An epidemic had carried away a number of the town's citizens, and Colonel Gray had read the Burial Office over several. Gray and the other Churchwarden, E. R. Perkins, had begun lay-reading on Sundays rather than have no services at all. Though Gray said that no other minister was working in Houston, he complained that the Episcopal Church was bringing reproach upon itself by failing to send ministers to Texas, when "Methodists and Presbyterians are spreading over

---

[24]*Ibid.*, 1840, pp. 32-3; *The Churchman* (New York), October 12, 1839, p. 120.
[25]*Ibid.*, October 26, 1839, p. 128.
[26]"Minutes of the Foreign Committee," October 10, 1839, p. 267; *Spirit of Missions*, 1840, p. 33.
[27]*Ibid.*, p. 159.

the country." At the same time he asked for full-time men both for Houston and Galveston. In the same letter Gray pleaded for a school-teacher to come out, for Houston had none; it seemed a good opportunity for the Episcopal Church to serve the community.[28]

By Christmas temporary help had arrived for Houston, but not from the Missionary Society. The Reverend Henry B. Goodwin of Maryland had come to Texas to locate land upon which to settle his wife's slaves, whom she desired to emancipate and establish in a place where they could sustain themselves. With occasional absences for services or business elsewhere, Goodwin ministered to the Houston congregation until after Easter, and his temporary ministry probably saved it from despair and extinction. When elected Rector, he declined; he was then fascinated with the idea of starting a University of Texas for which the Congress of the Republic had set aside a building site and a large landed endowment. When he went to New York, however, he was discouraged by the fund begging competition offered by Bishops McIlvane and Chase, who were seeking money to keep open their educational institutions in Ohio and Illinois.

> Drs. Milnor and Cutler begged me not to say 'University' in New York or Brooklyn, so I returned.—I expect to be home until late autumn, then hope to go to Texas for the winter.

But he did not return to Houston, nor did he go to England to raise money for the Church in Texas as he had told Gray he intended to do.

After Goodwin's departure from Houston, the Wardens continued to perform as layreaders, with fair response from the congregation. Gray wrote the Committee in June 1840, much less discouraged, expressing faith that the Lord had some purpose in their deprivation and in time would provide for them.[29] Their wait was not unduly prolonged, for on October 24 one of Bishop Kemper's Wisconsin missionaries, finding the climate there too rigorous for him, was appointed to the Texas Mission, to go to Houston or Galveston.[30]

This missionary was the Reverend Benjamin Eaton, a native of Dublin, Ireland. Eaton was ordained deacon March 15, 1839, in Saint Louis, Missouri, by Bishop Kemper, who put him to work and

[28]*Ibid.*, pp. 22-4.
[29]*Spirit of Missions*, 1840, p. 290; A. F. Muir, "William Fairfax Gray," *Historical Magazine*, XXVIII (1959), pp. 363-7.
[30]*Spirit of Missions*, 1840, 364.

later priested him at Green Bay, Wisconsin. Eaton arrived at Galveston on January 13, 1841, under most discouraging circumstances. After a very rough voyage from New Orleans he landed in the teeth of a typical Texas "wet norther." Galveston, by contemporary accounts, was anything but an object of beauty. The island, barely above sea level, in rainy weather was a morass of mud on the bay side, and its jerrybuilt board and batten houses must have looked as depressing as they were cold. Since no congregation could be gathered in that weather, Eaton went on to Houston, whence he wrote in great depression to Bishop Kemper, who had attempted to dissuade him from leaving Wisconsin.[31] Any one of the numerous gamblers in either place, betting on this man's spending the rest of his life ministering in Texas, might have ventured ten to one that he would leave on the next packet for New Orleans. As usual, however, the sun came out, and with it, Eaton's spirits revived. He set to work with a will.

Perhaps it was fortunate that Eaton's first services and efforts were in Houston, for there the zeal of Colonel Gray and the vestry gave promise of heartening response. The vestry invited him to make his home in Houston, and, without leaving Galveston unattended, to give most of his time to the former city. He himself was inclined to believe Houston the more promising field, but he arranged to spend two weeks of each month in each of the places, with layreaders taking the services for the Sundays on which he was absent. Back in Galveston after his first sojourn in Houston, Eaton sought out the Church's supporters and began officiating. A meeting on February 6 resulted in the organization of a parish, the selection of a vestry, and Eaton's election as Rector. Two days later he reported to the Foreign Committee that he had conducted services six times in Galveston and three times in Houston.[32] By mid-April he had revised his evaluation of Galveston and thought that he ought to spend the major part of his time there,

> as this is, and must continue to be, the principal city in the republic, where a larger congregation may be expected than anywhere else.

A scheme was on foot to erect a church upon the very good property which had been obtained, and in spite of hard times, around $1000

[31]William Manning Morgan, *Trinity Protestant Episcopal Church, Galveston, Texas: A Memorial History* (Houston, 1954), pp. 1-13. This work will be cited hereafter as W. M. Morgan, "*Trinity Church, Galveston.*"

[32]*Spirit of Missions,* 1841, pp. 82-3.

had been subscribed for it. The vestry wished him to go to the United States to solicit contributions for its erection.[33]

Meanwhile the prefabricated church building had arrived in Matagorda harbor, as Ives wrote the Foreign Committee in July 1840, and was soon to be brought ashore by lighter, but difficulties would begin again for there was no money for its erection. The veteran missionary was not downhearted; he told the Committee that he had written "to such of our friends in the United States as have heretofore done nothing for us," to ask for funds to pay for unloading the materials and erecting the building. He reported that the Church was growing greatly in its influence on the community, doing much to improve the moral tone, and gaining adherents. "Texas," he wrote in his letter,

> is one of the best missionary fields on the face of the globe for laborers who have good common sense, are well educated, are industrious, active, economical, and who will not easily be disheartened at the inconveniences and privations of a new country.[34]

A few months later Ives made a plea for just $100 to begin erection of the church, the materials for which were lying unused and exposed to rotting on the lot. Times were so hard that the people could raise no money themselves and must have help.[35] But by October two local donors had promised $200, Mr. A. C. Horton had made a gift of 600 acres of land to be sold, and the crew had commenced erecting the building. Ives hoped the remaining $800 would be sent by way of the New York office of the Society.

Ives at this time was distressed that the needs of other communities were not being met by the Church. He had, he said, been besieged by people from other towns to go and preach to them. Because he had adopted a strategy of intensive, long-range missionary work, emphasizing the schools which he and his wife were operating, he thought that he could not answer these calls, yet felt strongly that they should find an answer.[36] Late in 1840 recurrent attacks of fever made Ives decide he should have a temporary change of climate, and, encouraged by his vestry, he made a journey upriver to Austin. He wrote,

> I found the country exceedingly interesting, and much more densely populated than I had supposed. There are many towns and settlements on the banks of the Colorado River, between

[33]*Ibid.*, pp. 180-1.   [34]*Ibid.*, 1840, pp. 289-90.
[35]*Ibid.*, p. 387.   [36]*Ibid.*, 1841, pp. 31-2.

Matagorda and Austin, where an *itinerant* missionary of the Church could do great good, and where the Gospel can be preached to the people in no other way.

He found Austin a town of about 1000 people, totally lacking provisions for religious worship save by those ministers happening to visit in the town as he had done. There was no Sunday School, and no day school except a small one for girls. Here was a very good field for a missionary of our Church. "It is a most beautiful location," he said, "and one, as regards health, where I would as soon trust my family, as in New England." He preached while in Austin, he reported, on one Sunday "all day long," celebrated the Holy Communion, and performed three baptisms. Great interest in the Episcopal Church seemed evident. He yearned for a good clergyman to come and occupy the place.[37] That was not soon to be.

EFFORTS TOWARD A NATIONAL EPISCOPATE

The cause of the Church in Texas meanwhile had not been forgotten by the Missionary Society. Measures of help were proposed at the annual meeting of the Board of Missions, held at St. John's Chapel, New York City, in June 1840. In view of Polk's recommendation that a missionary bishop be sent to Texas, the Reverend Doctor William Rollinson Whittingham of the General Theological Seminary introduced a resolution that the Society request the next General Convention to elect three presbyters of the Church to be consecrated bishops of the Episcopal Church in the Republic of Texas, thus to give start to a new national church. The proceedings of the Board of Missions did not disclose whether there was debate on the proposal, but show that an effort to defeat it failed; the resolution was referred to a committee to report upon at the next annual meeting, in time for the next General Convention.[38] Unrealistic as the scheme may have sounded, it put the problem before the clergy of the Church, to whom the *Proceedings of the Board* were distributed free. At the next annual meeting at St. James' Church, Philadelphia, in June 1841 this resolution was withdrawn on the request of the special committee, of which Whittingham, now Bishop of Maryland, was chairman, but the annual report of the Foreign Committee stated of Texas, "the way is now prepared for the presence of a Bishop—that an independent church may be at once organized."[39]

[37] *Ibid.*, pp. 80-2.
[38] *Proceedings of the Board of Missions,* 1840, p. 5.
[39] *Ibid.*, 1841., p. 77.

Two congregations in Texas quickly reacted to this report. A petition from citizens of Galveston was circulated by the wardens and vestry of Trinity Church asking General Convention to elect the Reverend Benjamin Eaton as Bishop of Texas. A resolution of the wardens and vestry, to the same effect, pleaded the good work Eaton had done in their midst and the virtue of electing a presbyter already in the field. A letter from President Lamar and other officers of the government of the Republic accompanied these documents.[40]

The vestry at Matagorda, evidently meeting before knowing the action of the 1841 meeting of the Board but having in hand the *Proceedings* of 1840, petitioned the House of Bishops on July 31, 1841, rejoicing in the resolution to confer the Episcopate upon the Texas Church, giving their opinion that the Church in their nation was *"too new for an independent Episcopacy,"* recommending that when constituted it be "attached to and acting auxiliary to the Church in the United States," and nominating in the most earnest and laudatory way their own Rector, the Reverend Caleb Smith Ives, to be one of the bishops if three were selected or the Bishop if only one.[41]

Bishop Polk had not visited Texas during 1840, having concentrated his energies on the dioceses of Alabama, Mississippi and Louisiana on his second missionary tour.[42] At the end of November he started on his third visitation, which took him through Arkansas and Indian Territory and then back along the Red River. At two points he visited families in the Red River country of Texas, finding the influence of his former visit to have been fruitful. He recommended that the new Bishop of Texas, if General Convention elected one, should take thought for placing a missionary in this region. Reaching Louisiana, he visited the Reverend William Steel, a priest of the Diocese of Tennessee who had followed his daughter to that region with the intention of settling there. The Bishop thought him too aged to serve as a missionary and recommended that the Society place a man there.[43] In point of fact Steel did settle on the Texas side of Caddo Lake in the Leigh community, where he established a congregation which, although on Texas soil, was long reckoned in the Diocese of Louisiana, on whose clergy list Steel's name was afterward carried.[44]

[40]*General Convention Journal,* 1841, pp. 152-4. The Lamar letter is printed as Illustration No. 3.
[41]*Ibid.,* pp. 154-5.
[42]*Ibid.,* 1841, pp. 162-9.
[43]*Ibid.,* p. 172.
[44]Ms. account of Steel's ministry in Texas, Archives, Diocese of Texas.

Polk reached New Orleans at the end of February 1841, intending to sail for Matagorda by appointment to consecrate Christ Church, but a letter from Ives informed him that the building would not be ready for another month. Polk's appointments would not permit this change of schedule, and he made no further Texas visitation on this journey.[45]

Eaton had believed at first that by appeals in the Church press he could raise enough funds from the United States to supplement what the poverty-stricken Texans could give to finance the building of a church in Galveston. Therefore he declined the invitation of his vestry to go East.[46] Later in the year, however, he became convinced that only a personal tour would serve. By the time of the General Convention in New York he was there. On the way he had solicited successfully the churchmen of Charleston, South Carolina. The presence of so many clergy and leading laity at the Convention enabled him to enlist their support for the Galveston building.[47]

Christ Church, Matagorda, meanwhile had completed their building, which was opened for services on Easter Day, 1841, too late, as noted above, for Polk to consecrate it that season. In the spring and summer of that year Ives ministered in other parts of the country.[48]

Houston had not fared so well. Eaton came to feel that the great amount of time lost by travelling between the towns prevented much profitable work in either, and communicated to the Foreign Committee his determination to put most of his energies into Galveston and only occasionally to minister in Houston. Colonel Gray's death in April 1841, a severe blow to the congregation, left little hope that the Church could carry on without clerical leadership. Eaton requested the Committee to send out another missionary.[49]

When General Convention met the Missionary Society requested the election of two missionary bishops, one for West Africa, and the other for Texas[50] The House of Bishops complied by nominating to the House of Clerical and Lay Deputies the Reverend Nicholas Hamner Cobbs of Virginia as Missionary Bishop to exercise jurisdiction in the Republic of Texas and the Reverend John A. Vaughn, D.D., as Bishop of West Africa.[51] There was no objection to either

[45]*General Convention Journal*, 1841, p. 172.
[46]*Spirit of Missions*, 1841, p. 236.
[47]*Ibid.*, pp. 286, 319; W. M. Morgan, *Trinity Church, Galveston*, pp. 24-5.
[48]A. F. Muir, "Caleb Smith Ives," *Historical Magazine*, XXVIII (1959), pp. 332-3.
[49]*Spirit of Missions*, 1841, pp. 180-1.
[50]*Ibid.*, p. 325.
[51]*General Convention Journal*, 1841, p. 114.

of these worthy clergymen, who were well known and held in high esteem. Nevertheless an immediate objection to holding an election was made in the House of Deputies, ostensibly on the ground that neither the constitution nor the canons of the Church could assure that bishops consecrated for foreign lands and clergy they should there ordain would be bound by the laws of the Church.[52] This was peculiar ground for the councils of the American Church to occupy, since every deputy was aware of the difficulty encountered in securing bishops for America. One is led to suspect other reasons for wishing to delay, and they are not far to seek, since the financial affairs of the missionary endeavor were in deplorable condition. No bishop was elected, but an amendment to the Constitution was proposed for the action of the next Convention.[53] The situation of the Texas Church was left worse not better; the Diocese of Louisiana asked General Convention to elect a bishop for them, Polk was elected,[54] the Missionary Episcopate of the Southwest was left vacant, and Bishop Otey of Tennessee was asked to care for Arkansas and Indian Territory.[55] The entire vast region still fell to Otey and Polk as before, except that neither was designated to take care of Texas.

WITHOUT CLAIM ON ANY BISHOP

The cause of the Church in Texas must have seemed especially hopeless to the Galvestonians the next year, for, after they finally completed their church building in June 1842, they lost it in a hurricane the following September. The town itself was so stricken that no prospect existed for local means to rebuild. But help was on the way. There was a volunteer for Texas who, having graduated from the Virginia Seminary and been ordained Deacon and Priest by the Bishop of Virginia, was about to depart for the field. He was Charles Gillett[e], a man destined to contribute much of his abundant talent to the life of the young mission. The Board of Missions requested Gillett to delay his departure by touring the Churches in the States to collect money for the rebuilding of the Galveston Church.[56] The effort was so far sufficient that Eaton was able, by careful superintendence of the building operation, to rebuild with the very small amount Gillett brought with him. The rebuilt church was opened on Palm Sunday, 1843; Gillett and Ives were present with Eaton for the joyous occasion. While together, the three priests determined to take the affairs of the Texas Church in hand; they passed resolutions,

[52]*Ibid.*, pp. 74, 76.   [53]*Ibid.*, p. 82.   [54]*Ibid.*, pp. 113, 116.
[55]*Ibid.*, p. 117.   [56]*Spirit of Missions*, 1842, pp. 341-4. See below, p. 48, n. 52.

to be circulated in the United States, informing communicants of the Church who intended to move to Texas that they should bring testimonials of good standing from their local clergy, since, for the sake of the reputation and purity of the Church in Texas, the signers agreed to admit no other immigrants as communicants. The missionaries also decided to meet in Matagorda on May 8 "to organize the Church in Texas."[57]

Upon his arrival in Houston Gillett, through the kindness of the Presbyterian pastor, Mr. Atkinson, and his flock, was able to gather the congregation of the Houston Church and resume regular services. Episcopalians and Presbyterians used the Presbyterian building on alternate Sundays.[58] In April the Presbyterian minister left, whereupon the officials of his congregation invited Gillett to use the building regularly until they found another pastor. The Episcopalians needed a building of their own to assure permanent work, however, and the City Corporation offered to donate a lot, should they build a $6000 church building on it. This condition was quite beyond their means, so the congregation bought the lot for $200 and determined to put up a temporary

> lecture room, or chapel, large enough to hold 200 or 250 people; this would accommodate our present congregation, and probably for some time to come. It will be a building some 40 by 25 feet.

(Gillett must have planned to have them sit in one another's laps!) Pledges were secured that could be depended upon, amounting to $800, most of it in "lumber, labor, and orders on stores." Cash was very scarce in Texas; people were land poor, the finances of the government desperate, taxes very high, in short, money was needed from the Church in the States.[59]

San Antonio was captured by the Mexican army early in 1842. In consequence, the seat of government was moved by President Houston, now back in office for his second term, first to Houston, then to the hamlet of Washington-on-the-Brazos, where Texas independence had been proclaimed.[60] The Foreign Committee had asked Gillett to visit the little capital which he did shortly after his arrival in Houston, making the journey on horseback facing a wet norther. There he found that a communicant of the Church had gathered a Sunday School. Gillett was able to provide Prayer Books. He also conducted services at Independence, and learned of several Church

[57]*Ibid.*, 1843, pp. 200-1.   [58]*Ibid.*, p. 201.   [59]*Ibid.*, p. 391.

[60]Stanley Siegel, *A Political History of the Texas Republic, 1836-1845* (Austin, 1956), pp. 191, 196, 211-2.

families in the vicinity. Having thus spied out the land in Washington County, he returned to Houston, leaving again only for the Galveston church opening on Palm Sunday and for the meeting with Ives and Eaton in Matagorda on May 8.[61]

When the three clergy met in Matagorda, the planned organization of the Church in Texas did not take place. The most that they felt could be done realistically was to form themselves into a "Committee of Correspondence" for the welfare of the Church in the Republic. Gillett was as impressed with Ives' work in Matagorda as he was with the character of the town, whose society "taken as a whole, is confessedly better than that of any other town in Texas . . . ." On his return journey Gillett tarried at Richmond to preach and perform a baptism. Then he set to work in Houston to lay the foundations for the life of that parish.[62]

The year 1843 was a time of testing for Texans. The threat of Mexican reconquest remained; in consequence, immigration slowed up and many left the country. Ives wrote in July reporting the discouragement of many of the people, but asserting his own faith that the country's difficulties would be surmounted.[63] That faith was well founded. President Houston, for whom Ives held no high regard, maneuvered the English government to press Mexico into a virtual armistice with Texas, thus opening again normal trade and immigration from the United States; in the meantime he was negotiating for annexation to the United States.[64] The other two missionaries, meeting in Galveston in September, concluded that the stability of their congregations demanded parochial schools, like that at Matagorda; they sent a circular to the Church in the States to solicit assistance for the erection of school buildings. Eaton asserted that the uncertainties of the political situation and the unsatisfactory economic state of the Republic made it sure that funds could not be had in Texas,[65] while Gillett warned that Roman Catholic missionaries were coming in and planning schools; should the Church care to keep her own children, she would have to help provide their schooling. Gillett's letter is an eloquent reminder of the unsettled character of the country. He had planned further exploration of the field in order to look at La Grange, Bastrop, Austin, Bexar (San Antonio), Gonzales, and Columbia, but the trip had to be deferred;

> as this would be a journey of several hundred miles, a portion of it through an Indian territory, where it is not considered safe

[61]*Spirit of Missions*, 1843, pp. 363-5.   [62]*Ibid.*, p. 365.
[63]*Ibid.*, pp. 390-1.   [64]Siegel, *op. cit.*, pp. 222-30.
[65]*Spirit of Missions*, 1843, pp. 478-9.

The Reverend Benjamin Eaton, First Rector of Trinity Church, Galveston.

—From Morgan, *Trinity Church, Galveston*

The Reverend Charles Gillette, Rector, Christ Church, Houston, Founder, St. Paul's College, Anderson, Rector, St. David's Church, Austin.

Christ Church Matagorda, Texas, Mother Church of the Diocese.

Epiphany Church, Austin, Texas. A portion of the west wall still stands as a part of St. David's Church.

to travel, except in parties, I have been obliged to delay it for want of company.

Austin would be unimportant, he thought, until peace was concluded with Mexico and San Antonio made safe from both Mexican and Indian. When this happened, both places would be fields fruitful for missionary work, for the seat of government would return to Austin and San Antonio would become the center for the Mexican trade.

Gillett reported that our Church, which seemed to be the one Texas people really wanted, was not keeping up with the demand:

> the Presbyterians have about ten ministers in the country, the Methodist upwards of forty; Roman Catholics about six; while our own Church has only three.[66]

POLK'S SECOND VISITATION

Bishop Polk had been released from his obligations toward Texas since becoming Bishop of Louisiana in 1841, but his interest in the Texas Church had not diminished. When he received a request from the Right Reverend Alexander V. Griswold, who became Presiding Bishop following Bishop White's death, Polk planned another visitation. He arrived in February 1844. By spending several days at each station and by gathering all three of the clergy at Galveston at the close of the journey, the Bishop was able to gain a thorough knowledge of the progress that had taken place. At Houston he found Gillett doing very good work, although no building belonged to the Church. Matagorda, to which Gillett accompanied him, he found deeply influenced by Ives' ministry in both Church and school. Polk was particularly pleased with Ives' students, whom he catechized before confirming, and found outstanding in knowledge and understanding. Ives was pastor and teacher to the entire community, not only of the whites, but also of the negroes, several of whom were confirmed. At Galveston Polk found the Church doing well. He confirmed thirteen persons at Houston. He consecrated Christ Church and confirmed twenty persons at Matagorda, then he consecrated Trinity Church and confirmed twenty persons at Galveston.

Polk agreed with Gillett and Eaton that their stations, too, should have parochial schools in order to rear a generation of serious churchmen in those places as Ives was doing in Matagorda. The need for a few more missionaries, for San Augustine and Nacogdoches, for Brazoria, Columbia and Independence, was urgent. Austin, Bas-

[66]*Ibid.*, 1844, pp. 25-7.

trop, Gonzales and San Antonio would have to wait for more stable conditions. A regular provision for episcopal supervision should be made at the next General Convention. Polk knew that one of the alternative suggestions of the Board of Missions for accomplishing this object would be that he, as the Bishop of the closest domestic diocese, should be entrusted with the care of Texas. Hence, while not recommending what provision should be made, he insisted that it should be regular.

Texas, he believed, was particularly open to the Episcopal Church, whose orderly, sober and enlightened ministrations appealed to the translated Anglo-Americans, offering an anchor of stability in the midst of the uncertainties, disorders and hardships of life in that feeble new country. The new ardor for foreign missions in the American Episcopal Church should certainly be directed to include concern for people of the same origin, blood and tongue in this closest foreign field. Polk, having had personal experience of missionary work without the leadership of the episcopate, held it beyond debate that a bishop should head a mission.

Armed with Polk's recommendations, both Gillett and Eaton went to the United States in the summer of 1844, the former to attempt to raise money to erect the long-planned church building, the latter to solicit money for a school building.[67] Gillett was outraged and incredulous that many clergy denied him the privilege of presenting his cause to their congregations. He wrote:

> I confess I was sometimes pained and grieved beyond measure, to find some of my clerical brethren, who, placed over large and flourishing congregations, had never known what it was to want, either personally, or in any arrangement connected with their stated seasons of public worship, and who consequently could know nothing of the *wants* or the *trials* of Missionary life, inveighing against such of their brethren as placed on the outposts, felt themselves called upon to make an effort to sustain and comfort their feeble parishes, by asking aid from those to whom God has given an abundance. . . .

Not all, by any means, were thus minded; sufficient money was pledged or given to make a start seem probable in the near future. But Gillett, upon his return to Houston, learned that the building erected for a school by the City of Houston several years before was up for sale, and quickly took the bargain; the schoolhouse was purchased and moved onto the church lot for a sum of $500, and the congregation at last had a home, however temporary, of its own.

[67]*Ibid.*, pp. 268-70, 279-81.

Gillett planned to replace the $500 in the church fund as soon as possible, so that when the church was built, the building just purchased could be used for the school.[68]

Eaton's pleas met with more success. St. Michael's Church, Charleston, South Carolina, made the most generous contribution. In June 1844 Eaton was in Boston, whence he wrote the Foreign Committee. He was present at the triennial meeting of the Board of Missions coincident with the General Convention of October 1844 in Philadelphia. On returning to Galveston he found a yellow fever epidemic in progress, and was too busy ministering to its victims to begin his schoolhouse until spring; in April he reported the building in progress, and he expected to open sessions of the school in the Fall.[69]

THE GENERAL CONVENTION OF 1844

The General Convention of 1844 faced a new situation. In 1841, with its treasury exhausted, the Board of Missions had pressed the Convention to elect foreign missionary bishops, and had been checked by the House of Deputies' ostensible doubts as to the sufficiency of constitutional safeguards. By 1844 the Dioceses had acted to assure that those safeguards would be voted into law, and the Church had both renewed its support of foreign missions and become convinced that the episcopate should lead any mission.[70] Members of the Foreign Committee did not have to look hard to find fields in which the opportunities for work would justify electing bishops. The African mission had grown in scope, and most urgently needed direct supervision. It was felt that episcopal rank was needed for the head of the mission to Constantinople. Meantime the "mission to China," threatened with withdrawal at the last triennial meeting of the Board of Missions, because it could not enter China itself, gained a new prospect when the British forced open the doors of China, and was now being reinforced to the degree that it certainly needed episcopal supervision.[71] Measured against these needs the claims of Texas seemed small, especially since the annexation of that country by the United States, as the Board believed, would soon take place.[72] Foreign Missionary Bishops there would be, but the Board did not

[68]*Ibid.*, 1845, pp. 313-4.
[69]*Ibid.*, 1844, pp. 368-9; 1845, p. 184; W. M. Morgan, *Trinity Church, Galveston,* pp. 34-5.
[70]*Spirit of Missions*, 1843, p. 202.
[71]"Report of Foreign Committee," *ibid.*, 1844, pp. 390-5.
[72]*Ibid.*, pp. 394, 406, 415.

recommend that Texas receive one. Instead, there would be another provisional arrangement.

It would have been perfectly logical to ask Polk to care for the Texas congregations. From New Orleans he could reach Galveston readily by water, much more conveniently than any other bishop could reach Texas. But this simple solution, which, as his report suggests, Polk expected and would not have resisted, was not utilized. Other problems weighed heavily. Something had to be done about Arkansas and Indian Territory, since Otey of Tennessee had now resigned his temporary jurisdiction over these areas.[73] Polk had cared for Alabama during the triennium; he scarcely could be asked to resume the care of the Southwest again, particularly since he served Louisiana without salary but derived his income from vast plantation operations. He had been a cotton planter on a large scale before moving to Louisiana, and his well planned and supervised operations did not interfere overmuch with his episcopal responsibilities. But in Louisiana he embarked upon sugar planting at Thibodeaux. He made his home at this plantation, and soon learned how much of the owner's time and attention was demanded by this business, even with the best of supervision. In addition to the business cares of the plantation, he was concerned for the spiritual nurture of hundreds of slaves on the place. Though he employed a chaplain there whenever possible, he felt an obligation to minister to his own servants. Thus the demands upon his time were too great to expect him to resume the vast jurisdiction he held before 1841.[74]

At the same time that Texas failed to obtain a bishop of its own, the long agitated proposal of the Domestic Committee for an episcopate to the American Indians was voted down in the House of Bishops. That House decided instead to elect a new Missionary Bishop of the Southwest, with jurisdiction in Arkansas and Indian Territory south of the 36½ parallel, and to give him provisional charge of the Church in Texas. To this office the Reverend George Washington Freeman, D.D., Rector of Emmanuel Church, Newcastle, Delaware, was elected.[75]

The results of the first six years of the foreign mission to Texas was certainly meager, from any viewpoint. Only in two places, Mata-

[73]General Convention Journal, 1844, pp. 43, 137, 218-24.

[74]Ibid., p. 206; Joseph H. Park, General Leonidas Polk, Fighting Bishop (Baton Rouge, 1962), pp. 98-111; William S. Slack, "Bishop Polk and the Diocese of Louisiana," Historical Magazine, VII (1938), p. 370. For the hazardous nature of sugar planting, see J. Carlyle Sitterton, Sugar Country: The Cane Sugar Industry in the South, 1753-1950 (Lexington, Ky., 1953), passim.

[75]General Convention Journal, 1844, pp. 113, 179, 180

gorda and Galveston, had deep roots been put down; there were promising results also at Houston since Gillett had settled there. All the other openings for the Church which Bishop Polk had called to the attention of the Society had been neglected, except for the few exploratory journeys which the three missionaries had made occasionally as they were able. These did not, of course, extend to all the localities which the Bishop had mentioned. Had the Society been able to finance the dispatch of more clergy, it is possible that the Church might have taken deeper root in places like San Augustine and Nacogdoches than it did after a belated beginning in those places. Had Texas received the undivided attention of a bishop, undoubtedly much more would have been accomplished. Had Cobbs been elected, the great results that he later produced as Alabama's first bishop might have been Texas'.

Yet these six years were times of trouble in Texas. Any work that might have been begun at San Antonio, Austin or Bastrop would have been aborted when the threat of renewed war with Mexico and the menace of Indian raids caused the western frontier to roll back.[76] The chaotic financial affairs of the Republic would have made work in more sheltered places disappointing. Adverse results of attempts to use Texas rivers as channels of commerce caused many places for which high hopes had been held out to wither and die.[77] Whatever the disappointments and losses of these first years, it seems true that the devoted attention of Freeman began just as the time of larger opportunity for settled work was arriving.

III. The Unorganized Mission Under Freeman

GREAT DIFFICULTY beset the task assigned to the man the House of Bishops would nominate as Missionary Bishop of the Southwest. The territory was vast; settlements were far apart and transportation between them primitive, not only in Arkansas and Indian Territory, but in the Texas Republic. The job would demand physical stamina, courage and patience. The areas were in the South, largely a plantation region with numerous slaves.

---

[76]Following the capture of San Antonio. See above, p. 23.
[77]W. R. Hogan, *The Texas Republic*, pp. 68-74.

THE NEW BISHOP AND HIS FIELD

In view of these facts, the choice of George Washington Freeman seems strange, since he was fifty-five years of age at the time of
his election, a native of Massachusetts, and the rector of an eastern
seaboard parish. Yet he had first-hand experience in planting the
Episcopal Church on the frontier. After his ordination by Bishop
Ravenscroft in 1826 in North Carolina, Freeman had served not
only in that diocese but in Tennessee and Mississippi in the days
when the Church was little known. He was thoroughly acquainted
with the problems of the Church in the South, and had written
on the responsibilities of Christian slaveholders to their slaves.[1]
He was devoted to old-fashioned, strict church principles learned
from Ravenscroft, and he intended to hold forth the banner of the
Church without compromise. All this was known to Bishops Otey
and Polk, his old friends. They probably felt that his experience
and proven wisdom qualified him better than most for this difficult
and delicate position.

Freeman was consecrated to the episcopate during the sessions
of the General Convention at the same time as Boone of China
and Southgate of Constantinople, October 26, 1844. Freeman then
set to closing out his affairs in Delaware preparatory to entering
upon his new duties. He turned his attention first to Texas, which
he reached in March 1845. Because he had been delayed for ten days
in New Orleans waiting for a ship, the Bishop could visit only the
three established congregations.[2]

But those visits opened a new era for the Church in Texas.
Although it was unfortunate that he could not be assigned solely to
Texas and live there, Freeman gave the infant Church much attention and energy. He was a devoted pastor in his career in the Priesthood, and he continued the same pattern of ministry as a bishop.
On his first visit to Houston, he accompanied Gillett in visiting from
house to house amongst the congregation.[3] The Bishop made a deep
impression on Caleb Ives, who wrote of him:

[1]John N. Norton, *Life of Bishop Freeman of Arkansas* (New York, 1867), pp.
1-114. The tract on the duties of slaveholders was published by the Society for
the Advancement of Christianity in South Carolina around 1831. *Ibid.*, p. 94.
Norton stated that Freeman went to Columbia, Tenn. from Raleigh, and the clerical
directories of the period so state, but the *Journal of the Diocese of Mississippi* lists
him as Rector at Columbus, Miss. at this time. As Mississippi was under Otey's
provisional charge at the time, it is possible that his report was misread by the
editors of the yearbooks.

[2]*Spirit of Missions*, 1845, p. 252.

[3]*Ibid.*, p. 253.

> This visit, I doubt not will do good; so much modesty and Christian humility; so much good sense and piety, accompanied by manly learning cannot fail to do good in any community.[4]

Even though pressed for time, and prevented by unfavorable weather from receiving the full number of attendants upon the services he could conduct, Freeman was well received by the Texas Church, and he formed a good idea of what had to be done. His recommendations to the Foreign Committee followed in the main those of Bishop Polk and the three clergy at work in Texas; more missionaries were needed, and partial support awaited their arrival in some of the communities where they were particularly desired.[5]

All three of the Texas Priests meanwhile had been ranging abroad to extend the Church's ministrations. Eaton had preached before the Texas Congress at Washington-on-the-Brazos, and had officiated at Independence.[6] Gillett kept in touch with the people to whom he had previously ministered in Richmond.[7] During the 1843 summer vacation of his Matagorda school, Ives had gone to visit at Gulf Prairie on the Brazos Stephen F. Austin's sister, Mrs. Emma Perry, who had become a communicant during a visit to Matagorda the previous winter. Although prevented by weather from gathering a congregation, he was encouraged to believe that a parish could be established in that neighborhood. On that journey he also visited in Velasco and Quintana, where he met an encouraging response. The same summer, visiting in the home of Judge Dinsmore, "Well Point," thirty miles west of Matagorda on the bay, he preached and administered Holy Communion to the neighborhood. In the following year he began holding services at the Gibson plantation on Caney Creek, and in March 1845, he began services at Brazoria, where he continued to officiate occasionally until a missionary was obtained.[8] These encouraging signs of growth made the field promising for the work of the new Bishop.

Uncertainty about the status of Texas, however, made the Missionary Board cautious. Thus far the operation of the Texas mission had been a charge upon the treasury of the Foreign Committee. At the annual meeting of the Board in June 1845 a resolution was offered:

[4]Manuscript Common Journal of the Reverend Caleb S. Ives, March 29, 1844. This journal is in the archives of the Diocese of Texas at the Seminary of the Southwest, Austin, Texas. Cited hereafter as "Ives' Common Journal."

[5]*Spirit of Missions*, 1845, pp. 252-5.

[6]*Ibid.*, p. 184.

[7]*Ibid.*, pp. 344-5.

[8]Ives' Common Journal, March 29, 1845.

Resolved, That in the event of the annexation of Texas to the United States during the ensuing year, the Foreign Committee be charged with the care of the Church Mission in that country until the next annual meeting of this Board,

for which an amendment was offered to make the effective date of transfer the first of the year.[9] Although action on this measure was indefinitely postponed, the prospect of planning work for Texas, in view of the heavy obligations of the Domestic Committee to which the burden must pass, was dim indeed.[10] The Congress of the United States had passed and President Tyler had signed the Joint Resolution allowing the annexation of Texas, the Texas President delayed calling his Congress or a constitutional convention for some months. Ives, a devoted American who longed to see the Stars and Stripes flying over Texas, agonized over the delay. When the formalities were completed he entered in his Common Journal on January 7, "Today we received the intelligence that Texas is annexed to the U. S.," and on Sunday, the eleventh, with an overtone of joy, "had the Collect for the President of the U. S. for the first time."

Annexation itself could not bring the influx of settlers needed to cure Texas' ills; war with Mexico, made inevitable by this action, must be prosecuted successfully to give the security necessary for the development of the country. The Foreign Committee, reporting to the Board in 1845, said of Texas:

> The unsettled condition of the country continues to offer a serious obstacle to the success of missionary labors in it; still, the reports of the Missionaries there are encouraging, and satisfy the Committee that they are not laboring in vain.[11]

In addition the Foreign Committee, which at the June meeting had been confident of receiving plenty of money to meet its commitments, was seriously embarrassed by December.[12]

In view of these difficulties, it is not surprising that no additional missionaries were appointed for Texas even in 1846. Indeed,

[9]*Spirit of Missions*, 1845, p. 224.

[10]The Domestic Committee, with three bishops, one hundred and four clergy and three laymen employed, was $10,000 short of meeting its full budget of some $43,000. The budget of the Foreign Committee was slightly higher, $46,000 in round numbers. It is interesting that a correspondent of the *Banner of the Cross,* calculating the cost of the Church's extra-parochial program, arrived at the figure of one dollar and seventy-four cents per annum for each of Pennsylvania's 8,865 communicants. The total number of communicants in the United States he reckoned as 72,000. He recommended each rector keep account of the outside giving of his parishioners, and exhort them to come up to or exceed this modest figure. This letter, signed "X.Y.Z.," was reprinted by the *Spirit of Missions*, 1845, pp. 223-4.

[11]*Spirit of Missions*, 1845, p. 252.

[12]*Ibid.*, p. 407.

the Domestic Committee laid down the rule that none would be appointed. This action elicited a strong protest from Freeman. He received the circular of the Committee just when he had returned from his second visitation to Texas, a visitation that took him over new ground which promised a fair field of work for the Church; he had accompanied Ives to Brazoria County, where their ministrations met with a great welcome.[13] Freeman was anxious that Brazoria County be made a missionary appointment of the Board, and was understandably upset when he thought the Committee intended to appoint no new missionaries.

The situation was saved not by contributions to the Domestic treasury (which actually diminished the next year) but by the Texas Church itself. Both Houston and Galveston became self-supporting Parishes on July 1, 1846, and released their appropriations for new work elsewhere in the State. The town of Matagorda, hampered by its shallow harbor and by the log raft obstructing navigation of the river, had not grown as the others had; hence its Church, almost ideal in its inner life and its embrace of the entire community, was unable to do without the stipend its missionary received from the Society. The Board of Missions responded to the generous action of the Houston and Galveston congregations by designating three new missionaries stations for Texas: the first, Brazoria County; the second, Independence, Brenham, and La Grange; the third, San Augustine and Nacogdoches.[14] But another serious problem for the Episcopal Church rose up to confront the Bishop; no clergy came forward to accept the positions offered. Ives, who at length built up his school to the point that he could afford to employ assistant teachers, now devoted enough attention to Brazoria and adjacent points to keep the prospect alive, but he rejected the tempting offer the planters of that area made him to remove there.[15] About the same time Ives declined a call to Livingston, Alabama; he could not contemplate leaving his friends and parishioners, even though the Alabama offer would have paid much more than he received in Matagorda.[16]

---

[13]*Ibid.*, 1846, pp. 288-9; 326-8; Ives' Common Journal, March 27, 1846. The visit to Brazoria was a harrowing one for Ives and the Bishop. They were accompanied by a clergyman named Purdy, who had several epileptic fits on the journey, falling from his horse twice.

[14]*Spirit of Missions*, 1846, p. 358.

[15]Ives' Common Journal, 1846-7. One of the male teachers, William L. Sartwell, was the father of one of the first native sons to be ordained in Texas. The school situation in Matagorda was so promising that a project for a university under Church auspices was underway in 1846. *Spirit of Missions*, 1846, p. 154.

[16]Ives' Common Journal, August 2, 1846.

The first two new missionaries for Texas, remarkably enough, came from Florida, and both were future bishops. John Freeman Young had gone to Jacksonville, Florida, as missionary directly after graduation from Virginia Seminary.[17] He moved to Texas in January 1848, having as his companion, on the voyage from New Orleans to Matagorda, Ives, who had been to Mobile and New Orleans to solicit funds for plastering the interior of the Matagorda church.[18] Young had been appointed missionary to St. John's Church, Brazoria, which had been organized that year.[19] A short while later Henry Niles Pierce, a Candidate for Holy Orders of the Diocese of Florida, moved to Texas and was ordained Deacon on Easter Sunday 1848 in Christ Church, Matagorda, by Bishop Freeman. He was assigned to Independence, Brenham, and La Grange.[20] The third appointment was that of the Reverend Henry Sansom, Deacon, to San Augustine and Nacogdoches. Sansom, a native of England, possessed a good education and many gifts. He had been ordained in New York by Bishop Alonzo Potter of Pennsylvania on April 16, 1848, and reached San Augustine with his family on May 23, after a journey saddened by the sickness of his boy, who contracted scarlet fever on the trip and died the day after the family arrived.[21]

The addition of these three missionaries completed the roster of clergy who were to be canonically resident at the organization of the Diocese in 1849.

GROWTH TOWARD DIOCESAN STATUS

Christ Church Parish in Houston, after many trials, at length completed its church building in time for consecration by Bishop Freeman on Sunday, May 9, 1847.[22] By April 1848 Freeman was reporting that since completion of the church, the increased attendance had made it already too small; he commended the mem-

---

17John Freeman Young was born in Pittston, Maine, October 30, 1820, entered Wesleyan University in 1840, graduated from Virginia Seminary in 1845, and was ordained Deacon by Bishop Henshaw that year. He was Bishop of Florida from 1867 to 1885. *Appleton's Cyclopaedia of American Biography, en loc.*; Burgess' *List of Deacons*, 1845.

18Ives' Common Journal, January 31, 1848.

19*Spirit of Missions*, 1847, pp. 463, 253.

20*Ibid.*, 1848, pp. 256, 258-9. Pierce was born in Pawtucket, Rhode Island, October 19, 1820, and studied for orders privately. E. Clowes Chorley, "The Church in Arkansas and its Bishops," *Historical Magazine*, XV (1946), pp. 335-6.

21George L. Crocket, *Two Centuries in East Texas* (Dallas, 1932), pp. 288-9; *Journal of the Diocese of New York*, 1848, p. 33; *The Churchman*, April 22, 1848, p. 31. The invaluable book of Crocket's has recently been brought back into print by the Guild of Christ Church, San Augustine, Texas.

22*Spirit of Missions*, 1847, p. 252.

bers of the parish, now self-supporting, for having borne almost the entire expense themselves but suggested that help from the stronger churches of the East would be in order to enable them to carry out an enlargement of the church.[23] Trinity Church, Galveston, continued to flourish under its popular Rector, and the need for a larger building was being felt.[24]

Bishop Freeman's visitations for the first three years of his oversight over the Texas Church were taxing to the extreme. On his second visitation in 1846 he had gone by horseback across the Gulf prairies in the midst of the rainy March cold on his way to Brazoria and Matagorda. The exposure had so sickened him that he was several months recuperating. He recommended to the Board that the field be divided, since it was too vast and scattered to allow one bishop to extend the Church effectively. Texas, he thought, could be placed in charge of a neighboring diocesan bishop (the only neighboring one was Polk!)[25] In 1847 he reported having travelled in the year past 7,195 miles, 665 by land and the remaining 6,530 by water.[26] In 1848, after returning to Houston from a journey of two hundred miles overland through Brazoria and Matagorda counties, the Bishop set out in company with the Reverend J. F. Young, intending to go as far as San Antonio and Austin. The Bishop related (writing, as he did in his reports, in the third person):

> After the first day's journey, which was made in a splendid Albany coach drawn by six horses, they were transferred to a vehicle peculiar to the west, consisting of a rectangular box of the coarsest kind, resting upon the bolsters of a wagon carriage, without even an apology for springs, and uncovered. In this conveyance they were hurried along, faster in proportion as the way became more rugged, under the unmitigated rays of an almost tropical sun, for a distance of more than thirty miles, to Independence, in Washington county, where, in consequence of the severe indisposition of Mr. Young, occasioned by this rough mode of travelling, they were compelled to stop.

It was the young clergyman, not the old bishop, who broke under the roughness of the travel, and made the journey beyond Washington county impractical.[27]

By 1847 the Bishop's visitations began to take on something of an institutional cast; the clergy, assembled in Houston, "all in their surplices," assisted the Bishop in the consecration of the church. Gillett and Ives travelled with him overland to Matagorda and back

[23]*Ibid.*, 1848, p. 257.   [24]*Ibid.*, 1847, p. 253.   [25]*Ibid.*, 1846, pp. 285-91.
[26]*Ibid.*, 1847, pp. 253-4.   [27]*Ibid.*, 1848, p. 258.

through the Brazoria County settlements to Galveston, where in a
meeting they considered but rejected the proposal to organize a
diocese, for fear that such an organization as yet could not be
financed.[28] But the meeting created a sense of solidarity and achievement. In 1848 Matagorda was the scene of the greatest activity; as
noted above, Henry Niles Pierce was ordained on Easter Day. The
visit was made memorable for Ives, who at that time was disturbed
by the effort of some Baptist preachers to break the solidarity of the
community, by the fact that daily services were conducted throughout
Holy Week, with all the clergy except Eaton present from Maundy
Thursday.[29] To crown the festivities, Bishop Freeman on Easter
Monday performed the marriage rites for the Reverend Charles Gillett and Miss Mary Ann Wharton.[30]

Events were indeed moving forward so rapidly that the prospect
for organizing a diocese seemed bright. Though he does not mention it in recording his fourth visitation to Texas, Freeman seems
to have agreed with the clergy and representative laity to have a
meeting in Matagorda during his fifth visitation to consider the
matter again.[31]

Freeman's visitation of Texas in the fall of 1848 was even more
encouraging. He entered Texas from the Louisiana border, visited
San Augustine for the first time, and there made the acquaintance
of the Reverend Henry Sansom, Deacon. He reported that this Missionary was doing a good job at Nacogdoches as well as at San
Augustine, and the prospects of the Church at both places seemed
promising. After he had completed his visitation of these two congregations the Bishop took Sansom along with him, and stopped
next at Huntsville, where they met with a good reception. Huntsville and the settlement of Cincinnati, on the Trinity River, would
constitute, in Freeman's judgment, a hopeful missionary field. At the
new town of Anderson the Bishop and Sansom were welcomed
by a member of the Church of England, Henry Fanthorp, who
produced the names of a number of members of the Episcopal
Church in the vicinity. Anderson, too, appeared to be a useful
base for a mission.

Arriving in Washington County, the Bishop found the other
Deacon, Henry Niles Pierce, hard at work. He had begun regular
services in the three principal settlements, Washington, Brenham,

---

28*Spirit of Missions*, 1847, p. 253; Ives' Common Journal, May 24, 1847.
29*Ibid.*, April 20 ff.
30*Spirit of Missions*, 1848, p. 256.
31*Ibid.*, 1849, p. 264.

and Independence, and had also once visited Columbus in Colorado County.[32] At Brenham one of the candidates for Confirmation was Lindsey Peter Rucker, a man who was to contribute years of devoted labor in the ministry of the Episcopal Church in Texas up to the day of his death. Described as "late a highly respectable member of the Campbellite Baptist denomination,"[33] Rucker had come to Texas at the age of twenty-two, after graduation from Clinton College and ordination in the Methodist Episcopal Church in his native Tennessee. He had resided and taught school at various places in Washington County since 1838.[34] Rucker had been attracted to the ministry of the Episcopal Church through his association with Pierce while they taught in the same school in Brenham. Rucker applied for admission as a Candidate for Holy Orders, and was admitted as such following the adjournment of the primary Convention of the Diocese in Matagorda, January 3, 1849.[35]

West of Washington County the Bishop and Gillett conducted services at La Grange and Bastrop, which with Columbus, they felt, would afford a field for a missionary. They then tarried in Austin for several days and discovered a strong desire for the establishment of a parish there. At San Antonio, the next stop on the visitation, the same wish was expressed by a number of the inhabitants who attended the services. In both Austin and San Antonio confirmations were held.[36] From observations made on his journey from San Antonio to Matagorda, the Bishop believed that another field, including Victoria, Port Lavaca, and Indianola, was ready if only a missionary could be provided.[37] As Freeman saw it, eight more missionaries ought to be appointed for Texas, including one for Clarksville in the Red River Valley.[38]

But this fair opportunity could not be exploited for lack of money. Funds were indeed so short that Freeman had been delayed two weeks at Philadelphia in departing for his visitation; he had relied on the Domestic Committee to pay his back salary and trav-

[32]*Ibid.*, p. 265.

[33]*Journal of the Diocese of Texas*, 1850, p. 25. Cited hereafter as *"Texas Journal."*

[34]Lucy Rucker, *A Brief Sketch of the Rev. L. P. Rucker, with a Detailed Account of His Thrilling Adventure with the Indians* [n.d., n.p., published in Washington County, place unnamed], [2.] This book is in the Texas History Center, Library of the University of Texas, Austin. Cited hereafter as "Lucy Rucker, *Rucker.*"

[35]*Texas Journal*, 1850, p. 25.

[36]*Spirit of Missions*, 1849, p. 265.

[37]*Ibid.*, p. 267.

[38]*Ibid.*, p. 273.

elling expenses and found that body with an overdrawn treasury.[39] Shortly before this time the same Committee had been unrealistic enough to commend to Bishops Freeman and Kemper respectively the requests for episcopal attention coming from California and Oregon, stating that the jurisdiction of the Missionary Bishops extended to the Pacific Coast![40]

Thus on the eve of its organization as a diocese, the Texas mission faced the prospect of diminished support from the Missionary Society. If the cause of the Church in Texas was to prosper, the Church people of Texas must themselves perfect an organization in order to muster their own resources, seek more frequent episcopal supervision, and take more responsibility for conduct and support of the work of extension within the borders of the State.

[39]*Ibid.*, pp. 261-2.   [40]*Ibid.*, p. 217.

ADDITIONAL NOTE ON THE ORGANIZATION OF CHRIST CHURCH, HOUSTON, TEXAS.

Miss Marguerite Barnes has found the agreement to unite as a parish under the date of March 16, 1839. This information reached me after type was set for this work. The date reported by Chapman, April 1, 1839, was that on which the vestry was organized. Miss Barnes will deal with this fully in her forthcoming history of Christ Church Cathedral.

PART TWO

THE FIRST DIOCESAN DECADE

IV. Diocesan Organization and Program

O N NEW YEAR'S DAY 1849 Bishop Freeman presided over a meeting at Christ Church, Matagorda, to consider afresh the feasibility of organizing the Episcopal Church in Texas into a diocese. The appointment had been made on December 5 at Washington-on-the-Brazos, where the Bishop and Henry Sansom arrived from Nacogdoches to meet Henry Niles Pierce and Charles Gillett. It was arranged that Sansom should go to Houston to supply services at Christ Church while its Rector, Gillett, accompanied the Bishop on a visitation of the western settlements of the State; afterward they were to meet in Matagorda.[1]

ORGANIZATION OF THE DIOCESE

The attendance must have been disappointing to those present, considering the advance notice that had been given. Only three clergy beside the Bishop were present, if the minutes are correct; Ives of Matagorda, Young of Brazoria County, and Gillett of Houston.[2] It is possible that Pierce arrived before the adjournment of the Convention, for he was ordained to the Priesthood in Matagorda on January 3, the day after adjournment.[3] Of the laity, Matthew

---

[1] Spirit of Missions, 1849, p. 264.
[2] Texas Journal, 1849, p. 5.
[3] Spirit of Missions, 1849, p. 267.

Talbot, James Dennison, Thomas C. Stewart and William L. Sartwell represented Matagorda, and Dr. P. A. Davenport, the only out-of-town delegate at the opening of the meeting, St. John's Church, Brazoria County. Before the afternoon session was over William M. Taylor of Christ Church, Houston, appeared and gave his assent to the proceedings.[4] Two difficulties had hindered a full attendance; tremendous winter rains had flooded low places in the roads and delayed those who ventured to travel, and an epidemic of cholera which first appeared among the United States troops at Victoria had broken out at Houston.[5] These two circumstances kept Sansom in Houston, and may account also for the absence of Eaton and his Galveston delegation.

In spite of the small attendance the Diocese was organized, a constitution and set of canons were adopted, and a Standing Committee and Deputies to General Convention were elected. The Standing Committee, all clerical after the Connecticut model, consisted of Ives, Gillett and Young. Deputies to General Convention were Ives, Eaton, Gillett and Young in the clerical order, and P. A. Davenport, E. S. Perkins, R. D. Johnson and W. L. Sartwell in the lay order. This delegation was instructed to apply to the General Convention of 1850 for the admission of the Diocese into union with the Protestant Episcopal Church. Realizing that it would be impossible to support a bishop and carry on missionary work with local resources alone, the Convention requested Bishop Freeman to take the Diocese under his provisional care, and asked the Board of Missions to continue its appropriations for missionaries.

Six organized congregations were listed as members of the Diocese:

Matagorda, Christ Church, organized 1839
Houston, Christ Church, organized 1839
Galveston, Trinity Church, organized 1841
Brazoria County, St. John's Church, organized 1847
San Augustine, Christ Church, organized 1848
Nacogdoches, Christ Church, organized 1848

The Washington County field had as yet no organized congregations.[6]

After the adjournment of the primary Convention, Freeman made an intensive visitation of Brazoria County. He found the work of the Reverend John Freeman Young quite effective. At Columbia, under the zealous leadership of Dr. P. A. Davenport, the people were making plans to erect a small church building. The Brazoria

[4]*Texas Journal*, 1849, pp. 4, 8.
[5]*Spirit of Missions*, 1849, p. 267.
[6]*Texas Journal*, 1849, pp. 5-8.

church members were hoping for the same thing, though their plans were not so well advanced. Freeman officiated several times in both these towns, and at Gulf Prairie as well. These communities at that time were enjoying prosperity, due to successful experiments with sugar cane culture. The Bishop held out great hopes for the future of the Church in this area.

Reaching Houston over roads deep with mud, Freeman found that city practically submerged in it. Few services could be held, for the church building could be reached only with the greatest difficulty between frequent torrents of rain. After waiting a week in hope of assembling a full congregation, the Bishop proceeded to ordain the Reverend Henry Sansom to the Priesthood in the presence of those who could be assembled; he went to Galveston to visit the flock there and then returned to Houston for Confirmation, allowing as much time as possible for the Rector to get his candidates together. After another visit to Galveston, Freeman departed from the State on February 11, after the most thorough visitation he was ever able to give the Diocese.[7]

In the summer after the primary Convention, the Diocese had to mourn the death of its first clergyman and missionary, the Reverend Caleb S. Ives. Failing in health for some time, Ives had gone first to Sour Lake in East Texas to try the mineral waters; Sour Lake had developed into quite a mineral spa, drawing people from all over coastal Texas. Ives estimated about one hundred and fifty people were there at any one time during the summer. They bathed in the water, and drank it as well. Despite great pain from a rheumatic condition in his legs, Ives conducted services every Sunday while at Sour Lake, where there were numerous Episcopalians from Houston, Galveston, and even Matagorda and Brazoria Counties. Ives and his eldest son Angus made the trip in a buggy. Though he felt much better when he started home than he had before coming, the trip home undid all the good; he said that he was worse off than he had been before, and found himself too feeble to preach on Sundays.[8] Disappointed in the hope of recovering in Texas, Ives obtained a leave of absence in order to spend the summer in Vermont, where he hoped a respite from Texas' summer heat would

[7]*Spirit of Missions,* 1849, pp. 267-9.

[8]*Spirit of Missions,* 1849, p. 104; Ives' Common Journal, II, June 21, 1848 to August 14, 1849. This second volume of Ives' Journal turned up in Price Daniel, Junior's rare book shop in Waco in 1961, and was purchased by J. Cooke Wilson, Jr., who presented it to the Diocese of Texas. There are only a few pages of diary entries, starting where the first volume ended, and ending on the date on which Ives and his son Angus took ship from Mobile to the East. Most of the book is filled with Bible study notes of uncertain origin.

restore him.[9] He died in his native town of Tinmouth, Vermont, July 27, 1849. His death was lamented, not only in Matagorda and the surrounding country to which he had ministered directly, but by the entire Diocese, to whose very being he had contributed so much in energetic work, in wise counsel, and in steadying leadership.[10] Of all the lost opportunities of the Church in Texas in its first decade of life, perhaps the greatest was the failure to place this good and wise man in the office of Foreign Missionary Bishop to Texas, where his talents probably would have been more widely effective.

Until January 1850 the Matagorda Church was kept open by its layreader, W. L. Sartwell; then the Reverend S. D. Dennison of the Diocese of Massachusetts, "seeking temporary relief from parish labors in a voyage to the South," accepted the rectorship, and was appointed missionary by the Domestic Committee.[11] The services of one additional clergyman fortuitously were secured through the action of the United States Army in stationing Chaplain J. F. Fish, a Presbyter of the Diocese of New York, at San Antonio, where he organized Trinity Church.[12] At the same time the services of another were refused; a certain Ambrose Smith, residing in San Antonio and claiming orders in the Church of Ireland, was inhibited from officiating in the Diocese when he failed to exhibit credentials sufficient to satisfy Bishop Freeman. He ceased officiating, and subsequently left the State.[13] Smith had appeared in Matagorda during Ives' illness, and had preached for him a few times, to the satisfaction of the congregation, Ives said. While there he had become acquainted with John Freeman Young of Brazoria. Evidently both Ives and Young believed Smith was an Irish clergyman, and were willing to give the endorsement of the Standing Committee to his officiating in the Diocese.[14] Smith appeared in Mississippi some time in 1854, and promised Bishop Green to produce his letter of orders, but evidently was unable to do so.[15]

Freeman's generous expenditure of time on his visitation to Texas in the year of the primary Convention, and the sense of achievement in the organization of the Diocese, gave the work of the

[9]*Spirit of Missions*, 1849, p. 267.

[10]*Ibid.*, pp. 331, 357-9; *Texas Journal*, 1850, pp. 18-9, 26, 33.

[11]*Ibid.*, p. 9; *Spirit of Missions*, 1850, p. 141.

[12]*Texas Journal*, 1850, pp. 3, 19.

[13]*Ibid.*, pp. 19-21.

[14]Ives' Common Journal, II, March 16-18, 1849.

[15]*Journal of the Diocese of Mississippi*, 1855, p. 31; he is neither mentioned nor listed in subsequent Journals.

Church a new impetus in the ensuing convention year. There was much to report when the Bishop came again.

BISHOP FREEMAN'S PROGRAM

The first Annual Convention of the Diocese was appointed to meet on the second Thursday in December 1849 in Houston,[16] but because of illness in the Bishop's family, it was postponed to Ascension Day, May 9, 1850. Then the situation appeared much brighter than it had the previous year; four new congregations were admitted to union with the Diocese: Trinity, San Antonio; St. Paul's, Washington; St. Peter's, Brenham; and St. Paul's, Fireman's Hill, Polk County.[17] The Bishop presented a program of action which he believed would do much to forward the work of the Diocese. First in importance, he felt, was the appointment of a general missionary, who could travel about the State, look into promising situations, and officiate in places where members of the Church were found. Freeman was asking for the appointment of seven more missionaries by the Domestic Committee for fields ready to be occupied. These fields were Marshall, Harrison County; Clarksville, Red River County; Huntsville, Walker County with Fireman's Hill, Polk County; Austin; Columbus, with La Grange and Bastrop; Victoria with Port Lavaca; and Brownsville. But the Bishop believed that the Diocese itself should be able, through the exertions of its present congregations, to support the work of an additional man to act as the general missionary.[18]

The next important need of the Diocese, the Bishop felt, was a diocesan school. Since his election he had realized the need for such a school in his jurisdiction; he believed that if a sufficient supply of clergy was to be maintained, it would have to be recruited and educated locally. The school's principal function would be to educate young men for the ministry, and it must, therefore, be under the Church's control. Realizing that the Diocese of Texas had not the resources to begin such an institution, the Bishop suggested that some clergyman might make a start at his own risk and expense; indeed, he reported having received such an offer in a letter from a competent clerical educator. Should the Convention give its authority and encouragement, a beginning might be made.[19]

To both the Bishop's proposals the Convention gave approval. A Diocesan Mission Committee was charged with raising means to

---

[16] *Texas Journal*, 1949, p. 8.   [17] *Ibid.*, 1850, pp. 9-10.
[18] *Ibid.*, p. 22.   [19] *Ibid.*, pp. 22, 24.

employ a general missionary, and equip him with Prayer Books, Bibles and tracts for distribution.[20] Going beyond the Bishop's proposal, the Convention elected a committee of five to which it committed the business of the school, and gave them authority to select a site, find a teacher, put a school in operation, and report to the next Convention. To this committee were elected as clerical members Gillett and Eaton, and as lay members Guy M. Bryan, George Butler and General James Pinckney Henderson.[21]

One other forward-looking action, so far the the Texas Church itself was concerned, was taken by the Convention in passing a motion, introduced by the Reverend Henry Sansom, urging Bishop Freeman to transfer his residence to "some central and convenient point within the bounds of this Diocese."[22] Had it proved possible for the Bishop to accede to this request, many of the blunders connected with the school project and much of the consequent ill feeling might have been avoided, and perhaps the life of the Bishop prolonged.

Texas was admitted as a new diocese by the General Convention meeting in Cincinnati, Ohio, in October 1850,[23] where Texas was represented by Eaton, Gillett and Young as Clerical Deputies, and James Reily and Peter W. Gray as Lay Deputies.[24] The Board of Missions at its meetings during General Convention once again was unable to take advantage of the openings discovered by its missionaries. Though rescued from its desperate financial plight of the previous year sufficiently to prevent cutbacks in appropriations to work already established, the Domestic Committee of the Board refused to make additional appropriations to Texas or to other jurisdictions. By appropriating in cash all but one of the legacies received during the year it was possible to pay the missionaries still in the service of the Committee, but only because the number of domestic missionaries had been reduced in the previous year by resignations and deaths from one hundred to ninety.[25] Any new work to be started in Texas would have to be financed there.

In view of these facts, it is rather surprising that four new congregations had been organized by the time of the meeting of the Second Annual Convention on May 1, 1851; only one of these was in a community that Freeman had visited. During the summer of

---

[20]*Ibid.*, pp. 30-1. [21]*Ibid.*, pp. 28-9. [22]*Ibid.*, p. 32.
[23]*General Convention Journal*, 1850, pp. 11, 18, 104.
[24]*Ibid.*, pp. 2, 3. Gray was elected by the Standing Committee in place of W. L. Sartwell. *Texas Journal*, 1851, p. 20.
[25]*Spirit of Missions*, 1850, pp. 385 402.

1850, Lindsey P. (Rucker,) who was ordained Deacon following the Convention in the Spring of that year,[26] was engaged to supply services for the Reverend Charles Gillett during the latter's absence in the North. His route between his home in Brenham and Houston passed through the new Washington County settlement of Chappell Hill (spelled "Chapel Hill" in many of the early Church documents, but now and for a long time "Chappell"). He was urged by some of the local residents to conduct services for them. This he did, and soon found a movement underway to organize a congregation, build a church, and support a clergyman. When Gillett returned to his Parish, Rucker asked and received the Bishop's permission to organize St. Luke's Church there,[27] which was done in time for it to be admitted to the Diocese at the convention in Galveston, May 1, 1851.[28] Appointed to represent the new Parish at the Convention, but not recorded as being present, were W. L. Tunstall, William H. Sherman and John C. Wallis.[29]

Even more remarkable was the desire of a group of members and friends of the Episcopal Church in Brownsville to have their congregation admitted to the Diocese of Texas. No clergyman of the Church had yet visited there, yet the two wardens, Joseph P. Couthouy and John S. Rhea, attended the Convention and handed the petition for admission to the Bishop, together with the request that the Bishop make a visitation to Brownsville. The Parish was admitted under its present name, "Church of the Advent."[30] Because of the great length of time required to make a trip by steamship and because of his busy schedule, Freeman had reluctantly to excuse himself from visiting Brownsville that year.[31]

Another congregation would have been admitted at the 1851 convention had its application reached Galveston in time. This was Trinity Church of Marshall, Harrison County. On the previous Christmas, Sansom, missionary at San Augustine and Nacogdoches, had visited Marshall, and had organized the new Parish on January 4, 1851.[32] Being called as its Rector, Sansom had resigned his missionary appointment effective April 1, 1851,[33] and begun officiating in Marshall. Neither Sansom nor any of his flock attended the Convention.[34]

[26] *Texas Journal*, 1851, p. 9.   [27] *Spirit of Missions*, 1851, p. 418.
[28] *Texas Journal*, 1851, p. 9.   [29] *Ibid.*, p. 4.   [30] *Ibid.*, p. 9.
[31] *Spirit of Missions*, 1851, p. 377.
[32] Max S. Lale, *As It Was in the Beginning* (Marshall, Texas, 1950), p. 3.
[33] *Spirit of Missions*, 1851, p. 173.
[34] *Texas Journal*, 1851, p. 4.

The last of the four new parishes was Epiphany Church, Austin. Ever since Caleb Ives' visit to Austin in 1840 had disclosed the presence of some communicants of the Church in that town, the strategy of the Texas mission had been to establish a station there, although the removal of the government in 1842 diminished the importance Austin had enjoyed as the capital of the Republic under President Lamar.[35] With the return of the seat of government following Texas' admission to the United States, the town began to grow again. The Reverend Charles Gillett, who in 1845 had visited Austin in company with the Reverend Benjamin Eaton, returned in 1847 and organized a parish under the name of Christ Church.[36] Since Freeman's appeal for missionaries for this and other stations did not prevail with the Domestic Committee, the Austin parish seems to have lapsed for want of a minister, though layreaders performed services.[37] Nevertheless when Freeman visited Austin in December 1848, on his way to the organizing convention for the Diocese, his services met with enthusiastic response, and he was requested to send a missionary.[38]

Austin's desire for an Episcopal minister was at length satisfied when a former resident and religious worker, Edward Fontaine, now an Episcopal clergyman, returned, and reorganized the Parish, renaming it "Church of the Epiphany."[39] Fontaine had first come to Austin as Secretary to President Lamar. Then no religious services of any kind were being conducted, and although he "belonged to no church" at that time, Fontaine organized a Sunday School and an adult Bible Class in which he taught and preached each Sunday to both white and negro citizens.[40] Though he spoke of his temerity in doing this work, Fontaine was no uninstructed layman; he had been a Methodist minister.[41] After Lamar's term expired and President Houston moved the government from Austin, Fontaine moved to Independence, where he taught school for some time,[42] later moving to Mississippi. In the interval he was confirmed in the

---

[35]Writers' Program, Works Project Administration, *St. David's Through the Years* (Austin, 1942), pp. 12-16. This work will be cited hereafter as "*St. David's.*"

[36]*Ibid.*, pp. 17-18.   [37]*Ibid.*, p. 20.

[38]*Spirit of Missions*, 1849, p. 265.   [39]*St. David's*, p. 20.

[40]*Spirit of Missions*, 1852, pp. 46-8. This fascinating letter of Fontaine's gives his description of pioneer days in Austin, when the recurrence of Indian attacks made life in the town exciting if dangerous.

[41]Samuel Wood Geiser, "Note on Edward Fontaine," *Southwestern Historical Quarterly*, XLVII, No. 2 (October, 1943), pp. 181-3. I owe this reference to Mr. Weldon Hart of St. David's, Austin.

[42]*St. David's*, pp. 19-20.

Episcopal Church, and was ordained Deacon in June 1847 and Priest in May 1848, by Bishop Otey; he served as a missionary of the Domestic Committee successively at Aberdeen and Canton, Mississippi, before moving again to Austin.[43] When Freeman visited Austin on his way to the 1851 Convention, he learned that Fontaine had gone to Mississippi to remove his family to Austin; the Bishop conducted the Easter services for the flock.[44] As a consequence of the Rector's absence at the time of the Convention, the requisite papers were not placed before the Convention; thus is was necessary to delay admission of the Parish to union with the Diocese until the following year.[45]

Looking to the advancement of the work of the Diocese, Freeman recommended in his Convention Address that, even though there was not yet the canonical number of clergy to make possible the election of a bishop,[46] advance measures should be taken for financial support in the hope that an election would be possible at the next convention. Two matters the Bishop thought important for the advancement and well-being of the Church. First, the clergy must set forth the whole Gospel, as they had received it. There must be no compromise, no holding back for fear of prejudice, in presenting the Church

> as a divine institution, as apostolic in its character and organization, as Catholic as well as Protestant in its doctrines, and as the Body of Christ, of which all who would be saved must ordinarily become members.

The services of the Church must be conducted in strict obedience to the rubrics of the Prayer Book. To omit portions, to make changes, as some were disposed to do, was to violate the vows of ordination, the Bishop believed, and further, was to gain nothing at all, for the liturgy in its integrity commended itself to people better than watered-down versions. In the second place, since the scheme of employing a general missionary had not been carried out, the system used in some other dioceses should be tried; each parochial clergyman should give a part of his time in missionary work outside his own Parish.[47]

---

[43]*Spirit of Missions*, 1848, pp. 143, 344; Geiser, *loc. cit.*

[44]*Spirit of Missions*, 1851, p. 376.

[45]*Texas Journal*, 1851, pp. 4, 13.

[46]Six regularly settled in parishes or churches were required by Canon II of 1844. *General Convention Journal*, 1850, Supplement, Constitution and Canons, p. 39. Only five were qualified in Texas at convention time. *Texas Journal*, 1851, p. 4.

[47]*Ibid.*, p. 15.

Decisive action was taken by the Convention before its adjournment. The Reverend Charles Gillett proposed to undertake the Diocesan School at his own risk, with such help as the appointed committee and the members of the Church would afford him, and with the question of location to be decided by the committee. Then a committee was formed to canvass the congregations for pledges toward the support of a resident bishop, to be elected at the next Convention. The 1852 Convention was invited to meet at Washington-on-the-Brazos if the church building then being erected were completed in time; if not, it would meet at Chappell Hill in the same county, where the building project seemed farther along.[48]

The ranks of the clergy increased considerably in the ensuing convention year. Before the Galveston meeting adjourned, the Reverend D. D. Flowers of Alabama, who had accepted the rectorship at Matagorda, appeared at the Convention. The Reverend William Passmore of the Diocese of North Carolina was appointed missionary to the Church of the Advent, Brownsville, September 1, 1851.[49] The Reverend Elisha H. Downing of Mississippi was appointed to San Augustine and Nacogdoches December 1.[50] Charles F. Rottenstein, a former Methodist minister, was ordained Deacon at the 1852 Convention, and was assigned to assist in the Washington County field.[51] But there was considerable displacement and rearrangement. Flowers stayed only a few months at Matagorda before he returned to Alabama. Henry Niles Pierce accepted the call extended him by the Matagorda vestry. This left all four of the congregations in Washington County to be cared for by L. P. Rucker. Though he had been advanced to the Priesthood at the convention of 1851 and was thus qualified to stand alone, Rucker was burdened with the duties of a school; the assignment of Rottenstein to assist him was timely. Gillette[52] resigned the rectorship of the Houston parish upon becoming head of the Diocesan School, and the Christ Church vestry called Sansom to Houston to succeed him, and the new parish at Marshall was left without a Rector.[53] Finally, Trinity Church, San Antonio, was without clerical services because of the transfer of Chaplain J. F. Fish with his Army unit to Fort McKavitt, a frontier post on the San Saba River.[54]

[48]Ibid., pp. 23-6, 28.   [49]Spirit of Missions, 1851, p. 451.

[50]Ibid., 1852, p. 51.   [51]Texas Journal, 1852, p. 15.

[52]Sometime between the 1851 and 1852 Conventions both Gilletts, Rev. Charles and Henry F., changed the spelling of the name by adding the final "e." See the Journals of the Diocese for both of these years, including reports signed by each of these men.

[53]Texas Journal, 1852, p. 15.   [54]Ibid., pp. 13, 45.

With a more adequate clergy staff to attend to the Church's primary duty of the conduct of worship in the several congregations, the Diocese turned to bringing into effect the program which had been adopted in the last two Conventions. The matter of first importance was the establishment of a school.

THE ANDERSON SCHOOLS

Events moved swiftly in the establishment of the Diocesan School after the 1851 Convention. Armed with the Convention's authorization, Gillette and the committee met several times to consider possible locations, after circulating requests for proposals among the congregations. Only three concrete propositions were received. One was made by Mr. M. A. Bryan of Brazoria County, offering a location at the mouth of the Brazos River, at either Quintana or Velasco. A Mr. T. T. Baily, proposed a site at "the Sulphur Springs" in Gonzales County. More definite was the offer made by Orphan Friend Lodge Number 17, Ancient Free and Accepted Masons, and some citizens of Anderson; there were two buildings with sufficient grounds, a Female Academy already in being, and pledges of support from the citizens of Anderson who had joined in making the proposal. Other citizens of Grimes County pledged to assist in meeting the deficit incurred in the operation of the Female Academy as it was being run on the Lodge's responsibility. Gillette was sent by the committee to investigate; he reported to an adjourned meeting in August of 1851, that the buildings were inadequate for the purposes without substantial additions, which would cost between $3000 and $4000, and that he was unable to undertake so heavy a responsibility personally. The other members of the committee present, Eaton and Pierce of the clergy and Gray of the laity, voted, on the motion of Eaton, to undertake the establishment of the Diocesan School and continue the Female Academy, apparently at the risk of the Diocese, and so to inform the Lodge and the Bishop. They obligated themselves to begin the school by January 1, 1852.

Without waiting for a reply from the Bishop, Gillette set out to raise the necessary funds. He obtained pledges, totaling $1900, due in three annual installments, from seven persons in Texas; then he headed for Cincinnati, where Freeman had spent the Summer, intending to proceed to New York on a begging campaign. The Bishop put a stop to his trip, objected to the heavy obligation involved in the promise to continue a female department at the risk of the Diocese, and would only consent to accepting the Lodge's offer if the girls' school could be undertaken by some clergyman at his own risk. Gillette could do nothing but return to Texas and attempt to re-negotiate the matter with the Masonic Lodge. Gillette was able to meet the conditions set by the Lodge and by the Bishop only by agreeing to operate the girls' school at his own risk. By dint of monumental physical labor and by piling up a considerable debt he managed to get the schools into operation by January 1852.[55] When the Convention of 1852 assembled, a Diocesan School had been in operation for four months, but it appeared that it had both exceeded the authorization given by the previous Convention and incurred financial obligations which that body had not voted to undertake. Gillette had not stopped with the creation of a boys' secondary school; he had applied to the State of Texas for a charter for a degree-granting college. He and the committee justified this step by taking the ground that there was a general understanding at the 1851 Convention that the institution projected there was to be "the collegiate and theological school of the Diocese."[56]

A need for a school of collegiate rank was evidenced by the fact that by the time of the 1852 Convention the school had attracted some qualified college and seminary students. Two of the latter were acting as tutors in the secondary school while pursuing their theological studies under Gillette's direction; they were Joseph Wood Dunn and Hannibal Pratt.[57] Rottenstein apparently had completed his studies there in preparation for his canonical examinations. Although the amount of study that was possible in a new school, in a frontier community, with an inadequate library, and with students' time limited by tutorial duties, was less than desirable, this effort was certainly better than nothing. There several able men were prepared for the ministry, and others, who gained some of their schooling there, went elsewhere for college and seminary. No doubt several parishes rejoiced in years to come over the training that members of their congregations had received in the Anderson schools.

Yet the failure of the schools was almost inevitable from the start, because of inadequate financial backing from the outside, and because the schools were situated in a small community where previously the Episcopal Church was hardly known. Gillette was relieved of some obligations upon his time and financial resources when the Reverend J. B. F. Smith took over the girls' school at his own risk.[58]

[55]Ibid., 17-24.

[56]This was evidently called in question later, and Gillette offered another explanation in his "Brief History of St. Paul's College," printed in Texas Journal, 1856, pp. 28ff.

[57]Texas Journal, 1853, pp. 4, 21.

[58]Ibid., 1854, p. 19.

But Gillette had incurred so much debt for the new buildings for
the Diocesan (boys') School that it could not survive without help
from the outside. A group of five laymen had guaranteed to pay this
debt, but they never secured the needed funds, even when suit was
filed upon Gillette by the school's creditors.[59] The truth was that the
Church in Texas was not equal to building and operating a boarding
school without a substantial endowment, and no such endowment
could be raised in the frontier community that Texas then was.
Help from the older states was essential, yet in the hard times of
the early 1850's this help was difficult to get; the haste with which
the project had been undertaken had prevented a thorough effort to
secure such funds.

Had the Episcopal Church been known and accepted in Anderson and the surrounding area, revenue from day students might
have proved sufficient to keep the venture alive. In the beginning,
there were many day students, since there was no other school in
the place. But when the Church began conducting public services in
the courthouse on Sundays, it was discovered that the great majority
of the population possessed such ingrained prejudices that the sight
of a surplice or a Prayer Book threw them into panic. The local
Baptists united to found a rival school, to which most of the day
students transferred.[60]

Gillette worked unbelievably hard against great odds to keep
the institution in Anderson alive. During 1853 he made two trips on
horseback, one of 140 and the other of 360 miles, and secured for the
school pledges of only one thousand dollars, payable in three annual
installments. When he was away acting as financial agent he had
no one with whom to leave the direction of the schools, hence he
was unable to make more trips.[61] In June 1854 he resigned as Professor of the College and Principal of the "Primary Department" in
order to devote his full time to solicitation for the institutions;
some members of the Board persuaded him to withdraw his resignation as Professor, but he insisted upon giving up the boys' school
in order to travel more. The financial panic of that year made a
planned trip to the eastern seaboard seem inadvisable. He therefore
made another circuit of the Diocese, with negligible results. While
soliciting in San Antonio and Austin he several times had broached
to him the possibility of receiving significant support should the

[59]Gillette incurred all the debt himself; technically, the Diocese owed nothing.
He was indebted for $1,122 in 1854; he received no salary from any source during
this two year period. *Texas Journal* 1854, pp. 17-21.
[60]*Ibid.*, p. 18.   [61]*Ibid.*, 1853, pp. 20-1.

schools be removed to either place. He reported to the Board of Trustees, who encouraged him to sound out the prospects in Austin, where he received pledges of support, contingent upon transfer, totaling between $20,000 and $25,000. Bishop Freeman was notified of the proposal, but could not come to Texas to hold a special meeting; at his suggestion the meeting was called by a majority of the Board.[62] The removal to Austin was approved.

Freeman, alluding to the action of the Trustees in his 1855 Convention Address, called it "hasty." A long controversy on the floor resulted in the repudiation of the Board's action, and in the resolution to sustain the institutions in Anderson. The same Convention denied the petition of the Reverend Hannibal Pratt to be relieved of the debt he had incurred in the operation of the Primary Department of the School, but Pratt was commended to the generosity of the members of the convention![63]

Eventually the Anderson property was reconveyed to the Masonic Lodge, and the Diocese received a small cash compensation for the new buildings which had been erected. This sum was invested in land for the benefit of St. Paul's College when it should be reestablished, and trustees were elected from year to year in order to protect the title.[64] The interest of the Diocese shifted to the proposed new university, promoted by the dioceses in the South, which eventually located at Sewanee as the University of the South. The principal interest in the closing years of the life of the schools at Anderson lies in the missionary work performed by the clergy serving on the faculties, and in that of its trainees elsewhere in the Diocese.

V. Missions Stemming from St. Paul's College

THE ESTABLISHMENT of the Diocesan School at Anderson and the Reverend Charles Gillette's residence in the community naturally led to the organization of the Church of the Redeemer in that town. It was admitted to the Diocese at the Convention of 1852, being represented by C. B. Olney and J. B. Harris. J. Lawrence and B. B. Goodrich, the other elected delegates, were not in attendance. Named to the Board of Trustees of the Diocesan School were D. C.

---

[62]Gillette, "Brief History," *Texas Journal*, 1856, pp. 34-5.
[63]*Ibid.*, 1855, pp. 20, 43.
[64]*Ibid.*, 1857, pp. 30-4.

Dickson and Henry Fanthorp of Anderson.[1] It is notable that this number of men were elected to represent the Church of the Redeemer, although Gillette reported but three communicants.[2] Neither the constitution nor the canons of the Diocese at that time required vestrymen or delegates to be communicants,[3] probably because in many places no organization could have been effected under such a requirement.

By 1854 Gillette was reporting a fund of about $2000 in hand for the erection of a church building, around fifty children, including the students in the Diocesan School, in the Sunday School, and thirty communicants. This much had been accomplished in spite of determined opposition; during his first year there, Gillette had been able to conduct but one public service a month because of the vast majority of professing Christians—"nineteen-twentieths," he estimated—were Methodists and Baptists severely prejudiced against the Episcopal Church and therefore not ready to lend the use of their places of worship. The problem was solved temporarily by purchasing suitable seats for the County Court House, where the congregation could gather every Sunday until their church should be built.[4]

In June 1854 Gillette, having resigned as Principal of the Diocesan School in order to act as financial agent for the School and College,[5] resigned the rectorship of the Church at Anderson. The Reverend J. B. T. Smith, Principal of the Female Academy, having been received from the Diocese of Alabama, became the Rector, and that interesting and energetic nephew of Caleb Ives, Hannibal Pratt,[6] ordained Deacon at the 1854 Convention in Anderson, was made Smith's assistant in the rectorship as well as Principal of the Diocesan School.[7] In 1856, with the collapse of the schools at Anderson, Pratt removed to Columbus,[8] leaving Smith with a rapidly diminishing congregation, hard hit by the financial crisis in the State and by

---

[1] *Texas Journal*, 1852, pp. 5, 8, 9.

[2] *Ibid.*, p. 36.

[3] *Ibid.*, pp. 38-9. For example, Anson Jones, former President of the Republic, was a vestryman of St. Paul's Washington, delegate to several Conventions of the Diocese, and trustee of St. Paul's College. Yet, according to Gambrell, he was not a communicant. Herbert Gambrell, *Anson Jones, The Last President of Texas* (New York, 1948), pp. 422-3.

[4] *Texas Journal*, 1854, p. 33; *Spirit of Missions*, 1854, p. 179. The church was never built.

[5] "Brief History of St. Paul's College," *Texas Journal*, 1856, p. 34; see above, p. 51.

[6] For Pratt's ministry at Columbus and other points, see below, pp. 61-3.

[7] *Spirit of Missions*, 1854, p. 511.

[8] *Ibid.*, 1856, pp. 211-4.

removals.[9] Some time between the Conventions of 1856 and 1857 Smith himself left Anderson, being received into the Diocese of North Carolina within the 1858 convention year.[10] The Reverend Lucius H. Jones, a Deacon from the Diocese of Connecticut, who as early as June 1856 was applying to the Domestic Committee for appointment as a missionary to Texas, with the recommendation of Gillette, urged that because he had been to Texas he could be useful there. He was a college classmate of Hannibal Pratt, apparently at Trinity College, Hartford, Connecticut, and a graduate of Berkeley Divinity School.[11] He was appointed missionary at Anderson by the Domestic Committee effective August 1, 1856,[12] and he reported to the Board from that station. He made reference to that letter in a report from Columbus in 1857, but the former report was not printed in the *Spirit of Missions,* and the manuscript has not been located. In the latter report he related that the Masonic Lodge had taken possession of the Diocesan School property, which Jones and his brother had planned to manage jointly for the Diocese. After checking with clerical members of the Standing Committee (which involved a one-hundred-mile ride on Hannibal Pratt's mule to see the Reverend J. W. Dunn at Lockhart), Jones decided to spend the winter in one of the missionary stations under Dunn's care.[13] From this time the work in Anderson must have become dormant; there is no further report in the diocesan or Missionary Board records before the arrival of Bishop Gregg in the Diocese.

ANDERSON AS A MISSIONARY BASE

The establishment of the Diocesan School at Anderson gave occasion, as was expected, for the clergy therewith connected to carry on some missionary work beyond the town of Anderson. While Gillette was Rector, he reported organizing a congregation in Huntsville, by the name of St. Stephen's Church, with ten communicants.[14] He extended his labors to Fireman's Hill, on the east side of the Trinity River in Polk County, where he had visited and organized St. Paul's Church during his tenure as Rector of Christ Church,

---

[9]*Ibid.,* p. 16.

[10]*Journal of the Diocese of North Carolina,* Clergy List, 1858.

[11]Manuscript letter, Jones to Secretary, Domestic Committee, Wolcottville, Conn., June 13, 1856; *Spirit of Missions,* 1857, p. 180; 1858, pp. 119-20.

[12]*Ibid.,* 1856, p. 417.

[13]*Ibid.,* 1857, p. 180. For Jones' ministry at Seguin and San Antonio, see below, pp. 60-1, 65-6.

[14]*Texas Journal,* 1854, p. 33; *Spirit of Missions,* 1854, p. 179.

Houston,[15] sometime before the Convention of 1850, at which the congregation had been admitted to the Diocese.[16] His interest in this remote community no doubt arose because of the removal of his nephew,[17] Henry F. Gillette, to Fireman's Hill in 1848, to engage in teaching school and in farming.[18] Charles Gillette reported eight or ten communicants there, and intended to keep up his visits. In 1853 he reported having baptized twenty-seven infants there, all but one of them colored,[19] but he made no report either for this flock or for that at Huntsville in 1854. The next report was submitted to the Convention of 1857 at Austin by Henry F. Gillette, who was in attendance as delegate.[20] He reported that although the congregation had been in existence for eight years, it had "never had the stated services of a clergyman," but lay readers had conducted monthly services. Four communicants were listed. During the year the only clergyman who had visited them was a Reverend Mr. Bulkley of Virginia, who while there had baptized one infant. Mr. Gillette signed the report as junior warden.[21]

Before the end of the next convention year this congregation's long wait for a clergyman was over. The Reverend J. W. Dunn reported from Lockhart that a Presbyterian minister in his locale had applied to him for help in entering the Episcopal ministry.[22] He was Nathaniel Peck Charlot, who was admitted a Candidate for Holy Orders by the Standing Committee March 23, 1857.[23] Presumably studying under Dunn's direction in the interval, he was ordained Deacon by Bishop Polk of Louisiana, acting for the Dio-

[15]*Ibid.*, 1854, p. 179. The Texas Legislature in 1870 took the portion of Polk County west of the Trinity River, along with a portion of Walker County, to form San Jacinto County. Act of August 13, 1870, p. 79, cited on plat in State Land Office. Cold Spring (formerly Fireman's Hill) became the County Seat. J. de Cordova's Map of Texas, drawn by Robert Creuzbaur (Houston, 1849), shows the location of Fireman's Hill as the same as old Cold Spring, on the western bank of the Trinity, in Polk County. This map is on file in the State Land Office. This note is occasioned by the mystery surrounding the location at the time Du Bose Murphy wrote his *History of the Episcopal Church in Texas* (Dallas, 1935), n. 16, Ch. II, p. 147.

[16]*Texas Journal*, 1850, pp. 9-10.

[17]The only place I have found a reference to this kinship is in Hogan, *The Texas Republic*, p. 139.

[18]Walter Prescott Webb and H. Bailey Carroll, eds., *Handbook of Texas* 2 v. (Austin, 1952), "Henry Gillette," en. loc. This work will be cited hereafter as "*Handbook of Texas.*"

[19]*Texas Journal*, 1853, p. 36.

[20]*Ibid.*, 1857, p. 5.

[21]*Ibid.*, p. 40.

[22]*Spirit of Missions*, 1857, p. 215.

[23]*Texas Journal*, 1857, p. 16.

cese of Texas, on January 4, 1858, and Priest on January 2, 1859,[24] and was appointed missionary for Cold Spring (for the Fireman's Hill community had changed its name in the interval) and Huntsville. He fixed his residence at Cold Spring, and divided his time equally between the two places. Reporting on St. Paul's parish, he said:

> The parish at Cold Spring has been organized some eight or nine years, and has been sustained almost exclusively by the perservering efforts of Mr. H. Gillette, lay reader, (whose influence, as a practical scholar and devoted Christian, is widely felt, and acknowledged in this portion of Texas), for it had never enjoyed the services of an ordained minister more than two Sundays previous to my settlement here.

Gillette was superintendent of a Sunday School with some fifty pupils; Charlot reported having baptized forty infants, all but one of them colored. The Parish did not own a building.[25] Charlot considered that Huntsville had more potential for the Church than Cold Spring, but since he had living quarters for his family at the latter place, he could give Huntsville only such time as the distance of twenty-eight miles between the towns allowed. Charlot during 1859 extended his work to Danville, eighteen miles south of Huntsville, where he held services once a month, and to Moscow, thirty-five miles east of Cold Spring, and to Montgomery. All these towns were new territory for the Church, and promised good response.[26]

Another place which was able to enjoy the services of the Church on account of the schools at Anderson was a settlement known as Groce's Retreat, twenty miles below Anderson on the Brazos River; the Reverend H. Pratt reported in 1855 that he and the Reverend Mr. Smith had maintained monthly services which were very well received, with little appearance of the prejudice which had developed against the Church in Anderson.[27] After Pratt's departure from the vicinity nothing more is known of the Church at Groce's Retreat in this period.

Thus four congregations came into being or were nurtured from the collegiate center of Anderson during the life of the College. Two of them survived through the period covered by this book, and one, St. Stephen's, Huntsville, still exists. Meanwhile men who re-

[24]Manuscript Register of Clergy, Diocese of Texas.
[25]*Spirit of Missions*, 1858, p. 467.
[26]*Ibid.*, 1859, p. 224; *Texas Journal*, 1859, p. 27.
[27]*Ibid.*, 1855, p. 51; *Spirit of Missions*, 1855, p. 392.

The Right Reverend George Washington Freeman, Second Missionary Bishop of the Southwest, Provisional Bishop of Texas.

Emmanuel Church, Lockhart, Texas: Joseph Wood Dunn's "Concrete Church."

Trinity Church, Galveston, Texas.   —From Morgan, *Trinity Church, Galveston*

ceived training for ordination at the college went out into the Diocese to carry on a vigorous and interesting missionary program.

THE MISSIONS OF DUNN AND PRATT

In the area between San Antonio and Richmond two intensely interesting missionary fields were developed between 1852 and 1860, both of them by men who had received much of their training at St. Paul's College, Anderson. The first in point of time included Seguin, Lockhart and Gonzales, with Bastrop added for a part of the time. The other embraced Columbus and La Grange.

One of the two tutors assisting Gillette at the beginning of the Diocesan School at Anderson was Joseph Wood Dunn who had been preparing for the ministry of the Presbyterian Church before becoming interested in that of ours.[28] He was admitted a Candidate for Orders at the 1852 Convention,[29] and was ordained, after some hardship, the following year; he was compelled to follow the Bishop's route of visitation from Anderson, where he had passed his canonical examinations, to San Augustine for his ordination to the Diaconate, because he had not completed his minimum time of one year as a Candidate when he was examined at Anderson.[30] After apparently spending the remainder of the school year at Anderson, Dunn visited Lockhart in mid-August, where he found five people who claimed to be Episcopalians, as well as some others who expressed interest in the Church. He organized Immanuel Church on August 19, and two days later held what he believed to be the first Prayer Book service in the town. Dunn opened a school at Lockhart, and made the town his headquarters, but he reached out to organize congregations and hold services in Seguin and Gonzales. He received appointment from the Board of Missions as missionary to Lockhart and Seguin effective October 1.[31] In his first report to that body he described his field as "an equilateral triangle," about thirty miles to the side, embracing the county seats of Caldwell, Guadalupe and Gonzales counties; he regarded Gonzales as his responsibility even if the Board did not mention it.

In the nine months between Dunn's arrival and the Bishop's visitation in 1854 a remarkable beginning was made. Of the nine persons presented for Confirmation all but two were males, and

28*Ibid.*, 1853, p. 501.
29*Texas Journal*, 1853, p. 23.
30*Spirit of Missions*, 1853, p. 501.
31*Ibid.*, 1854, pp. 312-3. The name of the Parish was spelled "Immanuel" in the first year of its life.

two of them became Candidates for Holy Orders. While using his schoolroom as a place of worship, Dunn was already thinking of the possibility of erecting a church in Lockhart.[32]

The Church of the Redeemer, Seguin, was organized by Dunn August 25, 1853. By holding four services per month, and by working very hard during his visits to the town, Dunn had eleven people for the Bishop to confirm in Seguin in 1854, and he won Freeman's unstinted praise for the hearty response of the congregation, and for their good performance in singing the chants even though they had no instrument to accompany them.[33] Dunn also organized a parish in Gonzales in February 1854, but was able to visit and conduct services only once a month. There were no Confirmations at the Bishop's visitation in that year. Services had been held also at Prairie Lea and San Marcos, but without effecting organized congregations.[34] The Convention of 1854 voted to admit Emmanuel Church, Lockhart, and the Church of the Redeemer, Seguin, into union with the Diocese, but no petition seems to have been submitted from Gonzales. Dunn was advanced to the Priesthood during the Convention.[35]

Shortly after Bishop Freeman's visitation to Lockhart, intense opposition to the Episcopal Church sprang up in the town, with the result that the only building in the place available for public worship was denied to Episcopalians. With no other alternative but surrender, Dunn and his people determined to erect their own church building although they had no money. Dunn wrote the Board of Missions:

> After a few weeks of anxious solicitude and earnest effort, the foundation of a small, neat church edifice was laid; and I trust it was done in humble trust in God that He would aid those who help themselves. Four gentlemen agreed to put the roof on and the windows in, if I could get up the walls; and I, with nothing but my slender missionary stipend to depend upon, (for it takes all we can make besides to pay our board,) because personally responsible for six hundred dollars, the cost of the walls.

At the time of writing, Dunn had received from "two noble Christian ladies, one of them living in Eastern Texas and the other in Philadelphia" (almost certainly Mrs. J. Pinkney Henderson of San

---

[32]*Ibid.*, p. 313.
[33]*Texas Journal*, 1854, p. 14; *Spirit of Missions*, 1854, pp. 29-30.
[34]*Ibid.*, p. 313; *Texas Journal*, 1854, p. 15.
[35]*Ibid.*, p. 24; 1855, p. 16.

Augustine and some friend or relative of hers in her native Philadelphia) almost enough to meet his down payment of $300 for the walls, and was having the walls constructed of "concrete."[36] The late Tom Gambrell of Lockhart learned from a venerable resident of that town that the native concrete used in the walls was derived from a stratum of material dug out of a pit located in the east end of the town; this stuff, mixed with gravel and water, set up like concrete made from portland cement.[37]

Dunn found it necessary to make a begging tour of the older states in order to raise the funds to complete the church; response in some parishes in the South and East was almost sufficient to complete the job, though delays occasioned by a severe winter and hard times postponed opening the building for worship until some time before Bishop Freeman on his visitation of 1857 officiated in it and praised its excellent design.[38] It was the first church edifice completed by any denomination in Lockhart,[39] and probably is, as its people claim, the oldest standing non-Roman church in Texas.

Dunn by no means confined his attention to Lockhart. The congregation at Seguin was able to act as host to the 1955 Convention of the Diocese. To this Convention the Church of the Messiah, Gonzales, made its application and was received into union with the Diocese,[40] and during the sessions Dunn's brother, Ballard S. Dunn, was ordained Deacon and assigned as assistant in the field, which was enlarged by the inclusion of Bastrop.[41]

Ballard Dunn took up his residence in Gonzales. During the course of the year a large upper room in the male college building was equipped for a chapel (services previously having been held by courtesy of the Methodists), a melodeon bought, and a choir formed. More frequent services naturally increased interest.

The same improvement in the life of the Church in Seguin was noted by the Rector; the assistant missionary devoted part of his

[36]*Spirit of Missions*, 1855, pp. 10-11.

[37]*Emmanuel Protestant Episcopal Church, Lockhart, Texas* [n.d.], pp. 12-13. This booklet supplements Gambrell's article about the church in *Under Texas Skies* for June, 1951, and together they present much material about the history of Emmanuel Church.

[38]*Texas Journal*, 1855, p. 51; 1856, p. 22; *Spirit of Missions*, 1855, pp. 600-1; 1856, pp. 70, 214, 358; 1857, p. 599; manuscript letter, J. W. Dunn to Secretary, Domestic Committee, Lockhart, September 4, 1856.

[39]*Spirit of Missions*, 1857, p. 180.

[40]*Texas Journal*, 1855, p. 29.

[41]*Spirit of Missions*, 1855, p. 601; for the relationship between the Dunns, *Spirit of Missions*, 1857, p. 215. B. S. Dunn had been a member of the original vestry of Lockhart. Gambrell, *Emmanuel Protestant Episcopal Church*, p. 6.

time to this station, and made it possible to conduct Sunday services more regularly.[42] Here, however, the authorities of the Academy, where services were being held, threatened to charge a high rent or deny the premises to the congregation.[43] In November 1856 the Reverend Lucius H. Jones, having been ejected from the property of the Diocesan School at Anderson by the Masonic Lodge, became the resident assistant at Seguin under the Rector, the Reverend J. W. Dunn, who anticipated having to be absent from the field in order to take his wife to the North for the sake of her health.[44] The situation at Seguin improved rapidly with a resident minister, so that the prospects were good for self-support for the Parish in a short time, and the erection of a church was contemplated as soon as the current "hard times" would permit.[45] The Seguin Church changed its name to "St. Andrew's" at the Convention of 1858.[46]

J. W. Dunn's fine field was disrupted by misfortune. The adverse financial situation, occasioned by a severe drought, finally made it impossible for him to remain at his post; Jones later reported to the Board that the population of Lockhart had been cut in half by the exodus of people from the drought-stricken region. Seguin was so hard hit that Jones and his lay assistant, Mr. Monges, had moved to San Antonio.[47] Dunn had represented the Diocese at the meeting which selected Sewanee as the site for the Southern University, and thereafter resigned.[48] He was transferred to the Diocese of Louisiana by the Standing Committee in April 1858.[49] His brother Ballard, seeking an opportunity to progress more rapidly in his studies for the Priesthood, had moved to that Diocese the previous year.[50] Thus the remarkable missionary work of Joseph Wood Dunn in Texas was ended, and might even have seemed in vain, were it not now evident that many of his foundations were as sturdy as the concrete walls of his church in Lockhart. By the wise direction he gave his two assistants, he did much for the life and vigor of the churches they served. When he had secured assistance, he extended his field to Bastrop, where he organized a congregation and offi-

---

[42]*Texas Journal*, 1856, p. 22; *Spirit of Missions*, 1856, pp. 358-9; manuscript letter, J. W. Dunn to Secretary, Domestic Committee, Lockhart, March 11, 1857.

[43]*Spirit of Missions*, 1856, p. 70.

[44]See above, p. 54. *Spirit of Missions*, 1857, p. 180.

[45]*Ibid.*, pp. 215, 468.

[46]*Texas Journal*, 1858, p. 9.

[47]*Spirit of Missions*, 1859, p. 20.

[48]*Texas Journal*, 1858, pp. 10-11.

[49]*Ibid.*, 1859, p. 10.

[50]*Ibid.*, 1858, p. 13; *Spirit of Missions*, 1857, p. 215.

ciated for a short period, before having to give up the effort because of the difficulty in finding a place in which to conduct services.[51] A conscientious pastor, Dunn once made a trip of ninety miles to a frontier settlement he called "Attascosa Settlement" (possibly Atascosa in southern Bexar County) to visit a family of three whom he had baptized in Lockhart, but who had moved to the frontier before the Bishop arrived in Lockhart for Confirmation. Dunn wrote of preaching "in a little cabin schoolhouse, built by placing pieces of timber on end, after the manner of making a picket fence, and daubing the interstices with mud."[52]

The Dunn brothers' departure left Lucius Jones, still a Deacon, the only missionary in the field. Fortunately, his people were not left entirely without priestly ministrations, since the Reverend R. H. Ranney, formerly of Louisiana, had moved onto a farm nine miles out of Seguin, and had been transferred to the Diocese of Texas in 1856.[53] Unable to support his family by his ministerial work, Ranney resorted to farming, but was glad to conduct services when Jones needed him.[54]

Gonzales seemed to be the one town in the field in which the Church was not crippled by drought and hard times; upon the departure of B. S. Dunn the vestry called the Reverend H. N. Pierce as their Rector, with a salary of $700 per year. When unable to secure his acceptance, the congregation kept itself alive by the occasional services of Jones until the arrival of the Reverend J. M. Goshorn, Deacon, from Kentucky in March 1859.[55] Probably due to the long vacancy, the congregation had to have a missionary apportionment to supplement Goshorn's salary.[56]

Columbus and La Grange comprised the missionary field selected by the Reverend Hannibal Pratt when, after his departure from Anderson, he visited various parts of the Diocese, both to inform the Board of the needs of the mission, and to select the place where he felt his efforts would contribute most to the upbuilding of the Church.[57] The choice of Columbus and La Grange certainly was not dictated by self-interest; though unmarried, Pratt was supporting his mother,

[51]Manuscript letter, J. W. Dunn to Secretary, Domestic Committee, Lockhart, Sept. 4, 1856.

[52]*Spirit of Missions*, 1856, p. 70.

[53]*Texas Journal*, 1856, p. 13. See above, p. 11.

[54]Manuscript letter, Jones to Secretary, Domestic Committee, Seguin, July 20, 1857; *Texas Journal*, 1859, pp. 33-4.

[55]*Ibid.*, p. 11.

[56]*Spirit of Missions*, 1859, p. 322.

[57]*Ibid.*, 1856, pp. 211-4.

a sister of the late Caleb Ives.[58] Perhaps he was still burdened with
a debt incurred in the operation of the Diocesan School, for which
the 1855 Convention failed to take official responsibility, recommending Pratt to "the liberality of the Convention"[59] (which at this
point in the life of the Diocese of Texas was not very notable!).
Certainly Pratt must have been tempted by the generous offers made
by the planters of Brazoria County.[60] Thoroughly conscious of the
difficulties to be encountered he chose Columbus and La Grange,
where the Church had never had a chance to take root. As the
doughty missionary probably expected, the ministrations of the
Church were met with "much ignorant prejudice." Pratt wrote:

> My station . . . is settled almost wholly by planters and
> "stock raisers," from those parts of the Southern and Western
> States where our Church is least known.
> Few of these were raised in cities or large towns, to which, in
> their native States, our congregations are almost wholly confined.
> The majority received their education in "old-field schools,"
> and their religious impressions among the swarming sects of
> the West, which are all represented here—Mormans included.
> They are all, consequently, profoundly ignorant of the Episcopal
> Church, save, to use their expression, "It was started by an
> English king, who had a mighty heap of wives."

As the Church became better known, opposition increased. Moreover, once people were enlisted they were apt to pull up stakes to
move out to the frontier at any time.[61]

In spite of all the difficulties of the station, Pratt worked quite
successfully in both places. Parishes were organized in April 1856;
St. John's, Columbus, and St. James', La Grange, were admitted
into union with the Diocese at the Convention of that year.[62] His
friend L. H. Jones gave a good account of his work after a visit
to Columbus.[63]

Pratt, not neglecting any opportunity for doing good, following
the example that had been set by his uncle at Matagorda, and
encouraged by masters, began work among slaves. Although he reported that considerable success attended his efforts, with several
negro candidates under instruction for Baptism, Pratt wrote that

[58]*Ibid.*, 1858, pp. 119-21.

[59]*Texas Journal*, 1855, p. 43; see above, p. 52.

[60]See below, p. 86.

[61]*Spirit of Missions*, 1857, pp. 255-6.

[62]Manuscript letter, Pratt to Secretary, Domestic Committee, Columbus, Oct. 6,
1856; *Texas Journal*, 1856, p. 18.

[63]*Spirit of Missions*, 1857, p. 180.

the negro's idea of "getting religion" was to "get happy," with the
result that some worship services had threatened to turn into emotional orgies, with hand clapping, body swaying and singing of
strange songs which the missionary had never heard before. Pratt
asserted that this idea of religion, which he had to control if not
overcome, was shared by many white people. Undismayed, he sensed
all the more a need for missionary work, and begged for more work-
ers to carry it on.[64]

Pratt might have accomplished much more in Columbus and
La Grange and might have been spared for more years of efficient
work, had not his already delicate health been broken by the additional burden of stage rides to Richmond to conduct services. He
was accustomed to the lowlier but more independent mode of travel
by muleback, with the opportunity of stopping in to warm up and rest
anywhere along the road, and the rigors of the primitive stageline
were too much for him. Pratt's brother-in-law, Mr. Wright, told
L. H. Jones that Pratt had often got off the Richmond stage at Columbus at nighttime in winter "so cold, completely chilled through,
that he could scarcely crawl to the fire." Thus weakened, he fell
victim to the old malady which had made him drop out of college
six years before; "he died with hiccough."[65]

No church buildings were left as monuments to Pratt's work,
but perhaps a better memorial was the resolution of the Convention of 1858, which said in part that he,

> . . . though young in years, was giving noble proof of his min-
> istry by faithful and devoted labors, and that amidst many dis-
> couragements and hardships. Perhaps no better expression of
> feeling on the part of this Convention could be adopted than
> to repeat the words which, we are told, were oftenest on his
> lips—"All is well. All is well. It is the Lord, let Him do as
> seemeth Him good."[66]

To the next Convention the senior warden of St. John's, Columbus,
Mr. R. Robson, reported, "The parishoners are very anxious to pro-
cure another minister . . ."[67] They were unable to do so until after
the coming of Bishop Gregg.

SAN ANTONIO AND NORTH TEXAS

Trinity Church, San Antonio, bereft of its organizer and volunteer pastor, Chaplain Fish, seemed too important a place to be left

[64]*Ibid.*, 1858, pp. 75-6.   [65]*Ibid.*, pp. 119-20.
[66]*Texas Journal*, 1858, p. 14.   [67]*Ibid.*, 1859, pp. 31-2.

vacant. Charles Rottenstein's need to find a climate more congenial
to his health than Washington County prompted the San Antonio
vestry to call him to officiate for one year. Entering upon his duties
April 1, 1853, he found the prospects quite encouraging.[68] The vestry's ability to obtain sufficient subscriptions to pay the rector's full
salary made a missionary appropriation unnecessary after the first
few months. Shortly after entering into the rectorship of Trinity
Church, Rottenstein was ordained to the Priesthood at the Diocesan
Convention.[69] On the next year's visitation Bishop Freeman learned
that the congregation had fitted out as a chapel an upper room in
a rented house, and was shocked to learn that they held no Sunday
evening services, even though they controlled their place of worship. They and one other (unnamed) city congregation in the Diocese did not seem to realize, he told the Convention, that the main
object of Church people in assembling together was to offer worship
to God; two or three gathered together could do so. There need
be no sermon in the evening. The point in holding services was
to worship and praise God. Freeman assumed that since the Prayer
Book provided for Morning and Evening Prayer, both were required
when it was possible to conduct them. When he called for Prayer
Book loyalty, he meant it![70]

Rottenstein stayed in San Antonio a year longer than he had
contracted, before transferring to the Diocese of Louisiana in 1855.[71]
Trinity Church was left without a rector. Shortly afterwards an abortive missionary experiment brought to San Antonio Charles' father,
the Reverend George Rottenstein. This gentleman, described by
Bishop Freeman as "of Houston, late a Methodist preacher and
editor of *The Wesleyan Banner*," was confirmed at Anderson by
Freeman, and admitted as a Candidate for Holy Orders. Presumably
he remained at St. Paul's College to receive tutorial help in preparation for ordination from Gillette, who at the same time was
tutoring Hannibal Pratt for canonical examination.[72] The elder Rot-

[68]*Ibid.*, 1853, pp. 15, 35.

[69]*Spirit of Missions*, 1853, p. 497.

[70]*Texas Journal*, 1854, p. 14.

[71]Manuscript Register of Clergy, Diocese of Texas.

[72]*Spirit of Missions*, 1853, p. 499. Murphy said that the Rottensteins were
brothers, but he was almost certainly wrong. *Op. cit.*, p. 29. George wrote of his
former opposition to the Episcopal Church, "You know that I wandered long
in mases [*sic*] dark in the sectarian field, . . . (notwithstanding) my own son was
a clergyman of the Church." A search of the clerical directories for the period
shows only two clergy by this name, Charles F. and George. The quotation is from
a letter, George Rottenstein to Secretary, Domestic Committee, Covington, La.,
Sept. 25, 1857. Claude A. Beesley, *The Episcopal Church in Northern Texas Until
1895* (Wichita Falls, 1952), p. 26, calls Charles the son of George Rottenstein.

tenstein was ordained Deacon at the Convention in Anderson May 28, 1854, and was appointed "Missionary to the German population in and around San Antonio" beginning in June.[73]

Reporting to the Domestic Committee on his new field of labor, the new Deacon went into considerable detail. He estimated the population at around 7000, of which he said one quarter were Germans, most of them Protestants whose religious needs went unmet. The Roman Catholics did have a sermon in German once in a while, and the Methodist Church for some years had kept a German missionary at work between New Braunfels and San Antonio, but Methodism was so uncongenial to the Germans that no congregation could be organized. These people welcomed Rottenstein but feared that he did not intend to stay long, or that the small but determined "association of Infidels and Socialists" would cause him to leave. Ten German Prayer Books had been given him by Benjamin Eaton of Galveston, and he requested more of the Board, because some Germans in the congregation responded favorably to the Prayer Book services.[74]

By the next annual Convention it had become apparent that the mission would fail; the Germans would not attend religious services in a court house or private residence. Unless a church building could be provided, and the minister's salary too, there was no hope. Rottenstein, having been ordained to the Priesthood at the 1855 Convention, was transferred to Corsicana.[75]

In 1857 the Reverend J. W. Dunn reported to the Board that he and the assistants in his field made occasional visits to San Antonio, "a vacant parish."[76] Lucius H. Jones of Seguin, the assistant closest to San Antonio, most often performed this duty. In the year following Jones apparently devoted considerable time to reviving the work in San Antonio, with the result that a petition was presented to the Convention of 1858 asking the admission of a new parish, under the name of "St. Mark's." After proper inquiry the Committee on New Parishes satisfied themselves that Trinity Parish was in fact extinct; they therefore recommended the admission of St. Mark's, which the Convention granted.[77] There was something strange in this situation, for Jones, who presented the petition of St. Mark's, said in his report to the Convention:

[73]*Texas Journal*, 1855, pp. 16, 18.
[74]*Spirit of Missions*, 1855, pp. 102-3.
[75]*Ibid.*, 1856, p. 140; *Texas Journal*, 1856, p. 13.
[76]*Spirit of Missions*, 1857, p. 215.
[77]*Texas Journal*, 1858, pp. 12, 15.

The state of affairs in San Antonio cannot be well understood by one not acquainted there. They have been much misrepresented on both sides. It would not be wise to attempt a permanent arrangement there, except under the advisement of a Bishop. A new Vestry was elected at Easter, which it is hoped will result in unity, harmony and strength."[78]

Yet a permanent arrangement was soon made. Jones reported to the 1859 Convention as the resident Rector of St. Mark's, San Antonio, that activity was in full flow; funds were rapidly accumulating for the erection of a church building, which he hoped would begin soon.[79]

Another field was opened for the Church when George Rottenstein, after admitting defeat in his effort to minister to the Germans in San Antonio, was authorized by the Bishop to establish work in "Corsicana and other places in Navarro and neighboring counties." In the rich but sparsely settled country north of Austin he found a most promising field for the Church, especially should the hope of railroad construction materialize. But he himself labored under a disadvantage when he preached at Waco. He wrote:

> I arrived the 1st of June in Wacco [sic] . . . and preached there several times . . . presenting the claims of the Church, and performing services hitherto unknown to the people. But I saw no prospect of a firm establishment in Wacco. Politics and Know-Nothingism excited the people, and, as I am, "unfortunately," a foreigner, my good Methodist Brother of the place being a zealous K.N., took the advantage, and left me without a congregation.[80]

Rottenstein went east to Corsicana, where he found three Church families and other interested persons, and started services. Also in "General T's neighborhood (Chamber's Creek), and in Ellis county," thirty-five miles southwest of Corsicana, he ministered once a month to the white people in the morning and to the colored people in the afternoon, with very encouraging results. Another Sunday in the month the missionary ministered at a place called Taos, or Porter's Bluff, seventeen miles east, on the Trinity River, where he drew in some English families from a distance of twenty miles whenever the weather allowed them to travel that far.

St. Bartholomew's Parish was organized in Corsicana on August 16, 1855. On the fifth Sundays of the months, Rottenstein looked about for other communities to develop for the mission, and asked

[78]*Ibid.*, pp. 29-30.   [79]*Ibid.*, 1859, pp. 32-3.
[80]*Spirit of Missions*, 1856, p. 141.

if he might have a deacon to assist in reaching more places. He had run into debt by having to buy a horse and saddle, and appealed for enough salary to enable him to pay for them.[81] He was very pleased to learn that he was to have $400 per year; he considered the salary generous but too little to pay for moving his library from San Antonio.[82]

The hazards of missionary work, involving long journeys on horseback, formed the theme of one of Rottenstein's numerous letters to the Board. He was mystified by the number of times he found a beautiful Saturday on which to make the journey to an outstation, only to have the Sunday congregation kept away by a veritable cloudburst. It was not so bad when this misfortune precluded a service at one of his regular stations, but the occurrence was particularly frustrating when he was making his first visit to a town. It happened at Fairfield, Freestone County, in February 1856, but he stayed over for a Monday night service, and reported a good chance for a Church there, if a missionary could be sent.[83]

Corsicana was truly the frontier in those days, if uncertainty of mail and supplies indicates frontier conditions. During his first year there, Rottenstein wrote repeatedly for an additional supply of Prayer Books and tracts, which evidently were lost in transit. The drafts for his salary were often lost, and had it not been for generous laymen, like General Nichols of Galveston, who were willing to advance the money and draw on the Board through a New York bank, the missionary would have been in a bad way.[84] He learned that it paid to go all the way to Houston or Galveston to lay in supplies, since provisions in the much nearer supply center of Dallas cost twenty per cent more.[85]

In mid-1856 Rottenstein encountered difficulties in preaching regularly in Corsicana, for lack of a public building. With the consent of Bishop Freeman he moved to Dallas, then a town of five hundred people. Here he found some Church people and a ready welcome. A vacant storehouse was fitted up for services. He officiated in Dallas two Sundays a month. St. Matthew's Parish was organized, and was admitted into union with the Diocese at the 1857 Convention.[86] On other Sundays Rotterstein continued to care for his con-

---

[81]*Ibid.*, pp. 141-2; manuscript letter, Rottenstein to Secretary, Domestic Committee, Corsicana, Oct. 10, 1855.

[82]Same to same, Corsicana, Dec. 31, 1855.

[83]Same to same, Corsicana, Apr. 12, 1856.

[84]Same to same, Apr. 12 and June 4, 1856.

[85]Same to same, Houston, Dec. 16, 1856.

[86]*Texas Journal*, 1857, p. 14.

gregations at Corsicana and Chambers Creek. The desire of the Dallas congregation for a church building was great, but money was extremely scarce, and the little they could give would not suffice. Most of them pinned their hopes on the coming of a railroad, and invested all they could spare in land; unless the railroad arrived they were ruined.[87] Rottenstein appealed for outside aid for the Dallas church building, but response was poor. Someone gave the Dallas congregation two city lots in Fort Worth to be sold for the benefit of their building program, but the Dallas vestry thought it better to preserve these for the future needs of the Church in Fort Worth. Finally Rottenstein conceived the idea of taking leave of absence from his post to officiate temporarily at Covington, Louisiana; the Dallas people would be able to apply their payments toward his salary to the building fund, and perhaps he could solicit funds for them in Louisiana. He could return to his flock when the funds were in hand to build and when money was more plentiful.[88] Money did not come rapidly enough; he could not officiate indefinitely in one place and retain office in another; he was constrained to resign his Dallas appointment to accept the call to become Rector of the Covington Parish.[89] But his heart remained with Texas friends. When it became possible again to finance the work in Dallas, he returned as Rector.[90]

VI. Missionary Work and Pastoral Care Elsewhere

APART from the missionary work carried on from St. Paul's College, several other new missions were established during the decade preceding Gregg's election. Older congregations extended the pastoral care over their increasing members, and thus contributed to the mission of the Church. Two new fields were opened, Brownsville and the Red River Valley; the former was worked and the latter neglected. During the decade under consideration, the Brownsville field affords an exciting missionary story.

[87]*Spirit of Missions*, 1857, p. 129.

[88]Rottenstein to Secretary, Domestic Committee, Covington, La., Oct. 5, 1857; Houston, Nov. 5, 1857.

[89]Same to same, Houston, Nov. 5, 1857.

[90]See below, pp. 173-4.

BROWNSVILLE AND THE RED RIVER VALLEY

The story of Episcopal missionary activity in Brownsville stands first among all the stories coming out of Texas in the first ten years of the life of the Diocese. The Reverend William Passmore of the Diocese of New York was appointed to Brownsville in response to the urgent call of the Church and the Bishop. He arrived at his station and got settled in June 1851. It did not occur to him that it would be troublesome to travel to Chappell Hill for the Diocesan Convention of 1852. That was a clergyman's duty! (How often some other clergymen did not attend unless the place of meeting was close by!) Writing to the Secretary of the Domestic Committee on July 30, Passmore described his harrowing experience. He left Brownsville on April 13 in company with another American. They rode Mexican ponies and led a pack-horse laden with their baggage; this seemed the only way to go, since no stage lines operated. Warned by the Army commander to avoid the mainland route because of of recent raids by Indians and Mexican bandits, the travellers started up Padre Island toward Corpus Christi. They first had a scrape with a band of Mexican herders who probably planned to steal their animals while they were camped for the night, but the herders were discouraged by the vigilance of the two. Passmore and his companion next fell victims to a herd of wild mustangs rushing through their camp; this lured away one of the saddle ponies and the packhorse. Passmore's fellow traveller set off on the remaining pony to track the herd, hoping to retrieve beasts and baggage. After a wait of three days, the clergyman set out afoot with a bundle of crackers and a gallon of water in his carpetbag, following the beach to reach Corpus Christi before starvation overcame him. He walked about a day and a half; he shed his boots after his feet became blistered and walked on wet sand at the surf's edge. He managed to catch a couple of sandcrabs for food, but, exhausted and disheartened, saw little prospect of surviving. Thoughtfully he had left signal sticks along his route. When hope seemed dimmest, his companion returned with their animals and all their possessions. After a chase of seventy miles the man had found the beasts, which apparently were unable to keep up with the wild herd that had stampeded them.

Even then the perils of the journey were not over. The two travelers had to swim their horses across the usually shallow pass to Corpus Christi. Passmore was nearly drowned in the Aransas River on the way to Refugio. From Goliad, Passmore went on to Victoria, San Antonio, Austin, and thence by stage to the Convention at

Chappell Hill.[1] Did ever another clergyman have so difficult a trip to Convention? It is not surprising that Passmore returned to Brownsville by way of New Orleans, in order to get steamship passage over the difficult distances.

Passmore was greatly impressed with the missionary opportunity for the Episcopal Church in Texas, and put in a strong plea for more men and more money from the Board.[2] Most of all he believed in the importance of his isolated station as strategically located at the door of Mexico. He rightly assayed the condition of Christianity in Mexico to be even more deplorable than in Spanish days, he prophetically foresaw a calling for our Church there, and believed the Brownsville Parish an important example to the Mexicans to numerously in touch with the border city.[3] A church edifice was needed to make the Church's life in Brownsville secure, but as usual in Texas money was not available locally, and as usual the clergyman went East to beg. But Passmore was no usual clergyman; if his letters are any guide to his vocal effectiveness, no purses were safe on the persons of his eastern auditors. He returned to Brownsville with $1500 in cash and with promises of $200 more if needed. He had all he wanted, for he intended to erect "only the shell of a church." The local people could finish it. Twenty-three rectors of Churches besides those already contributing had offered future help, but Passmore did not want everything done from the outside. He hoped that interest displayed in the Brownsville mission would spread to aid the whole Domestic Mission program.

The prospect of having a Protestant church erected in Brownsville stirred the Roman Catholic Church from its lethargy. Hitherto indifferent to Brownsville, the Roman Catholic Bishop of Galveston dispatched six priests and an equal number of nuns to the place, and the building of a convent was begun.[4]

After many difficulties in securing labor and materials, and many broken promises of aid from the older states, Passmore's new building was almost ready for occupancy when yellow fever struck to blast the fair prospects of the missionary. The senior warden, almost half the vestry, and a quarter of the congregation were gone; not all died, but when the breadwinner of a family died, the rest had to leave that precarious community. Still the new church, incomplete as it was, attracted people as Passmore had hoped; the mem-

---

[1]*Spirit of Missions*, 1852, pp. 320-4.   [2]*Ibid.*, p. 324.
[3]*Ibid.*, 1853, pp. 11-14.   [4]*Ibid.*, pp. 139-40.

bership of the Parish was restored rapidly to its former level. The Church was making a real impact upon the community.[5]

Within the year Passmore resigned his appointment as missionary, but not to leave the community. He had brought the Parish to full self-support, and became Rector. This he accomplished without the bane of most parishes of the time—pew rents; the Parish was supported by contributions.[6]

Brownsville was not a stable community. The convention year ending in April 1856 saw a decline in its population; since those departing included some of the most substantial members of the Church of the Advent, it was a year of anxiety for Passmore. It was a sorrowful one, too; an accident befell the family as they returned from a vacation in the North. The Mississippi River steamer on which they were passengers caught fire and was destroyed. Passmore's mother died of burns, and he, his wife, and baby were badly burned. Back at his post, the Rector labored to pay the last of the debt on the church, that it might be consecrated—if ever a bishop would visit Brownsville! To that date no clergyman of the Church had been in Brownsville except Passmore himself, and he was beginning to be a little cross about it![7]

After the discouragements of 1856, the church building suffered storm damage the next year. Then it was discovered that the title to the Church lot was worthless, and the property had to be paid for again. But the Parish membership grew even as the population was falling. Passmore had not lost courage. He recommended to all weak parishes the system of offerings he used at Brownsville. The first Sunday offering was for Communion Alms, the second for Parish and Sunday School expenses, the third for Bishop's salary and convention expenses, the fourth for missions. On fifth Sundays, the offering was given to some less fortunate small congregation toward their building fund.[8]

Another yellow fever epidemic struck Brownsville before Passmore reported to the 1859 convention. It carried off as many communicants as the congregation had reported a year before; had not the growth been so rapid, there would have been no Parish! The most somber news, however, was that the long-suffering Rector was forced to leave Texas because of business affairs to which he must attend in the North; he only hoped that when Texas secured a bishop, the Bishop would not forget little Brownsville![9]

[5]*Ibid.*, 1854, pp. 260-1.   [6]*Ibid.*, 1855, pp. 9-10.
[7]*Texas Journal,* 1856, pp. 24-7.   [8]*Ibid.*, 1857, pp. 37-8.
[9]*Ibid.*, 1859, pp. 28-9.

The Red River Valley of Texas constituted a potential missionary field of real promise, as Bishops Polk and Freeman successively had urged the Board of Missions; they had pleaded in vain for an appropriation and a missionary.[10] An occasional visitation was made by the Bishop, with baptisms, confirmations, and communions; but no congregations were organized, and hence there was opportunity neither for habitual corporate worship nor for that responsibility for others which organized Church life made possible. Boston, Clarksville, and Paris,[11] places visited and officiated in by Bishop Freeman, had no contact with the Diocese of Texas.

WASHINGTON COUNTY

The development of the work in Washington County makes a story less exciting than Brownsville and less discouraging than the Red River Valley. All four of the County's congregations were in existence when the diocesan program of expansion and development began, and a great deal of work produced encouraging results. Symbolic of the energetic nature of that work is the fact that the Diocesan Convention of 1852 was able to meet in a church building in the County. The Convention was scheduled to meet at St. Paul's, Washington; instead it assembled at St. Luke's, Chappell Hill, since the new building at Washington was not yet complete. The building at Chappell Hill was new. In his annual report to the Board, Freeman wrote:

> The Convention assembled in St. Luke's Church, an edifice which has been erected since my last visitation. It is a plain but substantial structure, 52 by 25 feet, built entirely of red cedar, and reflects great credit upon the small community by whose enterprise and liberality it has been erected. . . . It has been built without foreign aid, and, and what is more and better, without incurring a debt, and that in a small village which was not in existence four years ago, and in a community among whom the services of the Church were unknown until within the last two or three years.[12]

Elsewhere in Washington County no permanent buildings were yet completed. The Reverend H. N. Pierce reported that work on a stone church begun a year before by the Brenham flock had been suspended because of poor crops and tight money. In the mean-

[10]Annual Reports of Missionary Bishops of the Southwest, *Spirit of Missions*, 1838-1857.

[11]*Spirit of Missions*, 1853, pp. 489-93.

[12]*Ibid.*, 1852, p. 422.

The Right Reverend Alexander Gregg, First Bishop of Texas.

Christ Church, San Augustine, Texas

St. Luke's Church, Belton, Texas.

time they had erected for temporary use a small, wooden building, which was to be sold when the church could be complete. At Washington some of the lumber was on the ground, but no one could be found to haul the remainder "at any price."[13] Rucker removed his residence to Washington at the beginning of the year and assumed the principalship of an academy "in order to relieve the parishes of the burden of supporting me while building." He continued to officiate at Washington and Chappell Hill as missionary of the Society.[14] When Pierce removed to Matagorda, the new Deacon, Charles Rottenstein, located at Chappell Hill, and he and Rucker shared the work of the four congregations in the County.[15] This arrangement lasted but a short time, for Rottenstein's health failed, and with the Bishop's approval he moved to San Antonio to take temporary charge of Trinity Church,[16] which was without a minister since Chaplain Fish's departure. All four of the congregations fell to Rucker's care. He conceived the idea of establishing a Church school at Washington and went on a six-week journey to solicit funds for the purpose, without the consent of the Bishop or the Board of Missions.[17] Rucker personally assumed the indebtedness of the Masonic Lodge for the academy in which he had been serving. Of $700 to be raised, he had realized $400, and expected to obtain the rest by January 1854.[18]

By the time of the Bishop's visit in 1853 the church building in Washington, another red cedar structure, was far enough along to use for services, though that at Chappell Hill still had not received its finishing touches. These congregations evidently were proud of living within their own resources, for the Bishop recorded his sense of amazement at their modesty in failing to make their necessities known abroad:

> Not one of the Churches in Washington County, I believe, has anything better than a glass pitcher and a tumbler, and an earthen plate, for the celebration of the Holy Communion, nor any more decent Font for Holy Baptism than an earthen or glass bowl. . . . They have, perhaps, hitherto done what they could, and their unpretending efforts are, in my judgment, worthy of high commendation.[19]

Another missionary was expected to arrive in October 1852 to

13*Ibid.*, p. 290.   14*Ibid.*, p. 291.   15*Ibid.*, p. 422.
16*Texas Journal*, 1853, p. 15.
17*Spirit of Missions*, 1853, pp. 233-4.
18*Texas Journal*, 1853, p. 35.
19*Spirit of Missions*, 1853, p. 499.

help Rucker, but he did not come.[20] Rucker had to labor alone in Washington County until 1855, in spite of the efforts made by the Bishop to give him relief. Brenham and Chappell Hill had been struck by the frequent affliction particularly liable to cripple small congregations on the frontier in the last century—the removal of several families of means; then there was no salary to supplement the small stipened the Domestic Committee was prepared to offer. Freeman did not expect Rucker to do more than hold the line.[21] That doughty laborer was not discouraged, however, for he reported at the beginning of 1855 substantial progress in commending the Church to the people of the County, was well as on the building program. Chappell Hill had been cleared of all debt, and St. Paul's, Washington, had at length been completed.[22] Unfortunately a burdensome debt was incurred by St. Paul's, Washington, during the last stages of its completion.[23] The congregation at Brenham had bought a building erected by the Presbyterians who were unable to pay for it. Only the Independence congregation lacked a building, and they were collecting a fund to erect one. What happened there is not clear. It appears that Mr. and Mrs. James A. Burton made available a plot of ground on which either they or the congregation as a whole erected a building sometime in this period. The Burtons evidently retained title to the property, making a certain T. C. Clay, Mrs. Burton's brother and an Episcopalian, their attorney-in-fact. In 1859 this property, then described as "generally known as the Episcopal Church," was sold by Clay to three purchasers. The sale was witnessed by G. R. Seward, another Episcopalian.[24]

The division of the Washington County field was made necessary by the experience of two seasons of heavy rainfall. Frequently it was impossible for Rucker to travel across the swollen creeks on the route between the two settlements on the Brazos River, Washington and Independence, and Chappell Hill and Brenham. The Reverend Elijah H. Downing, who had been missionary in the San Augustine-Nacogdoches field, was transferred to Brenham, with Chappell Hill as his second charge.[25]

Rucker resigned his missionary appointment in 1856.[26] His daughter wrote of him:

[20]*Ibid.*, p. 498.   [21]*Ibid.*, 1854, p. 510.

[22]*Ibid.*, 1855, pp. 101-2.   [23]*Texas Journal*, 1855, p. 19.

[24]This information, taken from the records of Washington County, was furnished to me by Miss Margaret Blakey of Dallas.

[25]*Texas Journal*, 1855, p. 18; *Spirit of Missions*, 1855, pp. 15, 600.

[26]*Ibid.*, 1856, p. 269.

> In 1855 [sic], Father decided to take his bunch of six boys
> out on a farm. He bought a farm in the rich soil of Milam
> Co., 17 miles north of Caldwell. He lived there nine years. . . .
> During all these stirring times, Father never lost an opportunity
> of preaching the Gospel. . . . He often held services near home,
> at a country schoolhouse. . . .[27]

The prosperity of the communities in the County must have declined, for in the following year Downing also resigned and left the
Diocese.[28] All these Churches remained vacant until Bishop Gregg
arrived to get them manned again.[29]

AUSTIN

The work in the capital city of the State, once started, gave
great promise. Epiphany Church was growing and planning for
more growth under the leadership of the Reverend Edward Fontaine.
But Bishop Freeman was not altogether happy with the situation,
for he said in his address to the 1852 Convention:

> The Church appears to be making good progress in Austin. An
> upper room has been neatly fitted up as a Church, and affords
> comfortable accommodations for the present, though not ca-
> pacious enough to hold at all times those who desire to attend
> our services. The subject of building a Church is seriously agi-
> tated, and no doubt one might speedily be erected, could the
> congregation be satisfied with such a structure as would be
> within the compass of their own means. It is a mistake, but
> too often made by our congregations, to try to do without a
> Church of their own until they shall acquire the means of
> erecting something grand and imposing, forgetting that one of
> the most important requisites for the growth of a congregation,
> after the acquisition of an efficient minister, is the possession
> of a place of worship entirely under our own control.[30]

Nevertheless the congregation held to its plans. The Convention
of 1853 met in this same "Church Room" of Epiphany, Austin.[31]
At that time all seemed to be going well with the Rector and his
flock; $6000 had been collected toward the erection of a church
building, and all other expenses paid[32] The cornerstone of the
new church had been laid April 7, 1853.[33] Construction dragged

[27]Lucy Rucker, *Rucker,* p. 3.
[28]*Spirit of Missions,* 1857, p. 182; *Texas Journal,* 1857, p. 13.
[29]*Spirit of Missions,* 1860, p. 477.
[30]*Texas Journal,* 1852, p. 14.
[31]*Ibid.,* 1853, p. 7.
[32]*Spirit of Missions,* 1853, p. 497; *Texas Journal,* 1853, p. 36.
[33]*St. David's,* p. 22.

along endlessly; in spite of a bond furnished by the contractor guaranteeing completion by September 1, 1853, the building was not finished, though it was roofed in, when Fontaine wrote his report to the Convention of May 1854. Disliking to enter a court suit, the congregation had not attempted to collect the bond.[34] Although there were eleven people waiting for Confirmation, both Fontaine and the Bishop felt that no episcopal visitation was necessary that year.[35]

On his way to the Convention of 1855, Bishop Freeman made what was for him a prolonged visit to Austin, arriving Friday night and departing on Monday. Services were held Friday and Saturday, and the consecration of the new church on Sunday was the highlight of the visitation.[36] The occasion, the culmination of the Rector's longtime dream, was saddened for him by the death of his wife, the former Ann Swisher.[37] The Bishop's terse comment in his convention address seems almost unfeeling:

> Services were held on Friday and Saturday nights, although the Rev. Mr. Fontaine was prevented, by sickness and death in his family, from being present with us.[38]

Eaton and Gillette appropriately were on hand to join in the services; both of them had conducted services in Austin before the organization of Epiphany Parish.[39]

Freeman thought the cost of the new Austin church excessive, and made no comment about its excellence or beauty. And indeed the subsequent course of affairs in the Parish worked out like a textbook case. The building could be consecrated free of debt because the vestry (apparently as individuals) assumed the last $1000 of debt themselves.[40] This debt was evidently made a charge on the offerings of the congregation, for in the next two years Fontaine cited the expense of the church and its furnishings, and the burden of the debt, as reasons for the failure of the Parish to aid other struggling congregations or to take up offerings for mission.[41] Things went badly for the Rector. His living expenses exceeded his salary each year. He could get no desirable results from his Sunday School because he could not enlist teachers, and parents

[34] *Texas Journal*, 1854, p. 33.   [35] *Ibid.*, p. 14.
[36] *Ibid.*, 1855, pp. 17-18.   [37] *St. David's*, p. 25.
[38] *Texas Journal*, 1855, p. 17.
[39] *Ibid.*, pp. 17-18; *St. David's*, p. 25.
[40] *Texas Journal*, 1856, p. 24.
[41] *Ibid.*, 1855, p. 49; 1856, pp. 24ff.

would not compel their children to attend;[42] even when he got enough ladies to teach, "the difficulty of getting male teachers has prevented the attendance of the boys."[43] From the outside, Epiphany Parish displayed all the symptoms of an ingrown, parochially minded congregation, which was just what the Bishop had feared (but just what he had encouraged in Galveston!).

Against this background it becomes easier to understand why a new congregation should have been formed in Austin. Doubtless the cause assigned by many, sectional feeling between Austinites of Northern and Southern sympathy, played its part;[44] yet dissatisfaction with the leadership of Fontaine must have been the decisive factor. Perhaps the effort made by a group in Austin to arrange the transfer of St. Paul's College to their city was not favored by Fontaine, but the records of the proceedings of the Diocesan Convention in 1855 disclose no instance in which he was particularly active in opposing the move.[45] The sequence of events is not altogether clear, but it seems possible that the failure to move the College and the almost certain prospect of failure for the schools in Anderson, suggested to men—already discouraged with their Rector's performance and out of sympathy with his political alignments[46]—the desirability of attracting to the city a clergyman who was a good teacher, pastor and preacher. Perhaps the men interested in a new parish also had a concern to keep alive the effort for theological education that was foundering at Anderson.

In any event Fontaine said in early April in his parochial report to the 1856 Convention at Galveston that the troubles of the congregation were at an end,[47] but some twenty of the communicants of Epiphany Church withdrew to form a new parish. They took the name used by the congregation that Gillette had organized in 1848, Christ Church.[48] Gillette was called as Rector, perhaps while he was in the East attempting to find funds to save the schools in Anderson.[49] He began his work in Austin December 20,

---

[42]*Ibid.*, p. 24.   [43]*Ibid.*, 1859, p. 30.

[44]Murphy, *History of the Episcopal Church in Texas*, p. 28; *St. David's*, pp. 26-7.

[45]Fontaine indeed voted to disapprove the action of the new Board of Trustees of St. Paul's, which proposed, among other things, an eventual move of the College to Austin, but so did such staunch advocates of the College as Rucker, Pratt, J. W. Dunn and Geo. Rottenstein. They, with Eaton, overrode the clerical votes of the Bishop, Gillette, Downing and Nicholson. But it was Rucker, not Fontaine, who was the stormy petrel in this fight. *Texas Journal*, 1855, pp. 26-7, 32-44.

[46]For Fontaine's Know-Nothing Party membership, see *St. David's*, p. 26.

[47]*Texas Journal*, 1856, p. 24.

[48]*Ibid.*, 1857, p. 36; see above, p. 46.

[49]*St. David's*, p. 27.

1856, and reported to the 1857 Convention (at which Christ Church was admitted without dissenting vote) that things were going well; a Sunday School had fifty pupils and ten teachers, and there were twenty-two communicants.[50] A year later he reported seventy-eight pupils and forty communicants. Only because of the long-continued drought and the stagnation in business was there no building in progress. Christ Church was having many more baptisms and larger attendance than Epiphany.[51] The new Parish and its Rector were doing what Epiphany had failed to do; they had a missionary outreach. In 1859, $100 was reported as collected for misions and $50 for relief of sufferers from the epidemic in Galveston.[52] Gillette was also holding monthly services at Wilbarger, a point in the County twelve miles from Austin.[53]

The resolution of the Diocesan Convention precluded moving the diocesan schools from Anderson to Austin, so Gillette began a boys' school in the capital city. It evidently met a real need, for the enrollment reached at least sixty.[54] By the Spring of 1858 Gillette was able to begin collegiate classes with the assistance of Walter R. Richardson and Frank R. Brown, men who, while teaching in the college, continued their studies for Holy Orders under Gillette's direction. The college was chartered in 1860 as "Wharton College," named for Gillette's wife, Mary Ann Wharton.[55]

The income from his school enabled Gillette to support his family without overburdening his congregation, and freed him to carry out his major commitment to education for the Church. Fontaine was also relieved of some financial embarrassment when elected Chaplain of the Texas Senate in 1857.[56] Austin, however, was too small for two parishes. In 1859 the situation was relieved when Fontaine married a wealthy widow and moved to her Mississippi plantation. The congregations soon agreed to unite under Gillette's leadership, and the united Parish took the name of St. David's in honor of the Bishop-elect, whose only parochial charge had been St. David's, Cheraw, South Carolina. The Church in Austin now had a building, and an energetic Rector was carrying on the educational and missionary program needed by the Diocese as well as the Parish.[57]

[50]*Texas Journal*, 1857, pp. 14, 37.   [51]*Ibid.*, 1858, p. 30.
[52]*Ibid.*, 1859, p. 32.   [53]*Ibid.*, 1858, p. 30; 1859, p. 32.
[54]*St. David's*, p. 29.
[55]*Loc. cit.; Handbook of Texas*, "Wharton College," *en. loc.*
[56]*St. David's*, p. 29.
[57]*Ibid.*, pp. 30-1. Fontaine did not leave the active ministry, but ministered effectively in Mississippi and Louisiana for years.

FAR EAST TEXAS

Far to the east of the other work of the Diocese, the Church was thriving in a relatively old culture in the three towns of San Augustine, Nacogdoches and Marshall, set amidst the beautiful pine-clad red hills of East Texas. The Churches at San Augustine and Nacogdoches, which had prospered under the pastorate of the Reverend Henry Sansom, were discouraged when Bishop Freeman visited in 1851. The new church building in San Augustine was far enough along to be used, however,[58] and when the Reverend Elijah Downing arrived, interest and activity revived. By the time of Freeman's 1853 visit the church building in Nacogdoches was usable, though not quite complete. There and in San Augustine Downing was doing good work in spite of many discouragements.[59] His health soon seemed impaired, and he was transferred in October 1854 to Washington County, leaving the East Texas congregations again bereft.[60]

The means taken to secure the next clergyman for the two East Texas congregations makes one of the most unusual stories in the history of the Texas Church. A zealous member of Christ Church, San Augustine, was Mrs. James Pinkney Henderson, *nee* Frances Cox of Philadelphia, a niece of Bishop Kemper. She had obtained the plans and solicited the funds from her friends in Philadelphia for the San Augustine church building.[61] Mrs. Henderson was in Philadelphia in 1855, armed with a letter from the San Augustine vestry. She went to see the Bishop of Pennsylvania, the Right Reverend Alonzo Potter, and asked him for the privilege of making an address to the clergy of the Diocese; such a request was unheard of at that day. Evidently she was persuasive, for she obtained a recruit, a Deacon of the Diocese, Charles H. Albert.[62] He did not stay long in this field but moved in 1856 to Marshall as missionary to that place and Jefferson.[63] This move coincided with the migration of Governor Henderson and his wife to Marshall, so the San Augustine congregation suffered a double loss.[64]

[58]*Spirit of Missions*, 1851, pp. 214, 378; 1852, p. 418.

[59]*Ibid.*, 1853, p. 501.   [60]*Ibid.*, 1855, p. 15.

[61]Crocket, *Two Centuries in East Texas*, pp. 288-9; Benj. Eaton to Bishop Kemper, Houston, January 20, 1841, cited in Morgan, *Trinity Church, Galveston*, pp. 6-8.

[62]Crocket, *op. cit.*, p. 291. A search of the *Journals of the Diocese of Pennsylvania* and of the *Episcopal Recorder* of Philadelphia has failed to yield any confirmation of the story. But this is not surprising; what man would want to record such boldness in a woman in the 1850's?

[63]*Spirit of Missions*, 1856, p. 501.

[64]Crocket, *loc. cit.*

Not until the Fall of 1857 was the vacancy filled, but the man who came was worth waiting for. One of the real saints of the Texas Church was the Reverend John Owen of Maryland, appointed missionary to San Augustine and Nacogdoches September 1, 1857.[65] An Englishman by birth and a former Congregationalist, Owen had a long and distinguished missionary career in the Diocese of Maryland before coming to Texas. He had applied to Bishop Freeman to go to Texas four years previously.[66] Nothing dismayed at the decline in life and interest which had come about in his new congregations during the long vacancy in the rectorship, Owen set to work with zest to build the flocks up again. Owen was a great reporter of travel difficulties, in which he seemed to glory. His letters to the *Spirit of Missions* almost take one onto the road with him. Some months after reaching his new post he wrote that his trips between San Augustine and Nacogdoches every two weeks not only cost him seven dollars a month at half price, but involved an all-night stage ride to San Augustine on the return trip. On one occasion he had no sooner reached home after this ride than a messenger arrived to bid him return to Nacogdoches for a funeral. He then had to ride horseback until one o'clock in the morning to get back to Nacogdoches. But he rejoiced that his own health and that of his wife and three children was good, and that their privations were worth the cause they served.[67] Owen's most amusing travel account concerned his journey home from the Convention of 1859 in Galveston. He rode a mule, and got to the Convention without too much trouble, but on the way home the mule balked finally and decisively, and Owen had to trade it for a horse; he gave $75 boot on credit, for which he had to leave his gold watch as security. In the letter recounting this incident, Owen recorded the loss of the family's house by fire, but still he seemed undismayed.[68] In such hands the missionary work of the Church was certainly safe.

Trinity Church, Marshall, to which the Reverend Henry Sansom had moved in 1851, had begun with good promise. The way for the Church in Harrison County had been prepared through the ministry of the Reverend William Steel, a canonical resident in the Diocese of Louisiana who lived and ministered in the Leigh com-

[65]*Spirit of Missions*, 1857, p. 620.

[66]Crocket, *op. cit*, p. 292; *Journal of the Diocese of Maryland*, 1836, p. 6; 1837, p. 13; 1839 Special, 1839, p. 10; 1841, pp. 7, 47, 102; J. Owen to Secretary, Domestic Committee, Aug. 1, 1857.

[67]*Spirit of Missions*, 1858, p. 278.

[68]*Ibid.*, 1859, pp. 318-19. Note that the printer started two monthly issues with p. 305 in that year. The reference is in the July issue.

munity close to Caddo Lake. On Bishop Freeman's first visitation to Marshall in June 1851, Steel was on hand to greet his old friend whom he had known many years before in Virginia.[69] This fact certainly indicates good communication between the "Louisiana" Episcopalians of St. Paul's Chapel, Leigh, and the new "Texas" Episcopalians of Marshall. But in Marshall, either things did not work out as they promised to do, or the lure of a larger and better established parish was too much for Sansom, for he accepted the rectorship of Christ Church, Houston, in the following year, and Marshall was left without a minister.[70] Not until 1856 was it to have another, when the Reverend C. H. Albert was made the missionary for Marshall and Jefferson.[71] He found that Marshall could use the full-time services of a clergyman, and he thought, could soon afford to pay his entire salary. Instead of starting work at Jefferson, for which he had been appointed, Albert decided Port Caddo was a likelier prospect, and began holding services in that vicinity twice a month. The erection of church buildings was planned at both places, Albert reported early in 1857.[72] But his stay in this field was a short one, for he became Rector of Christ Church, Matagorda, in January 1858.[73] Not until Bishop Gregg brought in more clergy was the Marshall field regularly supplied. But it was not left entirely without attention. After John Owen settled at San Augustine, he visited Marshall and conducted the first services in "the new gothic church built mainly through the untiring efforts of Mrs. Henderson, who had done much for the Church in Eastern Texas." On the same journey Owen conducted services at Henderson, the first services of the Episcopal Church to be held in that town.[74]

Almost nothing is known of the congregation organized in Liberty, whose application for admission to the Diocese under the name of "All Faith" was presented to the Convention of 1852 by Sansom. Mr. H. E. Perkins was the lone representative of the congregation at that Convention; it was never again represented, nor did it file reports during the rest of the decade. A Mr. H. E. Perkins appeared as a delegate for Christ Church, Houston, at the 1856 Convention; likely this was the gentleman who had provided leadership for the organization of the Parish at Liberty, and upon his removal to Houston the flock did not hold together. The Reverend Robert B. Croes of the Diocese of New York reported

[69]*Ibid.*, 1852, p. 418.

[70]*Loc. cit.* Lale's dating is wrong: *As It Was in the Beginning*, p. 5.

[71]*Spirit of Missions*, 1856, p. 501.   [72]*Ibid.*, 1857, p. 179.

[73]*Ibid.*, 1858, p. 633.   [74]*Texas Journal*, 1859, pp. 26-7.

having officiated at Liberty one Sunday in May 1857, while he was temporarily supplying at Christ Church, Houston. He held services at Sour Lake on another Sunday that month.[75]

THE COAST COUNTRY

In the congregations on or near the Gulf Coast the Church had its greatest strength, as was to be expected, since population and wealth were more concentrated here, the earliest work of the Mission was performed in this area, and it was settled before most of the interior Anglo-American settlements.

Trinity Church, Galveston, was by any accounting the strongest parish in the Diocese, and its Rector, the Reverend Benjamin Eaton had been the senior Presbyter of the Diocese since the death of Caleb Ives. In 1856 the Reverend Hannibal Pratt wrote:

> At Galveston is the citadel of Episcopacy in Texas. The parish was organized about sixteen years ago by the present incumbent. He has continued at his post through storm and pestilence, and consequently is greatly endeared to his people.[76]

In view of its leading position, the Galveston Church and its Rector took surprisingly little part in the affairs of the struggling Diocese for the two years following the 1852 Convention. Neither the Rector nor any lay delegate was present at the 1853 Convention in Austin.[77] In the following year Eaton attended the Convention at Anderson, but no lay delegate was present.[78] Not even a perfunctory report from the Parish was submitted for printing in the *Journal of the Convention*. Eaton attended the 1855 Convention at Seguin, accompanied by Mr. D. Wakelee, Jr., as lay delegate, and there he played a quite negative part by opposing not only the election of a bishop at that Convention but also the proposal to elect one the next year.[79]

There could have been at least two reasons for this apparent withdrawal from interest in the Diocese. Eaton had gone to the 1852 Convention as President of the Standing Committee,[80] which had heretofore consisted of three Presbyters. At that meeting an amendment to Canon Two was adopted. Proposed by Mr. H. Baily, a lay delegate from St. Paul's, Washington, the canon enlarged the Standing Committee to include two laymen. Moreover, Eaton was not re-elected to the Committee.[81] Then Bishop Freeman for some rea-

---

[75]*Ibid.*, 1852, pp. 8, 9; 1856, p. 4; 1857, p. 40.

[76]*Spirit of Missions*, 1856, p. 211.   [77]*Texas Journal*, 1853, p. 5.

[78]*Ibid.*, 1854, pp. 5, 7.   [79]*Ibid.*, 1855, pp. 5, 7, 34, 44.

[80]*Ibid.*, 1851, p. 5.   [81]*Ibid.*, 1852, pp. 28, 32.

son decided to include a criticism of the Galveston congregation in his address to the Convention of 1854. Remarking that their church building was much too small for those wishing to attend, and in a state of decay, he went on to say that it was

> . . . a matter of surprise and regret that no movement has yet been made toward the erection of a church commensurate with the wealth and size of the city, and adequate to the increasing demands for accommodation.[82]

This must have started things going, for in his annual report to the Board of Missions, filed later in the year, Freeman said of Galveston:

> vigorous efforts are being made to erect a new church of larger dimensions and more elegant architecture.[83]

These efforts indeed were being made, but the Galveston congregation might well have resented what seemed a public rebuke from the Bishop. When the plans were adopted for the new and magnificent Trinity Church, the first proposed cost must have seemed staggering, but subscriptions, to be paid over several years, were obtained.[84] More than anything else, anxiety over payment for this building must have motivated the worthy Rector's votes against an episcopal election at the Convention of 1855.[85]

Ground was broken for the new Galveston edifice on November 29, 1855, but it was two years in building, and it cost in the neighborhood of $40,000. At the completion of the building the Parish was in debt, not only to the builders and financiers, but to the Rector for his salary as well. Not until 1866 was it possible to clear the debt and have the building consecrated.[86] Perhaps Eaton and his Parish had been wiser than the Provisional Bishop; a weak and struggling Diocese could ill afford to have its strongest Parish so burdened by building that it could lend little or no aid to the general effort. Yet the spur given to the Galveston congregation by its accomplishment in erecting such a beautiful new church did great good. Ten years after the completion of the building the communicant strength had increased from 90 to 150, and the Sunday School from 50 to 360.[87]

As for Eaton himself, whatever were his disappointments about his position in diocesan affairs in the two convention years follow-

[82]*Ibid.*, 1854, p. 12.   [83]*Spirit of Missions*, 1854, p. 508.
[84]Morgan, *Trinity Church, Galveston*, pp. 50-4.
[85]See below, p. 91.
[86]Morgan, *op. cit.*, pp. 54-9. This is an excellent account.
[87]*Texas Journal*, 1867, p. 38.

ing the Chappell Hill Convention, prominence and approval lay ahead. The Convention of 1856, which met in Galveston, elected him President pro tem, and he presided until the arrival of the Bishop on the second day of the meeting. He also headed the list of Clerical Deputies to the General Convention at Philadelphia in September of that year.[88] At the Diocesan Convention at Austin the following year, the Bishop became ill and could not attend on the second day of the meeting; Eaton was called to the chair. He was also returned to membership on the Standing Committee by the Convention, and by vote of that Committee became its President.[89] He served as President of the Convention at its meetings in 1858 and 1859 and received the thanks of the house for his able and impartial chairmanship at the latter Convention. He also continued as President of the Standing Committee through these years, and was a Clerical Deputy to the General Convention of 1859 in Richmond, Virginia,[90] where he attended the consecration of Alexander Gregg as Bishop of Texas during the sessions of that body.[91] Certainly when Bishop Gregg arrived in his new Diocese in late 1859, Eaton as rector of the leading Parish in Texas was its most prominent clergyman.

The only self-supporting Parish beside Galveston in 1852 was Christ Church, Houston. Under the energetic leadership of the Reverend Charles Gillette it had come to number 74 communicants, and had a Sunday School enrollment of 63. The Reverend Henry Sansom succeeded Gillette as Rector January 1, 1852,[92] but he stayed only one year before being transferred at his own request to the Diocese of Mississippi.[93] The Parish was without a rector and deprived of regular services at the time of the 1853 Convention, but the Sunday School increased through the interest of the laity, according to the report of the junior warden, Mr. J. D. Andrews.[94] Early in 1854 the Reverend Joseph J. Nicholson of the Diocese of New York accepted the vestry's call to become Rector, and was present at the Convention at Anderson that year. He reported that the actual number of communicants had declined when he arrived to 46, but he had hopes for better things.[95]

---

[88]*Ibid.*, 1856, pp. 4, 8, 11, 12.   [89]*Ibid.*, 1857, pp. 3, 23, 24.

[90]*Ibid.*, 1858, p. 3; 1859, pp. 3, 9, 21.

[91]Letter requesting publication of the sermon preached by the Rt. Rev. John Henry Hopkins at Bishop Gregg's consecration, signed by Benj. Eaton, W. T. Dickinson Dalzell, P. W. Gray and Isaac E. Nicholson, Deputies of the Diocese of Texas in Attendance: bound up with the sermon, printed by Pudney & Russell, New York, 1859.

[92]*Texas Journal*, 1852, p. 41.   [93]*Ibid.*, 1853, p. 16.

[94]*Ibid.*, pp. 33-4.   [95]*Ibid.*, 1854, pp. 7, 12, 30.

Nicholson took an active part in diocesan affairs from the start. He was made Secretary of a new Society for the Diffusion of Christian Knowledge at the 1854 Convention, and was praised for the report he made for that body at the subsequent Convention. At the same time the Convention commended

> the plan of the Rev. J. J. Nicholson, to publish a paper in Houston or Galveston, advocating the principles of true Christianity, as taught by the Church to which we are atttached, and we recommend his proposed plan to the support of the members of our communion in Texas, and throughout the Church.[96]

Tragically, the great promise of usefulness in the energetic plans of this great Priest was cut short by the breakdown of his health which caused his resignation and removal to Alabama.[97]

Christ Church was then unable to secure a rector, but at the request of the vestry was served for the first half of 1857 by the Reverend Robert B. Croes of the Diocese of New York.[98] In mid-May of that year the Reverend William T. Dickinson Dalzell of the Diocese of Pennsylvania arrived in Houston to become Rector of Christ Church.[99] An able and energetic man, Dalzell set to work vigorously in the Parish which, as Bishop Freeman said, needed "uniting and edifying." In addition Dalzell held monthly services in Richmond. A move was on foot in Houston to build a rectory and a new church building, and measures were already taken and some funds raised for a building in Richmond.[100] At the time of the 1859 Convention the church in Houston had reached such a state of decay that services had to be transferred to the Court House, but a subscription had been started for a new building. In Richmond the new church was complete, about a third of its cost having been contributed by one of its members, Mr. William E. Kendall. The Parish had been organized as Calvary Church, and was admitted into union with the Diocese at that Convention.[101] Dalzell also had begun missionary endeavors at Hempstead.[102]

The real groundwork for Dalzell's work at Richmond had been laid by the Reverend Hannibal Pratt while he was in charge of the missionary field of Columbus and La Grange. Bishop Freeman had received the request of some members of the Church that services be provided at Richmond. It would have been natural for the Rector of Christ Church, Houston, to take care of this point, since the rail-

---

[96]*Ibid.,* p. 28; 1855, p. 38.   [97]*Spirit of Missions,* 1855, p. 523.
[98]*Texas Journal,* 1857, p. 40.   [99]*Ibid.,* 1858, pp. 13, 24-5.
[100]*Ibid.,* p. 25; *Spirit of Missions,* 1857, p. 600.
[101]*Texas Journal,* 1859, pp. 8, 24-5.   [102]*Ibid.,* p. 25.

road from Houston had reached Richmond, but the Houston pulpit was vacant at that time. The field was white for harvest in Richmond, so the Bishop asked Pratt to make the effort. For him to work there involved a sixty-mile stage ride each way, and that at night; such an extra burden had wrecked Pratt's health before Dalzell relieved him.[103]

The inability of the Brazoria County Church people to secure a minister during the period between the departure of the Reverend John F. Young and the end of the decade forms one of the strangest chapters in the story of the Texas Church. High expectations of many for rapid growth and development of commerce were disappointed, mainly through the failure to surmount the difficulties of navigating the bar of the Brazos River. Nevertheless this County was the seat of a rich plantation economy. Here, as much as anywhere in the State, it could be expected that at least one and perhaps two clergy could find support without missionary appropriation. Yet they did not come. Bishop Freeman was unable to visit the County on his 1852 visitation, but cited its need for a missionary.[104] In the following year he expected a missionary to report to Brazoria,[105] but was disappointed. He planned to visit in Brazoria himself, but was frustrated, as in the previous year, by heavy rains.[106] In the two following years the Bishop did not even attempt to visit the County, and his list of recommended mission stations did not include it.[107]

In 1856 Pratt visited Brazoria County, and reported:

> In Brazoria County . . . great interest is felt to have the services of the Church—an active clergyman among them. One is needed *now*. The county is large, populous and wealthy— the garden of Texas. The citizens are most hospitable, intelligent and refined. The Church is better appreciated than where there is less intelligence. . . . Three planters offered $1000 per annum to teach their children. . . .

Pratt refused their offer because he preferred the pastoral ministry, but he was told of generous offers of support for a rector, too. Pratt appealed for a clergyman to accept the opportunity. One man, he believed, could care adequately for Columbia, Brazoria and an unnamed point; at the last place a Churchman had fitted out a building for worship, but for want of a clergyman of our Church was giving its use to Methodists and Presbyterians.[108]

[103]*Spirit of Missions*, 1857, pp. 180, 255-6; 1858, p. 75.
[104]*Texas Journal*, 1852, pp. 12, 16.   [105]*Ibid.*, 1853, p. 16.
[106]*Ibid.*, p. 14; *Spirit of Missions*, 1853, p. 495.
[107]*Ibid.*, 1855, p. 601.   [108]*Ibid.*, 1856, pp. 211-12.

Evidently no clerical reader of the *Spirit of Missions* felt moved by Pratt's appeal. Without a resident Bishop to bring eager congregations and prospective pastors together, nothing could be accomplished for a field that was not to be under appointment by the Domestic Committee of the Board of Missions.[109]

At the time of the Convention of 1852, the prospects of the Mother Church of the Diocese, at Matagorda, must have seemed brighter. Its members were twice disappointed by the early departure of clergy who had accepted appointment to the field. The Reverend Mr. Flower had just departed to become Rector of the Church at Florence, Alabama, after only a year as rector of Christ Church. Next, the rectorship was accepted by the Reverend Henry Niles Pierce, who had been ordained Deacon and Priest in that Parish. During Ives' rectorship, Pierce had frequently visited and preached in Matagorda. After assuming the rectorship, Pierce, with his usual missionary spirit, reached out beyond his own Parish to officiate at Indianola and Port Lavaca. The Bishop reported such a renewal of life and vigor in Matagorda itself as promised early self-support should Pierce continue in the charge.[110] But, alas for Matagorda, romance intervened. The new Rector was married to Miss Nannie H. Sheppard of Matagorda on Easter Tuesday, 1854; Bishop Freeman performed the ceremony. The Bishop reported that year to the Convention that the Matagorda Parish had grown during Pierce's ministrations, and that he held Pierce in great affection. The people feared, as did the Bishop, that the responsibilities of marriage might motivate Pierce to move to a larger parish. And so they did. Pierce sent in his resignation effective June 1, 1854 to the Board of Missions, and accepted the rectorship of Trinity Church, New Orleans, Louisiana.[111]

Matagorda went off the missionary rolls and became self-supporting at this point.[112] The vestry called the Reverend Stephen R. Wright of Uniontown, Alabama, as Rector. Then disaster struck. A hurricane destroyed almost the entire town, including the beautiful building of the Mother Church.[113] The new Rector's first duty was to solicit funds to rebuild the church, and he spent some fifteen months out of his Parish doing it. Lay services were kept up in his absence. He succeeded in obtaining for the purpose $3000, which

[109]Ironically, the *Spirit of Missions* listed St. John's Brazoria, as a former mission, now self-supporting; 1856, p. 191.

[110]*Ibid.*, 1853, pp. 495-6.

[111]*Texas Journal*, 1854, p. 13; *Spirit of Missions*, 1854, pp. 337, 508.

[112]*Ibid.*, 1856, p. 191.   [113]*Texas Journal*, 1855, p. 18.

was matched exactly by the stricken Matagorda folk, and the reconstruction began. But after a few months back in his Parish,
Wright died of a stroke on January 28, 1857, much mourned by his
people.[114]

The Parish remained vacant until early 1858, when the Reverend
C. H. Albert was transferred from Marshall; Matagorda was restored
by the Domestic Committee as a station for a missionary.[115] Albert
reported to the Convention of 1858 that the congregation had dwindled during the long vacancy and during the period that the Parish
had been without a regular meeting place; but the new building
should be occupied in a short time.[116] It was completed in time to
be consecrated by Bishop Gregg at the 1860 Convention. Reporting
to Convention the next year, Albert said that the population of the
town had dropped drastically since the hurricane, and now numbered only about 450; as a consequence, the future of the Parish
was in some doubt. Albert was present at the Convention of 1860
which met at Matagorda, but was not listed as Rector;[117] he must
have resigned in the meantime.

Indianola and Lavaca (often then called Port Lavaca) were
opened up as a missionary field, independent of the Board of Missions, through the generous offer of a layman in Cincinnati, Ohio.
This man had no means other than his monthly salary, but out of
it he proposed paying the stipend of a clergyman for some field in
Texas. Bishop Freeman interested the Reverend C. S. Hedges of
Louisiana in accepting this appointment and took him along to visit
Indianola and Lavaca. Hedges decided to settle at Indianola and
undertake the mission.[118]

Congregations had been formed in both towns, and an encouraging response was being made when yellow fever struck with such
violence that the two places were almost depopulated. In Port
Lavaca only one of the seven members of the vestry survived. The
worthy missionary stuck to his post to minister to the sick and dying,
then he himself contracted the fever and barely survived. When he
recovered, the new beginning that had to be made in the work
demanded a concentration of time that forced him to discontinue
the work he had started at Victoria. The Parishes reorganized and
recouped their strength enough to petition the Convention of 1854
for admission, under the names of "Grace Church, Lavaca," and

114*Ibid.*, 1857, pp. 35-6, report of W. L. Sartwell as senior warden.
115*Spirit of Missions*, 1858, pp. 633, 640.
116*Texas Journal*, 1858, p. 23.   117*Ibid.*, 1860, p. 5; 1861, p. 9.
118*Spirit of Missions*, 1853, p. 495.

"St. John's Church, Indianola." The petitions were laid on the table, and apparently not acted upon at that Convention; however, the Parishes were listed in the next *Convention Journal,* so perhaps the Secretary failed to note the action of the 1854 Convention in admitting them. The ladies of each congregation began accumulating money and furnishings toward the building of churches.[119]

At the Convention of 1855 Hedges reported that his congregations had been struck again by the epidemic, which caused many people to move out of the vicinity. Not much had been done. A begging tour of the East in that Summer had yielded Hedges little over $300 toward the building of churches in his towns; it was impossible to start construction. The settlement of Saluria, ten miles below Indianola, had been included in Hedges' sphere of labor. [120]

Some time in the Fall of 1855 an end was put to Hedges' efforts. His Ohio benefactor ceased paying his salary, and in view of the hardships which had overtaken the communities in which he worked, Hedges could not support his family without this subsidy. As the Reverend J. W. Dunn of Lockhart put it, "Brother Hedges has literally starved out and gone." Bishop Freeman requested the Board of Missions to place Indianola and Port Lavaca on the list as an official Domestic Missionary station, but that body had not the means to do so.[121] The two congregations remained without a minister for years thereafter.

The roll has been called of congregations which constituted the Diocese of Texas to which Alexander Gregg came as Bishop in 1859. The Diocese was significantly larger than it had been in 1849, when there were but six clergy, six organized Parishes, and another field in early stages of development. At the end of the period there were thirteen clergy and twenty-four congregations in union with the Diocese, not including various outstations where services were being held. Communicant strength had more than doubled, and of course many more people were under the influence of the Church.

Yet very much more could have been done with full-time leadership. The need for a general missionary to rove over the State, ministering to scattered members and founding new congregations, had been seen at the 1851 Convention, but the Diocese had been unable to afford one. When Bishop Gregg took charge of the Diocese he himself performed this function. A bishop responsible solely for Texas could have done so as well in the earlier period before other

[119]*Texas Journal,* 1854, pp. 13, 23-4, 34; 1855, p. 5.
[120]*Ibid.,* pp. 49-50.
[121]*Spirit of Missions,* 1855, p. 601; 1856, pp. 214, 665; *Texas Journal,* 1856, p. 13.

church bodies moved into the new settlements. Only a resident bishop could have stimulated the local contributions needed to augment the limited funds which the Missionary Society could spare for Texas. The Texas Episcopalians realized their plight and their opportunity, of course, and as early as 1852 began the long struggle to obtain a bishop of their own.

VII.   The Search for a Diocesan Bishop

THE MEMBERS of the Diocesan Convention realized the need for a resident Bishop quite early in the life of the Diocese. Before they were able canonically to elect a bishop of their own, they invited Bishop Freeman to remove his residence from Little Rock to Texas. They were extremely fond of Freeman, and believed that he, despite age and infirmities, could give the leadership they needed if he spent more of his time in Texas. But Freeman was primarily responsible for the unorganized work in Arkansas and Indian Territory, and was only Provisional Bishop of Texas. Though the Diocese of Texas had the greater potential for growth, his primary duty was to develop missions within the northern areas to which he was primarily assigned. Hence he urged the Texas Convention to take steps to provide support for a diocesan bishop, then to elect one. The Convention of 1851 passed a resolution requesting the clergy and wardens of each congregation to solicit contributions to the Episcopal Fund.[1]

The Convention of 1852 heard no report of funds raised by the appeal of the previous year, but unanimously resolved to go into an election and unanimously elected Freeman on the first ballot. Caught by surprise, the Bishop asked time to consider. The Convention voted to instruct the Rector of each parish to solicit contributions for the salary of the Bishop, adding the new provision that funds collected should be forwarded to the Standing Committee quarterly.[2]

Bishop Freeman gave earnest consideration to the call of the Church in Texas, to which he made no definite reply before the next annual Convention. When it assembled in Austin in May 1853, the Bishop had intended in his Annual Address to decline the election,[3] but the clergy prevailed upon him to defer a decision at that time. In the following year addressing the Convention at An-

---

[1] *Texas Journal*, 1851, p. 26.   [2] *Ibid.*, 1852, p. 34.
[3] *Spirit of Missions*, 1852, p. 425.

derson, he declined the election, feeling unequal to the sacrifices
acceptance would entail.[4]

All told, this was a strange and unfortunate proceeding. True
enough, not enough money was immediately available to support
a bishop. Nevertheless, an episcopal residence at Anderson—central
to the Diocese as then developed, connected by stage lines with
other Church locations, and site of the new schools—might have
quickened the tempo of the life of the Diocese enough to assure
increasing support. At his time of life and state of health Freeman
understandably would shrink from such a risk. In any case he should
have made an earlier decision. His delay in making public his refusal proved almost fatal for the Church in Texas.

The Convention of 1854 made no move to conduct another
election. The following Convention, meeting at Seguin in May 1855,
became involved in heated controversy between those favored an
immediate election and those who contended that, without advance
notice and with such a small representation of the clergy and congregation present, an election was unwise. In a minority report
dissenting from the recommendation of the rest of the Committee
on the Election of a Bishop, the Reverend L. P. Rucker urged an
immediate election, "that this fruitful source of strife, contention
and discord among brethren be as speedily removed as the nature
of the case will possibly admit."[5] The Convention eventually voted
to conduct an election at the next annual meeting in 1856, although
the Reverend Benjamin Eaton had moved to table the action. A
committee to devise means for the support of a bishop was to report
to the next Convention.[6]

Prior to the Convention of 1856 in Galveston, efforts had been
made to find a man suitable for the episcopal office, and to provide means for his support. The Reverend Arthur Cleveland Coxe,
rector of Grace Church, Baltimore, Maryland, and later Bishop of
Western New York, was elected by the clergy on the first ballot,
and his election concurred in by the laity on their first ballot.[7] The
minutes of the Convention do not disclose who placed Coxe in
nomination before the Clergy, but some years later Mr. Oscar Farish
of Trinity Church, Galveston, who had been a delegate to that
Convention, stated that it was done by Charles Gillette. Farish gave
this account. His own Rector, Benjamin Eaton, had been nominated
also; Gillette then asserted that Coxe had assured him that he would
accept if elected, that he was not concerned about the small salary,

---

[4] *Texas Journal*, 1854, p. 16.   [5] *Ibid.*, 1855, pp. 32-3.
[6] *Ibid.*, pp. 30-4, 44.   [7] *Ibid.*, 1856, p. 14.

and that he could bring from ten to fifteen young clergymen along for the field. Upon hearing this Eaton withdrew his name. Farish charged that Gillette was being untruthful, for "it was later proved that he [Gillette] had in his pocket a letter from Mr. Coxe declaring that under no circumstances would he accept if elected Bishop." Farish thought Gillette was acting only to prevent Eaton's election, but praised Coxe for his generous contributions he and his friends made toward the salary of the Bishop of Texas.[8] Whatever may be the truth of Farish's statement, Bishop Freeman thought Coxe would accept. Freeman wrote of the election in his Annual Report for 1856: "This result was extremely gratifying to me, as insuring me (I, in my simplicity, thought,) from a large part of the burden...."[9]

The Convention acted to secure a fund for episcopal support by taxing each congregation twelve and one-half per cent on the salary of its Rector, to be paid over to one of the vestrymen elected by the vestry as agent and transmitted by him to the treasurer of the Convention. This local agent was also instructed to solicit contributions to a permanent capital fund for the support of the Episcopate, with the provision that when a parish had collected an adequate amount for this latter fund, it should be released from the assessment.[10]

When the Convention of May 1857 met in Epiphany Church, Austin, Gillette presented a letter dated March 25, 1857, from Coxe, declining the election, but detailing an offer to support a Bishop of Texas to the extent of $1500 per year for three years, provided the Diocese should offer its Bishop $1000 per year and travelling expenses for this period; then two more years Coxe would supply $1000 per year, provided the Diocese would pay $1500 per year and expenses. This offer was made by a group of clergy consisting of the Reverend Doctors Hawks, Hobart and Bedell of New York, Morton, Stevens, Howe and Wilmer of Philadelphia, and Wyatt and Coxe of Baltimore with Coxe acting as secretary. The only other condition the group laid down was that the election of the new Bishop should be unanimous, or concurred in unanimously, in order to lay the suspicions of party or factional influence; the committee pledged to make no suggestion and drop no hint concerning a nominee.[11]

---

[8]This narrative was in Farish's unpublished manuscript, *A Short History of the Episcopal Church in Galveston*, from which Morgan quoted: *Trinity Church, Galveston*, p. 41.

[9]*Spirit of Missions*, 1856, p. 630.

[10]*Texas Journal*, 1856, p. 17.

[11]Printed in *ibid.*, 1857, pp. 18-19.

Responding with profound thanks to this generous offer, the Convention solicited cash contributions on the spot, then lay delegates assented to assessments upon each parish for the amounts necessary to make up the salary required by the offer.[12] The Reverend Alexander H. Vinton, D. D., Rector of St. Paul's Church, Boston, Massachusetts, was nominated by the clergy to be Bishop of Texas; one ballot resulted in non-concurrence of the laity, but another secured his election, which was then made unanimous.[13] It is not known who suggested Vinton to the clergy, or on what ground they believed he would accept, but the belief proved false. Freeman, once again convinced that the Bishop-elect would certainly accept, offered his resignation. He was presented with a resolution of appreciation for his long and arduous services, and with a request that he withdraw his resignation as Provisional Bishop; he did not make himself understood, but left the Convention and Standing Committee in doubt as to his—and their—status.[14] Was he, or was the Standing Committee the Ecclesiastical Authority? In any event, Freeman, worn out in body after so many years of travel under the most gruelling conditions, could hardly continue the oversight of the Texas Church. This visitation proved to be Freeman's last to Texas. He died in Little Rock, Arkansas, on April 29, 1858.[15]

The Convention of 1858 met in April in Christ Church, Houston, secured voluntary acceptances of assessments totaling about $1500 for the salary of the Bishop, and elected to that office the Reverend Sullivan H. Weston, assistant minister of Trinity Church, New York. He was elected on the first ballot, unanimously,[16] in the apparent belief that he would accept, but he, too, declined.[17] A letter to the Secretary of the Domestic Committee written by the Reverend John Owen, who had come from Maryland to the San Augustine and Nacogdoches missionary field early in the year, hints at Weston's reason for declining. He wrote of the general disappointment at Weston's refusal of the office:

> Our Church is so conservative in its character, that one might reasonably suppose the most northern man could not fail to give satisfaction, so far as he would have to do with politics in the episcopate of any Southern State. In saying this, I am sustained by experience, for I labored for twenty-two years in such

12*Ibid.,* p. 30 and Statistical Table.   13*Ibid.,* p. 27.
14*Ibid.,* pp. 28, 29; *Spirit of Missions,* 1857, p. 600.
15*Ibid.,* 1858, p. 279.   16*Texas Journal,* 1858, p. 13.
17*Ibid.,* 1859, p. 9.

a State, and most of the time under the jurisdiction of one from the North, whom no Southern State could have been otherwise than profoundly proud to acknowledge and revere as its Bishop.[18]

But when Whittingham became Bishop of Maryland, the issues and feelings were not so intense between North and South as to make a northerner unwelcome as Bishop. The past two Conventions elected rectors of important city parishes. Perhaps the hope in 1858 was that an assistant in a large parish—a fellow-assistant of the Reverend John Freeman Young,[19] veteran of the Brazoria County field in Texas—would be more likely to accept the call. Perhaps Young had given friends in Texas reason to believe that Weston would accept.

Four successive refusals of the Texas Episcopate left the Diocese in a serious predicament. The population of the State was increasing rapidly. New towns were rising overnight. Communicants of the older congregations were on the move and hoped the Church could follow them. It became imperative that a suitable man who would accept his election could be chosen for Bishop. When the Convention of 1859, meeting in Galveston in May, came to the election, three men were nominated to the clergy. The Reverend Alexander Gregg of St. David's Church, Cheraw, South Carolina, was nominated by the Reverend W. Dickinson Dalzell; the Reverend Benjamin Eaton of Galveston, by the Reverend Edward Fontaine; the Reverend Dr. James Craik of Louisville, Kentucky, by Eaton. Eight clergymen were eligible to vote. Four voted for Eaton on the first ballot, Gregg received three votes and Craik one; under majority rule there was no election. Eaton withdrew, but received two votes on the next ballot to four for Gregg and two for Craik. The third ballot dead-locked again: Craik four votes, Gregg three, Eaton one. On the fourth ballot Gregg received five votes to Craik's three, and then was nomi-nated unanimously to the laity, who concurred unanimously on the first ballot.[20] Texas at last had elected a man who would feel con-strained to accept its Episcopate.

[18]*Spirit of Missions*, 1858, p. 468.
[19]*General Convention Journal*, 1859, p. 418.
[20]*Texas Journal*, 1859, p. 16.

PART THREE

THE DIOCESE IN BISHOP GREGG'S FIRST YEARS

VIII. The New Bishop Meets His People

THE STORY of the nomination and election of Alexander Gregg to the Texas Episcopate is strange and wonderful. Up to the time that Weston declined his election to Texas, it is quite probable that Gregg was completely unknown to virtually all the leaders of the Diocese of Texas. Indeed, only in the last three or four years had the Diocese of South Carolina begun to realize that the self-effacing parson of the small upstate town of Cheraw was a man of great ability and to use his talents for diocesan work. His home town, Cheraw, was the only cure Gregg had served.

Born in Society Hill, South Carolina, in 1819, the future Bishop finished South Carolina College at the head of his class in 1838, and then read law in an office in Cheraw. He gained admission to the Bar in 1841 and made a brilliant beginning in courtroom practice. His family was Baptist, but he had never affiliated himself with any church. In Cheraw he met, courted and married a devout Episcopalian, Charlotte Wilson Kolloch. Shortly after his marriage he was baptized and confirmed; turning his back on his legal career, he applied for admission as a Candidate for Holy Orders.[1] Like all

---

[1]Wilson Gregg, *Alexander Gregg, First Bishop of Texas*, ed. & extended by the Rev. Howard Noll (Sewanee, Tenn., 1912), pp. 6-13. Cited hereafter as "W. Gregg, Gregg."

but two of the fourteen candidates in the Diocese of South Carolina at that time, Gregg had to forego study at a theological seminary and read privately under the Bishop's direction.[2] Retiring to a nearby farm which he owned, Gregg sustained his family and read through a formidable bibliography given him by that strict high churchman and scholar, Bishop Gadsden.[3] Omitting neither Hebrew nor Greek, nor asking any other dispensation,[4] Gregg successfully passed his examinations at the end of three years' study, and was ordained to the Diaconate in St. David's, Cheraw, on June 10, 1846.[5]

The Cheraw parish was without a rector at this time, so Gregg was appointed minister, and served the parish while studying another spate of doctrinal, historical and practical books assigned by the Bishop. He was ordained to the Priesthood in December of the following year, and was made rector of St. David's.[6] Systematic and disciplined in his use of time, Gregg did his ministerial work in a steady and tireless way rather than brilliantly; he struck a good balance between study, writing, pastoral work, and general leadership in community affairs. He held services and preached frequently in small communities in the area, endeavoring to forward the missionary work of the Church in that region. He was instrumental in reviving a congregation at Mars Bluff, holding monthly services there while helping them seek out a clergyman and gather the means to build a church. At the same time, his congregation's offerings for diocesan, foreign and domestic missions exceeded those of many churches several times larger.[7]

Gregg's interpretation of the catholicity of the Church required that its ministrations be extended to all classes of people. Bishop Davis, reporting his visitation to Cheraw in 1855, said:

> . . . . the congregations appears to be in an advancing condition. The Rector has devoted himself with faithfulness and success to the very poor members of his parish.[8]

A slaveowner himself, Gregg was zealous for the spiritual welfare the negro slaves, and ministered as regularly to them as to the

[2]*Journal of the Diocese of South Carolina*, 1846, p. 14. Cited hereafter as "*South Carolina Journal*."

[3]A. S. Thomas, "Christopher Edwards Gadsden," *Historical Magazine*, XXVIII (1959), pp. 306-8.

[4]W. Gregg, *Gregg*, pp. 17-19.

[5]Burgess, List of Deacons.

[6]W. Gregg, *Gregg*, pp. 19-21.

[7]*Ibid.*, pp. 25-7; *South Carolina Journal*, 1853, p. 48.

[8]*Ibid.*, 1855, p. 24.

whites.[9] Apparently he was content to give himself in this small sphere; he ministered among his friends and kinsmen, supported himself from the proceeds of his own property, and drew practically no salary from the Parish.[10] Gregg might have spent his entire life in Cheraw had not his new Bishop, the Right Reverend Thomas F. Davis, drawn him into active leadership in the Diocese and beyond.

South Carolina was a large and old diocese, with many clergy. Although it was one of the liveliest and most generous dioceses in the entire country, with an aggressive program of church extension and education, its leadership, both clerical and lay, tended to be vested in the tidewater parishes, particularly in Charleston. Only one who sought prominence stood any chance of winning his own way, and Alexander Gregg certainly was not that. In fact, he was not diligent about attending convention, appearing there only about every other year, as did several of the back-country clergy.[11] But Bishop Davis drew Gregg into the work of the Convention in two areas. Gregg served on a committee to look into ways of advancing the work of the Church amongst the slaves, and made an able report to the next Convention;[12] he was involved in a study of the educational program of the diocese. In the latter interest Gregg worked on a committee to survey the prospects for founding a diocesan college. He reported to the 1857 Convention, advising against the project. At the same time, he was appointed the clerical member from South Carolina on a board to consult between Southern Dioceses about founding a Southern University.[13] For the first time since his ordination, Gregg preached at the opening service of a convention in 1857.[14]

Gregg attended regional meetings at Montgomery and at Sewanee, deliberating the Southern University, and although he did not attend the 1858 Diocesan Convention, he sent a competent report which was read there, and he was re-appointed clerical trustee. He reported in person to the next Convention concerning both the laying of the cornerstone at Sewanee and the Trustees' meeting there which he had attended.[15]

[9]*Ibid.*, Parochial Reports for Cheraw, 1847-59. For his views on separate services or congregations, see below p. 104.

[10]W. Gregg, *Gregg*, p. 27.

[11]Here W. Gregg is wrong. See lists of clergy not in attendance at Conventions in *South Carolina Journal* for this period.

[12]*Ibid.*, 1857, p. 90.

[13]*Ibid.*, pp. 39, 90.

[14]*Ibid.*, p. 5. This quite able sermon, printed at the request of the Convention, may be seen in the C.H.S. Archives.

[15]*South Carolina Journal*, 1858, p. 34; 1859, p. 49.

Gregg's participation in the meetings of the Sewanee Trustees impressed Bishop Polk of Louisiana with his great ability. Stephen Elliott, Bishop of Georgia, already knew him well, having been one of his professors at South Carolina College. The Reverend W. T. D. Dalzell of Houston, visiting in New Orleans at the residence of Bishop Polk, discussed Texas' need for a bishop with Polk and Elliott. Elliott recommended Gregg for the bishopric of Texas, and Polk doubtless agreed then, as he did later by letter. Dalzell related this to Judge Gray of Houston, who wrote Elliott to find out more about Gregg. In a long letter, Elliott explained his enthusiasm for this unassuming country parson, and his conviction that Gregg could do better in a Southern frontier diocese than could an urban or Northern Priest. A strong man physically, over six feet in height and used to the out-of-doors, Gregg could stand the strain of endless and difficult travel over a vast territory. In reply to Judge Gray's inquiries, Bishop Davis of South Carolina backed Elliott's recommendation with a frank appraisal. Realizing that the Bishop's stipend might be uncertain, he added that Gregg had independent means. Bishop Polk also appears to have communicated his high opinion of Gregg to several Texas Church people.[16]

Against this background the outcome of the 1859 election can be understood. The opinion of the Southern Bishops was most important at a time when the entire South was intensely self-conscious and defensive. Judge Gray was perhaps the most influential layman in the Diocese. With his assurances, the laity were ready to approve unanimously the clergy's nomination of Gregg. Not having received the slightest hint that his name had been mentioned for the Episcopate, Gregg received the news of his election as a bolt from the blue. His son related:

> His first intimation of so much as the faintest allusion to him in such a connection was when he was in attendance upon the Diocesan Convention of South Carolina, at Charleston. He had been engaged in prayer and had just risen from his knees, when a gentleman sitting behind him leaned over and told him that he had been elected Bishop of Texas. It struck him almost dumb. With his retired habits, simple tastes, and unambitious purposes he was little likely to have anticipated such a mark of esteem.[17]

For Alexander Gregg and his wife, the thought of leaving South Carolina was sorrowful indeed; yet, impressed as they were by the

---

[16]W. Gregg, *Gregg*, pp. 45-52, where Elliott's and Davis' letters appear, but Polk's is only mentioned.

[17]*Ibid.*, p. 53.

great urgency of Texas' need and the great blow which another refusal of the Episcopate would deal to the Diocese of Texas, they were too conscientious to refuse this call of duty. By May 27 Gregg had accepted the election.[18] In his own unself-conscious way, he had considered the need, recognized his own inadequacy, come to the conclusion that God was calling him nevertheless, then trusted God to give him the sufficiency. In his address to the first Convention of the Diocese of Texas over which he presided, he began thus:

> I appear before you, on this occasion, the first assembling of the Convention since my consecration to the Episcopate of Texas, with emotions of no ordinary nature. Called, in the providence of God, to enter upon so great and responsible a work, and that in a field of labor for which I might well have feared my former experience had in no way peculiarly fitted me, you may well imagine the doubts and apprehensions, not to speak of other grounds of distrust, with which so new and heavy a charge was undertaken. Nor have the opportunities for observation thus far offered me, served in any wise, but to confirm the opinion entertained at first, and to show how well founded were the feelings which this call, from the Great Head of the Church, inspired in me. And yet, it was a call which could not well be declined. Your previous disappointments, and the sore trials through which you have been called to pass, only served to make the summons more imperative. There was but one thing left for me to fall back upon—that grace freely promised, and all-sufficient for the servant of Christ, into whatsoever state of life, or sphere of labor, it may please God to call him.[19]

Having opened his heart to his fellow-workers in the Diocese, and thanked them for the warm welcome that had been shown him, Gregg then took himself and his feelings out of view and turned the attention of his hearers to the work to be done.

Alexander Gregg did not allow his new dignity to change his modest pastoral approach to the laity. In a circular letter which he published in the press, he began, "Dear Brethren," and ended, "I am affectionately your friend and Brother in Christ, Alexander Gregg, Bishop of the Diocese of Texas."

In the time which elapsed before his journey to General Convention for consecration, Gregg secured and read every book he could obtain on the history and geography of Texas, studied the *Journals* of the Diocese, and wrote to many of the clergy and laity

---

[18]*Ibid.*, pp. 55-8. Gregg did write to inquire about the effect of the drinking water of Texas upon health before accepting: *ibid.*, p. 56.

[19]*Texas Journal*, 1860, p. 9.

of Texas, all by way of preparing himself to be as useful as possible upon his arrival.[20]

Gregg was consecrated Bishop in Monumental Church, Richmond, Virginia, October 13, 1859. John Henry Hopkins, Bishop of Vermont, was the Consecrator and Preacher, and Bishops B. B. Smith of Kentucky, James H. Otey of Tennessee, Leonidas Polk of Louisiana, Stephen Elliott of Georgia, William Mercer Green of Mississippi, Thomas F. Davis of South Carolina and Thomas Atkinson of North Carolina were Co-consecrators.[21] Three other services of consecration were taking place at the same time in other Richmond churches; none of the church buildings in the city was large enough to hold all the bishops, clergy and laity that would attend the consecration, and there were strenuous objections against the original proposal to consecrate all four men at an out-of-doors service on the grounds of the State Capitol.[22] Bishop Gregg's first duty was to attend the House of Bishops for the remainder of the Convention, which did not adjourn until October 22.[23] This delay undoubtedly afforded him many opportunities for consultation with the Texas delegation, as well as with fellow Bishops and with the Domestic Committee of the Missionary Society which was meeting daily between sessions of General Convention. In particular, he must have sought out Bishop Polk's knowledge of Texas and its Church leaders, and the problems of the frontier from Bishop Kemper, who knew them as no other did. Almost at the beginning of the manuscript journal which Gregg began before leaving for Texas, there is a memorandum of subjects which must be covered in his first convention address. Apparently these topics were brought together as a result of the good use of the time Gregg spent outside of meetings during the General Convention.[24]

After arriving home from the Convention, the new Bishop devoted three weeks to ministry to the Parish in which he had labored

---

[20]W. Gregg, *Gregg*, p. 60.

[21]*General Convention Journal*, 1859, p. 378.

[22]W. Gregg, *Gregg*, p. 59. This author is in error in his reference to Bishop Hopkins as the Presiding Bishop. Thomas Church Brownell of Connecticut, as Senior Bishop, still held that office, but was prevented by age and distance from attending. The next senior, William Meade of Virginia, presided over the House of Bishops, and made the arrangements for the consecration services. *General Convention Journal*, 1859, pp. 147, 166, 167, 170. As late as the day before, the Committee on Consecrations proposed holding them jointly at St. Paul's Church. The minutes of the House of Bishops do not reflect the proposal to hold a consecration service out-of-doors.

[23]*General Convention Journal*, 1859, pp. 212-23.

[24]Gregg, Manuscript Journal. This valuable source for Gregg's episcopate is owned by the Diocese of Texas, and is available in the Registrar's office.

so long as he made preparations for his first visit to his new diocese. He left Cheraw November 10, and travelled by way of Charleston to Savannah, where he hoped to see Bishop Elliott; but Elliott was not at home, and the committee meeting Gregg had come to attend had been cancelled. He travelled overland to Chattanooga, and thence to Oxford, Mississippi, where he spent six days at the University of Mississippi.[25] While the purpose of these visits is not mentioned in his journal, Gregg evidently was concerned with the business of the University of the South. The Bishop left Oxford by rail for New Orleans, but his train was held up at Jackson, Mississippi, for several days due to a yellow fever quarantine. At New Orleans he encountered another delay in sailing for Galveston, also in the grip of a yellow fever outbreak and probably quarantined. Not until December 7 was he able to set sail for Texas.[26] But all this time was not lost; Gregg recorded in his journal the letters and the interviews by which he sought to recruit men for the Texas clergy staff.

The Bishop was able to spend only about a month on his first visit to Texas, but he accomplished a great deal. After services in Galveston and Brenham, he spent four days in Austin and its vicinity. He held confirmations at Wilbarger and St. David's, conducted an examination for Walter R. Richardson, a Candidate for Deacon's Orders, and apparently arranged to purchase a home. At San Antonio, he laid the cornerstone for St. Mark's Church and confirmed a class, then visited Seguin, Gonzales, Columbus, Richmond and Houston for services, confirming everywhere but at Columbus. After confirming an additional class at Galveston, he departed for South Carolina to bring his wife and six children and some of their slaves to Texas.[27]

Before reaching Texas, the Bishop evidently had determined upon Austin as his seat of residence, for he planned his itinerary to allow the longest stay in that city, and on his return with his family went directly there. The Deed Records of Travis County for 1860 record his purchase of approximately thirty acres of land from James H. Raymond *et al.* for the sum of $2846. This property, adjoining the City of Austin, was bounded on the West by Shoal Creek, on the North by 12th Street, on the South by 9th Street, and extended eastward 1445 feet to West Avenue.[28] Gregg believed Austin,

---

[25]*Ibid.*, 1859 dates.   [26]*Ibid.*

[27]*Texas Journal*, 1860, pp. 11-14; Manuscript Journal; W. Gregg, *Gregg*, p. 64.

[28]Deed Records of Travis County, Vol. "O," p. 162. While no improvements are described, there must have been a roomy house already on the place, or else he arranged to have one completed before his family arrived.

as seat of the State Government, would be a good point from which to spread the influence of the Church widely through the State. His confidence in the ability of St. David's rector, Charles Gillette, allowed Gregg to envision Austin as "the center of important educational and missionary operations. . . ."[29]

The Bishop equipped himself for his travels by purchasing in New Orleans a good, sturdy carriage and a smaller buggy. By securing a fine team of horses for the carriage after reaching Texas, he could manage his own routing, regulate the length of his visits in many parts of the State, and remain independent of public transportation.[30]

The Gregg family were accompanied on their journey to Texas by the Reverend J. Hamilton Quinby, a young Presbyter whom the Bishop had persuaded to become his travelling companion on his visitations and his assistant in general missionary work. This position Gregg hoped to make permanent, should he be able to continue to find vigorous young clergy like Quinby. For many years much of the work of the diocese would consist in pastoral attention to scattered Episcopalians beyond the reach of organized Parishes.[31]

With this fact in mind, the Bishop lost no time after his arrival in Austin before issuing a Pastoral Letter to the Episcopalians of the State. He addressed principally those scattered members whom he wished to reach. Published widely in newspapers, the letter brought a good response;[32] it enabled the Bishop to write personally to those who responded and to plan in his travels to visit them. Gregg wished eventually to serve these isolated members by dividing the Diocese into missionary districts with itinerant missionaries in each, but the Bishop had already visited many of them by convention time and he looked forward to their zealous efforts as a means to stimulate the growth of the Diocese.[33]

Within a month of his settling in Austin, Gregg was on the road. He and Quinby first made a circuit to Lockhart, Prairie Lea and Seguin. The next week they broke new ground in Central Texas, holding what they believed were the first services of the Church in Georgetown, Belton and Marlin. Waco, also included in this visit, had just received one of the Bishop's new missionary recruits, the Reverend Daniel Shaver from the Diocese of Indiana. The notices for the visitation had included services at Cameron, but rain and bad roads prevented the Bishop from reaching the town in time. Fortunately the Reverend Lindsey P. Rucker had arrived to meet the

---

29 *Texas Journal*, 1860, p. 12.   30 W. **Gregg**, *Gregg*, p. 65.
31 *Texas Journal*, 1860, p. 15.   32 *Loc. cit.*   33 *Ibid.*, pp. 18-19.

Bishop and took the opportunity to conduct a service, with the result that Gregg arranged for him to minister there monthly.

Two weeks before the time appointed for the Diocesan Convention at Matagorda, the Bishop started in that direction, giving thorough attention to Bastrop, La Grange, Columbus, Columbia and Brazoria on the way.[34] While he had not tried to make a whirlwind visit to all the congregations, he worked with characteristic thoroughness the territory he covered.

It is symbolic of the new beginning the Diocese made under her own first Bishop that the Convention met this year at Matagorda, where the Diocese had been born. The Bishop laid out a program that was challenging but practical. First of all, the members of the Church must recognize the resources they possessed, and put them to work in the service of the Lord. Gregg said the financial means were available "to do much, *very much.*" Besides the abilities of the people in the organized congregations, many scattered churchfolk would contribute to the advancement of the Church's work in Texas if means were found to bring the appeal before them. Therefore what was needed was a Diocesan Missionary Society, similar to those in the older dioceses, through which most of the money needed for missions within the Diocese could be gathered. The Bishop believed that Texas should become self-reliant, and for this reason he urged most earnestly that such an organization be founded.

At the same time, the Bishop declared that funds thus raised should not have the effect of diminishing the contributions of congregations to the "Parent Society," to which the Church in Texas was so deeply indebted for support during its infancy, and to which it must still look for help until its own machinery for support could be perfected. If the Diocese must learn to depend upon its own strength for missionary money, it must do the same for manpower. It must recruit and train its own leadership within the borders of the Diocese. The Bishop had no immediate concrete proposal for an institution for training clergy, but he said, "nor should we rest until Texas has her Nashotah to do for the Southwest what has been so happily effected in other parts of our land." He recognized the outstanding combination of missionary work and educational training so successfully carried out by the Wisconsin institution in its early days under Bishop Kemper's able direction.

Education for the laity of the Church was equally important. Means were at hand to establish a Female Institute through the generous provision of a tract of land at Quintana and a cash be-

[34]*Ibid.*, pp. 16-18.

quest in the will of the late Mrs. E. M. Perry of Brazoria County. The Bishop declared his intention to proceed immediately to investigate the prospects for getting such a school started. For men, the University of the South would offer the finest education in the land if its grand design could be carried out through the generous support of the members of the Church in the South. Texas was already represented on its board, and the Bishop bespoke the liberal response of the Diocese to the appeal for this institution in which he himself was deeply interested.

As a medium of information on Church affairs, Gregg commended *The Church Intelligencer,* a magazine just begun in Raleigh, North Carolina, primarily to publicize the needs of the Church in the South and the interests of the University of the South. With no lack of appreciation for the work of older Church papers, the Bishop particularly desired his people to support this one, since he intended to publish in it matters of interest to the Diocese.

Beside these projects for the institutional life of the Diocese, the Bishop disclosed in his address something of his missionary strategy. He intended manning central points as men and money became available, and he expected the clergy to extend missionary efforts toward smaller settlements within their reach. This move was immediate and obvious. Ultimately he hoped the division of the Diocese into missionary districts, with itinerant missionaries in each, would establish the Church where it was not known before, even in the smallest settlements.[35]

As occasion arose in the course of the next few years, the full meaning of the program was made clear. The Bishop intended this missionary outreach to be directed to all the people. His objective included missionaries for the slave population in Brazoria County and perhaps in one or two other points of heavy concentrations of Negroes in the Diocese,[36] but he did not favor separate negro congregations or separate services as a general rule. More than once he urged that seating be provided for the slave population, so they might attend Church with their masters.[37] There should be no racial barrier in the Church, and the Bishop disagreed with those who maintained that the Episcopal Church was not adapted to all classes of the white population. The remarkable work accomplished by the Reverend L. P. Rucker among all and sundry, including the simplest sort of rural folk, exemplified Gregg's assertion that the Church

[35]*Ibid.*, Bishop's Address, pp. 9-21.
[36]*Ibid.*, p. 18; 1862, p. 18.   [37]*Ibid.*, p. 14.

would never fulfill its mission nor its nature until it strove to bring in all classes of the community.[38]

The program which Gregg presented to his first Convention was based upon careful thought and investigation. It was at once farsighted and practical. The eventualities of the war would delay much of it, and prevent the accomplishment of some goals. Essentially, Gregg marked out what should and could be done by the Episcopal Church in Texas, and called for dedicated efforts of its members to carry out the tasks to which they were called.

IX.   Implementing the Program

GREGG appealed to the members of the 1860 Convention to join him in carrying out an ambitious program, but the entire membership of the Church in Texas must hear and respond to his program. Attendance at the Matagorda Convention was not full,[1] but the very favorable response elicited from those in attendance was spread throughout the Diocese as the Bishop made the rounds of his visitations. The Diocesan Missionary Society especially caught the imagination of the Church. The Bishop delivered a missionary address in each Church he visited[2] and his private appeals to individuals met encouraging results. In spite of the excitements and anxieties of public affairs in the ensuing year, approximately $1500 was contributed. This sum approached the maximum hoped for; in view of the equal amount raised for the Bishop's salary (an expense the Diocese had never had to meet in any previous year), this was no mean accomplishment for a diocese with slightly more than 800 communicants.[3]

Much of the Bishop's program was now under way. He had appealed to the Domestic Committee for a larger appropriation, and that body, happily out of debt for the first time in years, responded with an increase of $500 to a total of $3000, the highest allotment to Texas up to that time.[4] Bishop Gregg was able to attract to the

---

[38]*Ibid.*, 1861, p. 15.

[1]Nine clergy were present; those absent were Chaplain T. H. Mitchell, U.S.A., of Ft. Chadbourne, R. S. Seely of Washington, only recently arrived and convalescent from illness, E. A. Wagner of Marshall, only recently arrived, R. H. Ranney, who was retired, and L. P. Rucker, whose non-attendance was not explained. Nine Lay Delegates from five congregations were officially recorded as present, though there were other non-accredited visitors.

[2]*Texas Journal*, 1861, pp. 9-25.

[3]*Ibid.*, 1861, pp. 27, 32, 46-7.

[4]*Ibid.*, 1860, p. 19.

Texas field two more clergy from South Carolina, old time friends of his. He appointed the Reverend E. A. Wagner to Marshall and Jefferson, and the Reverend Richard S. Seely to St. Paul's Church, Washington; the latter became principal of a female academy in addition to his church duties.[5] The Reverend Daniel Shaver was appointed to Waco, but soon transferred to Brenham, and the Reverend L. P. Rucker was put back on the missionary list in charge of Cameron and Belton; the missionary forces of the Diocese were considerably augmented. Still not content, the Bishop appealed for more clergy to volunteer for Texas, especially single men for whom full support was available in several places.[6]

The clergy corps was augmented within the next two years, but except for the Reverend Silas D. Davenport who came from North Carolina to be rector of Good Shepherd, Corpus Christi, in March of 1861,[7] the new men were fruits of the educational work of the Reverend Charles Gillette in Austin and the Reverend L. H. Jones at Seguin. Frank R. Brown and Walter R. Richardson had studied under Gillette and were ordered Deacons—Brown, on December 23, 1860, in Austin,[8] and Richardson, after a harrowing escape from the North where he had been studying at Berkeley Divinity School, in Christ Church, Houston, on February 23, 1862. Richardson was advanced to the Priesthood on June 5, 1864, in Christ Church, Houston.[9] Henry B. Monges was scheduled to have been ordained at the same time as Brown, but his health failed. Monges resided with Jones at Seguin, studying for Orders and assisting in the mission until Jones moved to San Antonio; he then served as lay reader for the Seguin flock. He was succeeded in the work at Seguin by Herman G. Batterson, another Candidate for Orders.[10] Monges recovered his health in time to be ordained April 14, 1861, at St. David's, Austin, and was put in charge of St. Andrew's, Seguin.[11] He appears to be the first of the "Perpetual Deacons" ordained by Gregg, several of whom were to render good service in the years ahead. Their service freed the always inadequate number of Presbyters to cover more territory. Batterson, who came to Texas as a Candidate of the Diocese of Pennsylvania and spent some time with Jones at Seguin,[12] was ordained at St. David's on November 17, 1861. Apparently before he could be assigned to a field, Batterson made his

[5]*Ibid.*, 1860, pp. 19, 33.
[6]*Church Intelligencer*, I, No. 10 (May 23, 1860), p. 85.
[7]*Texas Journal*, 1861, p. 26. [8]*Ibid.*, 1861, p. 21.
[9]*Ibid.*, 1862, p. 17; 1864, p. 11. [10]*Ibid.*, 1861, p. 20.
[11]*Ibid.*, 1862, pp. 5, 10. [12]*Ibid.*, 1862, p. 14.

way to the North. He was carried on the clergy roll as "Not in the Confederacy" throughout the war, and was then transferred to Minnesota.[13]

Two other Perpetual Deacons were ordained by Gregg during the Civil War. C. W. Stone was recruited and schooled by Rucker, and assisted him for some time in his extensive field before renouncing the ministry. Stone was ordained on April 6, 1862, at St. David's.[14] Daniel W. Chase, principal of the Female Academy at Independence, was ordained June 15, 1865, in Christ Church, Houston.[15] Another recruit was ordained during the war, the Reverend Stephen Kay, D.D., a former Presbyterian. He served his Candidacy as lay reader at St. Matthew's Church, Dallas,[16] and was ordered Deacon on January 31, 1864, at Belton, and Priest at Independence on November 20 of the same year.[17]

These significant gains in the number of clergy were important to the work of the Diocese, but they were offset by losses. When the Convention of 1861 met in April in St. David's, Austin, four clergy had left the Diocese during the year previous. The Reverend C. H. Albert, who had resigned the rectorship of Matagorda just before the 1860 Convention returned to Pennsylvania; the Reverend J. H. Quinby returned to South Carolina; the Reverend N. P. Charlot was transferred to Indiana.[18] The Reverend T. H. Mitchell had departed for the North with his regiment of the United States Army, but he waited too long in applying for a transfer; after the formation of the Church in the Confederate States, Gregg was unable to transfer Mitchell to the Bishop of Ohio on any terms which the latter would accept. Somewhat unfairly, Gregg included Mitchell among the clergy whom he blamed for being away from the Diocese during the war.[19] In truth Mitchell made no recorded contribution to the life of the Diocese during his stay in Texas, nor did the Diocese play any part in his work as Chaplain. Unlike Chaplain Fish, Mitchell was only a name on the list. In leaving with his unit he was only doing his duty.

The Reverend H. G. Batterson apparently had strong ties in the

[13]Gregg, Manuscript Journal, Clergy List; Manuscript Register of Clergy, Diocese of Texas.

[14]*Texas Journal*, 1862, p. 19.

[15]*Ibid.*, 1865, p. 7. For his ministry at Independence, see below, pp. 216-8.

[16]*Texas Journal*, 1864, p. 11.

[17]*Ibid.*, 1864, p. 9; 1865, p. 18.   [18]*Ibid.*, 1861, p. 26.

[19]*Ibid.*, 1864, p. 13. McIlvaine, of Ohio, was amongst the most aggressively anti-Southern of the Northern Bishops.

North and felt it best to return there shortly after his ordination
in 1861. He was transferred to the Diocese of Minnesota after canonical relations with the Northern dioceses were resumed in 1866.[20] His
was straightforward behavior, in contrast to that of the Reverend
Daniel Shaver. This clergyman left Brenham in August 1862 to accept the rectorship of the Church of the Advent, Brownsville, with
the Bishop's consent.[21] On October 21, 1863, he reported to the
Domestic Committee in New York that he had left his field under
"circumstances too painful and grievous for expression in this report."[22] In a later letter he did explain that he had left because of
threats made against him by secessionists in Brownsville.[23] He assured
the Domestic Committee that he, with two other clergy, had "strongly
opposed the separation of the Diocese from the General Convention."[24] Thus maintaining that he was absent from his post through
no fault of his own, Shaver petitioned successfully for his back
salary from the Committee.[25] Since Shaver did not attend the Convention of 1862 when the Diocese of Texas took action for separation,
and since the minutes of the 1861 Convention give no roll call of
votes on the motion to send delegates to the consultation of Southern
dioceses, Shaver's word must be taken for the assertion. Certainly he
had hoped to minister quietly in Texas and to avoid political matters.
In a letter written from Brenham, late in 1860 or early in 1861,
he stated:

> . . . And I humbly trust, in all supplication and prayer, that
> Divine Wisdom may so guide the chief pastors, her Bishops, that
> they may preserve her bond of unity inviolate. . . .[26]

On hearing of the Federal occupation of Brownsville, Shaver asked
reappointment and aid in returning to his field. In May 1864 he
wrote from Brownsville, relating his expectation of receiving an
Army Chaplaincy, and soliciting funds to aid in repairing the
church.[27] Though disappointed in his hope of Army appointment,
Shaver ministered a while, but upon the recapture of the region
by Texas troops on July 30, 1864, he went to Louisiana and did
supply work while awaiting another opportunity to return to his

[20]*Ibid.*, 1866, p. 25.   [21]*Ibid.*, 1863, p. 23.

[22]Shaver to Domestic Committee, [n.p.], October 21, 1863.

[23]Same to same, La Porte, Ind., March 8, 1864.

[24]Citing his report of Oct. 21, 1863, included with letter cited in n. 23.

[25]Shaver to Domestic Committee, Worthington, Indiana, December 16, 1863.

[26]*Texas Journal*, 1862, pp. 5, 33; 1861, p. 32; *Spirit of Missions*, 1861, p. 76

[27]Shaver to Domestic Committee, Brownsville, May 16, 1864.

post. He returned with the Army of Occupation by August 1865,[28] reported his presence to Bishop Gregg, and was recognized as Rector. He reported to the Council of 1866 for the period from August 1, 1865, and related that work was in progress to repair the church and to build a parsonage.[29]

The Diocese suffered a grievous loss when the Reverend F. R. Brown died of consumption in Austin on April 12, 1864. Though a native of Louisiana, he grew up in Texas and had been turned toward the ministry since boyhood.[30] His usefulness as a missionary operating out of Austin ended when he associated himself with the protest of his rector, Gillette, against the prayer set forth by the Bishop,[31] yet Gregg seemed genuinely fond of him and was deeply grieved at his death.

Another great loss was the death of the Reverend Lucius H. Jones. Jones was the only Texas clergyman to enter the Chaplaincy of the Confederate Army; he resigned his San Antonio Parish in October 1861 to become Chaplain of the Fourth Texas Cavalry ("Reily's Regiment").[32] Campaigning through Louisiana and Texas, he ministered to various parishes as occasion arose, and held what was almost certainly the first service of the Church in Jasper, Texas, on March 16, 1863.[33] Never of robust health, Jones seemed to thrive on Army life. Gregg said of him, "After a long course of hardship and exposure, which seemed only to develop his strength, he fell a victim at last to the influence of a malarial climate." He died at Washington, Louisiana, on October 10, 1863,[34] mourned by a grateful diocese to which he had contributed much in a gallant way.

The Diocese sustained another tragic loss in the death of the Reverend John M. Goshorn and his wife in the 1864 yellow fever epidemic in Galveston. Eaton had obtained a leave of absence from the rectorship in May of that year, and had gone to England. The vestry induced Goshorn to act as Rector pro tem, and were delighted at the energy and ability with which he set about reviving the Parish after its dispersal during Federal occupation. When the fever

---

[28]Same to same, Brownsville, June 9, 1864; Col. Harry McCorry Henderson, *Texas in the Confederacy* (San Antonio, 1955, xi; Shaver to Domestic Committee, Brownsville, Aug. 8, 1865.

[29]*Texas Journal*, 1866, p. 31.

[30]*Ibid.*, 1864, p. 13; Gregg, Manuscript Journal, Apr. 12, 1864.

[31]See below, pp. 118-20.

[32]Gregg, Manuscript Journal, Clergy List.

[33]*Texas Journal*, 1863, Jones' report as Chaplain, p. 27.

[34]*Ibid.*, 1863, p. 13; Gregg, Manuscript Journal, Clergy List.

broke out, Goshorn and his wife worked unafraid with sufferers, and both fell victim to the disease.[35]

The Reverend Henry B. Monges, Deacon, entered the Confederate Army between the Annual Councils of 1863 and 1864. Since he had acted as roving missionary over all the vacant congregations in the Seguin-Gonzales-Lockhart triangle during the early part of the war,[36] he must have been sorely missed. By Council time in 1864, Eaton was in England, and the Reverend E. A. Wagner, Rector of Christ Church, Houston, had obtained his vestry's leave in order to return to South Carolina to look after family affairs.[37]

These lossses in effective clergy strength were compensated in part by ordinations and accessions detailed above, and also by the temporary help of the clergy who were refugees from the theatres of war. In the Spring of 1863 the Reverend G. W. E. Fisse, a Deacon of the Diocese of Maryland, took charge of the Marshall-Jefferson field,[38] and remained there until close to the end of the war. When the Council met in 1864, both Joseph Wood Dunn and B. S. Dunn of the Diocese of Louisiana were present and had been officiating in the Diocese of Texas for some time.[39] Two more Louisiana clergy, T. R. B. Trader and Caleb Dow, had taken refuge in Texas and were officiating, Trader in Nacogdoches, and Dow in Palestine.[40] The Reverend R. H. Murphy of Arkansas supplied St. Mark's, San Antonio, after its Rector, the Reverend W. T. D. Dalzell, left with the Bishop's permission to go to England to raise money for completion of the church building.[41] One other clergyman, J. M. Curtis of Arkansas, was officiating without being canonically transferred, but he was Rector-elect of Christ Church, Houston, and was unable to secure letters dimissory because Bishop Lay was somewhere in the East and out of communication with his jurisdiction. Unable to find young clergy to open up new missionary work, the Bishop induced the Reverend R. H. Ranney to come back into active service. Operating from his home base at Elm Creek near Seguin, Ranney began holding services there and at Sulphur Springs and Concrete.[42]

Although Texas was blessed by not becoming a theatre of war operations on a large scale, its commerce was hindered and its economy dislocated by the naval blockade. This had serious effects

35 *Texas Journal*, 1865, pp. 12, 14, 25, 27-8.
36 *Ibid.*, 1862, pp. 47-8; 1863, p. 24.
37 *Ibid.*, 1864, p. 12.   38 *Ibid.*, 1863, p. 4.
39 *Ibid.*, 1864, pp. 6, 7; for J. W. Dunn at Orange, see below, p. 193.
40 *Texas Journal*, 1865, p. 24.   41 *Ibid.*   42 *Ibid.*, 1864, p. 22.

upon the Church.[43] Currency became so inflated in the last two years of the war that individuals were contributing to the Bishop to make up for the loss in value on the currency he received for salary.[44] So many men left for military service that some congregations, like those at Gonzales and Columbus, were almost broken up. Three congregations were scattered by warfare. After the bombardment of Corpus Christi in August 1862 the town diminished so that the Reverend S. D. Davenport found himself unable to accomplish anything and moved to Waco.[45] The threat of Federal occupation of Galveston caused the congregation of Trinity Church to scatter, and the church building was closed on May 25, 1862. The practical loss of the strongest Parish in the Diocese had a serious effect on the ability of the Church to carry on its work.[46] By a strange twist, the departure of the Rector during the ascendency of the Secessionalists in Brownsville closed the Church there, and Federal occupation reopened it.[47]

The weakening effects of war dislocation were counterbalanced somewhat by the influx of people from the less fortunate states of the Southwest and South; many Episcopalians moved to Texas and entered actively into the life of local congregations. The parish of All Saints', Crockett, was organized and a class of twenty-five colored persons was presented for Confirmation to the Bishop in 1864, largely through the zeal of a Mrs. Dorsey, a Louisiana Churchwoman.[48] Parochial reports from several congregations in East and North Texas during the latter part of the war contain grateful references to help given by people taking temporary refuge in these communities.

The program which Gregg set in motion in 1860 was difficult to carry out because of the dislocations of war. The good effect of the program upon the supply of clergy and upon the stability of the communities in which they worked has been surveyed in this chapter. This effect was incidental to the fact of war. The secession of Texas from the Union brought on a crisis in the Dio-

[43]*Ibid.*, 1862, p. 47.   [44]*Ibid.*, 1864, pp. 12, 17.

[45]*Ibid.*, 1863, p. 25. The Rev. W. R. Richardson many years later related that North Carolinian Davenport was no neutral spectator at the Federal attack upon Corpus Christi: "though by nature one of the gentlest and most peaceable of men, he doffed the gown and took up the sword, or more literally the shotgun ... and took part in the battle of Corpus Christi." *A Brief Sketch of the History of the Protestant Episcopal Church in the Missionary District of Western Texas* (San Antonio, 1902) , p. 7.

[46]*Texas Journal*, 1862, pp. 17, 43.   [47]See above, pp. 108-9.

[48]*Texas Journal*, 1865, p. 18; 1866, p. 19.

cese of Texas. The question of allegiance to the national Church, and its serious bearing upon the ability of the Diocese to carry on its work, comprise the subject of the next chapter.

X. The Diocese and the Crisis of Secession

THE HINDRANCES to the work of the Church occasioned by the Civil War were not merely those of clergy supply, money, and population dislocation. They were political and emotional as well. In spite of the conviction of some of the clergy that the Episcopal Church was "too conservative to share in the political excitements of the time," once Lincoln was elected and the secession of Southern States started, it was really impossible for anyone to remain neutral. When Texas voted to secede and the Diocese was confronted with the decision as to its ecclesiastical relations, it became apparent that Church members were not all of one mind. Bishop Gregg faced the first great crisis that was to test his capacity for leadership.

Gregg had been chosen Bishop of Texas very largely because he was a Southern man. He was also an upcountry South Carolinian of the planter class, and a graduate of South Carolina College where the Southern reaction to Northern radicalism developed strongly in the third and fourth decades of the century. Naturally some of the attitudes of the culture in which he was reared appeared in his thinking. Also the enlistment of the Greggs' eldest son, the nineteen-year-old Alexander, Jr., in the Confederate Army, and his death of pneumonia in 1862 near Richmond, Virginia, would not incline them to neutrality.[1] The Bishop was, indeed, a partisan, but not by any means a blind one. He had deep political convictions, and as the conflict between North and South deepened into war these were to show in his Church policy.

The Convention of the Diocese met at St. David's, Austin, on April 11, 1861. Texas had seceded on the first of February and popular vote had ratified the action on February 23.[2] But Travis County, of which Austin is the County Seat, voted against secession. The membership of the Austin Parish, lately reunited, was sorely

---

[1]W. Gregg, *Gregg*, p. 72. About the same time that the family received the sad news of Alexander's death, they also lost the infant son just born in Austin.

[2]E. Merton Coulter, *The Confederate States of America: 1861-1865* (Baton Rouge, 1950), pp. 2, 3.

divided in its attitudes toward this political action.[3] Fortunately, the Convention was in session one day before Fort Sumter was fired upon, and it dispersed before President Lincoln called for volunteers to fight the South, on April 16, 1861.[4] The Convention was not subject to the passion that might have seized it later in the year. It opened without reference to the course of current events, and elected deputies to General Convention.[5] When the Bishop read his address to the Convention, he made no reference to the political situation until he recorded having set forth several necessary documents. The first was a form of prayer to be used in public services during the troubled times, together with a form of service for Friday, January 4, which was proclaimed by President Buchanan as a day of fasting and public humiliation.[6] On January 8 Gregg had prepared a pastoral letter for distribution throughout the Diocese, a very moderate letter, counselling prayer for peace; zealous attention to the work of the Church, that the excitements of the time should not submerge its just claims for time and substance; and charity to be exercised by all churchmen towards those who differed from them, that party strife should not disfigure the Church. Its keynote was, "Let your moderation be known to all men." On March 4 and again on March 21, he had addressed the clergy to direct certain changes in the liturgy made necessary by the ratification of the ordinance of Secession by the people of Texas. In the first of these notices the Bishop ordered the substitution of "Governor of this State" for "President of the United States" and "this State" in place of "these United States" in the Prayer for the President; "Legislature" was to be substituted for "Congress" wherever used. These directions were appropriate to the situation. The State Convention had passed the ordinance of secession, but had not yet joined the Confederacy. This latter step was taken on March 5, and occasioned the second letter which made adjustments to accord with the new allegiance.

Toward the end his address to the Convention, Gregg recounted receipt of a letter circulated among the Southern Bishops by Elliott of Georgia and Polk of Louisiana, who, as senior Bishops in the seceding states, proposed a consultation at Montgomery, Alabama, on July 3, to attempt to cement a common course of action. Each diocese was asked to send its own bishop, three presbyters, and

---

[3] *St. David's*, pp. 33-4.
[4] Coulter, *op. cit.*, pp. 38-9.   [5] *Texas Journal*, 1861, p. 8.
[6] *Ibid.*, 1861, p. 21. This form is appended to the bound copy of the Journals of the Diocese in the Archives of the Diocese held by me as Registrar.

three laymen. This meeting would be consultative only, to plan a common approach to the General Convention and to arrange for an amicable accommodation between the dioceses in the two countries; it would not rupture communion with the parent body, and certainly would not depart from the Church's doctrine, discipline, and worship. At the most, an arrangement might be made for the government of the Church in the Confederate States.[7]

At the request of the Convention, the Bishop appointed a committee consisting of the Reverend Messrs. Eaton, Gillette and Rucker, and Messrs. W. P. H. Douglas and W. L. Robarts, to consider the proposal to send delegates to the Montgomery meeting. The committee returned a majority report presented by Eaton, and a minority report presented by Rucker.[8] The majority report, signed by all the men except Rucker, deplored the proposal of Bishops Elliott and Polk as based on the false assumption that "the dissolution of the civil government necessarily involves a division of ecclesiastical organization," and opposed any move to "connect the Diocese with any body or association not first recognized and approved by the General Convention . . . ." The committee expressed the belief that such a meeting was premature, apt to stir up controversy before General Convention could deal with the situation and put the Church in a false light as dealing with politics. It was urged, moreover, that since the Diocese was vitally interested in establishing the University of the South, and since the cooperation of Tennessee and North Carolina was so important to its success, the sentiments of those dioceses should be solicited before taking any step that might endanger the common enterprise. After offering these quite negative resolutions for passage by the Convention, the committee recommended that, since the consultation of southern dioceses possibly would assemble, the Convention should elect three delegates in each order to attend it under instructions "to oppose to the utmost any effort to disturb our present ecclesiastical union, or the formation of any other. . . ."[9]

The doughty Rucker, thoroughly accustomed to dissent from majorities, offered his own set of resolutions. He claimed the appropriateness and the necessity of the proposed consultation on the ground that primitive canons and the English Reformation established the principle that the Church must organize itself within

---

[7] *Texas Journal*, 1861, pp. 21ff. This letter is printed in *Journals of the General Councils of the Protestant Episcopal Church in the Confederate States of America* (Facsimile Edition, Church Historical Society, Austin, 1962), I, pp. 3-4.

[8] *Texas Journal*, 1861, pp. 28-32.   [9] *Ibid.*, 1861, p. 32.

the limits of nationality. He asked that the Convention elect delegates to attend the Montgomery meeting without instructions, but that the delegates report back to the next Diocesan Convention, which should have the power to ratify or reject the actions of the consultation.[10]

Ignoring the ideological conflict within the committee, the Convention, on the motion of the Reverend L. H. Jones, resolved:

> That in accordance with the recommendation of the Bishop, this Convention send three Clerical and three Lay delegates to the proposed Convention at Montgomery.

It further resolved:

> As the sense of this Convention, that the action of the said proposed Convention be returned to the Convention of this Diocese for ratification or rejection.

The Secretary of the Convention, Jones himself, did not record in the minutes whether this was passed by a voice vote or a vote by orders, but very remarkably it is recorded as the next item of business that this resolution, proposed by Mr. A. M. Lewis of Brenham, was passed:

> Resolved, That in the future, when a vote "by orders" is called for, the Bishop be called upon to vote first.[11]

Perhaps the enigmatic action records irritation generated by the Bishop's refusal to take sides in so heated a clash as the Convention had just witnessed; or perhaps the Bishop had been compelled to vote to break a tie. In any event, no record in the minutes of any Diocesan Convention shows that Bishop Gregg voted when a vote by orders was called for, much less that he allowed himself to be "put on the spot" by having to vote first.

The Convention elected as delegates to Montgomery the Reverend Messrs. Eaton, Gillette and Jones, and Messrs. P. W. Gray, S. M. Swenson and A. M. Lewis.[12] The Bishop was requested to circulate a letter reporting the action of the Convention with reference to the proposed Montgomery meeting,[13] incorporating in the

---

[10] The text of both reports is printed in Chas. Gillette, *A Few Historic Records of the Church in the Diocese of Texas, During the Rebellion, Together with a Correspondence between the Rt. Rev. Alexander Gregg, D.D. and the Rev. Charles Gillette, Rector of St. David's, Austin* (New York, 1865), pp. 9-11. (Cited hereafter as "Gillette, *Records*.")

[11] *Texas Journal*, 1861, pp. 32-3. The Rev. John Owen, then of San Augustine, was prevented from attending by flood waters. Had he been there, the vote would not have been so close. *Ibid.*, p. 43.

[12] *Ibid.*, 1861, p. 34.   [13] *Ibid.*, 1861, p. 33.

letter the section of his Convention Address relating to the call issued by the two senior Bishops and his remarks upon it. In his letter,
Gregg emphasized the concern which he and his fellow Bishops
shared, that the bonds of unity and charity between Episcopalians
of North and South should not be rent:

> The thought of a violent rending of the Church, or of a sep-
> aration, if such must needs be, otherwise than as brethren and
> friends, is not for a moment to be entertained. We bless God
> for the spectacle of union, and of unity, which the Protestant
> Episcopal Church in this country has ever presented to the
> world.[14]

These are not the words of a rabid political preacher. When Gillette attempted to make his case against the Bishop in his *Few Historic Records,* he understandably saw fit to omit this letter as well
as others of Gregg's which furnished similar material against his
contentions.

Before the proposed convention could meet in Montgomery,
Bishops Atkinson of North Carolina and Meade and Johns of Virginia had met during the Virginia Diocesan Convention; that was
immediately after Virginia had seceded and at a time when North
Carolina was undoubtedly on the verge of following suit. They
wrote to the Bishops of the States already in the Confederacy, requesting a postponement of the July 3 meeting. They also asked
that a meeting place more convenient than Montgomery be designated—Raleigh, Ashville or Sewanee they suggested as alternatives.[15]
Gregg was away from home on visitation when this letter arrived in
Austin; when he saw it at the end of June, it was too late to learn
whether or not the postponement had been granted. He therefore
notified the Texas delegates of the probability of postponement and
suggested that they should not incur the great expense and hardship of the journey, made difficult by the Federal blockade.[16] The
meeting was held, however, and Texas alone among the seven invited jurisdictions was not represented. Little was done at Montgomery beyond setting an adjourned meeting for October 16, 1861,
at Columbia, South Carolina, and appointing a committee to draw
up a constitution and canons to be proposed to the Columbia
meeting.[17]

---

[14]Pastoral Letter, Apr. 15, 1861, appended to the *Texas Journals,* 1860-69 in
volume in Registrar's file.

[15]J. B. Cheshire, *The Church in the Confederate States: A History of the
Protestant Episcopal Church in the Confederate States of America* (New York,
1914), p. 28.

[16]*Texas Journal,* 1862, p. 13.   [17]Cheshire, *op. cit.,* pp. 35-6.

Gregg departed for the South Carolina meeting in mid-September and was the sole representative of the Diocese of Texas at that Convention.[18] Reporting to the Diocesan Convention of 1862 on the Columbia assemblage, Gregg asserted that the actions taken did not include any theoretical considerations of the effect of secession of states upon ecclesiastical relations; the actions simply adjusted to the facts of secession and war, which made new governmental arrangements for the Church necessary.[19]

One matter brought before the Columbia Convention compelled the Bishops and Standing Committees of the Southern Dioceses to face the fundamental question of their authority as Dioceses, practically severed from the Church in the United States, but not yet formed into another ecclesiastical union until the Constitution set forth at Columbia should be ratified by the Dioceses. This question arose through the request of the delegates of the Diocese of Alabama. They were bereaved by the death of their beloved Bishop, Nicholas H. Cobbs, and sought counsel on the legality of the consecration of a new Bishop without securing consent of a majority of the Bishops and Dioceses of the Protestant Episcopal Church in the United States of America. The Convention of the Southern Dioceses at Columbia took no action on this request. Gregg told the Texas Convention that the matter was referred to a committee of the three senior Bishops of the Southern States for their decision.[20] Acting on their advice, the Diocese of Alabama elected the Reverend Richard Hooker Wilmer and applied to the Southern Bishops and Standing Committees for consent to his consecration. The Bishops and Standing Committees had to decide whether they could canonically give their consent.

Facing this question, Gregg took the line of diocesan independence, a position in harmony with the states' rights principles upon which he was nurtured. But this standpoint he maintained with historical perspective and searching thought. He later developed this thinking at length in his "First Triennial Charge to the Clergy." In accounting for his actions to the Convention of the Diocese, he simply said:

> . . . the ecclesiastical action of the Diocese, so far as there has been any within the past year involving the question, has been, as in other Confederate Dioceses, that of original diocesan independence; subject, of course, to those relations which every particular branch of it must ever maintain to the Church Catholic.

[18] *Texas Journal*, 1862, p. 14; Cheshire, *op. cit.*, p. 39.
[19] *Texas Journal*, 1862, pp. 24-6.   [20] *Ibid.*, 1862, pp. 25-6.

. . . I did not hesitate to give my consent to the consecration
of the Bishop elect of Alabama. And, upon receiving an official
communication from the Senior Bishop of the Church in the
United States, asking my consent to the consecration of the
Assistant Bishop elect of Pennsylvania, deeming a respectful
answer, under the circumstances, due to that venerable Prelate,
acting, as he doubtless did, in accordance with convictions of
duty; I simply informed him that I could not reply as a Bishop
in the Church of the United States, our connection having
ceased—a separation not only necessary, but highly expedient
for the best interest of our holy religion: adding the expression
of such feelings and hopes for the future of both branches of
the church as the occasion rendered proper. The connection
once existing was that of mere ecclesiastical union—a human
arrangement simply for the common good of all, and to the
advancement of their common work. It is based upon, and
fashioned after the previously existing civil union of sovereign
and independent States—a *union* which had been entered into
for the promotion of the general welfare. The questions now at
issue between ourselves and those of whom we are separate,
are not questions affecting the church and its Catholicity, the Diocese in its integrity, the member of Christ in his spiritual relations. *Not at all* . . .[21]

Gregg argued that the dioceses of the South would not involve
themselves in schism by organizing into a new national Church,
since, on the principles which he stated, the governmental union of
dioceses did not touch the essential core of the Church's life.[22]

Those present at the Texas convention of 1862 in Christ Church,
Houston, evidently agreed with their Bishop, at least in so far as
the expediency of the new union of dioceses was concerned, for
they voted unanimously to adopt the Constitution of the Confederate Church.[23] But missing from the Convention was Charles Gillette.
He had not changed the views which he shared at the last Convention with the majority of the committee concerning the Montgomery
meeting; he also had taken exception to the wording of the prayer
which Gregg set forth on June 22, 1861, for use in every service
of the Church during the war. A fervent but rather long prayer for
divine guidance and protection over the Armies of the Confederacy and for victory, it contained the phrase, "the unnatural war
which has been forced upon us . . ." Gillette objected particularly
to this phrase, and told the Bishop that, with some difficulty, he

21*Texas Journal*, 1862, pp. 26-7. It is interesting that Bishops Otey of Tennessee
and Atkinson of North Carolina sent their consent to the consecration of the
Assistant Bishop of Pennsylvania, but refused consent for that of the Bishop of
Alabama. Cheshire, *op. cit.*, p. 35.
22*Texas Journal*, 1862, pp. 26-7.   23*Ibid.*, p. 33.

could use the rest of the prayer; but he could not refer thus to the war, since he did not believe it had been forced upon the South. The Bishop consented to allow Gillette and his assistant to omit this phrase for the sake of their consciences.[24] In his publication, Gillette gave no reason for his failure to appear at the 1862 Convention, and it is difficult to guess how the action of that body might have been influenced by his voice. When the Convention's results were known to him, he was apparently shocked and grieved by not being re-elected to the diocesan offices which he had held for so long, and he chose to couple this with other acts of the Convention as evidence of persecution.[25]

Another act of the 1862 Convention at which Gillette took umbrage was the publication of a set of resolutions offered by a committee which the Bishop appointed to consider that portion of the Bishop's Address referring to the relation of the Diocese of Texas to the Confederate States and to the Church in the United States. One resolution of the committee affirmed as the mind of the Convention the statement in the Bishop's prayer that the war had been forced upon the South; moreover, the resolution requested the clergy, on the first Sunday after receipt of the printed copy of the *Journal,* to read to their congregations that portion of the Bishop's Address which referred to the matter of Church-State relations.[26] Although four other clergymen who could have attended Convention were absent, Gillette believed this action had been aimed at him,[27] and thereupon he entered into an acrimonious and extended correspondence with the Bishop, which was neither edifying nor of much credit to either of them. The only ground of agreement they found was that "higher lawism" among Northern Abolitionists had had much to do with the rise of sectional bitterness. The controversy, as related by Gillette, did have its amusing aspects. At one point Gillette borrowed the Bishop's copy of Hawks' *Commentary on the Canons,* and then extracted materials from it to attempt to controvert the points which the Bishop had made against him.[28]

A very strained relationship arose. The Bishop, when present at St. David's, used the prayer in its entirety, but did not withdraw the permission he had given Gillette and his assistant, Brown, to omit the clause to which they objected. But when they wished to officiate in other towns, the Bishop insisted that the permission

[24]Gillette, *Records,* p. 12. [25]*Ibid.,* p. 41.
[26]*Texas Journal,* 1862, pp. 32, 38. [27]Gillette, *Records,* p. 17.
[28]*Ibid.,* pp. 35, 102.

did not apply.[29] Finally on the motion of the Reverend John Owen the Council of 1864 resolved to request the Bishop to withdraw the permission to alter the prayer.[30] The vote on this resolution was by orders, and two of the clergy, Goshorn and Richardson, who voted in the negative, took occasion to record their entire assent to the prayer of the Bishop; but they said that their vote expressed the conviction that this legislation was "inappropriate and calculated to foster dissension in the Church . . ." The same protest was registered by the lay delegation from Christ Church, Houston.[31] In a Pastoral Letter issued immediately after the 1864 Council, Gregg asserted that since the action of the Council was advisory, the whole burden of decision was his alone. He therefore withdrew the permission which he had given three years earlier, and required the use of the prayer intact.[32] Gillette then ceased to officiate, and he finally resigned his cure until restored to it at the war's end.[33] Gillette was elected Deputy to General Convention by the Council of 1865, a fact which testifies to the regard held for him by the members of the Council. When Gillette reached the East, he resigned his parish and took work there.[34] He then published his account of the troubles he had experienced in Texas during the war.

With the possible exception of the case of Daniel Shaver, Gillette's was the one major wartime controversy with the Bishop; its principal cause appears to have been the indulgence shown Gillette's feelings. Had Gregg either altered the prayer for the whole Diocese upon the first objection, or refused to allow the exception in any case, this particular ground of controversy could not have been as magnified as it became. But given a divided congregation in Austin and two such strongminded men as Gillette and Gregg, a collision could hardly have been avoided amidst the passions of the Civil War.

One result of the controversy was a most remarkable episcopal writing. As the subject for this First Triennial Charge to the Clergy, delivered at the Council of 1863, Gregg took that of Church and State.[35] He first discussed an allegation that there was a move underway toward an established church in the Confederacy; this charge the Bishop denied with vigor. After making a rather thorough his-

[29]*Ibid.*, p. 55.

[30]*Texas Journal*, 1864, p. 14. This was after Brown's death.

[31]*Ibid.*, 1864, pp. 14-6.

[32]This letter is bound up with the *Journals* for these years in the Registrar's files.

[33]*Texas Journal*, 1865, p. 26; 1866, p. 29.

[34]*Ibid.*, 1865, pp. 3, 10; 1866, p. 29.

[35]*Ibid.*, 1863, p. 18.

torical analysis of the evils of establishment even under its best form in England, Gregg emphatically endorsed the American principle of separation of Church and State. He believed that separation was necessary for the health of both, and he expressed his faith in the attractiveness of the primitive Catholic principles of our Church as sufficient to win the allegiance of Americans. He stated his conviction that the American way rightly extended to all Churches equality of status and freedom from state interference. He pointed out that no separation could be absolute; if the State owed religious bodies impartial protection and non-interference, the churches and their members owed the duties of obedience and respect, even under persecution. The charge is a thoughtful and thorough treatment of a timely subject; it displays its author's judicious weighing of all the factors involved.[36]

Gregg unsparingly condemned the war profiteering being practiced by many in Texas. A sermon preached in St. David's Church, Austin, and printed by request of many of his hearers, treated directly of this practice, as did a section of his address to the 1862 Convention that refers to "the peculiar and fiery temptations which war brings with it." He signaled out as a prime example the sin of pricing articles necessary to the life of the poor up to what the market would bear, in spite of the cheap prices at which they were stored. The Bishop called upon Churchmen to extend Christian charity into their business dealings, for the love of Christ and country.[37] The Bishop, then, definitely was not on the side of those who felt that the Church should have nothing to do with politics or business, and apparently the majority of the membership of the Diocese supported him in this stand. How fearlessly he could face the defeat of his country, and mark the path of duty in a new situation, was to appear at the close of the war.

XI. Wartime Missionary Work and Finance

ONLY A FRACTION of the time and attention of the Bishop and the leaders of the Diocese was taken up with the affairs of the war. Despite dislocations which the conflict brought, the cause of the Church was advancing with encouraging results. A few

[36]Gregg, *First Triennial Charge*, printed in *Historical Magazine*, XXXI (1962), pp. 165-203.
[37]*Texas Journal*, 1862, pp. 23-4.

congregations were added to the rolls of the Diocese during the years 1860-65. In 1860 St. Philip's, Palestine, was admitted as a parish and St. David's, Austin, went on the rolls to replace Epiphany and Christ Church.[1] The minutes for 1861 do not contain a report for the Committee on New Parishes, but it is evident from the Parochial Reports and the Bishop's Address that Good Shepherd, Corpus Christi, was admitted at that Convention.[2] In 1862 Christ Church, Jefferson, and St. Mary's, Bellville, were added to the roll of Parishes, and in 1863, St. Luke's, Belton. Grace Church, Independence, was admitted in 1864, and All Saints', Crockett, in 1865.[3]

In this same period an effort was made to clear the list of extinct congregations: St. Luke's, Chappell Hill, was removed in 1860 (along with the names of the merging Austin Parishes, Epiphany and Christ); St. Paul's, Cold Spring, was dropped in 1863[4] The eight new Parishes did not represent the total growth, however, for a new category, "Mission Stations," appeared in the *Journal* in this period. Apparently now it was felt that a congregation should be given time to take shape and gain strength before being designated a parish, whereas in former years the rule was to organize and seek admission almost as soon as services were started; exceptions were Independence, where services had been conducted with some frequency since very early times, and Clinton, served with some regularity from Gonzales. There were Missionary Station reports from Cameron, Belton, Caldwell, Lexington, Jefferson and Fort Worth in 1861, and additional ones from Victoria, Goliad, Prairie Lea and Clinton in 1862. Hempstead and Danville were added to the list in 1863 and Concrete, Elm Creek and Sulphur Springs in 1864. Waverley, Harrisburg. Coffeeville, Columbia, Courtney, Millican, Navasota, New Braunfels, Sandy Point and Waxahachie appeared on the list in 1865.[5] Gregg's missionary program was gaining speed. Even this roll of Missionary Stations does not tell the whole story. Gregg's practice was to visit with people along the route of his visitations, and wherever he was requested to do so, he conducted services. He searched out members and friends of the Church wherever he stopped. As soon as there was enough interest, a Missionary Station was designated, but this sometimes did not come about for several years, sometimes never. Between 1860 and 1865 the Bishop recorded ministering in the following places:

[1]*Texas Journal*, 1860, p. 9.   [2]*Ibid.*, 1861, pp. 19, 44-5.
[3]*Ibid.*, 1862, pp. 34, 38; 1863, p. 7; 1864, p. 6; 1865, p. 8.
[4]*Ibid.*, 1860, p. 25; 1863, p. 16.   [5]*Ibid.*, Parochial Reports, 1861-1865.

Marlin	Clarksville	Fort Worth
Coffeeville	Georgetown	Hillsboro
Rusk	Honey Grove	Buchanon
Sandy Point	Carancahua	Harrisburg
Piedmont	Texana	Hempstead
Owensville	Concrete	Bellville
Millican	Sulphur Springs	Belton
Courtney	Yorktown	Casa Blanca
Goliad	Refugio	Paris[6]

Missions were formed in some of these towns later; in others Gregg ministered as he was able to the Church people he found from year to year.

The strenuous efforts of the Bishop began to show a cumulative effect upon the growth of the Church as the years passed. He described the council year 1864-65 "such as in its wondrous history as we shall never see again." The statistics of his ministry bore this out; he confirmed 269 people in that period, and baptized 29 adults, all but one white, and 145 children, including 31 colored. There were 400 scattered communicants, in addition to the 800 reported in the organized congregations by clergy and layreaders, a total of 1,205.[7]

Since he was unable to replace Quinby as his travelling companion and itinerant missionary, the Bishop adopted the method of taking with him on his visitation, whenever possible, one of the settled clergy, not only to assist in the services, but often to preach when more than one service was held in a town, and to substitute should the Bishop become ill. This was a necessity in the latter part of 1863, when Gregg had resumed his visitations too soon after a serious case of typhoid fever and was so weak that he had to walk with crutches.[8]

Wherever possible, the Bishop arranged to have clergy follow up his work in new places, even though this meant they spread their efforts thinner. Otherwise he tried to secure layreaders, whose office he prized, as serving to keep the Liturgy alive and to train the Church's youth in its use. During the war years he believed it to be "the most needed work in Texas at this time."[9] But layreaders had to be selected with care and instructed in their work. Commending the efficient layreading at Marshall in 1865, the Bishop remarked that zeal was not enough; the layreader had to have

[6]*Ibid.*, 1860-1865, Bishop's Addresses.   [7]*Ibid.*, 1865, pp. 13, 21.
[8]W. Gregg, *Gregg*, p. 77; *Texas Journal*, 1864, p. 10.
[9]*Ibid.*, 1861, p. 12.

a thorough knowledge of the distinctive principles of the Church, and a due appreciation of her whole system of Christian training and spiritual progress—a subject to which the attention of the Laity of every class is earnestly invoked.[10]

The effect of the Civil War upon the financial structure of the Diocese became severe, but the Bishop did not abate his purpose to carry out his program for the Texas Church. Faced with a reduction of thirty percent in the appropriation from the Domestic Committee for 1861, the Bishop applied outside contributions of $785, given by people of South Carolina, North Carolina and Texas, toward the salaries of missionaries; to this he was able to add the $1500 realized from membership dues and collections for the Diocesan Missionary Society.[11] The situation was more serious than it first appeared, for the promised funds from the Church in the United States were not forthcoming. Gregg reported to the 1862 Convention that the last payments on missionary stipends from that source were made in January 1861, except for some drafts that could not be negotiated. At the October meeting the national Society stopped all appropriations to its missionaries in the seceded states, but did not refund contributions from persons in those states. Gregg believed that the Southern Dioceses had contributed more than was spent within them; he thought this quite proper, since the money was given to be used where the Society believed it was most needed. His point was that the Church in the Confederacy was demonstrably able to carry its own weight in its missionary task. The withdrawal of support from abroad, coupled with a drastic decline in the receipts of the Diocesan Society in the 1861-62 convention year, made the situation grave. The Bishop was plainspoken in referring to the failure of Texas Church people to support the program of the Diocese, especially since many of them, he asserted, had grown rich on war profits.[12]

The response of many people in Texas to this reminder of their duty enabled Gregg to support his diminished corps of missionaries during the emergency. Meanwhile contributions to the Diocesan Society increased, but these came mostly from individuals, for some parishes did nothing—a situation which the Bishop deplored. The action of the Executive Committee of Confederate Bishops in appropriating $3000 for missions in Texas filled the gap,[13] and made it possible for the payroll to be met in spite of the effects of inflation.

Invasion and adversity doubtless cut the ability of the richer

[10]Ibid., 1865, p. 17.   [11]Ibid., 1861, pp. 26-7.
[12]Ibid., 1862, pp. 21-2.   [13]Ibid., 1863, p. 12.

Confederate dioceses to keep up their missionary giving. At the Council of 1864 the Bishop reported having received $2310 from the Confederate Church's funds, part of which was paid by Texas parishes. At the same time, the Diocesan Society had raised a sum "very much larger nominally, but given by two few, and depreciation of the currency makes it fall far short."[14] Evidently nothing came from abroad between this Council and that of 1865, for all the receipts listed by the Bishop in his report are credited to Texas donors. The sum equals the amount he paid to the missionaries.[15]

Before the 1861 Convention Bishop Gregg started another fund devoted to the relief of the widows and orphans of clergy, and of aged and infirmed clergy. This fund was to be accumulated by offerings taken at the Bishop's visitations.[16] Meeting public approbation, the fund prospered wonderfully, becoming, as the Bishop said, "a favorite charity of the Diocese." At the end of the war it had grown to over $9000; but, having been invested in Confederate bonds, it was almost a total loss. Only a few hundred dollars of specie uninvested was left.[17]

The Episcopal Fund, among others, suffered because of the war. In spite of secession, the donors of the A. C. Coxe pledge made their payments up to the time of the 1861 Convention,[18] but not after the outbreak of hostilities. Up to the 1863 Council, the Diocese met its pledge to the Bishop's salary with an excess of almost a thousand dollars. To make up for the loss of the Coxe pledge, the General Council of the Confederate Church gave $491. The resolve was expressed by the 1963 Texas Council to make up the $2300 still unpaid at that time on the Bishop's salary.[19] Some progress was made toward this objective during the year following; $2300 was paid by the Texas congregations, and over $1300 was given by the Confederate Church, leaving $1600 due the Bishop at council time in 1864.[20] At the Council of 1865 the Finance Committee had to report that only $1118 had been received for the Bishop's salary during the year, much of that in currency. The Diocese was indebted to him for almost $2000, not counting what had been expected but not received from abroad. The report continued, however:

> The Bishop, with his characteristic liberality and generosity, appreciating the condition of a people just emerging from the

[14]*Ibid.*, 1864, pp. 11-12.   [15]*Ibid.*, 1865, pp. 21-2.

[16]*Ibid.*, 1861, pp. 27-8.   [17]*Ibid.*, 1865, pp. 22-3.

[18]*Ibid.*, 1861, p. 47.   [19]*Ibid.*, 1863, p. 19.

[20]*Ibid.*, 1864, p. 17.

exhaustion of a four years war, has expressed a desire that a portion of the above indebtedness to him be suspended.

Advantage was taken of this offer. All unpaid assessments against the parishes were cancelled, and sufficient assessments were levied currently to care for the full salary for the upcoming year, with a private effort being promised to raise at least half of the unpaid balance due the Bishop.[21]

Though the circumstances of the war forced postponement of some of the program of the Diocese, Gregg would not allow any part of it to be forgotten. In regard to Christian education, he urged the 1865 Council to attend to the need for a system of schools, beginning at the parish level with elementary education, and extending to collegiate education on the diocesan level. Schools of all sorts had been neglected during the war, and the Church had an opportunity to make a new beginning with her own children by providing education under Church control, Christian in spirit as in name, or, as the Bishop phrased it, "in spirit and feeling, Church homes." There was need for Church education for boys and girls, particularly for the former. The Diocese had been about ready to organize a boy's school in 1860, but it was delayed because of the threat of war; now it would be opened as soon as money was in hand to start it without debt.[22]

Bishop Gregg faced the victory of the Union, and its effects upon ecclesiastical relations, with the same consistency of principle with which he had met the secession of the Southern States. He issued a pastoral letter to the membership of the Diocese on May 15, 1865, dealing with "the close of the war and the changes in our civil affairs."[23] Gregg's prompt action is seen in the fact that the letter was written the day before Generals Kirby-Smith and Magruder formally surrendered the Trans-Mississippi Department to the Federal Government.[24] The Bishop told the members of the 1865 Council that he took this action "in part, to throw the great moral power of the Church in the scale of law, order and Christian obedience—all which are solemnly enjoined upon us in Scripture." Recalling how he had emphasized the close relationship between a Christian's duties to the state and to the Church, and believing now, as he had in 1861, that the Church must recognize the government in being, he ordered the changes in Liturgy made nec-

[21]*Ibid.*, 1865, pp. 10, 11.

[22]*Ibid.*, 1863, p. 13; 1865, pp. 33-4.   [23]*Ibid.*, p. 20.

[24]Louis J. Wortham, *A History of Texas: From Wilderness to Commonwealth* (5v., Fort Worth, 1924), IV, p. 364.

essary by the change in government. He recommended, moreover, that the Council resume its relationship with the Church in the United States; this, too, was in accordance with that states' rights principle he had followed at the time of Texas secession. He did not think it necessary to wait for another meeting of the General Council of the Church in the Confederate States before taking this action.[25]

The Texas Council asked the Bishop to appoint a special committee to study and report on this recommendation. The committee offered a resolution that the Diocese accede anew to the Constitution and Canons of the Protestant Episcopal Church in the United States of America, that the Council elect deputies to the forthcoming General Convention, and that the General Council of the Confedrate Church meet and dissolve itself. This resolution was adopted, and the Council elected as Deputies to General Convention the Reverend Messrs. Eaton, Gillette, Davenport and Owen, and Messrs. P. W. Gray, William M. Taylor, E. G. Benners, and W. B. Grimes.[26]

Gregg as a private citizen faced the fact of Confederate defeat and the need to act responsibly in the situation that had come about, by taking the oath of allegiance to the United States at the first opportunity for doing so in Austin, August 4, 1865. He was the first citizen in Austin to take that action; his example encouraged many, but drew criticism from extreme partisans on both sides.[27]

When the General Convention assembled in Philadelphia on October 4, 1865, three of the four Clerical Deputies and two of the four Lay Deputies from the Diocese of Texas answered the roll and took their seats without any protest from the House. They were the only Deputies present from a former Confederate Diocese until the third day, when the deputations from North Carolina and Tennessee appeared.[28] Although some members of the Convention did introduce motions and resolutions designed to embarrass those from the South, no action of the Convention belied the welcome that had been accorded to the deputations from the three Dioceses of the South. Thus the unity of the Church was reaffirmed. This result contrasts strikingly with the continued "North-South" divisions of many denominations, some of which endure even today.

Gregg did not attend the 1865 General Convention. We are left to guess his reason. It was more likely the urgency he felt to exploit the opportunity to establish schools in San Antonio, than,

[25]*Texas Journal*, 1865, p. 24.
[26]*Ibid.*, pp. 9-10.   [27]W. Gregg, *Gregg*, pp. 86-7.
[28]*General Convention Journal*, 1865, pp. 22-3, 32. Tennessee never formally entered the Confederate Church.

as his son suggested, fear of facing a cool reception at the Convention.[29] The Bishop removed his family residence to San Antonio at the end of August, in order to oversee the foundation of St. Mary's School for girls and to supply services for St. Mark's Church, whose rector had not returned.[30] As soon as he completed his Fall visitation, on January 1, 1866, he left for the North to attempt to raise money for the boys' school he considered so essential. He closed his address to the next Diocesan Convention with a statement of his hearty satisfaction with the restoration of the unity of the Church.[31] With peace and unity restored, there could be a renewed effort to carry out more fully the mission of the Episcopal Church to the people of Texas. How well it was performed is to be seen in the growth and deepening of the Church in the years of Reconstruction.

[29]W. Gregg, *Gregg*, p. 89.   [30]*Texas Journal*, 1866, pp. 18, 25-6.
[31]*Ibid.*, pp. 21, 26, 28.

PART FOUR

THE DIOCESE
IN THE
RECONSTRUCTION ERA

XII. Efforts for Schools and for Negro Work

WITH THE RETURN of peace the Diocese faced two responsibilities which could not be evaded. Something had to be
done about the education of its youth, and some new means had to
be devised for ministering to the former slaves who were adherents or
(in much lesser numbers) communicants of the Church. These tasks
were made difficult by the economic disaster which accompanied
the war and the defeat of the South, and by the social upheaval
caused by the sudden emancipation of the slave population. The
entire Reconstruction decade between the end of the war and the
division of the Diocese was one in which conflicting forces, seeking
to shape a new South in one way or another, caused every social
and religious effort to be handicapped. In the face of these difficulties the Diocese moved again to meet its responsibilities.

SCHOOLS

In October 1865 the Diocese made a new beginning on its
educational program. The Reverend J. J. Nicholson returned to become founder and headmaster of St. Mary's School for Girls and

Rector of St. Mark's Parish in San Antonio[1] The school began with
great promise of prosperity, but after a few months, an epidemic of
cholera claimed Nicholson's life and so frightened the parents of
the girls that the school could hardly find pupils. The Reverend
E. A. Wagner, who had returned to the Diocese, took up Nicholson's
tasks in Parish and school.[2] The school, unable to overcome the effects of the epidemic upon its enrollment, closed after two years,
heavily in debt to Wagner for salary and outlay for improvements.[3]

Bishop Gregg meantime had received an apparently princely
gift toward establishing the projected Church Training School for
Boys in San Antonio. On his visit to New York he was given the sum
of $10,000 by Mr. John David Wolfe of that city, to be used for
the erection of the school's first building.[4] The gift was in New York
currency, subject to a heavy discount in Texas, which had maintained a specie standard even during the Civil War. Despite other
gifts from the East, the building was in debt when complete enough
for use, and apparently was turned over to St. Mary's School because
financial difficulties prevented the opening of the boys' school.[5]

Meanwhile other efforts for the schooling of the Church's youth
were being made elsewhere in the Diocese. In 1866 the Reverend
Mr. Chase opened a Church School for Girls at Independence, apparently at his own risk, and operated it successfully for several years.[6]
A boys' school was proposed for the same town; it seems to have
been found not feasible, or perhaps was not attempted because of
developments in nearby Brenham. In that town an approach was
made to the trustees of St. Paul's College by Graham Lodge No. 20,
A.F. & A.M., and a group of citizens, requesting the revival of the
College and its preparatory school in Brenham. The Academy building owned by the Lodge was to be deeded to the College to house
its preparatory department, and funds were pledged to erect a college
building. The Diocesan Convention of 1867 approved this proposal
and authorized the Board of Trustees of St. Paul's to enter into the
contract.[7] Once again, however, disaster intervened. The Trustees

[1]The former Rector, the Rev. Dr. Dalzell, deciding not to return, was transferred to the Diocese of Louisiana in 1866. *Texas Journal*, 1866, p. 25.

[2]*Ibid.*, pp. 25-6.

[3]See below, p. 155.

[4]*Texas Journal*, 1866, p. 26; Gregg, Manuscript Journal, account sheet, "Boys'
School," 1866.

[5]R. W. B. Elliott, "Historical Sketch of the Church in Western Texas," serially
in *Spirit of Missions*, 1885, gives details of the finances. Also, Gregg, Manuscript
Journal, gives some.

[6]*Texas Journal*, 1866, p. 20, and reports in following years.

[7]*Ibid.*, 1867, p. 14.

reported to the next Convention the following sequence of events: the contract was closed, the building was taken into possession, and Professor Ford, of Columbia, South Carolina, was employed to head the preparatory department. The school was opened with the highest hopes. Ford made the most favorable impression, and a full enrollment was secured. Within a week yellow fever had struck the town, and the new schoolmaster was one of its first victims. The Trustees acted quickly to appoint another head for the school, a Mr. Glass, who, though not an Episcopalian, was well qualified academically. Then Brenham was struck by fire which wiped out a large portion of the business section. Collection of pledges for the college building was impossible.[8] The preparatory school continued to operate until January 1870 under the charge of General John C. Moore and the Reverend John Rosenberg. General Moore left at that time, and Rosenberg held on, with one assistant teacher, until April, when he accepted a position with a Methodist school at Chappell Hill. The Convention could only approve the recommendation of the St. Paul's Board, to return the land and building to the Masonic Lodge, and to have the Trustees revert to the duty of holding the college's landed endowment in trust for the future.[9]

The 1867 Convention also accepted the offer made by some citizens of Hempstead to begin a boys' school in that town, and appointed a committee to carry through the project.[10] The yellow fever epidemic of that year destroyed this enterprise also; the Convention of the following year was told that one member of the committee died in the visitation, and another moved away, so that nothing could be done.[11]

The Reverend W. W. Patrick organized "The Episcopal High School" in Waco in September 1867, and in his report to the Convention of 1868 reported it progressing very well. Patrick was apparently assisted by Mr. R. S. Nash, who was licensed as lay reader by Bishop Gregg in 1869, and, after being ordained to the Diaconate in January 1870, remained in Waco for another year. With the departure of Patrick in 1871 the school apparently lapsed.[12]

In addition to his efforts to begin a diocesan school system, Bishop Gregg urged the establishment of parochial schools wherever possible.[13] Texas was without public schools in most places, and the

---

[8]*Ibid.*, 1868, p. 10.   [9]*Ibid.*, 1870, pp. 18-19.

[10]*Ibid.*, 1867, p. 15.   [11]*Ibid.*, 1868, pp. 11-12.

[12]*Ibid.*, 1868, pp. 34-5; 1869, pp. 14-19; Gregg, Manuscript Journal, 2 Jan. 1870; *Texas Journal*, 1871, pp. 23, 49.

[13]*Ibid.*, 1867, pp. 29-30.

Roman Catholic Church was establishing both boarding and day schools in many places in the State; the anxiety of the Church for the schooling of her youth is understandable. Yet the depressed financial condition of the people during Reconstruction made it difficult for the congregations to meet more than the minimal expenses, let alone build school buildings and employ teachers.

Trinity Parish School was organized in Galveston after the Reverend Stephen Moylan Bird, Sr., became Rector. The Reverend Albert Lyon was induced to remove to Galveston to take charge of this enterprise, at the same time to assist in operating the "West End Mission," another of Bird's new projects.[14] But this effort on the part of a parish was exceptional in Texas.

Schools in which the Church's influence was felt were mostly private ones taught by clergy in order to supplement their incomes so they might remain in the smaller places. While Bishop Gregg recognized the necessity for some clergy to teach, he regretted it, feeling that the time of a Presbyter was spent more fruitfully in pastoral and missionary work; he urged congregations to increase the salaries of their clergy.[15] On the other hand, Gregg had nothing but praise for the work of Perpetual Deacons like Chase, Carrington and Nash, for whom schoolteaching was a profession and conducting Sunday services was a labor of love.[16]

However disappointed Gregg might have been about the failure to establish diocesan schools for boys, he early recognized the desirability of reviving the University of the South as the means through which the Southern dioceses could pool their slender resources for the education of their sons and for training candidates for the Ministry. Immediately after becoming the second Bishop of Tennessee, Charles Todd Quintard set his indomitable will to revive this enterprise. Initially having been an effort of the Diocese of Tennessee, the revived school soon enlisted the backing of the surviving trustees of the University as it had been organized before the war. Bishop Elliott of Georgia, the senior Southern bishop, became the Chancellor. He called a meeting of the Trustees to meet at Sewanee October 11, 1866, at which time the deeds to the University domain were discovered to be intact.[17] Texas was not represented at this meeting, which took place several months after the Diocesan Con-

---

[14]*Ibid.*, 1874, p. 78; Morgan, *Trinity Church, Galveston*, p. 79; see below, p. 189.

[15]*Texas Journal*, 1869, pp. 20, 21; 1872, p. 24.

[16]*Ibid.*, p. 31; Gregg, Manuscript Journal, 8 Apr. 1870.

[17]Arthur Benjamin Chitty, Jr., *Reconstruction at Sewanee, 1857-1872* (Sewanee, Tenn., 1954), pp. 87, 96.

vention of that year, but at the next Convention, in June 1867, Gregg spoke with great emphasis in commending to the members of the Church in Texas the proposed new beginning of the Sewanee venture.[18] He engaged in the business of the Sewanee Trustees at meetings held during the sessions of General Convention in October 1868,[19] and then, beginning with the summer of 1869,[20] he lived during the summer months at Sewanee with his family. Since the school year there began in the Spring, extended over the Summer and Fall, and had its long vacation in the Winter (a custom which persisted until 1908), Gregg was able to join with Bishops Quintard and Green, who lived on the mountain the year round,[21] in the management of the affairs of the school. During his first Summer there, Bishop Gregg took personal charge of the construction of the library building.[22] Gregg himself, with Bishop John Freeman Young of Florida and some of their friends, contributed the funds for this building.[23] As soon as he was financially able, he built at Sewanee a summer residence,[24] which was much enlarged by his daughters in later years.[25]

Although the distance from Texas to the Tennessee college was great, the interest and support afforded it by the Diocese of Texas during Gregg's episcopate was remarkable. In 1869 ten students arrived from Texas, and thereafter they came in numbers which Arthur Ben Chitty called, "considering the distance, . . . outstanding. . . ."[26] Texas Episcopalians alone made the annual University Offering a regular feature,[27] equal in importance with the Diocesan Missions Fund and the Fund for Widows and Orphans. For the four years 1869-1872, the offerings from Texas exceeded those of any of the other owning dioceses;[28] in assessing this fact, Texas' less war-damaged economy must be balanced by the remoteness of the school from the Diocese. Individuals made contributions of note; Peter W. Gray of Houston gave most of the cost of the Grammar School Building in 1872.[29]

If the services of the Diocese of Texas to the University of the South were outstanding, the contribution of the school to the Diocese were valuable. Even before the School of Theology was officially established, Texas was sending candidates to Sewanee for

[18]*Texas Journal*, 1867, p. 31.   [19]Chitty, *op. cit.*, p. 115.

[20]Gregg, Manuscript Journal, June, 1869.   [21]Chitty, *op. cit.*, pp. 56, 132.

[22]Gregg, Manuscript Journal, 1869.   [23]Chitty, *op. cit.*, p. 131.

[24]*Ibid.*, p. 132.   [25]Seen by the writer in the summer of 1961.

[26]Chitty, *op. cit.*, p. 175.   [27]Vide *Texas Journals* for period.

[28]Chitty, *op. cit.*, p. 178.   [29]*Ibid.*, p. 151; *Texas Journal*, 1871, p. 31.

training. The first two theology students, Peter G. Rucker and Thomas J. Morris, were from Texas.[30] For many years Sewanee was the principal resource of the Diocese for the education of its candidates, as well as for the liberal education of young men not preparing for the ministry.

Perhaps more than any other factor, the connection with Sewanee ameliorated the problem of a supply of young Texas men available to be educated for orders. Repeatedly before 1871 Gregg insisted that the mission of the Church was being held back by the failure of parents and members of parishes to encourage young men to consider the ministry as a vocation. At the 1871 Convention he reported that the situation had changed. There was no longer a lack of boys ready to study for orders, nor of parents willing to dedicate their sons to the ministry; the lack was of funds to help men whose families could not afford the expense of sending them to school. Money was needed for scholarships. The Bishop had pledged himself to find means for two more students to begin study in 1872, and he needed help. He believed that each large parish should support one candidate.[31] His appeal did not go unanswered; each subsequent year's *Journal* contains an account of special contributions for scholarships, including the annual income from a scholarship endowment given by that generous benefactress of the Texas Church, Mrs. J. Pinckney Henderson.[32]

NEGRO WORK

The black population was not forgotten as the Diocese of Texas planned its educational and pastoral work for the post-war period. It was generally recognized that the Negroes' greatest need was for education, to enable them to benefit from emancipation. Gregg called the Diocese to dedication to the task of providing schools for freedmen. He told the Convention of 1866 that he had sought financial aid for this work on his trip to the East earlier that year. He met with most cordial welcome from the Bishop of New York, the clergy and the people of that Diocese, and the bishops and clergy of other Northern dioceses. Doors were thrown open to allow him to present his program to congregations, and a generous response was made to his appeals for other needs, but he could secure no help for Negro schools. Although he promised to cooperate in any way possible with the new Freedman's Aid Commission set up by the General Conven-

---

[30]In 1870. Chitty, *op. cit.*, p. 136; *Texas Journal*, 1871, p. 29.
[31]*Ibid.*, 1871, pp. 31-2.   [32]*Ibid.*, 1873, p. 46; 1874, p. 31.

tion, he evidently expected little to be done by it in Texas, and he urged upon the local congregations the duty of establishing Negro schools, under the direction of the clergy where possible, or at least under the supervision of laymen devoted to the Church.[33] No doubt sincere efforts were made in several places to carry out this responsibility, but the difficult financial situation of that time, the shortage of clergy, and the preoccupation of many people with the re-establishment of a way of life made the undertaking so difficult that it would be laid aside easily. In two places, however, sustained efforts were made which showed results justifying the wisdom of the Bishop in commending the program.

At Independence the Reverend Mr. Chase in 1868 began a Sunday School for oral instruction of Negroes; he reported to the Convention of that year an enrollment of eighty-five. This result no doubt was due to the pastoral attention which Chase was giving the freedmen of the community. Because of the removal of half the families who formed the clientele of his schools, and the inability of the others to pay, the Bishop approved his giving part of his time to this work;[34] he was aided by a missionary salary grant of $250 per year from the Domestic Committee, voted at Gregg's request.[35] In San Antonio, where the Reverend Walter R. Richardson became Rector of St. Mark's Parish on June 1, 1868, a Sunday School for colored children was organized with the Bishop's assitance in February 1869, and two years later was reported by the Bishop to be doing very well.[36] No doubt efforts were made in other places in the Diocese but did not get into the record; several parishes continued to report colored communicants, baptisms and confirmations, and it may be surmised that Negro children studied in the Sunday Schools in these places along with the White children.

The efforts of congregations to retain their Negro members met with indifferent success, save in exceptional circumstances, such as will appear in the subsequent narrative of the particular congregations' growth and development. There was genuine concern over the Church's inexplicable failure to hold colored members. After Bishop Gregg had alluded in several convention addresses to the need for pastoral attention to Negroes, he brought forward a new proposal to the Council of 1874. Several Southern Bishops had pro-

---

[33]*Ibid.*, 1866, p. 27. The Freedmen's Aid Commission was headed by the Rev. Charles Gillette.

[34]*Ibid.*, 1868, pp. 32, 21.

[35]Minutes of the Domestic Committee, Board of Missions, 1868, Minutes Book, p. 43.

[36]*Texas Journal*, 1869, pp. 31, 20; 1871, pp. 24-5.

posed that General Convention be asked to create the office of Missionary Bishop to the Colored Race, to work generally over the South; Gregg thought that one bishop for the four million Negroes scattered over the entire South could accomplish nothing. He proposed that the Council consider asking General Convention to authorize the election of an assistant bishop, "something like a Suffragan Bishop," to work among the freedmen in Texas. What was needed was a concentrated, long-term project.

> Schools would have to be established, congregations organized, churches built, and colored candidates educated and trained for the Ministry—for a colored Ministry would be absolutely indispensable—and, withal an extensive system of chief pastoral visitations carried out—a personal, living, sympathetic connection and oversight maintained.[37]

Bishop Gregg had changed his former convictions. Previously he had objected to separate congregations for colored people, because of his belief in the equality of all people before God. He had believed that the same pastors could minister effectively to people of both races. But now, in the interest of securing results, he was willing to try another expedient.

A special committee, appointed to consider this subject, returned a report asking essentially what the Bishop had recommended.[38] This memorial was presented to the General Convention of 1874. It was unclear who would pay the salary of such a bishop; likely it would have been a charge upon the funds of the Domestic and Foreign Missionary Society. Several dioceses were asking for similar bishoprics for racial and language groups, including German-speaking folk and Indians. Both Texas and California were asking the Missionary Society to take over parts of their territory, and to pay missionary bishops. No doubt the financial outlay involved caused hesitation. The memorial was referred to a special committee on bishoprics to racial and language groups, for report to a subsequent Convention.[39] So far as the Diocese of Texas was concerned, this was the end of this matter. Work with the Negroes remained a difficult duty marked by little success. The newly emancipated Negroes preferred ministers and congregations of their own race. The Episcopal Church in Texas was unable to meet their desires. Clergy of their race were very few in number, and, if available, would have to be provided with residences and church buildings. In the prevailing economic hardship there was no money available

---

[37]*Ibid.*, 1874, pp. 60-3.   [38]*Ibid.*, 1874, pp. 26-8.
[39]*General Convention Journal*, 1874, p. 342.

in Texas to meet these needs. Church work for Negroes in the Diocese of Texas was not forgotten, but new methods for carrying it out had to be deferred to more favorable times.

Thus in the two most urgent social responsibilities of the Diocese in the Reconstruction Period there was more failure than success, yet it is to the credit of the Church's leadership that valiant and self-sacrificing efforts were made to meet them. Meanwhile in its missionary and pastoral tasks the Diocese achieved results that strengthened the Church and enabled it better to discharge its other trusts.

XIII. Strategy for Missions and Pastoral Work

THE COLLAPSE of the Confederacy found the missionary program of the Episcopal Church in the South in a precarious position, unable to pay its few clergy still at work in parishes, let alone to employ men for work not yet established.[1] Reunion with the Church in the North placed the resources of the Domestic and Foreign Missionary Society again at the disposal of the Bishops of the South, provided the Domestic Committee looked favorably upon their needs. The wonderful manifestation of Christian brotherhood in the post-war reconciliation of the Episcopal Church eliminated any disposition on the part of the Committee to hold back from the Southern Churches the means they so desperately needed.[2] The Right Reverend Horatio Potter, Bishop of New York, was particularly active in raising money for the Southern clergy, and he gave generously from his own resources to succor his brother Bishops in the South.[3] Possibly some of the worst of these needs were made known to Potter by Gregg during his sojourn in the East early in 1866. There was raised the Southern Clergy Relief Fund, from which Gregg reported making allowances to his clergy during the next two or three years.[4]

[1] *Texas Journal,* 1865; Treasurer's report, pp. 32, 33.

[2] See *Spirit of Missions,* 1865-6 and subsequently for this spirit.

[3] Manuscript letter of Rt. Rev.. Horatio Potter, D.D., sent out by student messengers from General Seminary, N. Y., Feb. 2, 1866, copy in Rev. H. J. W. Fay collection, C. H. S. Archives, Austin. Potter mentions the desperate circumstances of Bishop Davis of South Carolina, and of Bishop Green of Mississippi, about whom Gregg, who was in New York that week, would have had information and great concern.

[4] He gave some account of the use of this fund in his annual addresses to Convention, printed in *Texas Journal.* A complete account is contained in his Manuscript Journal.

FINANCES

The Domestic Committee at their stated meeting on December 4, 1865, allotted $3000 to Texas for 1866.[5] The minutes of the stated meeting for February contain this entry:

> Bishop Gregg was present, and made some interesting statements in relation to the needs of his diocese, and other portions of the South, and also named stations and missionaries. Whereupon the $3000 appropriated was increased to $6000.[6]

This very generous appropriation made it possible to press forward with a program that went far toward meeting the challenge which the relatively favorable post-war condition of Texas presented. It was possible to retain clergy who otherwise might have had to leave the State when local ability to meet their salaries disappeared; it was possible also to offer employment to several clergy from other dioceses of the South whose situations had become insupportable.[7] Gregg preferred not to bring in married clergy, as he feared they would suffer privation. Insecurity, he felt, was the cause of frequent clergy changes.[8]

The Bishop was unwilling, however, for the Texas congregations to live on the largess of others. He told the Convention of 1866 that every parish should contribute to diocesan objects. "As a diocese, we are one body, though with many parochial members. There is a danger of parochial selfishness." He complained that only one or two parishes were giving to the Diocesan Missionary Fund; only $139.50 had been collected during the year, mostly from individuals, many of them not residents of the Diocese. About the arrearages in his own salary he was uncomplaining.[9] Through the decade the Bishop kept hammering away at the shells of self-centered and lazy parishes. He urged the need for congregations to become self-supporting, with adequate salaries paid to their clergymen. Meanwhile parishes should be giving gladly to support the missionary work of the Church in Texas and beyond. As the cities of Texas developed outlying residential districts remote from the par-

---

[5]Minutes, Domestic Committee, 4. Dec. 1865, Minutes Book, p. 350.

[6]Minutes, Domestic Committee, 1866, Minutes Book, p. 362.

[7]Clergy received, 1865-66 Convention year: from Alabama, J. Avery Shepherd, Joseph J. Nicholson and A. F. Dobb; from Arkansas, J. M. Curtis; from Mississippi, Geo. Rottenstein and Gideon B. Perry. One only came from the North, J. Wilkins Tays, from Pennsylvania. *Texas Journal*, 1866, p. 25.

[8]*Ibid.*, p. 26.

[9]*Ibid.*, pp. 24, 26-8; the Bishop was paid only $2,151.47 on his $3,000 salary that year. *Ibid.*, p. 43.

ish churches, Gregg urged establishing parochial missions. This plea fell on deaf ears except in Galveston, where the Reverend Stephen Moylan Bird, Rector of Trinity Church, sponsored a mission in the west end of town.[10]

While urging larger contributions for all Church purposes, the Bishop strongly opposed tricks and entertainments for fund raising. He contended that the work of the Church should and could be sustained by sacrificial giving. Even though he praised the great efforts of the ladies of the Church in the several congregations to raise funds for their church buildings, he much preferred that members of the Church provide what they needed by their own giving rather than by sale of articles to the general public. He commended the new offering envelope system through which the Parishes in Waco and Dallas achieved self-support.[11]

The generous support which the Domestic Committee granted to the Diocese in 1866 could not be kept up during the subsequent years of national financial hardship. The appropriation was $4400 for 1867, $2700 for 1868, $2000 for 1869, then down to $1500 for 1870 through 1872, then up to $2000 for 1873, and $2300 for 1874.[12] The decreases worked hardship upon the Diocese because of the rapid influx of immigrants into the State and because of the rapidity with which towns were being founded. Great pressure was put upon the Diocese to extend ministrations to these new people. Clergy who could reach new towns had to spread their efforts over more territory, and local support had to be found to employ more diocesan missionaries. But principally the effect was a much heavier burden upon the Bishop, both because he did most of the advance missionary work and because he bore much of the financial loss in the affairs of the Diocese. The *Journal* of the Diocese for 1867 was not published because the treasury was empty; it was published along with the current year's proceedings in 1868, but in 1869 the Council[13] voted to assess parishes separately for the contingent expenses of the Diocese and the salary of the Bishop. Some solicitous friends had discovered that the previous two years' proceedings had been published at Gregg's expense since the cost was deducted from the treasury before the Bishop received available portion of his salary. By 1870 arrears were due him of roundly $3500, but this amount

---

[10]*Ibid.*, 1867, pp. 16, 27; 1871, pp. 31-2; 1872, pp. 45-7; 1873, pp. 48-50; 1874, pp. 56-7. The Rev. Mr. Bird was the father of the Rev. S. M. Bird, Jr., now Rector Emeritus of St. Peter's Church, Brenham.

[11]*Ibid.*, 1873, p. 16.

[12]Minutes Book, Domestic Committee for these years.

[13]*Texas Journal,* 1868, p. 7; for change of name of meeting, see below, p. 144.

was reduced more than $1500 by the following year.[14] In 1872 the Treasurer of the Diocese, Mr. James H. Raymond of Austin, told the Council there was no fixed salary for the Bishop, but each congregation paid him what it had stored up for the purpose when he visited.[15] While this was in fact happening, the report incensed some of the members. The Reverend L. P. Rucker asked the Bishop at the 1873 Council to tell the members what his salary was; he replied that it was $3000 in coin.[16] The same meeting, with Rucker in the chair, decided to insure the life of the Bishop for $10,000, with his wife as the beneficiary; the cost of the premium was to be met by the Diocese through assessments upon the parishes.[17]

The Greggs, in fact, had lost their fortune, and depended mostly upon the Bishop's stipend for their livelihood. They lost their home in San Antonio as well; likely it was sacrificed to help the Diocese meet its obligations to the Reverend E. A. Wagner and other creditors of the school enterprise there. Instead of complaining, the Bishop sought to secure some income from his writings. He rushed to completion the *History of the Old Cheraw*, an account of the people of his old home district in South Carolina, upon which he had worked for years, and he took it to England for publication when he attended the Lambeth Conference in 1867. A year after his return, he removed his residence to Galveston,[18] where he and his family boarded for some years.

Stringency may not have been the only reason for the Greggs to break up housekeeping. Mrs. Gregg's delicate health for some time had caused considerable concern to the Bishop. The burdens of housekeeping with little domestic help, were probably more than she could cope with.[19] In addition, three Gregg children at considerable expense attended various boarding schools out of the State.[20] Besides, after the family's removal to Galveston, the Bishop's work of visitation increased so much that he was home for only a week or two at a time between his long journeys. Summer at Sewanee came to be the family's time together.[21]

---

[14]*Texas Journal*, 1869, pp. 10-11; 1870, p. 31; 1871, p. 12.

[15]*Ibid.*, 1872, p. 15.   [16]*Ibid.*, 1873, p. 22.   [17]*Ibid.*, p. 11.

[18]Gregg, Manuscript Journal, 3 Mar. 1869.

[19]W. Gregg, *Gregg*, pp. 115-6.

[20]The scanty and fragmentary personal accounts included here and there in the Bishop's Manuscript Journal reflect this, though they do not afford enough information to yield a clear picture of his financial situation as a whole.

[21]This is more clearly seen in the Manuscript Journal, which details every day's activities, than in the reports on official acts contained in his addresses in the *Texas Journal*.

The move to Galveston was strategic. After the war the rapid development of Texas railroads made either Galveston or Houston the most advantageous starting point for the visitation of the Diocese; before then Austin or San Antonio would do as well. Two considerations gave Galveston the advantage over Houston in this era. From the former place, the best seaport in Texas, vessels sailed frequently to Indianola and Corpus Christi, from which points short-range visitations could be made easily to nearby towns. There was also the advantage of prompter mail service to Galveston from New Orleans and the East. Beside this, the Galveston Parish was the wealthiest and strongest in the Diocese. From its members came the greatest contributions to the causes Gregg took in hand, a fact no doubt due to the greater influence he was able to have by residing there. By contrast, the Houston Parish was destined to struggle for some years more before gaining strength and taking up a position of stewardship and leadership in the Diocese.

At the outbreak of the war one could go from Galveston to Harrisburg, and from there to Alleytown, a few miles out of Columbus, on the Buffalo Bayou, Brazos and Colorado Rail Road, which reached Richmond by 1856 and Alleytown by 1859. The Galveston, Houston and Henderson was completed from Galveston to Houston in 1860 (and *never* went to Henderson)! From Houston one could go also to Orange on the Texas and New Orleans by 1861, or up the Central Railroad to Hempstead by 1858.[22] Navasota was reached by this road in September 1859,[23] and Millican by 1860, but its progress stopped until after the war.[24] It was extended to Bryan by 1867, to Corsicana by 1871, and to Dallas in 1872. Its further extension to Denison in 1873 provided a connection with the Missouri, Kansas and Texas Railway and through service to St. Louis.

Brenham was reached by a connecting line, the Washington County Railroad, which was completed from Hempstead to Brenham by 1860, but it did not go beyond Brenham until it was bought out by the Central in 1869, after which it extended to Austin

---

[22]*Handbook of Texas*, *en. loc.*, for each road.

[23]*The Navasota Examiner and Grimes County Review*, Centennial Edition, July 1, 1954, reprinted an article written by Dr. A. R. Kilpatrick of Navasota, (grandfather of J. Walter Kilpatrick of Houston), originally prepared for July 4, 1876, and printed in the *Navasota Weekly Tablet* July 20, 1876. There is much of historical interest in this article, and in the entire Centennial Issue of this paper, concerning Grimes and eastern Washington Counties, and the Episcopal Church in this area. Dr. Kilpatrick handed on a vivid picture of the arrival of the first train in Navasota.

[24]*Handbook of Texas*, "Millican, Texas," *en. loc.*

by 1871.[25] One other railway out of Houston was completed before
the war, the Houston Tap and Brazoria, which extended to Columbia
on the Brazos River by 1859; this made the Brazoria County congregations more accessible.[26] Railroad facilities available before about
1867 assisted persons like the Bishop of Texas who had to travel
over the settled parts of the State; but railroads only supplemented
stages, hacks, and private conveyances. By the 1870's railroads became
for the interior of the State the main form of transportation.

But Gregg's strategy did not view railroads merely as institutions
that could do something for him; from the beginning of their
expansion he looked for opportunities to serve the people who were
building them, and those who were moving into the towns which
sprang up along the lines. The keystone in the missionary program
for these years was to establish work along with or ahead of railroad
construction. Older towns not touched by the prosperity of the railroad era were not neglected, but the planned emphasis on serving
the territory opened up was sound, for there the population
gravitated.[27]

THE CHURCH SYSTEM

As the Episcopal Church in Texas moved vigorously to take its
place in the new towns, it maintained a loyalty to the doctrine,
discipline and worship of the Church that presented its true light
to people who had not known it before. Remarking the state of
affairs to the Council of 1869, the Bishop said:

> The tendencies are all in the direction of a sound and vigorous
> churchmanship, for which, with the unity in doctrine, uni-
> formity in practice and peace and quietness that prevail within
> our borders to a remarkable degree, we have abundant reason
> to thank God and take courage.

Speaking of the conflicts and divisions that had arisen elsewhere
in the Church, he went on:

> The extremes of departure from the standard of primitive
> Catholic truth have brought in a flood of error, which we will
> have to combat with increasing steadfastness to the end.[28]

This approach took time to show results. People had to learn

---

[25]*Handbook of Texas*, "Houston & Texas Central R.R.," *en. loc.*

[26]*Handbook of Texas*, "Houston Tap & Brazoria," *en. loc.*

[27]See my article on Bishop Gregg, *Historical Magazine*, XXVIII (1959), pp. 317-
319, for his strategy.

[28]*Texas Journal*, 1869, p. 26.

the "system of the Church," in its orderly round of observances
and thorough coverage of biblical and creedal teaching throughout
the year. Gregg declared that where the Church's system was well
administered over a period of time its true influence upon the lives
began to appear. Additional people were attracted to the Church
by its habitual way of life, not by sensational appeals.[29] To ad-
minister this system well, the parson had to instruct the people in

> the services and life and holy work of the Church—the living,
> mystical body of Christ—the only sure foundation for indi-
> vidual and collective growth "in Him who is the Head, even
> Christ, from whom the whole body, fitly framed and joined to-
> gether and compacted by that which every joint supplieth, ac-
> cording to the effectual working in the measure of every part,
> maketh increase of the body unto the edifying of itself in love."[30]

Evidently the clergy, in such opportunities as they had, were
so doing in those days. The Bishop praised the emphasis on catechizing and upon the use of Prayer Book worship in the Sunday
Schools; he invariably visited the schools in every congregation.[31]

The Bishop was not uncritical of parsons and congregations.
He rebuked them when he felt rebuke was needed. He deplored
the lack of hearty responses in services, and connected it with such
habits as failure to kneel for prayers, to remove gloves when receiving Holy Communion, and with general abandonment of what he
called "the old paths." He voiced his conviction that church music
was in need of a thorough reformation; when the music dragged, the
service became doleful. He urged the use of the Gregorian chant,
which he felt appropriate to the note of joy which the service should
maintain.[32] As distasteful as the dragging of chants and hymns by
the congregation was the choir's use of music too complicated for
the people to sing. Ever and again he encouraged the use of plain
song as most practical and appropriate.[33]

A stratagem used before the war was employed again after its
conclusion; the annual meetings of the Diocese were shifted around
to various towns, including many in which the Church had only
recently begun work. Local congregations thus gained a wider vision
of the nature of the Church, whose standing was enhanced amongst

---

[29]*Ibid.*, 1872, p. 23.

[30]*Ibid.*, p. 33; Ephesians 4:15b-16.

[31]*Texas Journal*, 1867, p. 23; 1873, pp. 53-4.

[32]*Ibid.*, 1867, p. 28.

[33]*Ibid.*, 1871, p. 35. There is an entry in the Bishop's manuscript Journal, on
one Saturday when he was in Clarksville on visitation, "Practiced with choir."

the people of those towns. Although the Convention of 1866 met,
as had all the war-time ones, in Christ Church, Houston, subsequent
meetings were held in Brenham, Austin, Galveston, Bryan, Navasota, Austin again, Waco and Jefferson, in that order from 1867
through 1874. To emphasize the spiritual character and dignity of
these meetings the name "Diocesan Council" instead of "Convention" was proposed in 1868 by the Reverend B. A. Rogers of Austin,
and adopted by the Diocese in 1869.[34] This move coincided with a
concerted effort to use "General Council" to replace "The General
Convention" as the name of the triennial meeting of the entire
Protestant Episcopal Church;[35] the Church in the Confederate States
thus had named its triennial meetings.

Fortunately the recourse of the Diocese to this name for its
annual official meetings did not re-introduce the confusion occasioned by the action of the 1863 meeting, which not only voted to
call itself "The Council of the Diocese of Texas" but confounded
future historians by abandoning the past sequence of numbers by
designating itself "The First Annual Council"; this new numbering
continued through 1865.[36] The 1869 *Journal* was marked as that
of the "Twentieth Annual Council," preserving the proper number
sequence.

After the war the annual meetings came to be attended more
faithfully by lay delegates, and much more regularly than in former
years by the clergy. Better attendance was due in part to improved
transportation, including the issuance of free passes on at least one
occasion by the railroads,[37] and a large factor must have been the
closer contact which the Bishop was able to keep with his clergy
after the war. He not only found it possible to visit them more often
and for longer periods of time; he brought them to know one another
by frequently calling several together in one of the places where
he was making a visitation of several days' duration, or by taking
two or three along with him as he visited the towns in the part
of the State in which they were working. With this objective in mind,
Gregg did not attempt to make the city of his residence into a See
city, or to centralize his work in a cathedral as some American
bishops were beginning to do. Many of the ordinations he performed
within the charge of the ordinand, or at some point nearby where a

[34] *Texas Journal*, 1868, p. 14; 1869, pp. 7-9.
[35] *General Convention Journal*, 1868, 1871, 1874, *passim.*
[36] 1863 was the 14th, 1864 the 15th, 1865 the 16th annual meeting.
[37] *Texas Journal*, 1874, p. 35.

sufficient number of Presbyters could be gathered to examine the candidates and assist in the service; other ordinations were held at the Annual Councils.[38] These gatherings of clergy and widespread ministrations of ordination made clergy and lay people from different localities well known to one another, and doubtless added to their joy in attending the annual gatherings of the Diocese.

Another device the Bishop used as a means for securing high morale and unity among the clergy was his custom to choose as his assistant and travelling companion for an entire visitation a new missionary clergyman, quite often a new Deacon. He waited to assign the man to a field until the visitation was ended. Such men received excellent training, had a great opportunity to learn the mind and method of their Bishop, met something like half of the membership of the Diocese, and observed the unanimity with which Texas Episcopalians welcomed the ministrations of their Bishop and revered and followed him. Gregg, a man of unfailing modesty, would not have taken thought for the last of these opportunities.

The idea of a cathedral system was broached in Texas, and a committee to study it was appointed at the 1873 Council,[39] but in its lengthy report to the next year's Council the committee, while extolling its virtues, recommended against its adoption in Texas because of the vast territorial spread and the scattered nature of the work.[40]

Another development of great assistance in holding the interest and strengthening the work of the people of the Diocese was the foundation of a monthly publication, authorized by the Council of 1872 with the provision that the project should be self-sustaining. To assist the Bishop in editing and producing it, the Reverend S. M. Bird and Mr. George E. Mann of Galveston were appointed, and, later in the session, the Reverend W. W. Patrick and Mr. George W. Jackson.[41] The paper, named *The Diocese of Texas,* was published in Galveston beginning with the issue of January, 1873, at a subscription price of $1.00 per year.[42] It carried a schedule of the Bishop's visitations, news notes from around the Diocese, editorials, and articles designed to teach the members of the Church about the nature and ways of the Episcopal Church. It ran almost continuously until 1875, missing a few issues in 1873 and 1874 because of lack of

[38]See *Texas Journal* for all these years.　[39]*Texas Journal,* 1873, p. 24.
[40]*Ibid.,* 1874, "Appendix B," pp. 98-105.　[41]*Ibid.,* 1872, pp. 9, 10, 18.
[42]A prospectus, also designated Vol. I, No. 1, was issued in Oct., 1872.

funds. It is a valuable source for the history of the Diocese in these years.[43]

The vigorous educational, missionary and pastoral work of the Texas Church in the decade following the Civil War came at an opportune time and produced results. Bishop Gregg assured the Council of 1871 that the feeling toward the Church from without was improving. The Vatican Council had declared the Pope to be infallible, and the cause of the Roman Catholic Church with thinking people was hurt. Sectarian strife raged on the other hand. Both these manifestations, the Bishop asserted, made clear "the true catholicity of the Church's middle ground." The task, he thought, was to educate, but never to denounce others.[44]

Through these methods of propagation, the Church grew enormously in Texas. An article in the diocesan paper quoted an unnamed source's figures on the growth of the Episcopal Church in Texas in the decade 1861-1871. While the Church had grown nationally by 38% in this period, its greatest rate of growth had been in Texas, from 700 to 2000—300%—"a rate of increase," the source was quoted as saying, "greater than that of any other denomination in the State." The source ascribed this amazing increase to the immigration of Episcopalians to the State, an assertion that article disproved. First, he claimed, there were no reliable statistics to determine the religious affiliations of those coming into the State; second, while refugees from the other Southern States during the war had included a few communicants, most of these had returned to their own homes and did not count in the figures; third, since the war immigrants, who had poured mainly into North Texas, came mostly from regions of the country in which the Episcopal Church was not well known, and included, as a known fact, many more members of other bodies than Episcopalians. Other bodies had made greater gains in those regions of the State most heavily settled from abroad than had the Episcopalian Church. Not over 25% of the gain of the Episcopal Church, the writer in the diocesan paper believed, came from immigration. Rather, he was convinced, the Church's increase resulted from full-time Episcopal supervision, which

[43]A file, not nearly complete, is in my custody as Registrar of the Diocese. It came into the collection when discovered in the attic of the old Crocket home in San Augustine by the Rev. Charles A. Sumners, then Archdeacon of the Diocese, after the death of the Rev. George Crocket.

[44]*Texas Journal*, 1871, pp. 32-4.

began only a year before the period under consideration and provided frequent opportunities for confirmation.[45]

In the next year the diocesan paper, quoting the *Church Journal
and Messenger,* gave figures which revealed that the Diocese of
Texas had shown the greatest rate of growth of any of the organized
dioceses, outstripped only by some of the new western missionary
jurisdictions;[46] most of the latter had started during the decade from
virtually nothing, so that small absolute increases would show an
amazing percentage growth. The growth of the Diocese of Texas in
the period 1859-1874, on the eve of the division of its territory,
is reflected not only in the increase in communicant strength but
in the number of congregations. In 1859 there were 24 Parishes,
with a few outstations, cared for by 13 clergy. In 1874 there were
40 Parishes in union with the Diocese (a few were only technically
Parishes), and there were 30 missionary stations where active work
was being carried on; clergy numbered 33.[47] But despite this success,
Gregg was distressed that so much needed to be done beyond present
achievement.[48] Opportunities were being lost because the work was
too great for one bishop to perform; more episcopal supervision
must be secured somehow. A division of the Diocese, long sought
and not easily achieved, provided the solution to this problem.

XIV.　The Campaign to Divide the Diocese

THE NEED for additional episcopal supervision had been per-
ceived as early as 1868. At the Diocesan Convention of that year
the Reverend B. A. Rogers offered a resolution to memorialize General Convention to take legislative action that would make possible
an easier method of dividing dioceses, and to authorize some provincial system in order to preserve unity of purpose, action, and
fellowship between the parent diocese and its offspring. This resolu-

---

[45]"X," writing in the *Diocese of Texas,* Feb., 1873, p. 5.
Total confirmations by years, for the decade are:

1865-6	96	1870-71	240
1866-7	255	1871-72	271
1867-8	271	1872-73	256
1868-9	239	1873-74	291
1869-70	302		

[46]*Diocese of Texas,* Apr., 1874, p. 2.
[47]*General Convention Journal,* 1874, p. 471; *Texas Journal,* 1874, p. 4.
[48]*Texas Journal,* 1869, p. 16; 1874, pp. 56-7.

tion had the wholehearted support of Bishop Gregg, and was adopted unanimously by the Diocesan Convention.[1]

Memorials to change the Constitution and Canons of the Church, to reduce the restrictive conditions under which a diocese could be divided, were presented to the General Convention of 1868 by the Dioceses of Tennessee, Illinois, and North Carolina.[2] These moves resulted in a proposed amendment to the Constitution reducing from forty-five to six the number of parishes that would be in the new diocese, and from thirty-five to six the number of clergy resident for at least a year and eligible to vote in the election of a bishop. Texas evidently took no part in this action, for the remaining condition that "suitable provision must be made for the support of the Episcopate in the contemplated new Diocese"[3] would prove unworkable in so thinly populated and poor a diocese as Texas. A resolution which might meet the needs of Texas was introduced by the Reverend Alfred A. Watson of North Carolina; it

> Resolved, That it be referred to the Committee on Canons to inquire into the expediency of establishing Missionary Organizations under the charge of Missionary Bishops, within the limits of any organized Diocese or Dioceses when request to that effect is made by the Ecclesiastical authority of such Diocese or Dioceses.

Introduced on the tenth day of the session, this subject was not reported by the Committee on Canons until the nineteenth day, and the recommendation that it lie over until the next Convention adopted by the House.[4] Since no memorial was presented from Texas, it seems reasonable to conclude that the Bishop and his delegation decided to let other jurisdictions desiring division pave the way by their memorials. No remedy was made available to Texas until the next General Convention.

In his 1869 Council Address, Gregg began laying the groundwork for a request to the next General Convention to reduce the Diocese's territory. Citing the fact that the Bishop had to do the missionary work in most places outside the organized congregations, Gregg asserted that the growth and wider spread of the population was making it increasingly impossible for him to keep up with this

[1]*Texas Journal*, 1858, pp. 8, 13. The provincial system was provided for in the Constitution of the Confederate Church.

[2]*General Convention Journal*, 1868, Appendix, IV-4-5-6, pp. 394-411.

[3]*Ibid.*, 1868, pp. 405, 411, 213. This amendment was finally adopted by the 1871 General Convention. *Ibid.*, 1871, pp. 242, 381.

[4]*Ibid.*, 1868, pp. 72, 157.

work. He proposed, therefore, that General Convention be asked to reduce the area of the Diocese, and make the territory taken away from it into missionary jurisdictions to be cared for by a missionary bishop. Making reference to the North Carolina resolution introduced at the last General Convention, he promised that the same solution would be pressed for in 1871.[5]

The special committee which considered this proposal in the Bishop's address brought back a report containing three resolutions. The first asked the Council to

> put on record its thankfulness to Almighty God for his loving-kindness and mercy, in preserving so long the health and strength of our beloved Bishop, in the faithful performance of the arduous duties of the Episcopate in this Diocese, duties as few men have ever undertaken or could perform.

The second resolution, after recognizing the unwillingness with which any portion of the Diocese would part with Bishop Gregg's ministrations, asked the Council to concur in his wishes, in order to bring some relief to him personally, and to secure "more Episcopal work within our limits." The third resolution approved the plan to petition for the erection of one or more missionary jurisdictions in territory to be ceded by the Diocese. These resolutions were adopted unanimously by the Council.[6]

The Diocese attempted to prepare the ground for the renewal of its plea to the forthcoming General Convention. The Council adopted the report of a committee of seven which resolved to confront General Convention with a definite proposition. The boundaries of the diocese were to be moved eastward to the Colorado River and its North Fork to 32° North, and everything westward of that line was to be made into the Missionary Jurisdiction of Western Texas as the responsibility of the Domestic Committee of the Board of Missions, under the supervision of a missionary bishop to be elected by General Convention. This proposal was adopted by the Council.[7]

A memorial incorporating this request was introduced into the House of Bishops by Gregg. Its language was similar to that of a memorial presented at the same time by the Bishop and Convention of California.[8] When referred to the Committee on Memorials, the proposal's constitutionality was questioned, but when the Committee

---

[5] *Texas Journal*, 1869, p. 16.
[6] *Ibid.*, p. 9. [7] *Ibid.*, 1871, pp. 9, 13-14.
[8] *General Convention Journal*, 1871, Ap. X, pp. 274, 602-4.

on Amendments to the Constitution studied it, they reported that
there was, in their opinion, nothing in Article V of the Constitution
to prevent the action.[9] This report never came to a vote. The House
of Deputies attempted to deal with the question by an amendment
to the Canons which set out a clumsy procedure. A diocese could
be temporarily divided and given either an assistant bishop elected
by the Diocese, or the assistance of a diocesan or missionary bishop
of another jurisdiction who would act as ordinary of the territory
temporarily set off from the Diocese so long as its diocesan consented.[10] The House of Bishops rejected this dubious measure, and
offered instead a simpler provision for the election of an assistant
bishop when, by reason of extent of territory, a diocese requested
one and received the consent of the General Convention.[11] Finally
adopted by both Houses, this canonical provision left the Diocese
of Texas under the necessity of finding a salary for an assistant
bishop. This arrangement would have been more feasible, since
current funds might be raised by assessing the entire undivided
Diocese, than would the raising of an endowment fund for the
Episcopate of a new diocese, which seemed to be required under the
amendment to Article V of the Constitution, finally passed at the
1871 General Convention.[12] The Canon allowing petition for permission to elect an assistant bishop was the only help immediately
offered to the Dioceses of Texas and California in their efforts to
relieve their over-burdened Bishops, and both Dioceses "took out
insurance" by asking for and receiving that permission.[13]

At the same time another amendment was proposed to Article
V of the Constitution, providing that the General Convention could

> upon the application of the Bishop and Convention of a
> Diocese setting forth that the territory of the Diocese is too
> large for due Episcopal supervision by the Bishop of such
> Diocese, set off a portion of such Diocesan territory, which shall
> thereupon be placed, within, or constitute a Missionary juris-
> diction, as the House of Bishops may determine.[14]

Adopted by the House of Deputies on October 25 and sent over to
the other House, it was received by the Bishops, but not reported
on by their Committee on Amendments to the Constitution.[15] Taking the ground that measures sent by the House of Deputies to the
House of Bishops had the force of law if not acted on by the Bishops

[9]*Ibid.*, pp. 281-2.   [10]*Ibid.*, pp. 81-2, 160.
[11]*Ibid.*, pp. 337, 342.   [12]*Ibid.*, pp. 164-7, 354.
[13]*Ibid.*, pp. 242, 381.   [14]*Ibid.*, p. 201.   [15]*Ibid.*, p. 278; 1874, p. 53.

within three days (as then provided in Article III of the Constitution), the Secretary of the House of Deputies circulated this proposed amendment to the various Dioceses, as required by Article IX, for final disposition at the next General Convention.[16]

Bishop Gregg and the Texas Deputies went home with the prospect—a forlorn one indeed in Reconstruction days in Texas— that should they improve sufficiently the financial affairs of the Diocese, they might elect an assistant bishop at the Council of 1872. No doubt a real effort was made to accomplish this objective, but when the Council met the Bishop had to tell its members that he thought the move inadvisable, and they agreed. The only remedy was to work for passage of the amendment to allow setting apart a missionary jurisdiction.[17]

The great growth of the work in Texas occasioned by the rapid settling of the northern part of the State threw a heavy extra burden of labor on the Bishop, and led to the realization that the scheme proposed by Texas at the 1871 General Convention was inadequate. Even if the territory west of the Colorado River were handed over to a missionary bishop, there would still be more work in the remaining territory of the Diocese than one bishop could do with thoroughness. Northern Texas was growing with great rapidity, and would continue to grow for some years as the railroads developed and opened rich wheat lands to markets.[18] Two new missionary jurisdictions would be needed. The Council of 1874 resolved to ask that two such jurisdictions be set up; the boundaries of the Diocese of Texas would be as follows: beginning at Matagorda Bay, at the Southwest corner of Matagorda County, thence northwesterly along the western lines of Matagorda, Wharton, Colorado, Fayette, Bastrop and Travis Counties to its point of contact with the Colorado River, thence up the middle of the river to the northwest corner of Lampasas County, thence northeasterly to the eastern boundary of the State, running along the northerly lines of Lampasas, Coryell, McLennan, Limestone, Freestone, Anderson, Smith, Gregg, Rusk, Harrison and Marion Counties, thence along the eastern boundary of the State of Texas southward to the Gulf of Mexico, thence along the coast to the point of beginning. This proposal, after full and free debate, was adopted by the Council.[19]

The Reverend Benjamin A. Rogers, Texas' spokesman for this

---

[16]*Ibid.*, p. 28.
[17]*Texas Journal*, 1872, pp. 8, 10.
[18]*Ibid.*, 1874, pp. 63-4.
[19]*Ibid.*, pp. 16-18. These are the present boundaries.

effort in the House of Deputies at the two previous Conventions, opened the campaign with a resolution declaring that since the amendment to Article V of the Constitution, proposed at the last Convention, had been distributed for consideration to the several dioceses, it should be declared agreed to and ratified.[20] His proposal ran a complicated and discouraging parliamentary course. The Committee on Amendments to the Constitution reported that, in its judgment, the amendment should not have been circulated to the dioceses, because the House of Bishops had adjourned before there elapsed the requisite three days for concurrence or non-concurrence. The committee asked the Deputies to resolve that the amendment "fell to the ground" on this account. When finally brought to debate, the resolution was sent back to the same committee to study.[21] Eventually the committee came back with a startling disclosure. Nothing in the Constitution of the Church, they said, made any provisions for Missions. But the General Convention, under the Canons, could elect missionary bishops for any territory that was vacant. The Domestic and Foreign Missionary Society was legal agent of the General Convention to carry out its missionary task; as such, under the authority of General Convention which established its constitution, the Society might be directed to take over territory vacated by dioceses with the consent of General Convention; neither the Society nor the Convention might infringe upon the ground of a diocese without its consent. Since Texas by action of its Council had consented to vacate the areas in question, the General Convention could erect for them missionary jurisdictions and direct the Missionary Society to appropriate funds for their support. The House of Deputies adopted this report and sent it on to the House of Bishops, which concurred.[22]

Some still entertained grave doubts as to the constitutionality of this step, and the difficulties encountered by Texas and California had pointed out defects in the constitutional provisions for organizing new dioceses; therefore two amendments, designed to facilitate future divisions, were proposed to the dioceses for action at the next Convention. The first, identical with the amendment adopted by the Deputies in 1871, spelled out clearly the constitutional authority to take over as missionary ground territory ceded voluntarily by dioceses. The second made division of a diocese possible without

[20]*General Convention Journal*, 1874, p. 28.
[21]*Ibid.*, pp. 53, 82.   [22]*Ibid.*, pp. 89-90, 191.

MISSIONARY DISTRICT OF WESTERN TEXAS

PROPOSED DIVISION OF 1871

Parish +   Mission •

The proposed division of the Diocese, 1871

—From Murphy, *Episcopal Church in Texas*

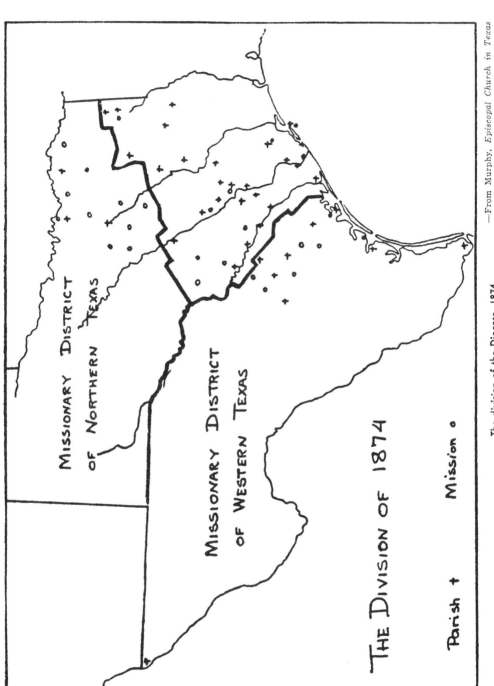

MISSIONARY DISTRICT OF NORTHERN TEXAS

MISSIONARY DISTRICT OF WESTERN TEXAS

THE DIVISION OF 1874

Parish +   Mission o

The division of the Diocese, 1874.

—From Murphy, *Episcopal Church in Texas*

the requirement of "suitable provision for the support of the Episcopate" in the new jurisdiction.[23]

Prior to this action the House of Bishops moved to define the new limits of the Diocese of Texas in accordance with diocesan wishes. The Bishops at first had refused to accept the opinion of the Deputies that action could be taken under the Constitution.[24] But in the later stages of the discussion, Bishop Gregg put a large map of Texas on the wall of the meeting chamber, and showed his brethren both the extent of the territory over which he was asked to travel, and how large would be his remaining Diocese should the two areas be detached. The doubters were convinced, and the measure passed.[25] The limits of the Diocese of Texas were reduced in accordance with the request, and the two new Missionary Jurisdictions, Western Texas and Northern Texas, were designated.[26] For the Missionary Bishopric of Western Texas the Bishops elected the Reverend Robert Woodward Barnwell Elliott, Rector of St. Philip's Church, Atlanta, Georgia, and for that of Northern Texas was chosen the Reverend Alexander Garrett, D.D., Dean of Trinity Cathedral, Omaha, Nebraska. In these choices the House of Deputies concurred.[27] Thus was won the long struggle to secure additional episcopal supervision over the vast territory of Texas. All three Texas bishops, in their respective territories, could give more time and attention to the individual congregations for which they bore responsibility.

The division had been made necessary by the very great success of the work of the Diocese of Texas since Gregg had entered upon the work of Bishop. Particularly in the years since the war the Church in Texas had grown and prospered, especially amidst people in towns where the clergy were at work, or where small groups of people did the best they could with their Sunday Schools and services conducted by layreaders between the annual visits of the Bishop. The careers of these several flocks are the subjects of the following chapters; first, those in parts of the Diocese which became new jurisdictions, and then those which remained in the mother Diocese.

[23]*Ibid.,* pp. 106, 101-2, 156.
[24]*Ibid.,* pp. 113-4.
[25]W. Gregg, *Gregg,* pp. 121-2.
[26]*General Convention Journal,* 1874, pp. 290, 299, 308-9, 312.
[27]*Ibid.,* pp. 319, 350.

PART FIVE

PLACES, PEOPLE AND
THEIR PARSONS,
1865-1874

XV. Western Texas

THE PORTION of the Diocese which was first considered for separation as a missionary jurisdiction was Western Texas. The development of parishes and missions proceeded more favorably in that part of the State than in the North. San Antonio was the natural base from which to expand the Church's work westward and southward.

SAN ANTONIO

San Antonio must have appeared to have a great potential for growth and importance when Bishop Gregg moved his family there at the close of the war. Since St. Mark's Parish was without a rector, he fulfilled the duties of that office until the arrival of the Reverend Mr. Nicholson in the Fall of 1865. That clergyman's tragic death in the cholera epidemic was related in an earlier chapter. Many deaths in successive outbreaks of the disease in San Antonio dimmed the prospects of the town, as well as of the Church and its schools.

Nicholson was succeeded by the Reverend Edwin A. Wagner shortly after his return to the Diocese. That diligent Priest set to work with a will to bring the Parish and St. Mary's School into good condition. The Parish lacked a building of their own in which to conduct services; their church, begun with such high hopes during the rectorship of L. H. Jones, was a partial enclosure of unfinished walls, often mistaken by strangers for an old Spanish ruin.[1] Harriet Brown Moore found in the minutes of the Dorcas Society, the ladies' organization of St. Mark's Parish, the records of Wagner's exhortation and encouragement to these ladies to persist in efforts to raise funds to carry forward the erection of the church. So well did they succeed that the vestry authorized Wagner to employ Major T. A. Washington to superintend construction work which was now resumed. Stone by stone the beautiful design of Richard Upjohn grew toward its intended shape.[2] With the Bishop in town, and a vigorous rector in charge, the Parish accelerated its rate of growth. On March 17, 1867, Gregg recorded that thirty-two people had been confirmed for the congregation within the year.[3] In January 1868, Wagner resigned the rectorship to become general missionary in the eastern part of the Diocese, with his residence in Marshall.[4] This move was made necessary by the failure of St. Mary's School, into which Wagner had poured his own money.[5] The mortgage given Wagner on Wolfe Hall was redeemed by St. Mark's Parish in purchase of the building; St. Mark's paid a considerable amount in cash and raised the balance through a mortgage given the Widows' and Orphans' Fund of the Diocese. The debt owed to Wagner was apparently satisfied but how deeply the Bishop himself was involved in loss does not appear.[6] Meanwhile the budget put at the Bishop's disposal by the Domestic Committee enabled him to grant a stipend to Wagner to do advance work in East Texas; Wagner was thus on hand to cover the vacancy at Marshall and Jefferson when Davenport moved from Marshall to Dallas.[7]

Upon Wagner's departure from San Antonio, Gregg again took temporary charge of the Parish; but only until June. At that time the rectorship was accepted by the Reverend Walter R. Richardson,

[1]Harriet Brown Moore, *St. Mark's Church, San Antonio: A Parish with a Personality* (San Antonio, 1944), p. 7.

[2]Moore, *op. cit.*, pp. 8-9: See also May E. Pumphrey, "History of St. Mark's Church," *St. Mark's Church, A.D. 1873, The Year Book of St. Mark's Episcopal Church* (San Antonio, 1933), p. 14.

[3]*Texas Journal*, 1867, p. 20.   [4]*Ibid.*, 1868, pp. 19, 25.

[5]Moore, *op. cit.*, p. 10. It would be interesting to know how Wagner had succeeded in salvaging any of his resources through his sojourn in war-torn South Carolina in the midst of the Civil War, and in what form he was able to bring them to Texas.

[6]Gregg, manuscript Journal, 25 Mar. 1870.

[7]Minutes, Domestic Committee, Minutes Book, p. 43.

then missionary at Huntsville.[8] St. Mark's gained a pastor who was to care for its people until his retirement in 1906.[9] The upper floor of St. Mary's (Wolfe) Hall was fitted up for services by January 1869, and though the congregation had been weakened by the departure from San Antonio of several Church families, fresh energy was being displayed under the new Rector's leadership. An appeal to the Church at large through Church papers brought over $400 toward the construction of the church building.[10] The congregation gave as it was able, seeking to collect a sufficient fund to enable another start toward completion of the building; by Council time in 1870 around $650 had been received, and a generous member had contributed about $400 to refurnish the Chapel in Wolfe Hall. By late 1873 it was possible to resume work on the church with the hope of bringing it to completion, many pledges having been made for the purpose. Bishop Quintard of Tennessee visited the Parish on behalf of the University of the South's Endowment Fund campaign and contributed the stone cross which was placed on the East gable. Another gift of great sentimental value was the bell, cast from a cannon from the Alamo.[11] Gregg found it necessary in April 1874 to persuade the vestry not to proceed so rapidly as to incur debt on the building;[12] consequently its completion was delayed until after the division of the Diocese.[13] The great growth of the Parish began after the completion of this beautiful building, which became the Cathedral of the Missionary Jurisdiction under Bishop Elliott, and the strong point for the life and growth of that jurisdiction toward diocesan status in the years ahead.[14]

THE WESTERN EDGE

Westward from San Antonio only Army Chaplains ministered in the first years after the war, when the United States Army again manned the chain of forts which controlled the Plains Indians and guarded the stage routes. Amongst these Chaplains were three Episcopalians, Elijah Guion, D.D., D. Eglinton Barr, and Norman Badger, all of whom reported their actions to the Council of the Diocese of Texas. Dr. Guion, after having "rendered good service"

[8] *Texas Journal*, 1868, p. 19; 1869, pp. 31, 32.
[9] Moore, *op. cit.*, pp. 23-30.
[10] *Texas Journal*, 1869, p. 32.
[11] *Ibid.*, 1870, pp. 28-9; 1874, pp. 84-5.
[12] *Ibid.*, p. 48.
[13] Moore, *op. cit.*, pp. 11-12.
[14] Brown, *West Texas*, Chs. I & II.

at the Church of the Advent, Brownsville,[15] ministered at Fort McKavitt to one part of the command to which he was attached, and to another part at Galveston. On his way from one point to another he held services at Columbus, which was vacant, and when in Galveston or San Antonio he assisted the rectors in their services.[16] Later transferred from his command to Indian Territory, Guion kept up his reports to the Diocese, and upon his transfer to San Antonio because of illness he again assisted the Rector of St. Mark's Parish in addition to his Army duties.[17] By 1874 he was at Fort Gibson, Indian Territory, doing what he could for the Church under adverse circumstances.[18]

Two reports of great interest were sent in by Chaplain Barr from his station at Fort Clark:

Chaplains' Report
Post Chaplaincy U.S.A., Fort Clark, Texas.

To the Rt. Rev. Alexander Gregg, D.D.:

In compliance with Canon XV, Sec. 1, I hereby respectfully submit a report of my services since I came to Fort Clark in June 1870.

In addition to the Divine Service for the troops, I have held a separate Divine Service every Lord's day for the families of the post and neighborhood. These services have been regularly maintained, sometimes in the open air, in a store house, in hospital tents, and more frequently, in places less convenient. The copies of the "Mission Service" kindly ordered for us by the Bishop of the Diocese, are in constant use, and exactly meet our wants.

Weekly Services, Good Friday, and Services introducing the duties of a Post Military School, three times a week. Holy Communion administered four times. Baptisms, children, 7; Sunday School children, white, 29, Mexicans 17—in all 46. I superintend and instruct the School every Sunday morning, using Beavens', and the Calvary Catechisms; Assistants 5—1 male and 4 female.

A gratifying result of these efforts is a growing respect for the Lord's day. At first we were annoyed by all the places of business being in full operation, and even by horse racing during the time devoted to Divine Service and Sunday School. Now these places are closed, and the horse racing is ended. Another gratifying fact is that this Missionary work has stood the most determined opposition of a Romish Priest, who claims nearly all the children, and publicly anathematized all who attend our Services or Sunday School, ordering them to return their Bibles, Catechisms, Scripture tickets, &c., but not one has

[15] *Texas Journal*, 1868, p. 22.   [16] *Ibid.*, 1870, p. 30.
[17] *Ibid.*, 1872, p. 74.   [18] *Ibid.*, 1874, p. 87.

been returned, and not one scholar lost. Besides striving for the education of the troops, as is my duty by law, I have devoted my leisure time to the education of the children. As there was no daily School in the neighborhood, I have succeeded, through the Superintendent of Education, in establishing one, under the charge of Mrs. Ballantyne, a member of the Church; and a suitable School house is soon to be erected.

I have the honor to be, very respectfully, your obedient servant,
                                        D. Eglinton Barr,
Fort Clark, Texas, May 10, 1871.   Chaplain U.S.A.[19]

FORT CLARK — POST CHAPLAINCY, U.S.A.

To the Rt. Rev. Alex. Gregg, D.D.:

I respectfully submit the following report of services rendered during the year:

Held service in the Chapel every Sunday, at 10 A.M., 3 P.M. and 6 P.M., also at Brackett's store, with Sunday School, at 1 P.M., and in the Hospital at 4 1-2 p.m.

The service appointed for the sick has been used with gratifying results. The number of pupils in the Sunday School has increased from five or six to fifty-eight. Much of my time during the week has been given to the teaching of a day school. I have succeeded in enlisting the co-operation of the Supervisor of Education for this District, who has procured a commodious room and appointed a teacher. This is chiefly for the benefit of the Mexican children. The school numbers 62.

I have baptized 9 persons, 6 adults and 3 children. Administered Holy Communion eight times in public and on four occasions to the sick and dying.

                      D. Eglinton Barr, Chaplain U.S.A.[20]
FORT CLARK, TEXAS, April 13, 1872.

Barr's outfit was transferred to Fort Davis, where he rendered such service that, upon his transfer in 1873 to Pennsylvania for the sake of his health, the officers and their families at the fort sent a testimonial letter to Gregg, extolling Barr for his effective and devoted work. His contribution at Fort Clark gave Bishop Elliott an anchor point for his work along the Rio Grande.[21]

Chaplain Badger, a Priest of the Diocese of Kentucky, reported to the Council of the Diocese of Texas in 1873 from Fort Concho (the present San Angelo), relating that he had taken an interest in the civilian population which had grown up around the fort. These people, mostly of Mexican blood, were neglected spiritually, and bore a bad reputation for lawbreaking and immorality. Badger's work among them bore fruit. He persuaded many couples who were

[19]*Ibid.*, 1871, pp. 49-50.   [20]*Ibid.*, 1872, p. 66.
[21]*Ibid.*, 1873, p. 43; *Diocese of Texas*, Apr. 1873, p. 5.

living together to allow him to conduct the rites of matrimony for them. He used Spanish or English for these services, as the occasion demanded. By his work the morals of the community improved[21a]

These three Chaplains labored as best they could far out on frontier. They founded no civilian parishes, attended no Councils of the Diocese, and they took no active part in the corporate life of the Diocese. Gregg was unable to take time from his grueling schedule of visitations in the settled parts of the Diocese to confirm their candidates and give them the encouragement of his presence. Yet they upheld the banner of the Church and gave help to those they reached.

The first organized congregation in far West Texas was founded by one of the real heroes of the Texas Church, whose earlier work in the Diocese will be noticed below. The Reverend Joseph Wilkins Tays reported by letter to the Council of 1871 that he had left his last position as Chaplain of the Texas Senate and gone to El Paso, reaching there on October 2, 1870. He began conducting services at once; no other services were being held by any group of Christians when he arrived, and his were well attended, even by Mexican people. St. Clement's Parish was organized on Christmas, 1870, and he was elected Rector. He also officiated at nearby Fort Bliss, with good response. Years later Tays related to Bishop Elliott that he had been persuaded to move to El Paso by a District Judge and other residents whom he had met in Austin, and that he derived part of his income from his appointment as Superintendent of Schools. He also acted as a land surveyor, and accepted parcels of land in payment for his services; these lands later brought him a measure of wealth, most of which he gave to the Church.[22]

St. Clement's Church was admitted to membership in the Council on June 1, 1871,[23] and continued to function during the rest of the period preceding the division of the Diocese. Tays' hopes for the town proved premature, for it languished until the railroads reached it;[24] but his hopes for the Church were amply justified. The strategic place the Church came to occupy by its early and strong beginning in that distant town proved what the Church can do on the frontier when it came first and was ably led.

[21a] *Texas Journal,* 1874, p. 77.
[22] *Ibid.,* 1871, pp. 41-2; *Spirit of Missions,* 1885, pp. 353-5.
[23] *Texas Journal,* 1871, p. 8.
[24] *Ibid.,* 1872, p. 65; also my "Beginnings of the Episcopal Church in Western Texas," *Yearbook of the West Texas Historical Society,* 1962, pp. 19-36.

THE EASTERN AND NORTHERN EDGES

Closer in and east of San Antonio, in that portion of the Diocese which was to pass to West Texas, the work at Seguin languished during the war. The Reverend H. G. Monges, Deacon, was stationed there following his return from the Confederate Army. Because of impaired health, Monges removed to Bellville in Austin County, leaving the veteran R. H. Ranney to tend the people at Seguin.[25] In February 1868 Gregg presided at a meeting to reorganize the congregation, and, in response to the interest shown, he promised every effort to secure a clergyman for the flock.[26] Not until 1871 could the promise be fulfilled; the Reverend Robert Carley, Deacon from the Diocese of Missouri, was appointed to reside and be in charge at Seguin, giving one Sunday a month to Gonzales. The congregation, heretofore without a building of their own, purchased "a substantial two-storied building," and arranged the upper floor as a chapel.[27] Carley, an Irishman by birth and an honors graduate of Trinity, Dublin,[28] proved to be just the man for the place. Bishop Gregg reported that "Mr. Carley has endeared himself here," had all things going very well, and was diligently instructing the people in "the distinctive principles" of the faith of this Church.[29] Ordained to the Priesthood in May 1872, Carley died suddenly on the following August 5, in the thirty-eighth year of his life; he was mourned by the entire Diocese as well as by the people of Seguin.[30] After several months' vacancy, the rectorship was filled by the Reverend J. T. Hutcheson from the Matagorda County field. By April 1874 the Bishop found on his visitation that "the Rev. Mr. Hutcheson has won the confidence of his people." Plans were being made to erect a church building, which was completed after the division of the Diocese. The foundations of strong and stable Church life which Dunn and Jones laid long before were not lost, but built upon, to make this congregation one of the points of strength for Western Texas. Carley and Hutcheson ministered to the settlements of Lavernia, near Seguin, as well as at Sutherland Springs.[31]

Emmanuel Church, Lockhart, had declined considerably by the end of the war. Only six communicants were reported in 1866, and no report was sent in the following year.[32] Although the Bishop

25 *Texas Journal*, 1866, pp. 5, 18; 1867, pp. 3, 32.   26 *Ibid.*, 1868, p. 19.
27 *Ibid.*, 1871, pp. 25, 29.   28 *Ibid.*, 1873, p. 27.
29 *Ibid.*, 1872, p. 33.   30 *Ibid.*, 1873, pp. 10, 20, 27.
31 *Ibid.*, 1874, p. 48; Brown, *West Texas*, Ch. I.; *Texas Journal*, 1872, p. 34.
32 Statistical Tables, *Texas Journal*, 1866, p. 67.

had included the town on his visitations for these two years, it was not until 1868 that his diary entry sounded the note of encouragement. The church building, so out of condition that it had been unusable, was being repaired, and would soon be ready for services. This show of interest meant that the parish was beginning to come to life again.[33] The following year services were held in the restored church. The Bishop was so stirred by the signs of renewed zeal that he laid aside his manuscript and made an ex tempore talk at the Communion Service, and the following day he called all around the parish.[34] With the coming of Carley to Seguin, the Bishop arranged for him to give Lockhart an occasional service, which seemed the best that could be done at the time.[35] Under that capable young clergyman the life of the parish quickened its pace, in spite of the infrequency of the services. Layreading was conducted on the intervening Sundays, E. Heppenstall being licensed by the Bishop for the purpose. After Carley's death lay services were continued. In 1874, the Bishop arranged for the Reverend R. J. Swancoat of Austin to conduct monthly services for the Parish.[36]

Gonzales, the other point on the old mission field founded by J. W. Dunn, was also prostrate by 1865; without a clergyman in the field, it seemed vain to hope that the people's desire to erect a church could be fulfilled.[37] By 1870, the expectation was that a building would be put up if there was a good crop.[38] When Carley took charge, the congregation arranged to get the exclusive use of a hall for Church services. The prosperity of the congregation, along with that of the town, lagged until it was reached by the railroad.[39] The development of strength in this Parish took place after Gregg handed it over to the new Missionary Bishop.

Other points in this general area at which Gregg held services on his visitation were Prairie Lea, Sutherland Springs, and Concrete; but in none of them were organized congregations formed. Farther south from Gonzales the Church people in the town of Clinton, De Witt County, showed interest. The number of Church people grew, but no minister could be secured, and it did not seem possible

[33]*Ibid.*, 1868, p. 19.

[34]Gregg, manuscript Journal, 15-17 March 1870. It was this kind of extemporate talk, to which the Bishop usually referred as "an address" in his manuscript Journal, which so greatly endeared him to his hearers. Letters in the *Spirit of Missions* and the *Diocese of Texas* at time refer to these talks, and express the sorrow the people felt at the Bishop's departure when he had thus intimately addressed the congregation.

[35]*Texas Journal*, 1871, p. 24.   [36]*Ibid.*, 1872, pp. 32, 38, 39; 1874, p. 47.

[37]*Ibid.*, 1867, p. 21.   [38]Gregg, manuscript Journal, 30-31 Mar. 1870.

[39]*Texas Journal*, 1872, p. 34; 1873, p. 39.

to organize a parish. By 1872, the Bishop was able to appoint Mr. H. C. Pleasants, "a very worthy gentleman," as layreader, and the life of the Church quickened.[40] Meanwhile the railroad being built from Indianola by-passed the town, making its terminus in the new town of Cuero, three miles away. A move was under way to transfer the county seat to Cuero from Clinton, since the new town seemed destined to draw Clinton's population to its advantageous location. Services were begun in a warehouse and were apparently attended by the Clinton Episcopalians. When Gregg visited Cuero in 1873, an effort was under way to buy lots for a church building.[41] In the next year the congregations were officially consolidated with the intention of organizing a parish. With the permission of the Bishop, the church building in Lavaca, where the town and the Parish were in a state of collapse due to the removal of the railroad, was moved to Cuero and readied for use. The Bishop was seeking a missionary to appoint to the field.[42] Grace Church, Cuero, was ready to contribute to the life of the new Missionary Jurisdiction.

Below Cuero, a trio of congregations in Calhoun County had a life of interest and vigor in this decade. With the end of the war and of the naval blockade, commerce returned to its natural channels. Freight entered the ports of Indianola and Lavaca for shipment inland as far as San Antonio, for the railroads had not penetrated the interior. By 1867, Gregg had organized a parish at Indianola under the name of "Church of the Ascension." The ladies worked hard to raise a building fund almost large enough to insure the erection of a church; only a little help was needed from the older congregations of the Diocese. The Reverend J. W. Tays was transferred from Columbus and Richmond to take charge of this congregation. The Parish was admitted to the Diocesan Convention in 1867.[43]

A year later the work of Tays was showing results. Congregations were large and plans were advancing for the erection of the church building. When Tays arrived in Indianola he was the only Protestant Minister. There was an abandoned Methodist building, which he arranged to use for Church services. In accordance with the needs of the community, he began conducting a union Sunday School, but when a Presbyterian Minister arrived the use of the building

40Ibid., 1867, p. 21; Gregg, manuscript Journal, 3 Apr. 1870; Texas Journal, 1872, pp. 34, 39.
41Ibid., 1873, p. 40.   42Ibid., 1874, p. 49; for Lavaca, see below, pp. 164-5.
43Texas Journal, 1867, pp. 6, 21. The former organization as "St. John's" was apparently ignored.

was denied to the Episcopalians. They therefore built their own church, "the prettiest wooden church in Texas," as Tays wrote, in spite of its lack of windows, paint, and proper seating. In its unfinished state the building had cost $2600, of which all but $300 had been paid by the local congregation, who expected to pay the remainder shortly and within the year finish and furnish the building. "This, I think," Tays said, "is not doing badly for a handful of Episcopalians in a little frontier town in the country, having the reputation that Texas has abroad."[44]

Tays also officiated occasionally at Lavaca, where the congregation built up to the point that they re-organized the Parish on March 31, 1866, and later called as their Rector the Reverend Robert Jope of St. Andrew's Church, Bryan.[45] Tays was left more time for his work at Indianola and for the extension of the Church's work to other towns. He wrote

> The only drawback to unaccustomed people coming here are the occasional visits of yellow fever, but this only extends from fifty to one hundred miles inland, otherwise it is as healthy as the South of France, and if anything more beautiful. I have suffered here all that it is possible for a man to suffer, and now I would not exchange it for any missionary field in the United States.[46]

Tays had indeed suffered; shortly after his arrival in Indianola, his wife and infant child died in a yellow fever outbreak, and he was left with two children to rear. He married again a year later; Gregg performed the ceremony.[47] In 1869, Tays found it necessary to leave the coast on account of the health of his family, and he transferred to the Parish in Bryan. Jope then took over the work of both Parishes, apparently moving his residence to Indianola.[48]

Jope did well in Indianola in his first years there. The new church, which Gregg found nearly ready for consecration and described as "a large and comely edifice" upon his visit in March of 1869[49] was destroyed by a tornado in August. Jope proceeded immediately to the East, where he raised sufficient funds to rebuild it. A new rectory was built, and the Rector was working to secure funds to erect a parish school. Lavaca was shrinking in population,

[44]*Spirit of Missions,* 1869, p. 90.
[45]*Texas Journal,* 1867, p. 21; 1868, p. 23.
[46]*Spirit of Missions,* 1868, p. 19.
[47]Gregg, manuscript Journal, 7 May 1868. The bride's name in the Bishop's Journal is illegible.
[48]*Texas Journal,* 1869, pp. 27, 30; 1870, p. 4.
[49]*Ibid.,* 1869, p. 21.

but the congregation was carrying on with lay reading by Dr. E. L. Beaumont on Sundays when the Rector was not present.[50]

Indianola was something of a headquarters for Gregg for parts of each year in this period; he would sail from there to Corpus Christi (and on to Brownsville, the one year he was able to arrange for the trip). Some years he went up the bay to Trespalacios, Matagorda, and Caney, and returned to Indianola to take ship home for Galveston; also Victoria, Goliad and Cuero were all easily reached from Indianola. He became intimately acquainted with the people of this flock, and expressed in his Journal his thankfulness for the great service they were rendering in the town. Entries for each visit showed the great hopes he held for the continuation of the Parish's happy and useful career. The new church was consecrated on April 14, 1872.[51] But in the next year there seems to have been some disaffection between Jope and his Indianola congregation. The details are obscure and seem irrecoverable. Jope, like Tays, gained a bride in Indianola. On May 9, 1871, Gregg performed the marriage ceremony for him and Mary Teymus [?] L. Lee.[52] At the Council of 1873, the Bishop made an oral statement (which did not get into the minutes) about the differences between Jope and his congregation. A special committee appointed to consider the matter reported that the Council had no power to intervene, but they proposed a canon to cover such cases in the future. The Council refused to pass a motion that Jope be asked to resign in the interest of the harmony of the Church.[53] On February 12, 1874, the Standing Committee of the Diocese, finally securing full attendance for the purpose, examined all the papers concerning the case, and

> unanimously adjudged that the evidence of the temporary insanity of the accused was conclusive; and that the Committee did not think it for the good of the Church, or in accordance with justice, that he should be put upon his trial. . . . [54]

Hence Indianola and its Rector passed to the new Bishop of Western Texas unreconciled, and so remained until the hurricane of 1875 destroyed the rectory and drowned its occupants.[55]

Economic tragedy befell the Lavaca congregation during Jope's tenure. Gregg entered in his diary for Sunday, April 12, 1871:

50*Ibid.*, 1871, pp. 44, 45.   51*Ibid.*, 1872, p. 35.
52Gregg, manuscript Journal, 9 May 1871.
53*Texas Journal*, 1873, pp. 10, 15, 18.
54*Ibid.*, 1874, p. 24.   55Brown, *West Texas*, p. 8.

This town, with its trade all gone, and a large portion of its population removed, presents a sad picture of change and desolation, such as, within the compass of a year, has seldom been witnessed. The Parochial organization must soon cease to exist, though provision will be made, as far as possible, for those who may remain.[56]

What happened to bring this ruin about was explained by Bishop Elliott in his "Historical Sketch of the Church in Western Texas";

Port Lavaca [was] once the most thriving seaport, Galveston excepted, in Texas—with a great wagon trade that extended three and four hundred miles into the interior. A railway was constructed into the county above, but as Port Lavaca was the port of embarkation, while damaged, it was still conducting an admirable traffic. But it suffered at the hands of the railways—one day they took up the track to Lavaca, and laid it to Indianola. Merchants, lawyers, doctors, clergymen and trade hastened away—Port Lavaca was struck by paralysis.[57]

Although our Church did not abandon the remnant that remained in the town (Bishop Elliott asserted that all other religious bodies did do so), there were so few to attend services and so little money to maintain a building that Gregg thought it wise to move the structure at Lavaca to Cuero.[58]

Much happier, but equally interesting, is the story of the third congregation in the County, St. Paul's, Chocolate. During Tay's ministry in the area, he was the first minister of any sort to visit the little settlement on Chocolate Bayou. No schoolteacher was there, so Tays secured one who, being licensed by the Bishop as a layreader, conducted services every Sunday. The teacher, Nelson E. Carrington, made application to be a Candidate for Holy Orders and was accepted.[59] The Bishop visited on Good Friday and Easter Eve, 1869, and confirmed nine (the head of every house, Tays said). "The patriarch of the neighborhood, eighty-five years of age, with his two sons, their wives, and a granddaughter all [partook] together of their first communion."[60] Captain Sylvanus Hatch was the "patriarch." At Hatch's death in 1886, Elliott wrote that the man had fought in the Battle of New Orleans and won battlefield promotion from Andrew Jackson. Apparently he was also a veteran of the Texas Revolution.[61]

[56]*Texas Journal*, 1872, p. 35.
[57]*Spirit of Missions*, Aug. 1885, p. 412.   [58]See above, p. 162.
[59]*Texas Journal*, 1869, p. 30.   [60]*Ibid.*, p. 21.
[61]*Journal of the Missionary Jurisdiction of Western Texas*, 1886, p. 32.

The little flock immediately began to plan for a church building;
on his visitation a year later, Bishop Gregg found it completed
through the labors of Carrington and members of his flock, and
ready for consecration.[62] Carrington was ordained to the Diaconate
June 9, 1870, at St. Andrew's, Bryan. On his visitation to Chocolate
in 1871, the Bishop reported, "Mr. Carrington is doing well here,
and the little community is united in love and devotion to the
Church."[63] The following year Carrington moved to Victoria, giving
two Sundays a month to Chocolate, and Charles Brett, a member
of the flock, was licensed to read lay services on the other Sundays.[64]
By 1874, the Bishop reported that the congregation had outgrown
their little church and were making plans to enlarge it. The rift
between Jope and the other two Churches had no adverse influence
here. Brett as layreader was holding the congregation together; Carrington's connection with them, as with that at Victoria, apparently
ceased with his removal inland.[65] Though small, this congregation
was a bright jewel indeed in the crown of the Diocese.

At Victoria the work done earlier in the decade by the Reverend
W. R. Richardson languished for lack of a clergyman to carry
forward the growth. But the spark of interest was not dead, even
though the only services were those conducted by the Bishop on his
annual visitations. By 1867, the ladies had started a building fund,
and by 1869 had secured lots.[66] Trinity Church Parish, organized that
year, was admitted to the Diocese on May 28, 1869, with a Council
delegation consisting of Messrs. P. J. H. Allen, W. J. Neally, and
N. A. Thompson (none of whom succeeded in attending.)[67] John
H. Allen, Senior Warden, was licensed as layreader, and was Sunday
School Superintendent as well.[68] In 1871, after Carrington arrived,
a small church was erected in two and a half months, the minister
doing most of the labor himself.[69] By 1873, Carrington was no longer
connected with the Parish, and William H. Allen was licensed to
read lay services. In the following year the Bishop reported that
Carrington officiated "when in town."[70]

At Goliad, the other point at which Richardson had begun
his ministry, the congregation was dispersed by removals. Gregg,
visiting there in 1871 after an interval of eight years, found only

---

[62]Gregg, manuscript Journal, 8-9 Apr. 1870.
[63]*Texas Journal*, 1871, p. 26.
[64]*Ibid.*, 1872, pp. 34-5, 39.   [65]*Ibid.*, 1874, p. 49; 1873, p. 39.
[66]*Ibid.*, 1867, p. 21; 1869, p. 20.   [67]*Ibid.*, 1869, p. 7.
[68]*Ibid.*, 1870, p. 29. Was this the Col. J. H. Allen whom the Bishop had licensed
in 1866 for Lamar, Refugio Co.? *Ibid.*, 1866, p. 24.
[69]*Ibid.*, 1872, pp. 34-5.   [70]*Ibid.*, 1873, pp. 39, 43; 1874, p. 49.

two families of the original congregation, but he reported that other earnest members had been added. He expressed the intention to provide as soon as possible for their nurture. The town was included in the Spring visitations for the years remaining until the division of the Diocese, with confirmations every year. Although no formal organization was effected, the Bishop reported of his visit in 1874: "The attendance was quite large, and increased interest evinced. With a few earnest Church women here, the Church will not fail to grow as the town advances in population."[71]

At Corpus Christi, the hopeful beginning made during the sojourn of the Reverend S. D. Davenport was vitiated by the decay of the town due to the Federal blockade. The Bishop made no visit in 1866; undoubtedly because his plans to go to Brownsville from Indianola by water was frustrated by the uncertainty of getting return passage on a steamer. The following year he made the trip, accompanied by the Reverend John Owen of Matagorda, and found the situation encouraging. Fifteen people were confirmed on the visitation. Gregg marked out Corpus Christi as a place where a clergyman should be stationed, and hoped to have one by Fall.[72] The Bishop was able to realize this hope. The Reverend A. F. Dobb was sent during the Summer, but for some reason did not stay long.[73] In 1868, the Bishop was accompanied to Corpus Christi by the former Rector, S. D. Davenport, and the two remained several days. Nineteen people were confirmed on this visitation, and arrangements were made to maintain lay services until another clergyman could be found. The layreader appointed was R. J. Denny.[74] All was well at the Bishop's next visitation in March 1869, when he noted that the flock was doing well under layreading. Denny demonstrated his interest by attending the Annual Council in May 1869.[75]

Something must have gone radically wrong in the intervening months. The nature of the trouble Gregg did not note in his Journal, but his anxiety became apparent from the amount of time he devoted to his next visitation in the midst of a busy schedule, and from the general tenor of the entries he made. He reached Corpus Christi from Indianola on April 13, Wednesday in Holy

---

[71]*Ibid.*, 1871, p. 25; 1872, p. 34; 1873, p. 39; 1874, p. 49.

[72]*Ibid.*, 1867, p. 21.

[73]Mr. Dobb was received from Alabama in 1866, and had no cure within the Diocese that year. In 1867 he was Rector of St. Peter's Church, Brenham, apparently going from there to Corpus Christi. He was transferred to the Diocese of Kentucky in 1868. *Ibid.*, 1866, pp. 5, 25; 1867, p. 3; 1868, p. 25.

[74]*Ibid.*, 1868, pp. 22-3, 24.

[75]*Ibid.*, 1869, pp. 3, 21. Mr. Arthur H. Edey was licensed in 1869. *Ibid.*, p. 24.

Week, and stayed through Easter Monday; he called on all the members of the congregation, met with the ladies of the Dorcas Society, and, he said, "settled all matters." He then had a congregational meeting, at which a vestry was elected. His last entry for the visitation was "Thank God for his mercy in results for Parish."[76]

During the course of the next year, two lots were purchased for $800, leaving a balance in the building fund, and the vestry issued a call to a clergyman to become Rector of the Parish.[77] The Reverend William Brittain assumed the rectorship of the Church of the Good Shepherd on July 16, 1871, and when the Bishop visited in April 1872, Brittain had won the affections of the people. The church building was going up, largely due to the self-sacrificing Dorcas Society members.[78] But by May of the following year, the new Rector had resigned and gone to Alabama. The Bishop again presided over a vestry election, and encouraged those elected to take measures to get a minister and go forward with the church building.[79] By January 1874, the Reverend Nelson Ayres, from St. Andrew's Church, Bryan, became Rector and moved into a good new rectory. The prospects of the town were better, with the promise of a ship channel and of a railroad to Laredo; the future of the Parish at last seemed secure.[80]

Gregg made a visit in 1870 to nearby Rockport, where he confirmed several people, then called on a Captain Ives at his residence, confirmed him, and gave him Holy Communion, since he appeared too ill to attend the regular service. Perhaps the Captain was the brother of the revered first missionary to Texas, the Reverend Caleb S. Ives. The Bishop also performed baptisms and confirmations at Mr. Bailey's and at Judge Talbot's.[81] The following year the Bishop visited again, and promised a monthly service as soon as a rector should be found for Corpus Christi.[82] M. Talbot, layreader, reported for the mission at Rockport to the Diocesan Council of 1871. For 1872, Frederick A. Bailey was licensed as layreader,[83] and the Reverend William Brittain wrote the report to the Diocesan Council, announcing the erection of "a very comfortable chapel" and stating his belief that the Church was firmly rooted in the community.[84]

[76]Gregg, manuscript Journal, 13-18 Apr. 1870.

[77]Texas Journal, 1871, p. 26.

[78]Ibid., 1872, pp. 35, 63. Mr. Brittain came from the Diocese of Ohio to Corpus Christi. Ibid., p. 40.

[79]Ibid., 1873, pp. 43, 40.   [80]Ibid., 1874, pp. 3, 50, 76.

[81]Gregg, manuscript Journal, 20-21 Apr. 1870.

[82]Texas Journal, 1871, p. 26.

[83]Ibid., p. 47; 1872, p. 39.   [84]Ibid., p. 73.

In April 1873, Gregg made his annual visitation, and reported that though the town was suffering from diminution in population and decline in business, the Church's prospect was not much changed. Bailey filed a report to the Council for "Church of the Messiah, Rockport,"[85] but the congregation seems not to have been organized as a parish, nor to have been admitted to the Diocese as such. Gregg's last visit to Rockport as their diocesan bishop was made on April 29, 1874; he reported large congregations and "a most becoming demeanor," but stated that the town had declined more, though the membership of the Church remained steady. The former layreader, Bailey, had moved to the neighborhood of Corpus Christi,[86] and no one was licensed to take his place. Though the Reverend Nelson Ayres made a report for Good Shepherd, Corpus Christi, that year, there is no report for Rockport in the *Journal*.

The only other point in the Corpus Christi area which Gregg recorded having visited in the post-war decade was Long Mott, twelve miles from Corpus, at which he celebrated the Holy Communion on April 17, 1871. But no other information about the Church people there was supplied in the Bishop's address.[87]

The only congregation south of Corpus Christi before the division of the Diocese was the Church of the Advent in remote Brownsville. At the war's end, no one of our Bishops had visited there, since it was nearly inaccessible from the settled parts of the State except by water. The Brownsville congregation was not visited by either Bishop Freeman or Bishop Gregg through no fault of their own.[88]

The return of the Reverend Daniel Shaver to Brownsville has been related previously.[89] In his report to the 1866 Convention, he hopefully recorded "a well organized Vestry, composed of the best element and talent in the place," and good feeling in the town; the disrepair of the church building would be remedied, and a rectory built.[90] The frustration of the Bishop's plan to visit Shaver and his flock in 1866 no doubt disappointed them. The warm presence and assuring manner of Gregg might have induced Shaver to remain longer; he must have felt qualms about the Bishop's attitude toward him, even though Gregg welcomed him by letter and recognized

[85]*Ibid.*, 1873, p. 75.   [86]*Ibid.*, 1874, pp. 49-50.   [87]*Ibid.*, 1871, p. 26.

[88]For Freeman's efforts to fit the place into his plans, see above, p. 45. Also, for the Rev. Wm. Passmore's hair-raising adventures in going to the Convention of the Diocese in 1852, see above, pp. 69-70. Bishop Elliott found great difficulty in reaching the place, as did Bishop Johnston also, in his early days in West Texas. See my *West Texas*, Chs. I, II.

[89]See above, p. 109.   [90]*Texas Journal*, 1866, p. 31.

him as Rector of the Church.[91] The Bishop likewise was distressed
by his inability to get to Brownsville not only because of his sense
of duty toward Rector and Parish, but also because he wished "to
do something in regard to work being contemplated for our Church
in Mexico."[92] This visit had to wait another year, however, since no
steamship was making the voyage when the Bishop reached Indianola
with a reservation on a steamer line.[93] On April 19, 1868, Gregg
at length succeeded in reaching Brownsville, and stayed at least
through April 22. His report of this visit is interesting:

> This was my first visit to the parish of the Advent, after anxious
> but fruitless efforts to do so before. A glad welcome was ex-
> tended, increasing interest manifested as the visit progressed,
> and most gratifying results were attained. I met the Vestry on
> several occasions as to the future of the parish. A determined
> effort will be made, with God's blessing, to rebuild the church
> (destroyed by the tornado in October last) and erect a parsonage
> and parish school house, all on the same lots. In connection
> with Mexico, this point is one of the highest importance. The
> friends of the Church here and in Matamoros, are fully alive
> to it, and of one mind as to the only effective mode in which
> the work can be carried on. I have written to the Foreign Com-
> mittee, New York, on the subject proposing a plan of operation.
> With wisely directed effort, under God, we look, at no distant
> date, for the happiest results. The Rev. Mr. Guion, Chaplain
> in the United States Army, has rendered good service here, but be-
> fore my visit was called away with his regiment. He is the
> only clergyman, except Rev. Daniel Shaver (for some time resi-
> dent here), who has served the parish since the departure of
> the Rev. Wm. Passmore from the Diocese, in 1859, the first and
> devoted Rector who laid the foundation of the work.[94]

The Bishop proposed to the Foreign Committee that they join
with the Domestic Committee in the support of a clergyman, who
would minister both in Brownsville and in the adjacent town of
Matamoros, Mexico. The Brownsville vestry with Gregg's consent, called Dr. Guion, U. S. Army Chaplain, to be their Rector.
The Foreign Committee adopted this suggestion, and requested
the Domestic Committee to join them in the project. The latter
body agreed, and proposed that the two committees jointly raise
subscriptions for the purpose by an appeal in the *Spirit of Missions*
and by other means.[95] The money was not soon forthcoming and the

[91]See above, p. 109.   [92]*Texas Journal,* 1866, p. 22.
[93]*Ibid.,* 1867, p. 21.   [94]*Ibid.,* 1868, p. 22.
[95]Minutes of the Domestic Committee, 5 October 1868, Minutes Book, p. 55.
Gregg's letter to the Foreign Committee is in the Missionary Society archives.

proposal died aborning. Thereafter, Brownsville was not included in the statistical tables in the *Journals* of the Diocese, though the *Journals* of the Missionary Jurisdiction after 1875 show that the work had not entirely ceased.

Congregations at New Braunfels and San Marcos, founded before the division of the Diocese, fell within the West Texas jurisdiction. The Church blunted more than one spear upon the shield of the predominantly German town of New Braunfels,[96] but it had members there for whom Gregg conducted services on several occasions.[97] After a visit on March 20, 1867, Gregg arranged for the Reverend R. H. Ranney, formerly residing at Seguin, to begin holding services at New Braunfels. That veteran Priest organized a Sunday School and held regular services until June 1869, when, as he put it, "finding no encouragement, I was constrained to yield to circumstances." He moved to Galveston and officiated at the military post until the arrival of the regular Army Chaplain, Dr. Guion.[98] G. H. Judson later was licensed as layreader at New Braunfels, and evidently services were continued prior to the arrival from Mississippi of the Reverend Albert Lyon to take charge of the Mission.[99] Of his visitation in March 1872, Bishop Gregg wrote:

> Mr. Lyon, with improving health, is making vigorous efforts for the Church. The responses and general decorum here, the congregation consisting chiefly of young persons, were worthy of special commendation.[100]

Lyon reported in great enthusiasm to the Council that year. He found not one communicant outside his own family when he came. A generous Jew rented a good building to the Church at a nominal figure, and a decent chapel had been fitted out. Sunday School and Church were well attended, and there were twelve communicants. Lyon felt that a parish would soon be organized.[101] His report of the following year was far different. Eight communicants had left, and one ceased to communicate; two had been added, only one by confirmation. The rent on the chapel was too much for the diminished flock, who were worshipping in the home of the missionary. Speaking of himself, he said: "He is the third Missionary who has failed in the Anglo-German community. . ."[102] About September, Lyon moved to Galveston to take charge of Trinity Parish School and to assist the Rector in the new West End Mission and

<hr>

96See above, p. 122.
97*Texas Journal*, 1866, p. 18.   98*Ibid.*, 1870, p. 30.
99*Ibid.*, 1872, pp. 39, 40.   100*Ibid.*, p. 32.
101*Ibid.*, pp. 71-2.   102*Ibid.*, 1873, pp. 73-4.

Sunday School.[103] No further report appears from the New Braunfels mission before it became a part of Bishop Elliott's charge.

At San Marcos, Gregg conducted a service on July 16, 1865; he reported:

> . . . preached and administered communion, a large and attentive congregation being present. This was the first service of the Church ever held in this place, at least since my connection with the Diocese. . . .[104]

Nothing more was heard of the town in the records of the Diocese until 1874, when the Bishop stated in his Council Address that a parish had been organized under the ministrations of the Reverend Wallace Carnahan. Evidently for the sake of his health, Carnahan moved from Mississippi in December 1873, and very quickly made a good start in San Marcos.[105] Nothing is said concerning the building in which services were conducted, but it was evidently under Church control, for an organ, given by some members of Trinity Church, Galveston, was installed to enhance the services.[106] Since the minutes of the Council do not record the admission of San Marcos as a parish, probably no application was made, and the congregation, with its excellent missionary, passed to the new jurisdiction as a mission.

Mention of this infant congregation rounds out the roll of parishes and missions that formed the core of the Missionary Jurisdiction of Western Texas at the end of 1874. Nine parishes and nine missions, with seven clergymen, Gregg reckoned to hand over to his successor in this portion of the Diocese.[107]

XVI.   Northern Texas

THE SECOND AREA of Texas that would be erected into a missionary jurisdiction was Northern Texas. The strongest congregation in the Northern region was St. Matthew's Church, Dallas, and it became the natural center of the new jurisdiction. By 1874, the need for more intensive episcopal supervision in this area had become apparent, but growth came much later than did the ex-

103*The Diocese of Texas,* Sept. 1873, p. 8; *Texas Journal,* 1874, p. 78.
104*Ibid.,* 1866, p. 18; for service by Dunn, see above, p. 58.
105*Texas Journal,* 1874, pp. 47, 52, 85.
106*Diocese of Texas,* Apr. 1874, p. 6.
107*Texas Journal,* 1874, p. 64.

pansion of the Church in the area designated as Western Texas. At the beginning of 1866 there was not a congregation holding services, nor a clergyman, in all of that part of Northern Texas that was to pass to Bishop Garrett as the developed portion of the area comprising his missionary jurisdiction. Not even from Dallas, where the most hopeful beginnings had been made, was a report for 1866 sent to the Secretary of the Diocese.

DALLAS

But the Dallas congregation was the first to revive. After a short period of work in the Brazoria County field following his return to the Diocese of Texas in 1865,[1] the Reverend George Rottenstein returned to his first love, St. Matthew's, Dallas, on July 1, 1866. He began his work anew with hopefulness and vigor that belied his age, as his report to the 1867 Convention indicates:

> The Rector took charge of this Parish July 1, 1866, and has been regularly engaged in his work since that time, except while accompanying the Bishop, at his request, on his visitations. Our congregations are good, considering there has been no regular Church service here for years past. The children are catechized in the afternoon of the first Sunday of the month, and we are thankful . . . for effective teachers and willing children. We now hope to be able to build a church, for which suitable lots and $1000 are secured; and in the expectation of help from abroad we hope to accomplish this herculean task, even in our present state of poverty, and thereby secure the permanency of the Parish.[2]

Bishop Gregg was there on October 7-8, 1866, and was pleased with the prospects for the Church. But the aged Rottenstein's strength was not equal to the task. He died, probably where and as he wished, in Dallas at work, in February 1868.[3] Gregg paid him warm tribute in his Convention Address of 1868, and the Convention mourned his passing.[4] The Bishop had licensed John M. Crockett as layreader in 1867, and Crockett signed the Parochial Report for 1868 as senior warden.[5] In October 1868, Gregg requested the Domestic Committee to approve the transfer of the Reverend Silas D. Davenport from Marshall to Dallas; the request was granted. Visiting

[1]See below, pp. 193-4.

[2]*Texas Journal*, 1867, pp. 33-4.

[3]Beesley, *Episcopal Church in Northern Texas*, p. 28.

[4]For the tribute of Bishop Gregg, *Texas Journal*, 1868, p. 27; for the resolution of the Convention, *ibid.*, p. 9.

[5]*Ibid.*, 1867, p. 25.

Dallas in January 1869, the Bishop said, "Mr. Davenport has won the confidence and affection of the people."[6]

A year later Gregg arrived for a visitation of the congregation that extended from October 22 to 26. He confirmed ten people and laid the cornerstone of St. Matthew's Church.[7] The process of building was to be slow, however. Davenport said in his parochial report for 1869 that, with room rent to pay for their chapel, the poor parishioners must take their time about the costly business of building. A year later the church was not complete, having been delayed by the high rates charged for hauling materials.[8] In November, the Bishop, recording his visit to the parish, wrote:

> The parish is advancing. It has now the first of our church buildings in course of erection in Northern Texas. This is a humiliating reflection, but gives earnest, we trust, of a better day to come.[9]

In the following November, Gregg found the Parish flourishing. The long awaited railroads, the Texas Central from Houston and the Texas and Pacific from Marshall, were about to reach town. They not only would cause growth for the community and the Church, but also would make St. Matthew's "a strategic center of the Church's work."[10] An article in the *Diocese of Texas* rejoicing in the opening of the new church said that in the past five years the congregation moved from a blacksmith shop, through rented quarters, to "quite a neat little church."[11] The next few years of growth were to seem the day of small things for the future Cathedral, but much indeed was accomplished. Davenport reported 121 communicants for 1874, where Rottenstein had counted 18 in 1867.[12] The congregation that year relinquished their missionary appropriation, having attained self-support through the use of the weekly envelope system for offerings.[13] Though there were yet difficult times to be faced, Davenport and his lively congregation were to be the strong anchor-point for Bishop Garrett's work. The only other point in Dallas County mentioned in the record in this decade was Lancaster, where Gregg conducted a service in October 1866, on his

[6]Minutes, Domestic Committee, 5 Oct., 1868, Minutes Book, p. 54; *Texas Journal*, 1869, p. 19.

[7]Gregg, manuscript Journal, 22-26 Oct., 1869.

[8]*Texas Journal*, 1869, p. 28; 1870, p. 25.

[9]*Ibid.*, 1871, p. 20.   [10]*Ibid.*, 1872, p. 26.

[11]Aug. 1873, p. 5.   [12]*Texas Journal*, 1874, p. 76, 1867, p. 38.

[13]*Ibid.*, 1874, p. 76; for the system in Waco, see below, p. 211.

way from Waxahachie to Dallas, but apparently he found no opportunity to exploit.[14]

THE NORTHEAST SECTOR

McKinney in Collins County was the next point at which Gregg held services on his swing through north Texas in the Fall of 1866. He conducted what he believed to be the first services of our Church, but was unable to make any future plans for work there.[15] In October 1869, he and the Reverend Francis R. Starr spent two days in McKinney. There were large congregations for the services both days, and a great deal of interest.[16] The following Fall the Bishop arranged that Starr, now Rector of the Church in Paris, and Davenport, of Dallas, should alternate in holding occasional services in McKinney. Of this plan the Bishop said, "not good, but the best that can be done."[17] J. L. Doggett was licensed as lay-reader in 1872, and the organization of a choir and Sunday School was reported.[18] Not until the end of 1873 was the congregation to secure regular clerical leadership when the Reverend E. W. Gilliam, who was received into the Diocese from North Carolina,[19] was appointed missionary for McKinney in addition to his duties as Rector of the Church at Sherman, where he resided.[20]

Sherman looked like a good prospect for the Church in 1866 when Gregg visited and held services. His tentative plan was to link it with the Red River Counties in a mission, if he could send a clergyman to the field. His next visit to this area was in 1869. Extremely wet seasons with floods disrupted his schedule in 1867, and the time taken in attendance upon General Convention curtailed his visitations in 1868.[21] In 1869 the Bishop recruited his first missionary for the area, the Reverend Francis R. Starr, who was accompanying him on his visitation. Though large congregations and much interest marked the visitation to Sherman, no arrangement was made for a share of Starr's time, perhaps because Paris and Clarksville required too much work to allow it.[22] The following October, the Bishop felt that the field did not possess enough promise to justify spreading Starr's field to include Sherman. But

[14]*Texas Journal*, 1867, p. 17.   [15]*Ibid.*, p. 17.
[16]Gregg, manuscript Journal, 27-28 Oct., 1869.
[17]*Texas Journal*, 1871, p. 20.
[18]*Diocese of Texas*, Jan., 1873, p. 5.
[19]*Texas Journal*, 1874, p. 52.   [20]*Ibid.*, p. 45.
[21]See Bishop's Addresses in Texas Journal for these years.
[22]Gregg, manuscript Journal, 29-31, Oct., 1869.

he did think that as soon as another man was available this should be his headquarters.[23] In May 1873, Gregg related that many Church people had moved to the town since his visit the previous November. Lots for a church building had been bought and a building fund started. The Bishop's plan was to enlist a clergyman to share time between Sherman and Denison, where he had just visited. In Denison he found a vigorous new town in which the Church was largely represented. There, as at Sherman, property was available.[24] With these good prospects Gilliam arrived late in the year to take charge of the work in Sherman. In February 1874 Gregg made his last visitation to this congregation, and of it he said:

> Rev. Mr. Gilliam has been here a little more than three months, and an established congregation was found, a hall temporarily fitted up for services, a newly organized Parish, and a comfortable Rectory nearly finished—encouraging results for so short a period. The town will be one of the largest and most important in Northern Texas, and we may look for substantial Church growth.[25]

St. Stephen's Church, Sherman, was admitted into union with the Diocese of Texas on May 28, 1874, at the Council at Jefferson, and was represented there by Emile Jouvenat and C. P. Field.[26] Thus another parish was added to the number which Bishop Garrett was to receive from the Mother Diocese. Denison was included in the field assigned to Gilliam. In his report to the 1874 Council he showed the communicant strength as nine, with the building fund increasing but not yet sufficient for construction to start. The Town Land Company had contributed a site for the church.[27]

Bonham was another place at which Bishop Gregg found "a good welcome and a desire for the services of the Church" on his visit in the Fall of 1866.[28] In November 1869, accompanied by Starr, Gregg spent four days in intensive calling and conducting several services. At a meeting to discuss the organization of a parish, good interest was displayed, but evidently no final action was taken.[29] In October of the following year, the Bishop on his visitation made arrangements for occasional services to be conducted by Starr.[30] That hard-working clergyman included in his 1871 report for the Clarksville Mission this paragraph about Bonham:

[23]*Texas Journal*, 1871, p. 20.   [24]*Ibid.*, 1873, p. 42.

[25]*Ibid.*, 1874, p. 45.   [26]*Ibid.*, pp. 11, 12.

[27]*Ibid.*, p. 76.   [28]*Ibid.*, 1867, pp. 17-18.

[29]Gregg, manuscript Journal, 1-4 Nov., 1869.

[30]*Texas Journal*, 1871, p. 20.

West of Paris, forty miles, is Bonham, where there are nine communicants, four of whom were confirmed last Fall. Here I officiate every quarter, remaining a week and reading services and preaching every night, and administering the Holy Communion on Sunday morning. . . .[31]

In November 1872, Gregg presided at another meeting called to organize the congregation as a parish,[32] but the minutes of the Council of 1873 do not reveal that a petition for admission was presented. The congregation was still listed as a mission in the *Journal* of the 1874 Council.

Paris was first visited by Gregg in June 1861,[33] but he was unable to return until October 18, 1866. Although the Red River country had been visited several times by Bishops Polk and Freeman, neither of them had been able to secure a missionary to exploit the opportunities found for the Church in this lovely region of the State. The outbreak of war shortly after Gregg took office circumscribed his opportunities for advance work and recruitment of clergy. Only at the war's end could he think of arousing the hopes of such Churchmen as might still be found in that region, far separated from the established work of the Diocese. In view of the long if inevitable neglect, the welcome the Bishop received in Paris must have been heartening. He must have told the people, as he recorded in his Journal, that he had tried in vain to secure a clergyman for this portion of the State.[34] In November 1869, nine people were confirmed by the Bishop during his stay of two days, and at a meeting between the men of the congregation and Starr, arrangement for that Priest's settlement there must have been made.[35] On Septuagesima Sunday, 1870, Starr returned from accompanying the Bishop on visitation and took charge of the field. A parish by the name of "Holy Cross" was organized, with seventeen communicants. It was admitted to the Diocese on June 9, 1870.[36] Starr's lengthy report to Council the following year was full of the flavor of missionary work for the Episcopal Church in essentially virgin territory:

Comparing this my second report with that of last year, the Parish shows some progress; not so much as could be desired or was expected, when, as the first Missionary of the Church in this portion of the Diocese, I took charge of Paris and Clarksville, on Septuagesima Sunday, A.D., 1870. Then we did not

[31]*Ibid.*, p. 57.   [32]*Ibid.*, 1873, p. 31; *Diocese of Texas*, January, 1873, p. 5.
[33]See above, p. 123.   [34]*Texas Journal*, 1867, p. 18.
[35]Gregg, manuscript Journal, 5-7, Nov., 1869.
[36]*Texas Journal*, 1870, pp. 8, 28.

know as we do now, the difficulties which would meet us in the struggle for parochial existence. We knew, of course, that we had to begin at the beginning, and depend mainly on ourselves to gather up those tools necessary for the effectual working of any part of the Lord's vineyard. We had no organization, no house in which to worship, no Prayer Books, but in the hands of the few who had been confirmed, no school for Catechumens, no Parish library, no well trained laymen to assist in the public services. In truth, there was no one except the Rector's wife who could readily "find the places" in the Prayer Book; not one who had ever taken part in singing the Chants, and the great majority had never even heard them sung. As to the citizens generally, the Church was a new and unheard of thing. It is not therefore surprising that much prejudice existed; that the excellencies of our unequalled Liturgy were and are still unappreciated. And yet, in spite of all this, and much more, by the grace of God, we have been permitted to organize the Parish under the name of the "Holy Cross," and to hold regular services two Sundays in every month and on Holy Days, a choir has been organized and trained to render the whole service in music; the children have been gathered together for instruction in the Church's ways, every Sunday; their offerings have been regular, and they are now partially supplied with Catechisms and Library books. A Church lot, on which is a dwelling now used as the Rectory, has been partially paid for . . . a foundation has been laid for future growth, which, by the blessing of God, will be neither slow nor meagre. . . .[37]

In the prospectus for the new periodical, *The Diocese of Texas*, of October 1872, there is an item from Paris reporting the laying of the cornerstone of the new church by the Rector.[38] In November the Bishop reported finding the "comely church building" nearing completion, "with valuable unencumbered grounds, the property of the parish."[39] On All Saints' Day, 1873, Gregg consecrated the new church, and the following day instituted Starr as Rector.[40] In the Parochial Report for 1874, Starr listed the value of the church building as $2500, that of the rectory as $3000, and his salary as $400 per year. The Church at last was brought to strength in the Red River country.

The attention of the Bishop of Texas was as much overdue to Clarksville as it was to Paris when Gregg made his second visitation to that town on October 21, 1866. He felt this keenly, as his diary entry shows: "Here again, the want of the Church is sadly

[37]*Ibid.*, 1871, p. 46.
[38]There were no page numbers in this issue.
[39]*Texas Journal*, 1873, p. 32.
[40]*Ibid.*, 1874, p. 40; *Diocese of Texas*, Dec., 1873, p. 5.

felt, and must as speedily as possible, be supplied."[41] Returning in 1869, Gregg found that considerable advance preparation had been made for his visit. He recorded that on his first night in town he "practiced with the choir." In addition to conducting services, preaching, baptizing and confirming two ladies, the Bishop met with the men, evidently to arrange for Starr's appointment to minister here in connection with Paris.[42] The arrangement was made and Starr had his first service on the First Sunday in Lent, 1870. He found two communicants, evidently the two ladies baptized and confirmed by the Bishop the previous November, and by Council time in June added three more.[43] Bishop Gregg was pleased with Starr's work in both congregations. On his visit of October 1870 he said:

> The Rev. Mr. Starr has worked very faithfully and effectively at both places, though with much to discourage, and is laying a good foundation for the future in this interesting field.[44]

In December of the following year he said of the work in both places:

> The Rev. Mr. Starr has laid a foundation here in thorough Church training and practice, which will tell largely, under God, in the future.[45]

Judge William H. Wooten was licensed as layreader for Clarksville in 1872. In November of that year the Bishop found that the congregation had secured a site and a building suitable for temporary use for services. He wrote, delighted: "Decided progress has been made, and the Church has now an encouraging future before it."[46]

In 1866, while on his way from Clarksville to Jefferson, Gregg conducted the first service of the Church ever held at Mount Pleasant, Titus County.[47] This visit evidently led to no great hopes, for no further visits are recorded.

Another point in Northern Texas where a congregation was formed was Kaufman, which Gregg visited in November 1870. Staying three days there, he organized a parish and arranged for Davenport to conduct services monthly.[48] The petition for admission to the Diocese evidently was not presented, however, as the congregation continued to be listed as a mission. The Bishop visited again

[41]*Texas Journal*, 1867, p. 18.
[42]Gregg, manuscript Journal, 8-10 Nov., 1869.
[43]*Texas Journal*, 1870, p. 28.   [44]*Ibid.*, 1871, p. 20.
[45]*Ibid.*, 1872, pp. 26-7.   [46]*Ibid.*, 1873, p. 32.
[47]*Ibid.*, 1867, p. 18.   [48]*Ibid.*, 1871, p. 21.

in 1871[49] and 1873; on the latter visit he remarked that the Texas and Pacific Railroad would miss this town in favor of Terrell, twelve miles distant. The mission would be shifted to the latter town, at which Gregg hoped to place a clergyman. The Reverend John Portmess went to Terrell in 1874.[50]

The latecomer among the towns in which the Church worked before this territory became part of the Northern Texas Jurisdiction was Sulphur Springs. Portmess, while schoolmaster and missionary at Hallville (now Hallsville), Harrison County, made a visit to Sulphur Springs in August 1873, and reported that, since reached by the Texas Central Railroad, the community had grown in only a few months from a small village to a town of between 2000 and 2500; it would grow more when the International and Great Northern should be built that far, at a near date. Though unable to remain for a Sunday and conduct services, Portmess learned of the presence of several Church families, and saw a good opening for the Church. Gregg, accompanied by the Reverend Messrs. Starr and Wagner, paid a visit in November 1872. Baptisms, confirmations, and an arrangement for further services by Starr resulted.[51]

THE REMAINDER OF THE JURISDICTION

At Fort Worth, where before the war a beginning was hoped for,[52] no work was found possible before the division of the Diocese. Gregg visited in October 1873, but found such discouragement on account of the delay in the extension of the Texas and Pacific from Dallas that he felt it imprudent to send a missionary at that time.[53] Fort Worth would have to await the arrival of the railroads, which occurred after Bishop Garrett took over the territory.

South of the Dallas-Fort Worth area there were several points at which the Church had work within what became the Jurisdiction of Northern Texas. At Corsicana, where the Reverend George Rottenstein had ministered before his removal to Dallas in the days of Bishop Freeman, the congregation apparently became extinct. Not until the construction of the Texas Central brought an influx of Church people to the town was the work revived. About the beginning of 1872, the Reverend Virginius O. Gee, newly received

[49]Ibid., 1872, p. 26.
[50]Ibid., 1874, p. 41; Beesley, Episcopal Church in Northern Texas, p. 51.
[51]Diocese of Texas, Aug., 1873, p. 5; Texas Journal, 1874, pp. 40, 86.
[52]See above, pp. 68, 122.
[53]Texas Journal, 1874, p. 39.

from the Diocese of North Carolina, was stationed there. Gregg found him "laboring faithfully" in February of that year and receiving a good response from the railroad people who were temporarily resident. Many of them were Churchmen who had learned at points reached earlier in the construction of the railroad how well the strategy of the Bishop of Texas met their needs. There was hope for a church building shortly.[54] The Bishop visited again in the Fall. By the first of 1874 Gee had become Rector of St. Andrew's, Bryan, and the Reverend J. Cooper Waddill of Calvert was making occasional visits to Corsicana;[55] the hope for a building was still alive.[56] In June of that year it was reported in the *Diocese of Texas* that the Reverend Heber O. Crane of Mississippi had entered upon general missionary work at Corsicana and other points on the Texas Central Railway.[57] It does not appear from the records that this clergyman was transferred to the Diocese, and he probably did not remain long in the work. The building of a church and the attainment of parochial status for Corsicana belong to the story of Bishop Garrett's work.

When Gregg made a visitation of St. Paul's Church, Waco, November 12 to 15, 1871, the class he confirmed on the last evening included two people from Hillsboro. He therefore stopped in that place on the 17th, administered Holy Communion, and preached. He found a few members of the Church "longing earnestly for [the Church's] services," and promised to make some arrangement for them.[58] A year later the Bishop visited Hillsboro again; no services in the interim are recorded. His last visitation, at which he confirmed one person, was made on October 14, 1873.[59] The place was not listed as a mission in the statistical tables, so it could not be counted as one of the congregations of the new jurisdiction.

Waxahachie was one of the places visited by Gregg on his northern swing in October 1866. Staying there two days, he conducted services, confirmed, and celebrated the Holy Communion. Beginning in 1869, the Bishop visited annually in the Fall, performing baptisms, confirmations, and celebrating the Holy Communion. He promised in 1871 to arrange for occasional services. The clergy reported no such services. Yet there was a statistical report for the Waxahachie Mission for each year after 1871. Davenport, who did not report the services he held in Kaufman and McKinney, possibly

[54]*Ibid.*, 1872, p. 29.   [55]*Texas Journal*, 1874, p. 73.
[56]*Ibid.*, p. 76.   [57]June, 1874, p. 5.
[58]*Texas Journal*, 1872, p. 25.   [59]*Ibid.*, 1874, p. 39.

occasionally ministered in Waxahachie.[60] Two other points in Ellis
County that Gregg visited from time to time on his rounds were
Tellico and Red Bank.[61] The Bishop also made a visit to Ennis
in 1874, and administered the Holy Communion to the few Church
members.[62]

The work in Cleburne, unlike most of the new work begun in
this decade, was not initiated by Gregg. In the council year 1870-1871
Bishop Gregg sent a layreader's license to P. Y. Brook,[63] who had
recently moved to the new town of Cleburne, and who wished to
start a congregation. The work was under way only a short time
when Brook suddenly died. Shortly thereafter the Reverend R. S.
Nash, Deacon, moved from Waco to Cleburne, where he opened a
school; he took charge of the infant congregation, as Bishop Gregg
put it, "as a labor of love." The Bishop visited Cleburne on
November 19, 1870, and was pleased with the progress made in
that "young and growing town." Gregg was not an entire stranger
to the neighborhood, since he had visited the nearby former County
seat, Buchanon, as early as 1860;[64] that town, like so many missed
by the railroads, dried up as population moved to the closest point
on the rails.[65] On October 19, 1872, the Bishop presided at a meeting
at Cleburne at which the Parish of "The Holy Comforter" was
organized; Nash was to continue in charge. Subscriptions for a
church building were started at this time.[66] At the Diocesan Council
the following Spring, the application presented by the Parish was
found to be so incomplete as to be inadmissible, and was ordered
to be laid over until complete.[67] Although the congregation went
ahead with the projected church building, which was being pressed
toward completion at the Bishop's visitation in October 1873,[68]
nothing further seems to have been done to perfect the organization
of a parish. Nash filed a report for "Cleburne—Church of the Holy
Comforter—Mission" at the Council of 1874. It reflected the value
of the church building as $3000, upon which an indebtedness of
$500 remained.[69] Thus for Cleburne, too, parish status was in the
future.

[60]*Ibid.*, 1867, p. 17; Gregg, manuscript Journal, 21 Oct., 1869; *Texas Journal,*
1871, p. 21; 1872, p. 26; 1873, p. 31; 1874, p. 45. See also Statistical Tables in *ibid.*,
1872-74.

[61]*Ibid.*, 1871, p. 21; 1872, p. 26; 1873, p. 31.   [62]*Ibid.*, 1874, p. 45.

[63]*Texas Journal,* 1871, p. 29.   [64]*Ibid.*, 1861, p. 16.

[65]*Handbook of Texas,* "Buchanon," *en. loc.*

[66]*Texas Journal,* 1873, p. 31; *Diocese of Texas,* Jan., 1873, p. 5.

[67]*Texas Journal,* 1873, p. 13.   [68]*Ibid.*, 1874, p. 39.

[69]*Ibid.*, 1874, p. 75.

Other points at which occasional services were held included Honey Grove, one of the towns visited by Gregg in 1861. Starr reported having held three services there in the 1872-1873 Council year. Sylvan Academy, Stacksville, and Robbinsville were other points at which Starr held periodic services. At a place called Savoy he received a deed to the Church for four lots valued at $300.[70]

In the most rapidly growing part of the State in the decade 1865-1875, the Church made great progress at points where Gregg was able to place clergy, and at localities within their reach to which they were able to give a little attention, at great sacrifice of time and energy. At other places a faithful few held together, sustained only by the Bishop's annual visitation, and waiting the coming of a better day. With a Bishop of their own in Northern Texas, these people would find more frequent opportunities to worship and to take their part in the work of the Church.

XVII. The Coast Country

OF THE TERRITORY retained by the Diocese of Texas after the General Convention of 1874, the coastal counties from the Colorado River eastward contained four of the six charter parishes of the Diocese. Three were original starting points of the foreign mission of 1838-39, Matagorda, Houston, and Galveston. Here the Church had taken deepest root in one of the oldest Anglo-American cultures in the State. Of the three places, Galveston was the largest and wealthiest. It became the strong home base for the Diocese of Texas after the division, as San Antonio became the base for Western Texas, and Dallas for Northern Texas.

GALVESTON

Galveston became prominent in the life of the Church when Bishop Gregg moved there in 1869. Trinity Church, Galveston, did not become a cathedral, as did St. Mark's in San Antonio, and St. Matthew's in Dallas. Yet the wealth and generosity of the Church members, stimulated no doubt by the intimate friendships which Gregg rapidly developed or deepened, made the congregation of Trinity Church the strong right arm of the Bishop in developing the self-reliance of the Diocese for its forward-looking missionary program. In every statement of funds for any extra-parochial pur-

[70]*Ibid.*, 1873, pp. 78-9.

pose in the ten years between the end of the war and the division of the Diocese, Trinity Church and individual members of the Parish topped the list of contributors. They gave sums far beyond the ability of San Antonio or Dallas contributors to match. After Stephen Moylan Bird became Rector in Galveston, the first neighborhood mission in the Diocese was founded, and one of the first real parish schools was opened.

The Rev. Benjamin Eaton returned as Rector of Trinity Parish on December 1, 1865.[1] In the interim since the death of the Reverend John Goshorn,[2] occasional services had been conducted by the Reverend John Owen of Matagorda and the Reverend J. M. Curtis of Houston,[3] after which the Reverend A. F. Dobb acted as supply minister for some months.[4] Eaton returned to face a grim financial situation. Total debts of the Parish amounted to $32,500; an attempt to secure a loan from Trinity Church, New York, for $22,000 was unsuccessful, and a committee was appointed to find some means to extinguish the debt. This committee was fantastically successful, for by June 17, 1868, the church building was free of encumbrance and was consecrated by Gregg.[5] In his report to the Convention which met at Houston just prior to the consecration of Trinity Church, Eaton announced, "The prospects of the parish are now brighter than at any former period."[6]

The consecration service was a great event in the life of the Parish. Almost all of the clergy who had been present at the Houston Convention joined the Bishop and Eaton in the service, which was attended by a very large congregation. With his usual felicity of expression Gregg said:

> This was an occasion of great thankfulness and rejoicing for the parish—a day to which Rector and people had long and anxiously looked forward as the cherished consummation of ardent hopes and untiring labors! May this spacious and beautiful edifice long remain in a city where others, though less imposing, must ere long spring up—the pride and ornament of the Church in Texas.[7]

[1] *Texas Journal*, 1866, p. 33.

[2] See above, pp. 109-10.

[3] *Texas Journal*, 1865, pp. 27-8.

[4] Morgan, *Trinity Church, Galveston*, p. 57.

[5] Morgan, *op. cit.*, pp. 57-8; *Texas Journal*, 1866, p. 33; 1867, p. 16.

[6] *Ibid.*, 1866, p. 33.

[7] *Ibid.*, 1867, p. 16; Morgan, *op. cit.*, pp. 58-9. Though much has been done through the years to maintain and improve the structure, this building is the present house of worship of Trinity Parish.

In the Summer of 1867 another outbreak of yellow fever caused Eaton to leave town, no doubt at the urging of the vestry. Mindful of the fearless and heroic services he had rendered in epidemics in the earlier years of his ministry, his friends felt that in old age and infirmity he should not be exposed again, since he had never contracted the disease.[8] The Reverend John Owen, beloved Rector of Christ Church, Matagorda, was called on again to supply the Parish temporarily. Ministering fearlessly to the victims of the fever, he contracted it himself, and died on October 16. The vestry of Trinity Church arranged his burial at their expense, and resolved:

> Whereas it has pleased Almighty God in His wise providence to take to himself the Rev. John Owen from his temporary field of labor amongst us, in which he officiated most devoutly, imparting Christian consolation to the sick and dying, administering the Sacraments and giving Christian burial, as well to the stranger as to our citizens, during the late epidemic.
>
> Resolved: That, we, the members of the Vestry, in common with the whole church, and this community, will hold in sacred remembrance the self-sacrificing character of our beloved spiritual father, who has gone to receive his reward in Heaven.[9]

A tablet on the south chancel wall of the church commemorates the sacrificial services of the two Priests who died in ministering to victims of the epidemics, the Reverend John Goshorn[10] and Owen. In his 1868 address to the Diocesan Convention Gregg bore testimony to Owen out of a full heart:

> We mourn the loss of many, and among the number, one who gave his matured energies, his excellent gifts, and at last, his life to the Church in Texas. The Rev. John Owen was a bright and shining light. Having taken the place temporarily of the Rector of Trinity Church, Galveston, he fell a victim there to the destroyer, after ministering faithfully to others, as he had ever been wont to do. A godly and well learned man, an earnest and instructive preacher, a sympathizing and indefatigable pastor, he was a rare example of those graces which adorn the minister of Christ and commend his religion most forcibly to the acceptance of mankind; self-denying, uncomplaining, ever cheerful, willing to spend and be spent in his master's service, it was his peculiar happiness ever to contribute largely to that of others, and amid many sore trials—for he was tried as few are—faithfully to endure to the end, that he might be saved.
>
> To myself, the loss of such a brother, of such a fellow-laborer,

[8]Chas. W. Hayes, quoted in Morgan, *op. cit.*, p. 73.

[9]Minutes of the Vestry, Trinity Church, Galveston, October 16, 1867, quoted in Morgan, *op. cit.*, p. 66.

[10]See above, pp. 109-10.

of such a devoted friend as he always was, is peculiarly heavy. You must all feel it as you look upon the vacant place which for years was radiant with the light of his presence, and in common with his afflicted parish and the Diocese at large, deplore the loss for many years to come.[11]

Eaton was back in the Parish before mid-December 1867, when the Bishop confirmed a class presented by him.[12] Though he was a Clerical Deputy to General Convention for 1868, he appears not to have attended its sessions.[13] Only a statistical report for the Parish was submitted to the Diocesan Convention of 1868, which met at St. David's, Austin, though Eaton was present and took part in its business.[14]

Affairs seemed to have gone on rather uneventfully for the aged Rector and his Parish for the next three years. No doubt the presence of the Bishop and his family in their midst quickened the tempo of the life of the flock; in January 1870 the Bishop recorded in his Journal twelve to thirteen calls made around town in company with Eaton, in addition to the many he made, either by himself or with Mrs. Gregg during the few weeks he spent at home that Winter.[15] Home again from May 5 to May 18, the Bishop confirmed seventeen persons, who with the fourteen confirmed in January made a total of thirty-one for the year.[16] Eaton was not inactive. He was present at the Diocesan Council at St. Andrew's, Bryan, June 9 to 11 that year,[17] and presented another seven persons to Gregg for Confirmation on June 14, before the Bishop departed for Sewanee for the Summer.[18]

On Sunday, March 19, 1871, Eaton was preaching in Trinity Church when stricken, and he collapsed into a coma while pronouncing the ascription. He died that afternoon at four o'clock.[19] His congregation was overwhelmed with grief. In his rectorship of over thirty years, he had baptized and given spiritual nurture to a great portion of his flock, married very many of the couples in the town, and buried their dead. The vestry began immediately to arrange for his funeral. They summoned the Reverend Messrs. J. W.

---

[11]Bp's. Address, *Texas Journal*, 1868, pp. 26-7. For Owen's ministry at Matagorda, see below, pp. 195-6.

[12]*Texas Journal*, 1868, p. 18.

[13]*Ibid.*, 1868, p. 2; *General Convention Journal*, Minutes, House of Deputies, for each day.

[14]*Texas Journal*, 1868, pp. 3, 5, 30.

[15]Gregg, manuscript Journal, 19-24 Jan., 1870.

[16]*Ibid.*, 23 Jan., 15 May, 1870.   [17]*Texas Journal*, 1870, pp. 4, 7, *passim*.

[18]*Ibid.*, 1871, p. 19.   [19]Morgan, *op. cit.*, pp. 69, 70.

Phillips, Lindsey P. Rucker, T. R. B. Trader, and Roderick H. Ranney to participate in the Service. The Bishop was in San Antonio in the course of his visitation, and could not get back in time for the rites. Eaton was buried beneath the chancel, which had been designed to make this possible.[20]

To meet the emergency until a new rector could be secured, the vestry employed the Reverend R. S. Nash, a Perpetual Deacon then teaching at Waco, to conduct services.[21] Later, the Reverend R. H. Ranney, who was then living in Galveston, took temporary charge of the Parish. One Reverend Dr. Lewis was there for a time. The Bishop returned from his visitation at the beginning of May, and confirmed a large class prepared by Nash, remarking that the death of the beloved pastor had made "a profound impression upon the parish."[22] At the Diocesan Council, held at Navasota June 1 to 3, the Bishop paid this tribute to Eaton in his Council Address:

> On the 19th of March, the 3rd Sunday in Lent, in his 66th year, the Rev. Benj. Eaton, D.D., Rector of Trinity Church, Galveston, fell at his post, with his armor on, his lamp trimmed, and his light burning—having been borne to his bed in the arms of weeping parishioners, expiring a few hours afterward. With the remarkable circumstances attending his death—and such an end has seldom, if ever, been witnessed in the Church —with the long and peculiar connection existing between himself and the community and Parish, and to which, from the infancy of the one and the incipiency of the other, more than thirty years of his life were devoted—and with his relations to the Diocese, in which he ever bore so prominent a part, and was so highly honored and respected—with all this you are familiar. It is a part of our common history which will ever remain an enduring monument of his rare gifts, his Christian integrity, his patient continuance in well-doing and his earnest devotion to the Church. His memory will never cease to be cherished by those with whom he was more immediately connected, and by the Diocese at large. The aged pastor had done his work faithfully, and finished it as we may well desire to do. He died well—with the words of blessing on his lips—and in the sight, as it were, of all his people. The Church was his only spouse—and from her altar he was borne, only to be brought back and buried there! "Blessed are the dead who die in the Lord: even so, saith the Spirit; for they rest from their labors."[23]

[20]*Ibid.*, p. 72-3; *Texas Journal*, 1871, pp. 24-5.
[21]Morgan, *op. cit.*, p. 76; *Texas Journal*, 1871, pp. 4, 49.
[22]*Ibid.*, pp. 42, 27; 1872, p. 67. Lewis was not otherwise identified.
[23]*Ibid.*, 1871, pp. 38-9.

Almost eleven months elapsed between Bishop Gregg's meeting with the vestry, on May 6, 1871, and the arrival of a new rector. The Bishop suggested three clergymen as likely to be suitable, but none of them was called. The vestry induced Stephen Moylan Bird, Rector of St. Paul's Church, Selma, Alabama, to come and look over the Parish in February 1872. He was called to the rectorship, but his Selma vestry refused to release him. After being refused by the Reverend J. S. Lindsey of Warrenton, Virginia, the vestry went back to Bird, this time successfully; he accepted their call, was released by his vestry, and took charge of Trinity Church on April 7, 1872.

At Eaton's death the Church was indebted to his estate for a considerable sum, since as a bachelor of simple tastes he had always been generous about arrears in salary.[24] In his will Eaton made several bequests to the Parish, including one for a wall plaque in memory of Goshorn and Owen.[25] to carry out the wishes of the late Rector, the vestry purchased from his executor, Mr. George Sealy, four pieces of property he owned, including his own residence and some other buildings, apparently rent houses; one of these became the new rectory.[26]

The Parish and the Diocese sustained another great loss November 30, 1872, in the death of General E. B. Nichols, who since his removal to Galveston in 1850 had been a mainstay of the congregation. His wealth was equalled by his generosity, energy and interest. A frequent delegate to the Diocesan Conventions and Councils and Deputy to General Convention, he contributed of his means and his thoughtful attention to the welfare of the Diocese and its causes. A boon companion of Eaton's, he was the Bishop's friend and backer as well. At his death Trinity Church owed him several thousand dollars, apparently advanced to clear the church building from debt.[27]

Trinity Church became quite lively under its new Rector. Bird, tall, good-looking and youthful, with a dramatic flair in the pulpit, seemed to take Galveston by storm.[28] In early May, Gregg returned from visitation to find a pleasing situation. He wrote:

It was most gratifying to me to find this Parish, after its sore privations and repeated disappointments, supplied with so earnest and devoted a Rector. He has entered on his work in this

[24]Morgan, *op. cit.*, pp. 76-7.
[25]See above, p. 185.   [26]Morgan, *op. cit.*, p. 77.
[27]Based principally upon Morgan, *op. cit.*, pp. 346, 350; *Texas Journal, passim.*
[28]Morgan, *op. cit.*, pp. 78-9.

noble field, which is white to harvest, with great energy, and the people are delighted.[29]

The two projects long cherished by the late Rector were taken in hand. A new pipe organ "of great capacity" was installed, the funds for which were raised by two of the choir members, George Sealy and a Mr. Roeck.[30] At the same time the "Ladies Society" began to raise money to build the Sunday School Chapel for which Eaton had wished so long, and which was now designed as a memorial to him. This latter project was to require a decade for its fulfillment.[31] But the Parish did not confine its efforts to its own immediate precinct; two more enterprises, for which Gregg had long asked, were initiated in Galveston. A branch Sunday School and mission were begun in the West End section of the city, and a parochial school was started.

A news item in the *Diocese of Texas* for February 1873 reported that funds were being sought for a "West End Mission" building, with the plea that segments of the population now being lost to the Church must be held.[32] The Reverend Albert Lyon was called from New Braunfels to assist the Rector with this work, and to be in charge of the parochial school.[33] The new building for "Trinity Chapel Mission" was being built with the support of "Trinity Church Guild," an organization of men of Trinity formed by Bird. Lyon reported a Sunday School with fourteen teachers and officers, and an average attendance in excess of sixty children, almost all of them from the poor of the neighborhood. With the completion of the chapel building, missionary services were planned.[34]

Trinity Parish School was Lyon's other responsibility which he took over with enthusiasm and flair. An advertisement in the *Diocese of Texas* for September 1873 gave notice of the beginning of its first term, and included the rates and the information that board was available in Galveston for out-of-town students.[35] The school was military in plan, for boys only; its daily schedule, including times for religious instruction, was printed in successive issues of the diocesan paper.

On March 30, 1873, Bird presented the largest confirmation

[29]*Texas Journal*, 1872, p. 38.

[30]*Diocese of Texas*, Jan. 1873, p. 4.

[31]*Texas Journal*, 1873, p. 66; Morgan, *op. cit.*, pp. 82-3.

[32]*Diocese of Texas*, Feb. 1873, p. 7.

[33]*Texas Journal*, 1874, p. 78; *Diocese of Texas*, Sept. 1873, p. 8.

[34]*Texas Journal*, 1874, p. 78; Morgan, *op. cit.*, p. 79.

[35]*Diocese of Texas*, Sept. 1873, p. 8.

class Gregg had so far had in the Diocese; the Bishop said 49, Bird said 48; Morgan, citing the *Galveston Daily News* as well as the *Journal of the Diocese,* said "fifty-six in all,"[36] perhaps including in that number others confirmed during the year. In any event this was the earnest of things to come in the ability of the old Parish to bear its witness in what was then the largest and richest city in the State. The list of contributions of the Parish to causes outside its own maintenance is a measure of the quality of the Christian conviction of the flock:

Trinity Church Mission	$2496.90
Eaton Memorial Chapel	1800.00
Diocesan Missions	261.10
Communion Alms	465.90
Education Beneficiaries	334.00
Louisiana overflow	109.10
Domestic Missions	72.00
Foreign Missions	28.00
Memphis epidemic	42.00
Columbus epidemic	60.00[37]

HOUSTON, HARRISBURG, LIBERTY AND ORANGE

Christ Church, Houston, did not fare as well as its sister Parish in Galveston in the decade following the war. It had begun in a promising way. The Reverend J. M. Curtis took charge shortly before the Diocesan Convention of 1865,[38] and by June of the following year Gregg reported that the church building soon would be ready (it seemed) for consecration, the congregation having spent in the convention year $5320 toward its repair and improvement.[39] The Reverend J. W. Tays said of Christ Church in 1866: "They have a nice brick Church almost completed, but quite too small for the wants of the place; the need of a second will soon be severely felt."[40] But Curtis resigned to go to Alabama in the Fall of 1866, leaving the Parish without a rector until he was succeeded in the Spring of 1867 by the Reverend Joseph Cross, D.D., from the Diocese of Tennessee. The Bishop wrote, on his visitation to Houston on April 28: "The Church here . . . is greatly blessed in the ministrations of Dr. Cross. He has come, I rejoice to say, to give his heart and life to the work in Texas."[41]

[36] *Texas Journal,* 1873, pp. 38, 65; Morgan, *op. cit.,* p. 78.
[37] *Texas Journal,* 1874, p. 77.   [38] *Ibid.,* 1865, p. 7.
[39] *Ibid.,* 1866, pp. 24, 33.   [40] *Spirit of Missions,* 1866, p. 438.
[41] *Texas Journal,* 1867, pp. 22, 26.

Dr. Cross indeed rendered good service; confirmations and attendance seemed impressive, but he soon resigned. Financial problems were apparently the difficulty; only $656.55 in contributions in addition to the $600 assessment was reported for 1868. Probably because of this problem, Gregg addressed "a meeting of the congregation for parish purposes" on April 13, 1868.[42] The parochial report for 1869 was signed by R. M. Elgin, layreader, who said:

> This parish has been without a Minister since the middle of July last. The services have been kept up regularly, however, by Lay-reading; so that, so far as membership is concerned, the parish has about held its own. The contributions have been mainly devoted to the payment of the debt due for the church building, which is now almost entirely liquidated.[43]

On April 23, Gregg noted that, despite the effectiveness of the "regular and efficient Lay Reading," the need for a rector was greatly felt.[44]

The next Rector of Christ Church, Houston, was the Reverend T. R. B. Trader, one of the clergy from Louisiana who had officiated in the Diocese temporarily during the Civil War. He took charge of the Parish on January 1, 1870, and remained until some time in 1873. Trader's work prospered in Houston; the number of communicants increased from "up to 150" in 1870 to 223 in 1873. But by that time the congregation was indebted to the Rector for $1900, almost a year's stated salary of $2000.[45] Once again, the trouble seemed to be the building fund; in 1872, $5000 had been subscribed for enlargement of the church, and in the year following $1200 had been spent for repairs.[46] Shortly after this Trader had to give up, and was listed as without a parish in the Clergy List of 1874.[47] Bishop Gregg wrote concerning his visit to the Parish on January 18: "The Parish was found in sore need of a Rector, with no early prospect of relief." On May 24, noting again the great need for clerical leadership and the absence of any to be confirmed, he was assured that steps were being taken to fill the rectorship.[48] In November 1874, the acceptance of the Reverend J. J. Clemens, rector of St. Paul's Church, Selma, Alabama, to be Rector of Christ Church, was reported; then began a decade of creative leadership that was to make Christ Church the Mother Church of Houston, accepting its

[42]*Ibid.*, 1868, pp. 22, 36.
[43]*Ibid.*, 1869, p. 29. Dr. Cross was transferred to Iowa. *Ibid.*, p. 25.
[44]*Ibid.*, p. 22.   [45]*Ibid.*, 1870, p. 26; 1873, p. 67.
[46]*Ibid.*, 1872, p. 68; 1873, p. 68.   [47]*Ibid.*, 1874, p. 4.
[48]*Ibid.*, pp. 43, 51.

responsibilities for the extension of the Church to the expanding
suburbs of the city.[49]

Prior to Clemens' tenure, one mission may fairly be claimed
as the child of Christ Church. Nativity Mission, Harrisburg, was
begun in 1864 by the Reverend J. M. Curtis, who reported to the
Council:

> The undersigned, about Advent, commenced officiating at
> this point regularly Sunday evening, once a month, which,
> from the interest manifested, he was induced, from and after
> Easter, to increase to twice a month.

Twelve baptisms, fifteen confirmations, and twenty-four communicants were reported.[50] The following year the congregation was
reduced by half, because people who had come there due to the
war returned to their homes or removed elsewhere. Curtis continued
to officiate in spite of reduced numbers.[51] No detailed reports were
rendered for the following two years, nor did the Bishop record
any visitations, and probably services were suspended with the departure of Curtis. Gregg visited the congregation and confirmed three
persons on April 20, 1869.[52] In January and again in May 1870
the Bishop made visitations of two days each time, calling on parishoners, and performing baptisms and confirmations.[53] The Reverend
T. R. B. Trader, in his 1870 parochial report for Christ Church,
Houston, noted that he had performed three baptisms, two marriages and one burial at Harrisburg, but he did not mention conducting Sunday services there.[54] The following year he rendered a
separate report for Nativity, Harrisburg, which reflected a measure
of activity. Arrears in assessments had been paid, almost $40 was
contributed to diocesan missions, and the communicant list had
grown to twenty.[55] No report was submitted for 1872. Visiting the
congregation May 13 and 14 of that year, Gregg said, "To a few
ladies here are we indebted, under God, for the work done."[56]
No report was rendered for 1873, and the Bishop visited but once,
May 22, and found no candidates for Confirmation.[57] Upon his
visit on March 3, 1874, the Bishop arranged for the Reverend T. J.

---

[49]*Diocese of Texas,* Nov. 1874, p. 5.   [50]*Texas Journal,* 1865, p. 28.
[51]*Ibid.,* 1866, pp. 33-4.   [52]*Ibid.,* 1869, p. 22.
[53]Gregg, manuscript Journal, 17-18 Jan., 17-18 May, 1870.
[54]*Texas Journal,* 1870, p. 26.
[55]*Ibid.,* 1871, pp. 42-3. This report says 50 communicants, but the statistical
table gives 20, obviously the correct figure, since there were two added that year,
with one added otherwise, and four by Confirmation the previous year. (Citations
above, and statistical tables for 1869 & 1870.)
[56]*Ibid.,* 1872, p. 38.   [57]*Ibid.,* 1873, p. 41.

Morris, recently ordained Deacon, to visit the congregation once a month in connection with his other duties along the Galveston, Harrisburg and San Antonio Railway.[58]

Eastward along the Gulf Coast toward Louisiana the only work attempted during the decade was at Liberty. In December 1865, Gregg held services there, and expressed the belief that a missionary could profitably give Liberty part of his time. An arrangement to that end was promised as soon as possible,[59] but apparently it could not be effected. Perhaps J. M. Curtis held occasional services there while he was Rector of Christ Church, Houston, but no record of services after that time has come to notice, excepting the Bishop's visit in December 1866.[60] From the time of Gregg's 1865 visit, Liberty was carried on the list of missions in the statistical tables of parishes and missions through 1868, after which it was dropped from the list.

The work at Orange, begun during the war by the Reverend Joseph Wood Dunn, then of the Diocese of Louisiana but temporarily resident in Texas, may have been continued after the war on an occasional basis from Dunn's base in Franklin, Louisiana, until he followed his brother, Ballard S. Dunn, to Brazil; the only record found is the list of missions in Gregg's manuscript Journal, which lists J. W. Dunn in charge of Orange from 1863 to 1867.[61] Dunn did not return to Orange as resident missionary until 1878.[62]

BRAZORIA COUNTY

The work in Brazoria County was one for which Bishop Gregg had often desired to make better provisions; after the departure of Dalzell for San Antonio, no one could be found for the field until the close of the war, when the Reverend George Rottenstein was appointed by the Bishop and given a missionary appointment by the Domestic Committee, with a salary of $400 per year, at the Bishop's request.[63] The Bishop visited the field in May 1866, entering the County from Matagorda County, accompanied by the Reverend John Owen. Rottenstein joined them at Brazoria, where

[58]*Ibid.*, 1874, p. 45. This mission included Richmond and Columbus.

[59]*Ibid.*, 1866, p. 20.   [60]*Ibid.*, 1867, p. 20.

[61]This is the source quoted by Crocket for the Register of Parishes and Missions before his time.

[62]*Texas Journal*, 1878, p. 2.

[63]Minutes, Domestic Committee, Board of Missions, stated meeting, 6 Feb. 1866, Minutes Book, p. 362; *Texas Journal*, 1866, p. 24.

services were conducted. At Columbia one person was confirmed.[64] Rottenstein reported to the Diocesan Council that there were about nineteen communicants in the two places. He had been officiating in each place on alternate Sundays. But by the time of the publication of the *Journal*, he was listed as Rector of St. Matthew's Church, Dallas.[65] No resident minister could be obtained for the places during the remainder of the decade. The impetus given the work of the Church by the veteran missionary was none the less not lost. Gregg and Owen visited the two towns in April 1867, and found life and interest in the Church. At Brazoria the Bishop baptized twelve white and four colored children, and, after catechizing the children of the Parish, pronounced their answers "amongst the very best that I have heard." This, he said, was the work of "an earnest churchwoman." Two people were confirmed here. At Columbia there were no candidates for Confirmation, but the Bishop reported:

> There is a settled determination here to erect a church building in due season. The Church has grown in strength, and the prospect for the future is encouraging.[66]

The following year very heavy rainstorms made it impossible for Gregg to get through from Matagorda to Brazoria; regretfully he omitted his visit, and perhaps for this reason he stayed four days in the vicinity on the following year's visit, confirming three in Columbia and one in Brazoria. In 1870, the Bishop went to Columbia from Houston by rail, accompanied by the Rector of Christ Church, Houston, T. R. B. Trader and the Reverend C. N. Spaulding, general missionary. Much interest was displayed in both places, and the Bishop was able to arrange for regular services by appointing John Adriance of Columbia as layreader.[67] With this continuity the work at Columbia developed to the point that a parish by the name of St. Luke's was organized and admitted to the Council in 1872. The Bishop found that hopes were still held for building a church, in spite of the constantly depressed economy in this plantation region.[68] At Brazoria, where the parochial organization had long since lapsed (though the *Journals* still listed the congregation as the Parish of St. John's), the Bishop presided over a meeting at which a vestry was elected and the Parish reactivated in May 1874. Although the members of the two congregations were

---

[64]*Ibid.*, p. 22.   [65]*Ibid.*, pp. 5, 30.   [66]*Ibid.*, 1867, p. 22.
[67]*Ibid.*, 1868, p. 23; 1869, p. 22; Gregg, manuscript Journal, 24-28 February 1870.
[68]*Texas Journal*, 1872, pp. 7, 38.

still afflicted with poverty, hopes that the Columbia Tap Railway ·· would be extended across the Brazos River toward the Colorado encouraged the people. Should prosperity return, it might be possible to support a clergyman between the two Parishes.[69]

MATAGORDA COUNTY

The Mother Church of the Diocese, Christ Church, Matagorda, was in much better condition in 1865 than were the Brazoria County flocks. With a faithful and efficient Rector in the Reverend John Owen, the congregation was trained in the Church's system of orderly worship, and involved in his missionary zeal. Because of the depression in agriculture and trade at the war's end, it was necessary for them to accept a Domestic Committee appropriation of $300 per annum to assist with Owen's salary for 1866.[70] but the following year Owen declined that salary. He stated that the Parish was able to keep him from want; he believed it his duty to circumscribe his desires to the measure of the ability of the Parish to pay its Rector.[71] Gregg made his 1867 visitation to Christ Church from Good Friday through Easter Monday, and reported thus to the Convention of that year:

> The devoted Rector of this parish has fully established daily services and weekly communion with the happiest results. Would the same were done in all our parishes with settled clergymen. Without it, the beauty, the life and power of the Church cannot be fully exhibited, or the spiritual life of her children developed as it ought to be, and enabled to overcome the evil of this naughty world. It is an example which very forcibly commends itself to imitation.[72]

Owen's zealous care was not limited to Matagorda itself. He apologized that his "labors were somewhat circumscribed" in the 1865-66 convention year because of his attendance at the General Convention of 1865, but he included in his annual report of services celebrations of the Holy Communion on Caney Creek six times, on Carancahua Bayou once, and on Trespalacios twice, then added, "three of the above [67] communicants reside out of the limits of the Parish, but are under the Rector's pastoral care."[73]

The tragic death of Owen, related earlier in connection with the account of Trinity Church, Galveston, closed this magnificent

---

[69]*Ibid.*, 1874, p. 50.

[70]Minutes, Domestic Committee, Board of Missions, stated meeting, 6 February 1866, Minutes Book, p. 363.

[71]*Texas Journal*, 1867, p. 35.   [72]*Ibid.*, p. 22.   [73]*Ibid.*, 1866, p. 37.

chapter in the life of Texas' first Parish. The economy of the area
was severely strained; like most Texas seaport towns without a railroad in that era, it was losing trade. To find a clergyman willing to
"circumscribe his desires" to the extent that Owen had done was
not soon accomplished. Gregg, on his visitation in May 1868, wrote,
"A determined effort will be made to keep this parish alive, notwithstanding the decline of the town."[74]

Fortunately a good layreader had been trained to fill the gap.
J. H. Cutler, undoubtedly influenced by the ideals and practice
of the late Rector, carried on as best he could. The Bishop said of
the situation on the following year:

> This parish is blessed with a faithful Lay Reader, and shows in
> its continuing life, under many privations, and notwithstanding
> the gradual decline of the town, the happy effects of the able
> and devoted ministrations it has enjoyed in the past.[75]

A leader in his community and county, Cutler had interested himself in diocesan affairs as well; he had represented the Mother Church
in Diocesan Conventions and Councils frequently since 1856, and
reported to the 1871 Council as senior warden.[76]

It seems unlikely that any clergyman was able to visit Matagorda
between the Bishop's visitations. The Parish Register does not reveal
this information except for baptisms or marriages performed during
this period. The only ones recorded are by the Bishop on his visitations.[77] Gregg tried to give as much time and attention to the Parish
as he could manage. In 1870, he was in the County for a full week,
and in Matagorda he prepared the candidates for Baptism and Confirmation himself, and visited all around the Parish.[78] The following
year he seemed pleased that the Sunday School was being maintained
in a good fashion, and layreading was regularly conducted.[79] The
standards maintained in the Christian education of the young in
this Parish came in for a glowing tribute from the Bishop at his
visitation in 1872; in it he saw a pattern for the rest of the Diocese.
The teachers had been well trained, and were devoted, and the
results were observable in the knowledge and attitudes of the
children.[80]

The Bishop was accompanied on his 1872 visitation to Matagorda by the Reverend J. T. Hutcheson, who, having been re-

---

[74]*Ibid.*, 1868, p. 23.   [75]*Ibid.*, 1869, p. 22.   [76]*Ibid.*, 1871, p. 45.

[77]The Parish Registers of Christ Church are intact, and are available on micro-
film in the Diocesan Archives at Austin.

[78]Gregg, manuscript Journal, 27 April-3 May 1870.

[79]*Texas Journal*, 1871, p. 27.   [80]*Ibid.*, 1872, p. 36.

ceived from the Diocese of Maryland that year, was acting as the Bishop's assistant for the Spring visitation.[81] Arrangements were made during their stay for Hutcheson to settle and become missionary for the entire County. He took up his residence in Caney, and got about on horseback. This able and experienced clergyman, whose many contributions to the work of the Church in Western Texas were to enrich its life for many years to come, did not get on well in Matagorda County. A prolific correspondent for the new diocesan paper, signing himself "Caney," he responded to the request for news items from the parishes with a sarcastic letter about the members of the Mother Church. He reported that they were, by their own account, very poor; they had no ponies to ride to Church, although they did not lack them for the numerous parties held over the County. He surmised that they really wanted the services of the Church only once a year, upon the Bishop's visitation.[82] Before the next Council meeting Hutcheson, his health impaired by the climate, had accepted a call to Seguin. The death of Mr. Cutler, in the same year, left the Parish without its chief lay leader. Hutcheson, reporting to the Council for the Parish, said:

> The parish is now in an encouraging condition. My connection with it closes with this report. There is a fine field for a clergyman who has the strength to do the work, and he will be liberally supported.[83]

Perhaps "Caney" had meant only to shake some of his parishioners out of their lethargy, or else the weather was in his bones when he wrote his piece. On his visitation in May 1873 Gregg licensed a young man, J. H. Selkirk, as layreader, to officiate in the absence of a clergyman.[84]

The vacancy in the rectorship was not protracted, however. The Bishop had been accompanied on his Spring visitation by the Reverend Edwin Wickens, who had been received from the Diocese of Missouri, where he had been Chaplain of St. Luke's Hospital and City Missionary.[85] In August it was announced that Wickens, who had gone back to St. Louis, would return to Texas the last of September to be in charge of the field in Matagorda County, with his

[81]*Ibid.*, p. 40 & *passim.*

[82]James Theodore Hutcheson was a native of the British West Indies, a graduate of Virginia Seminary, some years in the ministry before coming to Texas. See my *West Texas*, p. 38, and obituary in *West Texas Journal*, 1917. For Hutcheson's letter, *Diocese of Texas*, Feb. 1873, pp. 6-7.

[83]*Texas Journal*, 1873, pp. 41, 56, 72.

[84]*Ibid.*, p. 41; for the name, Gregg, manuscript Journal, 11 May 1873.

[85]*Diocese of Texas*, Feb. 1873, p. 7.

residence in Caney.[86] The principal object of his journey North was disclosed by the publication in the September issue of the diocesan paper of this letter:

> FOR CHURCH WORK IN MATAGORDA COUNTY, TEXAS. The undersigned having charge of Church work in the above mentioned county, appeals to churchmen everywhere for aid. Matagorda county is on the Gulf coast of Texas; for want of railroads, it is but sparsely settled; the chief points of labor are far distant from each other; and the residents of the county live on large plantations scattered over the county. The labors of the missionary are thus rendered very heavy, as he has to travel chiefly on horseback from point to point. Christ Church, Matagorda, one of the oldest in the State, was, before the war, a fine and commodious building. Now, it is almost in ruins. There is not one perfect window in the whole building; the tower is unsafe; and unless some speedy efforts are made to raise means to repair the building, the whole structure must fall. The congregation, in prosperous times, has always been noted for its liberality in helping forward the promotion of Church work in other places; but now they have to ask for help of others to save their beloved church from destruction.
>
> On Caney river, a point where services are held semi-monthly, there is no church building. The congregation have to worship in a very uncomfortable schoolhouse, quite unsuited for church purposes. The majority of the people are poor. Being chiefly ladies, they can do but little; but they cheerfully give that little, and do the best they can. A few hundred dollars would put up a small chapel to hold, say one hundred persons. If $500 can be raised, I am sure that we can put up all that we desire.
>
> At Tres Palacios River another congregation is forming. Here we worship in a school-house; if possible it is more miserable than that at Caney. This appeal is endorsed by the Bishop. Contributions will be thankfully received, and gratefully acknowledged. They should be sent to the address, the Rev. Edwin Wickens, care Bishop Gregg, Galveston, Texas.
>
> > (Signed) Edwin Wickens,
> > Missionary in Charge
> > Matagorda County.

Some response to this appeal was made within the Diocese, from parishes as small and struggling as those at Belton, Cleburne, and McKinney,[87] but it apparently did not yield much in St. Louis. Wickens reported to the 1874 Council:

> Some slight repairs on the old church building have been done. At least $1000 should be spent without delay, so as to prevent further decay.[88]

---

[86]*Ibid.*, Aug. 1873, p. 5.   [87]*Ibid.*, Nov. 1873, p. 5.
[88]*Texas Journal*, 1874, p. 83.

In spite of the delay in repairing the building, things otherwise went well in the old Parish. Gregg met with the vestry on his May visitation, and was satisfied with their resolve. Wickens' efforts were producing good response, as the congregation was increasing while the town itself was losing population. Caney and Trespalacios, the other (unorganized) congregations in the County, were doing well also,[89] although the plan to build chapels in these places was not to be fulfilled. The deep and strong foundations laid in the lives of the people in the three previous decades made them respond faithfully to the ministrations which the Church could extend.

XVIII.   From Matagorda to Austin

THE TOWN of Wharton received a visit from Bishop Gregg on May 5, 1867, but no work was started here within the decade.[1] Above Wharton, the Church folk of Columbus took heart again when in 1866 Bishop Gregg made the town the hub of a mission circuit embracing Richmond to the east and La Grange upriver from Columbus, with the Reverend Joseph Wilkins Tays in charge. Tays, then in deacon's orders, was received into the Diocese from Pennsylvania.[2]

Soon after being assigned to the field Tays wrote the Domestic Committee an acute summary of the situation of each of the three towns. The people in Richmond and Columbus had been prosperous —even wealthy—before the war; they now were prostrate from its effects. "Everyone pleads that the war has broken them up; and that with the present system of labor, they almost despair of being able to rally for some time to come." Tays had gone out by rail to Richmond from Houston for Sunday services shortly after his arrival in Texas. His were the first services in the congregation for six months, and some seventy-five people, mostly churchmen, turned up. He described the church building as neat, but in need of repair. A few hours after he left on Tuesday, a tornado completely wrecked the church. This left the members of Calvary Church in the same state as those of St. John's, Columbus, and St. James, La Grange; they had no place for their services but the county courthouse. Because of post-war discouragements, there was no prospect that the members of any of the three might build their own churches, Tays thought, and he appealed to Church people in the North to send

[89]*Ibid.*, p. 50.   [1]*Texas Journal*, 1867, p. 23.   [2]*Ibid.*, 1866, pp. 22, 23, 25.

contributions through Dr. Twing, Missionary Agent of the Domestic Committee.

Tays described La Grange as "a beautiful little town of twelve hundred inhabitants [with] much more of a business aspect than either of the other two." There were but thirteen members of St. James' Church, but they were earnest, and like the members of the other two congregations, they wanted the part-time services of a clergyman.[3]

St. John's congregation in Columbus were more ready to move toward building than Tays estimated. They secured a good site for a building and began making plans for it about the time he took charge. In La Grange, a good lot was given to the congregation, and an effort was begun for a building. The Richmond members aspired to rebuild their church within the council year.[4] But economic factors caused the people in all three congregations to be disappointed. At Richmond hopes for rebuilding were deferred for another year because crops failed. Columbus was generally depressed, though there was hope for a more prosperous state of things when the railroad should cross the Colorado River from Alleytown, for Columbus would become the terminus for some time.[5] Tays had to teach school in Columbus to support his family, and was unable to give more than one-fifth of his time to La Grange. Yet the Church in La Grange was showing great promise. There was a good Sunday School under the superintendence of Mr. Matthews, and the ladies were hard at work to build up their funds for the erection of a church. Tays thought the congregation could support a single clergyman before long.[6]

The financial situation was not the only measure by which the health of these two Parishes could be estimated, however. Bishop Gregg spoke in glowing terms of the revival of life at Richmond and La Grange, in which he confirmed thirteen and twelve candidates respectively. Tays' method of Christian Education made the Church Catechism the core of instruction; it was the method closest to the Bishop's heart, and he commended the example to others.[7]

But Tays labors were not spent in this field very long; in May of 1867 Bishop Gregg transferred him to Indianola and Lavaca.[8] That he went with mixed feelings is evidenced by his letter to the Domestic Committee; he was heartsick over leaving the three flocks unshepherded. Yet Tays recognized that the Bishop was right

[3]*Spirit of Missions,* 1866, pp. 438-9, 677-9.
[4]*Texas Journal,* 1866, pp. 23, 36, 38.   [5]*Ibid.,* 1867, pp. 36-7, 33.
[6]*Ibid.,* p. 35.   [7]*Ibid.,* p. 23.   [8]*Ibid.,* 1868, p. 30.

in his strategy of manning the places which were becoming more important through increase in trade and transportation.[9]

Columbus was the only one of the three congregations to report to Council in 1868, when Colonel Robert Robson reported as layreader. But he stated that ill health had intervened to prevent his continuing to hold services. Upon the Bishop's visit on May 22 a vestry was elected and the revival of the Parish noted. Mr. J. W. Phillips was licensed as layreader for the Parish.[10] La Grange, however, was very far from inactive; the Bishop, accompanied by the Reverend Messrs. Davenport and Richardson, spent three days there in May of 1868, and during the stay he confirmed twelve people, including six adults who were baptized on the same occasion.[11] The impetus given the Parish by this visitation was continued when Mr. John Rosenberg took charge as layreader in September 1868.[12] At the opening service of the Diocesan Council, May 27, 1869, "Professor John Rosenberg" was ordained to the Diaconate and assigned to continue his care of the La Grange flock, apparently teaching school at the same time. The prospects for the future seemed bright indeed.[13]

This happy state of affairs was soon rudely disturbed. A great flood on the Colorado River brought considerable damage to La Grange, so seriously disrupting the life of the town that Rosenberg could not remain there. With the consent of the Bishop he took a position as teacher in St. Paul's School in Brenham.[14] Bishop Gregg visited the congregation in March of 1870, confirming one man,[15] but no regular arrangement for services could yet be made.

In the Spring of 1872, appointments were made for monthly services to be conducted by the Reverend J. W. Phillips, who was then residing in Austin, and ministering to several flocks in Central Texas.[16] The following year the congregation purchased a two-story building, using the upper floor for a chapel, the lower for a school. In the Bishop's judgment Phillips' work was showing good results,[17] in spite of his time being so divided between stations.

---

[9]*Spirit of Missions*, 1867, p. 654.

[10]*Texas Journal*, 1868, pp. 30, 24.   [11]*Ibid.*, p. 24.

[12]*Ibid.*, 1869, 30. Mr. Rosenberg came from San Antonio to La Grange, *ibid.*, 1868, p. 24.

[13]*Ibid.*, 1869, pp. 5, 23, 30.

[14]*The Churchman*, Oct. 2, 1869, p. 322. For Rosenberg's further migration to a Methodist school at Chappell Hill, above, p. 131. He was transferred to Washington and Oregon in 1870. *Texas Journal*, 1871, p. 29.

[15]Gregg, manuscript Journal, 8 Mar. 1870.

[16]*Texas Journal*, 1872, pp. 3, 31.

[17]*Ibid.*, 1873, pp. 70, 38.

In neighboring Lee County Phillips extended his work to Giddings, the County Seat. He reported to the 1874 Council that he had conducted twelve services there during the council year, with good prospects for the future. The Bishop had reported "a small church element" there on his visit in March of 1874. Though the Bishop also visited Lexington on this occasion, his silence suggests that the same promise was not seen in this latter community.[18]

There is no record of ministrations at Bastrop between the end of the war and the Spring of 1869. The Bishop spent a Sunday there. He confirmed two persons, one of whom was Mr. J. W. Phillips, a former Methodist minister, whose missionary labors in Columbus, La Grange and Giddings have been mentioned above. The following day Gregg presided at a meeting for the organization of a parish, and made arrangements for "Professor Swancoat" to conduct services monthly. Swancoat had recently been ordained Deacon in the same Council Service with Rosenberg. Colonel Charles S. James was licensed as layreader.[19] It is probable that the Reverend B. A. Rogers, Rector of St. David's Church in Austin, had done the preparatory work in the community, as well as directed Mr. Swancoat's reading for orders.

Calvary Church was admitted to membership in the Diocesan Council on the 27th of May 1869.[20] Within two years the arrangement with Swancoat terminated; in the Spring of 1871 Bishop Gregg remarked on his visitation that the people were anxious for services.[21] Perhaps the burden of travel proved too much for Swancoat, who was Principal of the Academy in Austin. The roads must have been fantastically bad between the two points, for Bishop Gregg recorded of his journey from Bastrop to Austin in March of 1870 that the buggy upset twice, but by the mercy of God none were hurt![22] Between the 1871 and 1872 Councils, Swancoat was transferred to the Diocese of Missouri,[23] but he had ceased to officiate at Bastrop before that time.

In the Spring of 1872 the Reverend J. W. Phillips took charge of the Parish as a part of his missionary field and conducted monthly services.[24] The number of communicants increased from sixteen to

[18]*Ibid.*, 1874, pp. 78, 46.

[19]*Ibid.*, 1869, pp. 23, 5, 24. For Swancoat's ministry to Lockhart, see above p. 161.

[20]*Texas Journal*, 1869, p. 6.   [21]*Ibid.*, 1871, p. 24.

[22]*Ibid.*, 1870, p. 4; Gregg, manuscript Journal, 11 Mar. 1870.

[23]*Texas Journal*, 1872, p. 40. He was back in Austin, and listed as "Missionary" in 1874. *Ibid.*, 1874, p. 4.

[24]*Ibid.*, 1872, p. 61.

twenty-eight in the year which followed, and the congregation had under consideration the purchase of a small, unused church building, planning to add to it as they were able.[25] This project apparently was not carried through, as Phillips made no mention of it in his report for 1874; but he did remark, "The Church interest in this Parish is increasing,"[26] a state of things further verified by the comment of Bishop Gregg made in his Council Address. Gregg stated that the children in the Bastrop Sunday School were better prepared than those at any other place he had visited, for which the Church was indebted to a Church woman who, in spite of feeble strength, worked faithfully and effectively at the job.[27] While the day was still ahead in which Calvary Church would have its own house of worship and a resident rector, foundations were being laid which made those goals possible.

For St. David's Church, Austin, the decade 1865-1875 was a bright one. In late November of 1865 the Reverend Benjamin A. Rogers of the Diocese of Pennsylvania took temporary charge of the Parish, since the Rector remained in the East following the 1865 General Convention, to which he was a Deputy. Rogers supplied during the Winter; then with Gillette's cordial recommendation,[28] he was elected Rector when Gillette decided not to return. He reported to the Diocesan Convention of 1866:

> . . . Through the active mercy of God, St. David's is now in a united and prosperous condition, and the Church, congregation and Sunday School are all giving good evidence of increasing interest and growth. The Sunday School has recently more than doubled its numbers, and is continuing to grow. . . . In all matters pertaining to the interests of the Church, the minister finds himself well supported by his people.[29]

Bishop Gregg must have desired an end to the disputes in the congregation that had been his first home Parish in Texas; on his visit in October of 1866, he was immensely pleased to find Rogers so well received and the Parish united under his leadership.[30]

With the increased tempo of the life of the congregation an addition to the building became necessary. Rogers reported to the 1867 Convention that there were hopes for enlarging the church should the congregation's prosperity continue.[31] A more ambitious scheme for an entirely new building was considered, but this was abandoned when insufficient funds were forthcoming from the many

[25]*Ibid.*, 1873, p. 60.   [26]*Ibid.*, 1874, p. 72.
[27]*Ibid.*, p. 47.   [28]*Ibid.*, 1866, p. 29; *St. David's*, p. 40.
[29]*Texas Journal*, 1866, p. 29.   [30]*Ibid.*, 1867, p. 17.   [31]*Ibid.*, p. 32.

money-raising projects of the choir and the church ladies. Plans
were then prepared to enlarge the existing building. The addition
was to the south end of the building, giving it the present south
wall; the chancel was reversed to occupy this space, the present west
door on San Jacinto Street became the main entrance, and the
seating faced south (opposite to its original and present orienta-
tion). New stained glass chancel windows, a new pipe organ, a carved
wood altar and reading desk and the present pulpit were given during
the process of enlargement and beautification.[32] With its beautiful
hilltop site, the church stood out as one of the prominent features
of the Austin skyline; its congregation was equally prominent in
influence and leadership in the community.

Much more than numerical growth and the improvement of
the church building must be credited to Rector Rogers and his
congregation. Austin was the focal point for Reconstruction tensions,
with Federal military headquarters, reconstruction politicians and
"carpetbaggers" rubbing shoulders with returned Confederate vet-
erans and resentful Confederate ladies. St. David's itself had plenty
of opportunity—and tradition—to tempt the extension of consequent
quarrels into its fellowship. Its membership included Elijah M.
Pease, longtime parishioner and benefactor of the Parish, who had
returned to the Governorship by Federal appointment, and the much
despised Governor E. J. Davis, while on the other side there were
many men who had served in the Confederate forces, and were working for a Democratic victory. The opportunity for conflicts was not
stifled by a policy of silence about affairs of State on the Rector's
part. He condemned unsparingly the corruption of the Reconstruction State government during the Davis administration, with
the Governor seated before him. Even though Davis' name was not
used, the point could not be missed. Yet somehow Rogers led his
people to exemplify on the parochial level the reconciling influences
of the Church which had so quickly and effectively brought the
northern and southern dioceses back together at the General Convention of 1865.[33]

Another service which Rogers must have rendered (though it
goes unmentioned in the official record) is that of recruitment
and training of clergy. Two members of St. David's flock, Richard
Swancoat and Emir Hamvasy, were ordained during his tenure, and
he probably helped them prepare for their examinations.[34] In ad-

[32]St. David's, pp. 44-8; Texas Journal, 1871, p. 24.
[33]St. David's, pp. 42ff.
[34]For Swancoat, see above, pp. 161, 202; for Hamvasy, see below, pp. 246-8.

dition, the Reverend J. W. Phillips very probably had been in touch with Rogers before deciding to come over from the Methodist ministry, though he is first mentioned in Bishop Gregg's diary at his confirmation at Bastrop. He lived in Austin while caring for La-Grange and Bastrop, probably to better prepare for his examinations for the Priesthood. In any event, Rogers' influence upon these men is obvious, and the teaching role played by Gillette before him would easily have led to the expectation that Rogers would follow it himself.

St. David's numbered 76 communicants at Rogers' first report in 1866; by 1874, shortly before his resignation, he reported an even 200.[35] Sunday School teachers had increased from eight to twenty; scholars from sixty-five to one hundred and sixty-five. Bishop Gregg reported the largest congregations and the largest confirmation class he had known in Austin in 1874. He praised the Rector, for he wished to keep him, and he knew that Rogers was contemplating a change to another position.[36] The contribution Rogers made to the Parish and to the Diocese in this critical period was very great, and his name is held in honorable esteem even today, not only in St. David's, but in other places which he served in a later residence in the Diocese.[37]

No attempt seems to have been made to revive the work formerly carried on at Manor, the former Wilbarger, in Travis County. Bishop Gregg returned there in 1874, conducting services and confirming one person, but he made no comment in the record concerning prospects for regular ministrations at the place.[38]

In Williamson County, to the north of Austin, Gregg recorded that he conducted "the first services of the Episcopal Church" at Brushy Chapel on August 6, 1865,[39] but the congregation does not again appear in the record. In October of the same year, he held services in Round Rock,[40] but this effort was not repeated during the decade. At Georgetown, the County Seat, the Bishop, accom-

---

[35]*Texas Journal*, 1866, p. 29; 1874, p. 72.

[36]*Ibid.*, p. 47; *St. David's*, pp. 48-9.

[37]Rogers became Associate Secretary for the Society for the Increase of the Ministry, with headquarters in Connecticut in 1875, but remained canonically connected with the Diocese. *Texas Journal*, 1875, p. 25. He then transferred to the Diocese of Illinois, but returned in 1877, with residence in Austin, serving as Missionary at large. *Ibid.*, 1877, p. 11. He was Rector of St. Paul's Church, Waco, from 1880 to 1883. Luella Conger Boynton, compiler, *St. Paul's Episcopal Church, Waco, Texas, 1863-1963, A Hundred Years' Witness* (Waco, 1963), p. 9. This excellent centennial history was published when this present work was being readied for the press.

[38]*Texas Journal*, 1874, p. 47.   [39]*Ibid.*, 1866, p. 18.   [40]*Ibid.*, p. 18.

panied by Rogers, went to conduct services and preach in March 1868;[41] we may well speculate that the zealous missionary interest of Rogers had already extended here, as it had to Bastrop. Nothing more appears in the records of the Diocese concerning Georgetown until 1874. That year the Reverend J. W. Phillips reported for the "Georgetown Mission," stating that he had conducted four weekday services, and had found enough communicants and adherents in the town to justify further effort.[42]

If the revival of the work of the Church at Bastrop and George-town may presumably be credited to the work of the Rector of St. David's Parish, Austin, the beginnings of the Church in Lam-pasas surely trace to a layman from the same parish. Dr. Thomas S. Denny, a member of St. David's vestry from 1870 to 1872,[43] moved to Lampasas in late 1872 and found a few Church people who also had migrated to that town. Bishop Gregg licensed Dr. Denny to read services, and he gathered the flock for worship.[44] Dr. Denny reported to the 1873 Council for the mission, relating that there were eleven communicants, and that a Sunday School was soon to be organized.[45]

With its high altitude and its mineral waters, Lampasas was highly regarded as a health and summer resort in that period, at-tracting a number of visitors. Amongst them in the first Summer of the mission were two clergy of the Diocese, the Reverend T. R. B. Trader and the Reverend J. T. Hutcheson, both of whom made themselves available for ministrations, baptizing and celebrating the Holy Communion. The Bishop made his first visitation to the con-gregation in October 1873 and saw hope for the development of a parish there.[46] Thus at what was to be the very western corner of the reduced Diocese of Texas, a Hill Country congregation came into being to season the cotton-planting and piney woods majority with a dash of the flavor of the Old West.

XIX. Belton to Bellville

NORTHWARD, just beyond the sphere of influence of the Austin Parish the congregation at Belton was served by the Reverend Lindsey P. Rucker on a monthly basis until 1867. This was a year of heavy rainfall and flooding of the streams which the veteran

41*Ibid.*, 1868, p. 20.   42*Ibid.*, 1874, p. 78.
43*St. David's*, p. 74.   44*Diocese of Texas*, Jan. 1873, p. 5.
45*Texas Journal*, 1873, p. 70.   46*Ibid.*, 1874, p. 38.

Priest had to ford in his journeys from his home in Burleson County. Rucker had other fields of work already, and now he saw a new opening at San Antonio Prairie, Burleson County. Since this promised a better response than did Belton, Rucker obtained the Bishop's consent to transfer attention there.[1] This left Belton without a minister.

BELTON

In November 1871, Bishop Gregg visited the congregation, with the intention of going on to Gatesville before his appointment at Waco. High water prevented this journey, and gave the Bishop time to give the Belton congregation four days of pastoral attention. So much interest resulted that he requested the Reverend W. W. Patrick, who had just given up his school at Gatesville and returned to Waco, to conduct monthly services at Belton. General John C. Moore, who had recently been associated with the Diocesan School at Brenham, was licensed as layreader to conduct services on the other Sundays.[2]

Patrick did well in the field. The congregation was flourishing, the ladies were busy raising funds, and a contract had been let for a building. By Council time, Patrick reported the stone walls were up for the new church, but the congregation had run out of funds with which to complete it. Patrick was still residing in Waco and visiting Belton once a month.[3] Appeals for aid for the completion of the church were sent to other congregations in the Diocese, and contributions came in from Galveston, Houston, Waco, Navasota and Bryan, while the local congregation managed to raise almost $1500 in additional funds themselves.[4] In October of 1873, the Bishop found the church building almost completed, and plans well advanced for establishing a parish school. With the railroad construction rapidly approaching Belton, the prospects for the County appeared bright, and the future of the congregation was promising. When the church was completed Patrick moved to Belton to give his full time to that flock.[5]

Two other places at which Patrick ministered after he resigned as Rector of St. Paul's Church, Waco, were Howard and Gatesville. Howard, "a small village nine miles east of Belton," Patrick included in his missionary circuit in 1872, and he held services there once a month through the first half of 1873. Though he stated that

[1] *Texas Journal*, 1866, p. 30; 1867, p. 32.
[2] *Ibid.*, 1872, pp. 24-5, 1871, p. 29.   [3] *Ibid.*, 1873, pp. 30, 61.
[4] *Diocese of Texas*, Feb. 1874, p. 5.
[5] *Texas Journal*, 1874, p. 38; *Diocese of Texas*, Mar. 1874, p. 5.

attendance at the services was always good, it was decided for some reason not to continue them. Bishop Gregg preached at an evening service there in 1872, but no confirmation candidates were presented to him.[6]

Gatesville, the County Seat of Coryell County, obtained a mission of the Episcopal Church when Mr. Patrick moved there following his resignation from the Waco Parish in 1871. He held his first service in February and began regular Sunday services each week the following month. Though there were but six communicants in the town, a Sunday School with twenty children was begun, and attendance at Church services averaged around eighty persons. Patrick believed a parish could be built up in the place.[7] But, as so often was the case in frontier communities, people moved away; during his year of residence in Gatesville five of the six communicants left the town. Patrick moved back to Waco at the end of March 1872, to make that city his headquarters for missionary work in towns within reach. Before leaving Gatesville, however, he received the gift of "a beautiful lot for Church purposes" from Judge J. W. Maberry.[8]

WACO

At the end of the Civil War the Reverend S. D. Davenport was still in charge of the Waco mission. Many refugees from federally occupied territory lived there temporarily and were communicants. When many of them left, it was impossible to sustain a minister, so Davenport was transferred to Marshall and Jefferson.[9]

At his visitation to Waco in October 1866, Bishop Gregg discovered that the Church people wanted another minister, not only to maintain regular services, but to start a school for boys. Gregg was fortunately in touch with a clergyman competent for both tasks.[10] The new missionary was the Reverend W. W. Patrick from the Diocese of South Carolina, where he had been missionary to Negroes in St. Stephen's and Upper St. John's Parishes.[11] Though he was appointed missionary to San Augustine as of January 1, 1867, with a stipend of $200 from the Domestic Committee,[12] he

---

[6]*Texas Journal,* 1872, p. 67; 1873, pp. 30, 61. 1873, pp. 30, 61.

[7]*Ibid.,* 1871, pp. 23, 42.   [8]*Ibid.,* 1872, p. 67.

[9]*Ibid.,* 1866, p. 39; Minutes, Domestic Committee, Board of Missions, stated meeting 6 February 1866, Minutes Book, p. 362.

[10]*Texas Journal,* 1867, p. 17.

[11]*South Carolina Journal,* 1864, p. 5.

[12]Minutes, Domestic Committee, Board of Missions, stated meeting 4 Feb. 1867, Minutes Book, p. 7.

does not appear to have accepted this. He first appeared in the diocesan records in Bishop Gregg's 1867 Convention Address, where it was noted that at St. Paul's Church, Washington, on May 24th Patrick read service and the Bishop preached. Patrick was also present at the Convention at Brenham the weekend following. He may have been supplying at Washington, since the Reverend R. S. Seely had removed from that Parish in October of 1866.[13]

Patrick took charge of the Church in Waco July 10, 1867, and immediate results of his energy appeared. Two lots were acquired and a chapel building placed on them at a cost of $1260; only $500 was owed for this by convention time of 1868. In September of 1867, Patrick established the Episcopal High School in Waco. He boasted that the young men of the Diocese could "be thoroughly educated, and . . . they could learn to appreciate the advantages of the Church." He enrolled between thirty and forty-five pupils during the period covered by the report, and there was instruction in Latin, Greek, Mathematics and English.[14] The next step, the organization of a parish, was taken during Bishop Gregg's visitation on March 19, 1868. "Mr. Patrick," the Bishop wrote, "has labored faithfully and well for the Church and school, and his work has been blessed."[15]

St. Paul's Parish was admitted to the Diocesan Convention at Austin on May 28, 1868, and it was represented by its new Rector and F. S. Hawley and Fred Quarles.[16] The Bishop returned for another visitation at Christmas of 1868, and recorded:

> Notwithstanding the addition and heavy labor of his school, Mr. Patrick has continued to work faithfully in the parish, and entertains well-grounded hope for the future.[17]

These hopes were not illusory. The congregations were large; the Bishop praised the conduct of services as impressive, and he held up for special notice the excellent preparation given to children. Two layreaders were licensed to assist the Rector, Messrs. R. S. Nash and George W. Jackson.[18] Nash appears to have taught in the Episcopal High School, and he was a Candidate for ordination to the Diaconate. He was ordained on January 2, 1870, in St. Paul's Church, Navasota.[19] He returned to Waco to assist Patrick in the work of

---

[13]*Texas Journal*, 1867, pp. 6, 23, 36.

[14]*Ibid.*, 1868, pp. 34-5; the school was conducted in the church building; Boynton, *St. Paul's*, p. 8.

[15]*Texas Journal*, 1868, p. 20.   [16]*Ibid.*, p. 4.   [17]*Ibid.*, 1869, p. 19.

[18]Gregg, manuscript Journal, 16-19 Oct. 1869.   [19]*Ibid.*, 2 Jan. 1870.

the Parish and in the school. The church building was renovated in 1870, and a general strengthening both in numbers and in conviction was reported for the congregation.[20]

In January 1871 Patrick resigned and moved to Gatesville.[21] The Parish was still without a rector by council time, 1871, but regular services had been maintained; Nash officiated before his removal to Cleburne. Then George W. Jackson read lay services. Though the vestry was striving to secure a rector, it was endeavoring at the same time both to secure sufficient funds to be able to pay an adequate salary and to acquire a rectory.[22]

The Reverend Otis Hackett became Rector in the Fall of 1871, being received from the Diocese of Louisiana.[23] Very soon after his arrival Bishop Gregg was present for visitation, and wrote:

> The Rev. Mr. Hackett . . . it was very manifest, had gone earnestly and successfully to work, presenting, in a goodly confirmation class, the first fruits of his labor. The results of the faithful and self-denying labors of Mr. Patrick, in this place, will long be seen and felt.

The Bishop remarked upon the large attendance at the services during this visitation,[24] but not as vividly as did Hackett in the Church press. Hackett related that the church was entirely filled, and people outside crowded about the doors and windows in great numbers. He also gave an interesting account of Waco at this time, describing it as a contradiction; a growing and bustling town of 5000, prosperous and on the increase in spite of the lack of a railroad at a time when other towns so hampered were failing. He also reported that the church building then in use had been constructed after the second building fund for the congregation had been raised. In Davenport's day during the war, a sum of money had been raised and invested in Confederate bonds, which of course were worthless at the war's end.[25]

Since Hackett was receiving a stipend of $150 per annum from the Domestic Committee,[26] he sent them a report about this same time; the report was printed in the *Spirit of Missions* without date or author's name. It is eloquent of the situation of the Church in an "over-churched" community in that era:

> Our prospects are as encouraging as could be reasonably expected. We were late—among the last—in the field here. The

[20] *Texas Journal,* 1870, p. 29.   [21] *Ibid.,* 1871, p. 23.
[22] *Ibid.,* p. 49.   [23] *Ibid.,* 1872, p. 40.   [24] *Ibid.,* p. 25.
[25] *The Churchman,* N.S., V., No. 50 (Dec. 9, 1871), p. 395.
[26] Minutes of Domestic Committee, Minutes Book, 1872, p. 138.

ground was preoccupied by the Baptists and Methodists, and educational institutions founded, the "Waco University" by the former, and a "Female College" by the latter, before any persistent efforts were made to establish the Church. And besides these two dominant bodies, the Old School Presbyterians, Cumberland Presbyterians, Campbellites, Romanists, and German Methodists, are each struggling to gain or maintain a foothold in this little sect-riven community.

How sad that a house should be thus miserably divided and subdivided against itself—*eight* competing dispensers of the Gospel to a church-going population of a thousand souls! What a spectacle for an incredulous world! What a stumbling-block to the honest inquirer! Who can wonder that so many are driven into the extremes of Popery and Infidelity? . . .

The Church is taking root here. Overshadowed though it now is, and looked upon as a strange plant, we have no fear of its dying out or being stunted. It is needed, and sooner or later will be wanted and welcomed. The kingdom of God "is like a grain of mustard seed, which a man took and cast into his garden; and it grew and waxed a great tree; and the fowls of the air lodged in the branches of it."[27]

As good as their word, the vestry purchased a rectory for Hackett, even though it involved them in debt for part of its cost.[28] The new financial burdens of building payments and an adequate salary for the Rector brought the Waco congregation to search for new methods for securing contributions; the innovation of the envelope system emerged, apparently for the first time in the Diocese. Bishop Gregg commended it in his 1873 Council Address, following which a committee was appointed to report on it to the Council. The chairman, George W. Jackson of Waco, explained its operation and exhibited samples of the materials in use; the committee recommended that the system be generally adopted, and their report was accepted by the Council.[29] The following year it was reported that the Parish was self-supporting; only a larger church building was wanting to make its situation most favorable.[30] Upon his visit to Waco in October of 1873 the Bishop said:

> As I contrast the Parish, now, in its efficient organization and hundred communicants, with the prospect as it appeared in March, 1860, when the first visitation was made, and three

[27] *Spirit of Missions*, 1872, p. 594

[28] It must have been a fairly good house for that day; its cost was $2250 gold, with three lots. The original cost of the chapel had been $1260. *Texas Journal*, 1872, p. 76.

[29] *Ibid.*, 1873, pp. 16, 50-2. This Council met in Waco.

[30] *Ibid.*, 1874, pp. 38, 57.

Church families were found, and four or five communicants,
there is abundant reason to thank God and take courage.[31]

"RUCKER COUNTRY"

The work carried on by the Reverend L. P. Rucker in Burleson
and Milam Counties was strenuous enough, even after he had dis-
continued his efforts at Belton. The help he had previously received
from the Reverend C. W. Stone, Deacon, was no longer available
in the Convention year 1865-66. The latter's address was listed as
Lexington and his status as inactive in 1866; subsequently Stone
renounced the Ministry and was deposed.[32] This left Rucker alone
in the field. The doughty veteran was not easily discouraged, however. In his report to the 1866 Convention, apparently after Stone
had withdrawn from the work, and while Rucker was still making
the burdensome journey to Belton each month, he expressed himself
about his rural circuit:

> The Missionary reports . . . that since the first of January past
> he has been officiating regularly, when not prevented by bad
> weather, one Sunday in the month at each of the three places
> in the above Mission, viz: At a schoolhouse near Maj. Richards',
> in Milam county, on the 1st Sunday in the month; at Caldwell,
> in Burleson county, on the 3rd Sunday; and at Cameron, in
> Milam county, on the 4th Sunday. There has been no organiza-
> tion in either place, and no official acts have yet been performed
> beyond the regular services, and these have been somewhat *ir-
> regular*, owing to the continual floods of rain and high waters,
> there being no ferry on Little River. There are some fifteen com-
> municants within the Mission. Your missionary feels much en-
> couraged, however, at the general spirit of inquiry and marked
> interest shown at all three of these points, *not only, as heretofore,
> by the few church friends* in the community, but by the masses
> of the population. To meet the general desire for information
> about the Church, evening lectures have been commenced at
> Cameron and Caldwell explanatory of the most prominent dis-
> tinctive features of the Church; and these are being attended
> with very marked interest so far, in both instances. Your Mis-
> sionary hopes that, with God's blessing on his well meant efforts,
> he may have interesting statistics to report by the next Annual
> Convention.[33]

Rucker's hopes were, alas, doomed to disappointment. In the
following September Bishop Gregg had scheduled a circuit about

---

[31]*Ibid.*, p. 39.
[32]*Texas Journal*, 1866, p. 5; 1867, p. 25.
[33]*Ibid.*, pp. 31-2.

Rucker's field between his Austin and Waco visits, but he was taken sick; cholera, which had been epidemic in San Antonio and had struck in his family, began to show its first symptoms in Gregg. His son's account has it:

> While on the road between Austin and Belton the symptoms of the dread disease manifested themselves, but with his experience in nursing cholera, he knew what treatment to apply, and found relief. The following day he had a recurrence of the symptoms, which again yielded to treatment. Writing to his family, he expressed his dread of being abandoned on the road, and yet how he was constrained to proceed in the line of duty.[34]

Bishops must make their appointments on schedule if at all possible; thus Gregg regretfully passed Rucker's field by so that he could reach Waco and Dallas on time.[35] Rucker was still hopeful, as he wrote his next annual report, that there would be candidates for Confirmation when the Bishop could finally make a visitation. Cameron had by then only one communicant, though several were thought disposed to be confirmed. In the country surrounding Caldwell there were five or six communicants, but none in the town; nevertheless, response to the services was good, and an increase looked for. At Major Richard's neighborhood there were another six communicants and some candidates.[36] But before the next Convention Rucker was needed to shepherd a more densely populated area; the small flocks would be cared for more adequately only after the division of the Diocese.

Rucker was called to Brenham, where St. Peter's Church was in difficulties. This call must have been irresistible, for it was here that Rucker had first been attracted to the Episcopal Church. After Shaver's departure during the war, Rucker had included Brenham and Independence in his vast field, receiving some assistance from Stone in Burleson and Milam Counties.[37] At the Council of 1865, with the ordination to the Diaconate of D. W. Chase of Independence, Rucker received much needed relief; Chase became for a time responsible for Brenham along with Independence.[38]

The prospects for the Brenham Parish improved during Chase's tenure. The repair of the church building was a much-needed project ready to be undertaken under Rucker when the collapse of the Confederate cause forced its postponement;[39] it was now carried out

---

[34] W. Gregg, *Gregg,* pp. 99-100.
[35] *Texas Journal,* 1867, p. 17.   [36] *Ibid.,* p. 33.
[37] *Ibid.,* 1864, pp. 19, 22; 1865, pp. 27, 29, 30.
[38] *Ibid.,* p. 7; 1866, p. 5.   [39] *Ibid.,* 1865, p. 27.

before the Convention of 1866 met. Chase reported for the congregation:

> The church building in this place has recently been "put in order," and rendered comfortable and pleasant. The contributions for the purpose have been liberal, and made, in many cases, without solicitation. The congregation is large and attentive, and a deep interest manifested in the services. A small Sunday School has been organized with encouraging prospects. But what is still more gratifying, the Vestry is composed, in part at least, of that which is so much needed in every Parish, viz: active, zealous, "working men." Truly we have abundant reason to "thank God, and take courage."[40]

In September of 1866 the Reverend A. F. Dobb began teaching in Independence (presumably in Mr. Chase's "Church School for Young Ladies"), and taught there through December. At Christmas of that year, he became Rector of St. Peter's Parish, Brenham, allowing Chase to concentrate upon the Parish at Independence and upon his school.[41] The 1867 Convention met at Brenham amidst the most encouraging signs for the future of the Parish; these included the revival of St. Paul's College in its new location in Brenham. But the prospects of town, Parish and College were dashed by the twin tragedies which struck Brenham later that year—the yellow fever epidemic and the destructive fire which resulted from the friction between Federal soldiers and citizens.[42] Dobb left soon thereafter, being transferred to the Diocese of Kentucky.[43] Rucker was called back to pastor a stricken parish. He reported to the 1868 Convention:

> This parish was so devastated by destructive fires, and scourged by pestilence, during the past year, as to require time and patient, persevering labor to revive the spirits of the bereaved, heartbroken and afflicted few that were left to mourn over their desolate waste places. The rapid influx of population, and growth of the place, however, are adding steadily to the growth of the parish, and with a year or two of rest, and even a moderate share of prosperity, it is believed that St. Peter's Church will become one of the more interesting inland parishes of the Diocese.[44]

Rucker's prophecy was not too sanguine. In May of 1869 Bishop Gregg confirmed seventeen persons in the Parish, the largest single class up to that time for Brenham, and he reported that attendance was so great that an enlargement of the church building was

---

[40]*Ibid.*, 1866, pp. 30-31.   [41]*Ibid.*, 1867, pp. 33-34.
[42]*Handbook of Texas*, "Brenham," *en. loc.*
[43]*Texas Journal*, 1868, p. 25.   [44]*Ibid.*, p. 29.

urgently required.[45] Confirmations were held again in October, January and May, the Bishop reporting "good feeling in the Parish."[46] In May, 1871, the Bishop remarked upon his visitation, "The church building here has been enlarged and improved, and the Parish is doing well."[47]

The city of Brenham, and St. Peter's Parish with it, suffered a temporary setback in 1871 when the railroad, which so long had terminated there, was extended toward Austin. In spite of losses by removal, however, Rucker reported the general state of the Parish was good, and improvements were made on the church building to afford "a more 'decent and reverent' worship of God." With his usual hopeful disposition the Rector looked for an increase in numbers to offset the losses.[48] Recovery was slow in the era of hard times which fell upon the country. In order to support his family, Rucker had to return to his old profession of schoolteaching. He gave such time as he could find to the Parish, bravely staying with his people in bad times as well as good. He became the Senior Presbyter of the Diocese upon the death of Benjamin Eaton in 1871. He was elected President of the Standing Committee in Eaton's place that year, and for many years served well in that office.[49]

From the time Rucker returned to Brenham he was not content to confine his ministrations to that Parish alone; with his unfailing zeal for missions, he reached out to other places. The account of his ministry in these places will be related elsewhere. The careers of the other two congregations in Washington County meanwhile deserve notice.

WASHINGTON AND INDEPENDENCE

St. Paul's Church, Washington, was still under the care of the Reverend R. S. Seely at the close of 1865. He reported to the Convention of that year:

> We have been laboring for some time to establish a school of the first order in this Parish, but our numbers are still small. Our sons have been compelled to learn the arts of war instead of those of peace. We hope, however, as the war has now ended, that our numbers will be greatly increased.[50]

The year following he could report that the school was still able to operate successfully, but he had to relate a sad decline in the mem-

[45]*Ibid.*, 1869, p. 23.
[46]Gregg, manuscript Journal, 4 Oct., 1869; 11 Jan., 28-29 May, 1870.
[47]*Texas Journal*, 1871, p. 28.   [48]*Ibid.*, p. 40.
[49]*Ibid.*, pp. 43, 3.   [50]*Ibid.*, 1865, pp. 5, 18, 31.

bership of the Parish. Five communicants had died and ten removed from the community leaving only ten in the Parish.[51] While the effects of the railroad serving Navasota were not too serious during the war, they now began rapidly to undermine the economy of Washington.[52] As every southern plantation town, Washington faced the adjustment from slave to free labor. By the first of October, 1866, Seely had to give up; he removed to the small Robertson County community of Owensville where he opened a school; he did missionary work there, and at Stirling and Wheelock.[53]

For a time there were hopes that the town of Washington would be revived. Bishop Gregg conducted services there on May 24, assisted by the Reverend W. W. Patrick, and stated that the Parish showed signs of a return to vigor.[54] For the next two years the Bishop made an annual visitation to the Parish,[55] but if other services were conducted in the intervals between these visits, they have not been recorded. In April of 1870 the old church building, the beloved "red cedar church," was moved across the Brazos River to Navasota,[56] where it could be put to more frequent use. Thereafter St. Paul's Washington, disappears from the record, its members, if any remained, presumably attended services occasionally at Navasota.

The other Parish in Washington County, Grace Church, Independence, was served throughout the decade by the Perpetual Deacon, D. W. Chase, whose educational activities have been noticed in a previous chapter. In 1866 he said in his report:

> The congregation is steadily increasing in numbers and interest, although the Parish has still to contend against much opposition. . . . A church building is much needed, and is indispensable to the permanent prosperity of the Parish.[57]

It will be recalled that the small community of Independence was then the locale of Baylor University, with its Female Department; the town was a Baptist stronghold. The Episcopal Church and Episcopal schools must have aroused considerable opposition there.[58] There were, nevertheless, twenty-three communicants in 1866, and a Sunday School with five teachers and forty scholars.[59]

Chase, by all accounts a sweet and gentle man, was long on pa-

[51]Ibid., 1866, p. 39.
[52]Centennial Edition, Navasota Examiner (July 1, 1954), (n.p.)
[53]Texas Journal, 1867, p. 36; see below, p. 231.
[54]Texas Journal, 1867, p. 25.   [55]Ibid., 1868, p. 21; 1869, p. 23.
[56]Ibid., 1870, p. 27.   [57]Ibid., 1866, p. 35.
[58]Handbook of Texas, "Baylor University," en. loc.
[59]Texas Journal, 1866, p. 35.

tience and determination. Still unable during the year ensuing to
make a beginning on a church building, he secured a small organ
for church services, which evidently were conducted in his school,
and looked with hope to the future for a house of worship.[60] Hard
times intervened in the next year; half of the communicants had left
the vicinity, and the school was hard hit. Chase turned to meet another need in the community, the education of the freedmen, reporting eighty-five in a Sunday School in 1868.[61] Holding bravely on
with the work of the Parish in spite of diminished numbers, he lasted
through the bad times; in January of 1870 Bishop Gregg noted
that steps were being taken "to fix up a building for a church."[62]
In May of 1871 he wrote in his Journal:

> A neat church building is being erected here through the un-
> tiring efforts of Rev. Mr. Chase, and there are otherwise more
> signs of life and growth than for some time past.

Five white persons and one colored were confirmed at a night service
during this visitation,[63] which enabled Chase to report twenty-four
communicants; he reported, in addition twenty catechumens, undoubtedly colored adults in his Sunday School for freedmen. Concerning the new building he wrote:

> At the last Council I reported $214.30 for repairs of Church . . .
> making $1083.15 which has been expended on the new Church.
> We hope in a few months to have it so far completed as to be
> be able to occupy it, although from $900 to $1000 will be re-
> quired to finish it as we desire.[64]

The building was indeed occupied, and Bishop Gregg explained
why this was accomplished in his address to the 1872 Convention:

> the small but comely church building here will be an enduring
> monument to the persevering labor and self-denying devotion
> of Rev. Mr. Chase. Much of the work was done with his own
> hands, and under discouragements which would have paralyzed
> the efforts of most men. His little flock stood by him and did
> what they could. It is hoped the building will be ready for con-
> secration by another year.[65]

Chase became quite ill, and unable to officiate, late in 1872;
he was reported "about over his illness, and able again to officiate" in
January of 1873.[66] Probably during his sickness he lost the fol-

---

[60]*Ibid.*, 1867, p. 34.   [61]*Ibid.*, 1868, p. 32.
[62]Gregg, manuscript Journal, 11-12 Jan., 1870.
[63]*Texas Journal*, 1871, p. 28.
[64]*Ibid.*, pp. 43-4.   [65]*Ibid.*, 1872, p. 31.
[66]*Diocese of Texas*, Jan. 1873, p. 5.

lowing he had amongst the freedmen; in 1872 he had reported thirty catechumens, and but one in 1873, and there were no baptisms of colored people reported in the interval.[67] But his church building was consecrated by Bishop Gregg, assisted by Chase, Rucker and Wickens, on March 12, 1873. The Bishop observed:

> This was a joyous day for the faithful minister and his people, who had struggled hard to bring their comely building to completion, and will mark an era in the life of the parish.[68]

As Chase had predicted, the completion of the building set aside for worship accelerated the growth of the Parish and the devotion of the people; thirty-five communicants were reported in 1873, the greatest number the Parish had ever had.[69] Patience, sacrifice and hard work had proved their worth in establishing the Church in an unlikely environment.

BELLVILLE AND TRAVIS

South of Washington County, St. Mary's Parish, Bellville was apparently without a Rector in 1865, when the Bishop visited it in June,[70] but some time between that date and May of 1867 the Reverend H. B. Monges, Deacon, removed there from Seguin, and became the missionary in charge. Bishop Gregg reported that an attempt would be made to erect a church building, and that, in response to the desires of many of the people, a Church School would be started there.[71] Monges evidently did begin teaching school, and was trying, at the same time, to do sufficient reading to pass his examination for the Priesthood, having been admitted a Candidate for Priest's orders that year.[72] His health continued frail, however; he was able to conduct serivces only on alternate Sundays, but hoped to be able to have them every Sunday as his health improved.[73] He continued in charge during 1868 and 1869, but filed only statistical reports, giving no details, either of his own health and progress or of the reasons the congregation showed no growth. In 1870 the Reverend Mr. Rucker filed the parochial report as Rector, and Monges appended a supplementary statement that he had acted only as Rucker's assistant during the year. Rucker stated his belief that the Parish would soon be an interesting one, in spite of its

---

[67]*Texas Journal*, 1872, p. 69; 1873, pp. 68-9.
[68]*Ibid.*, p. 36.   [69]*Ibid.*, p. 68.
[70]*Ibid.*, 1865, p. 21.   [71]*Ibid.*, 1867, p. 24.
[72]Gregg, manuscript Journal, List of Candidates.
[73]*Texas Journal*, 1867, p. 32.

small membership (only eight communicants). The stability of the community had been disturbed by agitation for the division of Austin County, and the removal of the County Seat from Bellville.[74] Austin County at that time included a large tract of land on the East of the Brazos River, including Hempstead, and the inhabitants of that part of the County were restive about the distance to the County Seat.[75] If the question were settled in Bellville's favor, the future of the town and Parish should become good.

At the beginning of 1871 Rucker had to give up the charge of Bellville, as he had given up Hempstead, in order to devote his time to teaching; Monges was again in sole charge, but added nothing to the report that Rucker gave to the 1871 Council.[76]

The following year Monges was still listed in the Clergy List as Deacon in charge of St. Mary's, but he did not appear to have been present in February of that year, when the Bishop made his visitation.[77] Thereafter he disappeared from the record; strangely, Bishop Gregg made no mention of his whereabouts, nor of transferring him to any other jurisdiction, nor was his name carried on the Clergy List. In the manuscript Register of Clergy of the Diocese his dismissal to the Diocese of California is dated 1881. The likeliest conjecture is that he left for his health, always hoping to return, until the date of his transfer.

Bishop Gregg, visiting Bellville in February of 1874, reported that Rucker was again in charge, conducting a Sunday service every month.[78] The question of the County Seat was now settled in Bellville's favor, though the eastern portion of the County had been cut off, and, with some territory from Grimes County added, made into Waller County, with Hempstead as the County Seat.[79] The uncertainty that was now holding back development was the route that would be taken by the railroad now approaching the County; if Bellville won (which it did), the town would progress. The communicant roll had doubled since the last report, there now being sixteen names on it.[80]

Meanwhile, another locality in Austin County had secured a mission; Rucker had been working at the Settlement of Travis,

[74]*Ibid.*, 1870, p. 23.

[75]Frank MacDonald Spindler, "St. Bartholomew's Church, Hempstead, Texas," *Historical Magazine*, XXIX (1960), pp. 56-90, deals incidentally with the Bellville Parish, p. 57.

[76]*Texas Journal*, 1871, p. 39.

[77]*Ibid.*, 1872, pp. 3, 30.   [78]*Ibid.*, 1874, p. 43.

[79]Spindler, "St. Bartholomew's," p. 57.

[80]*Texas Journal*, 1874, pp. 43, 73.

effectively, as the Bishop remarked upon visiting it. Here Henry
Justus Brown, Jr., who was teaching school, was appointed layreader,
and also enrolled as a Candidate for the Priesthood.[81]

The work of the Church in the entire area, from Belton and
Waco to Bellville was carried on in a largely rural culture. With
the single exception of Brenham no town within it in which the
Church's work was being carried on was as yet served by a railroad.
Shortage of clergy had made necessary the abandonment of regular
work in Milam and Burleson Counties, yet Rucker's labors in them
had shown the capability of the Episcopal Church to work in the
open countryside in this part of Texas. The work at Travis in Austin
County indicated the same thing. It was the misfortune of the Diocese
to be so pressed for missionary funds and manpower during this
decade that most of the opportunities for work in this kind of setting
had to be neglected in favor of another much more strategic effort,
that of making the ministrations of the Church available to the
people involved in the great railroad boom accompanying the extension of the Texas Central Railroad northward.

XX.   The Texas Central Railroad Mission

THE CIVIL WAR had brought an end to construction of railroads
in Texas, but with the coming of peace it resumed. The railroad
which promised the greatest aid to the development of the interior
of Texas in the decade following the war was the Houston and Texas
Central, most often referred to in the documents of the Church
as the Texas Central, or just the Central Railroad. It was this road
which first resumed building at the close of the war.[1] Many people
were involved in the construction and in the business incident to it,
as well as in the operation of the completed portions of the road.
In a shattered post-war economy the outpouring of railroad money
drew a throng of job seekers and hangers-on to the area. There was
no more open situation in Texas into which the influence of the
Church could be directed.

The first junction point on the railroad above Houston was
Hempstead, where the Washington County Railroad joined the Central to serve Brenham and its trade territory. This made for important
activity in Hempstead, even before the former road was bought
by the Houston and Texas Central and extended to Austin in 1871.

[81]*Ibid.*, pp. 43, 51.
[1]*Handbook of Texas*, "Houston and Texas Central Railroad," *en. loc.*

HEMPSTEAD

When the Reverend L. P. Rucker returned to Brenham, his first outreach was to Hempstead, for which he reported in 1868, telling of its organization and its hope for building a house of worship, in spite of the setback which the epidemic had given the town.[2] St. Bartholomew's Parish had been admitted to the Diocese at the Convention of 1867, it being represented there by Messrs. D. W. Broadnax, J. W. McDade and F. J. Cooke.[3] The Bishop was even then attempting to find a pastor for the new Parish. Rucker took charge in February 1868.[4]

Rucker's work at Hempstead was as successful in the early days as was his labor at Brenham, and the Bishop found much about it to encourage him. The fund for the new building was growing, with promise for a beginning on construction within the year. The congregation was growing and boasted a choir, with a Sunday School in process of organization.[5] By May 1870 the building was commenced, with hopes to enclose it sufficiently for use within months, postponing its adornment and finishing touches until contributions from outside made them possible.[6] The following year Rucker reported to Council:

> For want of support, I found it necessary in March last, to engage in teaching, in Brenham, and consequently, was compelled to give up my appointment at Hempstead. I very deeply regret the necessity for taking such a step, but felt that my way was completely hedged up at Hempstead, and, therefore, reluctantly retired from the field.[7]

In November 1871, the Reverend J. T. Hutcheson took charge of Hempstead, and under his guiding hand the funds to ready the church for services were secured in the Parish. Though Hutcheson reported that strong prejudices existed against the Church in the town, the Parish nevertheless was in a favorable position for growth. The Bishop remarked that "the people themselves, who had been almost hopeless, were surprised and delighted at the results of his efforts." Hutcheson did not remain long, however; he accepted the rectorship of Christ Church, Matagorda in May 1872.[8]

[2]*Texas Journal*, 1868, pp. 30-1. For the collapse of the proposal for a Church School here, see above, p. 131. See also the Reverend F. M. Spindler's account of the history of St. Bartholomew's Parish, "St. Bartholomew's," *Historical Magazine*, XXIX (1960), pp. 56-90.

[3]*Texas Journal*, 1867, pp. 4, 7.

[4]*Ibid.*, p. 25; 1868, pp. 30-1.   [5]*Ibid.*, 1869, pp. 23, 29.

[6]Gregg, manuscript Journal, 24 May 1870; *Texas Journal*, 1870, p. 26.

[7]*Ibid.*, 1871, p. 43.   [8]*Ibid.*, 1872, pp. 68, 30; 1873, pp. 66, 72.

Hutcheson was succeeded at Hempstead by the Reverend J. Cooper Waddill, whose headquarters and principal charge was at Calvert, farther up the Central Railroad. He reported to the Council of 1873 that the church was now furnished with organ and pews, with debts so near liquidation that it should soon be consecrated.[9] Waddill's time was too limited to permit him to reach thus far for long, however, and by February Hempstead was in charge of the Reverend Virginius O. Gee, resident at Bryan, and serving Navasota and Millican along with Hempstead, an arrangement that was made after Gee had for a short time been resident Rector at Navasota.[10]

NAVASOTA

The year 1866 saw the quickening of the life of the Church in Navasota, where, on June 5, Bishop Gregg was present at the organization of a parish. The Railroad Company had donated a block of land for a church, rectory and school. It was the Bishop's hope to find a clergyman who would reside at Navasota, and take care of other points along the railroad as they developed. Meanwhile the Reverend R. S. Seely was conducting services once a month for the Navasota people. The Parish was admitted to the Diocese at the Convention in Houston June 14, 1866, with the name, "Church of the Holy Comforter."[11]

A clergyman was not soon found. During the first half of 1867 Mr. Andrew J. Yeater, a Candidate for Holy Orders, held services at Navasota and Anderson.[12] Some time in 1869 that missionary whirlwind the Reverend L. P. Rucker added Navasota to the long list of his commitments, affording the flock a regular monthly service, and his energetic leadership. He foresaw "the speedy erection of a church building and parsonage."[13] In May of the following year Bishop Gregg reported that interest was great, with hopes for a building within the year.[14] In April 1870 Rucker executed his great coup; the red cedar church building from Washington, for whose completion he had worked, prayed, begged and worried so long in the years before the war, was now rescued for a fresh career of usefulness in the new town. His mission accomplished, Rucker resigned the charge. The name of the Washington church was perpetuated by the Navasota vestry by changing the name of their Parish to "St. Paul's,"

[9]*Ibid.*, 1873, pp. 66-7.   [10]*Ibid.*, 1874, pp. 44, 79-80.
[11]*Texas Journal*, 1866, pp. 6, 23, 39.   [12]*Ibid.*, 1867, p. 25.
[13]*Ibid.*, 1869, p. 31.   [14]*Ibid.*, p. 24.

a move which precipitated a parliamentary wrangle on the floor of the Council in Bryan in June of that year.[15]

Bishop Gregg sent the Reverend John W. Phillips to take charge of the Navasota flock immediately upon Rucker's resignation. During the two months before his Council report he officiated regularly there, and at Millican and Anderson. St. Paul's Church, Navasota, was consecrated by Bishop Gregg on June 1, 1870.[16]

Phillips was indeed the Railroad Missionary during the subsequent years; at the Council of 1871, which was held in Navasota, he reported for Bryan, Calvert, Hearne and Millican, along with Navasota. In November 1871 he was relieved of Navasota by the Reverend J. T. Hutcheson, who remained in charge until Easter of 1872.[17] He was followed by the Reverend Virginius O. Gee, who resided in Navasota, and gave quarterly services to Anderson; he was able to minister regularly each Sunday, but complained that the heavy duties of school teaching prevented him from doing the amount of pastoral work that he thought the Parish needed. In the year following Gee added Hempstead to his charge; his report for Navasota reflected a much brighter prospect for the Parish.[18] In common with other towns that had been for a while the railheads of lines coming up from the coast, the time of bustling prosperity, with railroad engineers, officials and laborers jostling for room with teamsters and traders involved in freighting goods beyond the railhead, was followed by a time of stagnation, until a normal kind of growth around the point of shipment for agricultural products from the surrounding countryside set in. The boom crowd moved on from Navasota to Millican, thence to Bryan, and Navasota begun gradually to find its own level, and, with it, St. Paul's Parish.

MILLICAN

Millican was the first point at which Bishop Gregg aimed his post-war aggressive missionary policy of working along the routes of railroads that were being built. It is true that Millican was reached by the Central Railroad in 1862,[19] but it could be built no further

[15]*Ibid.*, 1870, pp. 10, 12-13, 27.

[16]*Ibid.*, pp. 27-8; Gregg, manuscript Journal, 1 June 1870. This building is still standing in Navasota, now a storehouse for a grain company. It was sold by the Parish when the new building was erected in 1891, according to statements made to me by several members of the Parish.

[17]*Texas Journal*, 1871, pp. 40, 43, 45; 1872, pp. 72-3.

[18]*Ibid.*, 1873, pp. 72-3; 1874, pp. 79-80, 83.

[19]Centennial Edition, *Navasota Examiner. Handbook of Texas* has 1860: "Millican," *en. loc.*

until after the war; in the general stagnation of business, there was little to do. Bishop Gregg visited the place in 1863, 1864, and 1865, but, with the shortage of clergy then prevalent, did not provide it a clergyman.

With the close of the war, and the resumption of activity in railroad building, the Bishop went into action. The following report appeared in the 1867 *Journal*:

> MISSION OF ST. ANDREW, MILLICAN. The undersigned, Lay Reader, by the Bishop's appointment, commenced in July holding divine service with much doubt, from a knowledge of his own unworthiness, and the poor prospect of any favorable result. God, however, has answered our prayers, and we trust to have a parish organized when we shall go to Bryan. We now have but the schoolroom, common to all, nevertheless we have held service about fifty times. We have an organ with a well organized choir, and our audiences are generally above the capacity of our place of meeting. Where opposition was at first, we now find friendly greetings and assistance.
>
> Our thanks are due to the Rev. Messrs. Rottenstein, Seely and Chase, for services held.
>
> Geo. D. Haswell, Lay Reader.[20]

Events moved rapidly from this time. Yeater began here with the same diligence he had displayed before his ordination; when the Bishop visited the place at the close of March 1868, he reported that a building had been purchased for use as a church; Yeater reported to the Convention in May that the building, secured through the liberality of the Bishop, was now ready for consecration.[21] But before this had come about, the community had been struck three heavy blows; the yellow fever epidemic of 1867 had reduced its population from 600 to 300;[22] then the railhead was extended to the new town of Bryan, taking many people beside Haswell with it; then Yeater's health broke, compelling him to leave in July 1868; he was transferred to the Diocese of Illinois.[23] The Reverend J. Wilkins Tays, then Rector of St. Andrew's, Bryan, reported that a layreader was occasionally conducting a service, and he proposed himself holding a weeknight service once a month, to try to keep the congregation in being. The Sunday School was well maintained.[24]

On his visitation in January of 1870 Bishop Gregg found that these stopgap measures had been of some effect; three people were confirmed, and the little chapel, though not then ready for consecra-

[20] *Texas Journal*, 1867, p. 36.   [21] *Ibid.*, 1868, pp. 21, 34.
[22] *Handbook of Texas*, "Millican," *en. loc.*
[23] *Texas Journal*, 1869, pp. 25, 31.   [24] *Ibid.*, p. 31.

tion, would be so in the Spring.[25] When Tays left Bryan for Calvert, the Reverend J. W. Phillips officiated occasionally at Millican.[26] The Chapel was consecrated by Bishop Gregg on June 3, 1870, its name being changed to "St. Luke's," evidently because the organized Parish in nearby Bryan had taken the name of "St. Andrew's."[27] Phillips reported for the mission in 1871 and 1872, in the latter year revealing a decline in communicant strength to nine.[28] When Phillips left this part of the Diocese, the Millican congregation owed him fifty dollars back salary, which, the Reverend Nelson Ayres said in his report, he doubted they could pay, for the communicant strength was now down to three persons, who were not able to contribute much.[29] No report was filed for Millican for the 1874 Council, though the Bishop, visiting the place on February 14 and 15, confirmed two persons, and remarked that the few earnest Church folk remaining would be cared for as opportunity afforded.[30] The work in Millican, meantime, had served its main purpose; it had ministered to the needs of those engaged in building the railroad, and as that moved north, other points had been used for the same purposes.

BRYAN

Bryan was the next railhead above Millican that received the Church's attention. The Church was there almost before the town. The Reverend A. J. Yeater reported:

> On the 10th of November, 1867, I conducted the first Episcopal services ever held in this energetic young city. I labored there two months as a missionary, and prepared the way for the organization of a parish, and the erection of a handsome church edifice.[31]

On December 17 Bishop Gregg visited the place, and recorded that a parish had indeed been organized the week before. He wrote the Domestic Committee:

> On the 17th of December, the Rev. Robert Jope [from the Diocese of Alabama] accompanied the Bishop to Bryan, a town

25Gregg, manuscript Journal, 4 Jan. 1870.

26*Texas Journal*, 1870, pp. 24, 28.

27Gregg, manuscript Journal, 3 June 1870.

28*Texas Journal*, 1871, p. 45; 1872, p. 71.

29*Ibid.*, 1873, p. 71.   30*Ibid.*, 1874, p. 44.

31*Ibid.*, 1868, pp. 29-30. The Bryan townsite was donated by William Joel Bryan (for whom the town was named) to aid the extension of the railroad. The former County Seat, Boonville, was three miles east of Bryan. *Handbook of Texas,* "Brazos County," *en. loc.*

which has sprung up as if by magic, at the present terminus of the Houston and Texas Central Railroad. A parish had been organized here the previous week, under the lead of a few zealous laymen. Mr. Jope received a call, accepted it, and immediately went to work with a strong arm and a stout heart. On the 7th of January, not twenty days afterwards, he reported that the parsonage was under way, and that in two weeks more he expected to have his family in it; the cost to be about two hundred and fifty dollars, with the responsibility on his shoulders, the work being also done in part by his own hands; and as to the church building, that it would be ready for consecration by the 22nd of March. . . . The Church is leading the way in this young town of about two thousand inhabitants—a new thing, almost, under the sun![32]

Later in the year Jope also reported on Bryan, giving an interesting view of the development of a railroad boom town:

Bryan is the nearest terminus of the Texas Central Railroad. One year ago there were not more than a dozen houses here; fifteen months ago it was all open prairie; now we have a population of four thousand to five thousand.

St. Andrew's parish was organized two or three days before last Christmas. Since that time we have erected a neat church building of rough boards, with seats for three hundred persons. We have also built a small parsonage, sufficient for the necessities of the Minister's family. This last has been built almost entirely by your Missionary's own hands.

On the 22nd of March—a day long to be remembered, we hope —our Church was consecrated by our worthy Bishop. The solemnities of that occasion were entirely new to the great mass of this population, and (together with the beautiful and forcible discourses of our beloved Bishop) we think they will tell upon the future of our Railroad Mission.

The services are well attended, being rendered quite attractive by the assistance of an efficient choir. We have to meet the hostility of the carnal mind to the Cross of Christ in general, but there is little opposition to the Church as such. Nay, we are daily receiving proofs of public favor which encourage and help us on, and we have good ground for hope that we have achieved a position for the Church which will be permanently maintained.

The terminus of the road will move thirty miles up the country this fall. At some point near Stirling, where there is not now one solitary habitation, there will, in all probability, be before Christmas a population of three or four thousand. As was the case at Bryan and Millican and Navasota, and all points below, this will be a promiscuous population, rushing from all points of the compass, intent upon building up their broken

[32]*Texas Journal,* 1868, pp. 18, 25; *Spirit of Missions,* 1868, pp. 245-6.

fortunes, but caring little for God's Church or their own souls. Our good Bishop is doing all he can to leaven interior Texas, and for this purpose he wishes to build a church and a school at every such point on the railroad.[33]

Not too long afterward Jope moved to Lavaca. After the Parish was vacant for several months, during which lay services were conducted, and the indefatigable Rucker appears to have given occasional services, the Reverend J. Wilkins Tays left Indianola to take over the mission to the railroaders, beginning with April 24, 1869. He expressed his purpose (with more zeal than geographical accuracy) thus:

> . . . as the railroad extends, and the population follows, they will carry the teachings of St. Andrew's with them. And our determination is, under the guidance of God's grace, to plant a scion from the parent stem at every Station, so that we will be able to point to a succession of Gothic churches, extending like a line of forts from the Gulf to the Rio Colorado [sic], which will be under God, not only a power, but a glory in the land.[34]

The boom time for Bryan lasted only a short while; the railroad offices shifted to Calvert, to which Tays turned much of his attention; he resigned as Rector of St. Andrew's after only a year's tenure.[35] The finances of the Parish were apparently so shaky, with the removal of many of the railroad people, that Bryan had to share the time of Reverend John W. Phillips with Calvert (until the arrival of the Reverend J. Cooper Waddill), Hearne, Millican and Navasota.[36]

Recovery came soon, however; in 1871 the Bishop reported that the interior of the church had been done over, a bell had been purchased, and things looked bright for the Parish once again.[37] More communicants removed from the town in the following year, however, making it still necessary for Phillips to spread his energies over too many places; he resigned in late 1872 to confine his attention to Bastrop, Giddings, and La Grange,[38] being succeeded at Bryan by the Reverend Nelson Ayres, who had been ordered Deacon October 6, and, after accompanying the Bishop on his Fall visitation, was assigned to Bryan, with Millican his only other work.[39]

During Ayres' tenure the Church evidently began to take root

[33]*Spirit of Missions*, 1868, pp. 687-8.

[34]*Texas Journal*, 1869, p. 27.   [35]*Ibid.*, 1870, p. 24.

[36]Parochial Reports, *Texas Journal*, 1871.

[37]*Texas Journal*, 1871, p. 28.

[38]*Ibid.*, 1872, pp. 61, 62, 68-69, 70, 71; *Diocese of Texas*, Jan. 1873, p. 5.

[39]*Texas Journal*, 1873, pp. 70-1; *Diocese of Texas*, Jan. 1873, p. 5.

in the rich plantation class in the Bryan vicinity; Bishop Quintard of Tennessee lectured there on the University of the South in 1873, and raised over $1000 in cash and notes. At that time he expressed astonishment at the church building which had been so glowingly described when it was erected; his reporter quoted his somewhat untactful remark, "a barn is better." Evidently rough board churches, whitewashed inside and out, had gone out of fashion in Tennessee.[40]

In January 1873, Ayres became Rector of the Church of the Good Shepherd, Corpus Christi, and was succeeded by the Reverend Virginius O. Gee, who moved his residence to Bryan, with half of his Sundays given to Navasota, and such attention as he could spare to Hempstead.[41] The live part of the railroad mission had long since moved far to the north, leaving the Parishes behind it to gain enough strength to be able to afford full-time clerical services when their local economy allowed.

CALVERT

Calvert was the next mission founded along the railroad after Bryan. On the first of September, 1869, the Reverend J. Wilkins Tays took charge of the mission and conducted services at Calvert on alternate Sundays. By great efforts on the part of the ladies funds were raised for the erection of a church building. On Bishop Gregg's visit, January 1870, services were held in the schoolhouse; by council time the church was already built and consecrated.[42] At the latter visitation, a parish was organized, under the name, "Church of the Epiphany," which was admitted to the Diocese at the Council three days later. By this time, however, Tays had resigned to become Chaplain of the Texas Senate;[43] the Bishop was assisted at the consecration of Epiphany Church by the Reverend R. S. Seely.[44]

The Reverend John W. Phillips had charge of Calvert for a few months after Tays' departure; he was relieved of this charge by the arrival of the Reverend J. Cooper Waddill from Alabama in mid-March 1871. He set to work vigorously, and in his first report to the Council related holding missionary services "three times at Port Sullivan, once at Cameron, and three times at Maysfield." The congregation labored to improve the church building at Calvert; the

40*Diocese of Texas*, Apr. 1873, p. 5.
41*Texas Journal*, 1874, p. 44.
42*Ibid.*, 1870, p. 24; Gregg, manuscript Journal, 7 January and 5 June, 1870.
43*Texas Journal*, 1870, p. 8; 1871, pp. 41-2.
44Gregg, manuscript Journal, 5 Jan. 1870.

Bishop remarked on it at his visit of May 1871;[45] but even more was done in the Fall of the following year, when the scheduled ordination of Nelson Ayres made the parishioners particularly anxious to have their church in applepie order. A new bell was given by four young men.[46]

Waddill continued to divide his time with other missions in the vicinity; he took over the Corsicana mission after the departure of the Reverend Virginius O. Gee for Navasota. Before this he had ministered part time at Hempstead. He was also burdened with a school, a fact which Bishop Gregg deplored.[47]

Waddill was assisted at Calvert by a very zealous and generous layman, Mr. J. W. Beard, who was senior warden as well as layreader. The yellow fever epidemic of 1873-4, which hit Calvert with great force, carried away Beard and two other communicants. Although Epiphany Church's losses were small as compared to the great number of deaths in the community—Waddill himself performed eighteen burials that year—the death of so good a leader was a hard blow. The ladies, however, continued their efforts, aiming now for a parsonage, for which they had accumulated $300 by council time, 1874.[48]

HEARNE AND COURTNEY

Hearne, in southwestern Robertson County, did not seem an important point for the work of our Church when the Central Railroad was built through it, but when the International Railroad was begun to form a junction with the Central at that point, another look was taken. The Reverend J. W. Phillips made a report for "Mission, Hearne, Robertson County" to the 1871 Council, but did not indicate when he began ministering there, or how often he held services. His report, something of a classic in sacerdotal statistics, read:

> Communicants 7; Sunday School—Teachers, male 1, female 1—
> total 2; Scholars very few; Contributions—Rector's salary $31.[49]

---

[45]*Texas Journal,* 1871, pp. 28, 40.

[46]*Diocese of Texas,* (Prospectus, October, 1872), n.p.; *Texas Journal,* 1873, p. 62.

[47]*Ibid.,* 1872, p. 24.   [48]*Ibid.,* 1874, p. 74.

[49]*Texas Journal,* 1871, p. 43. The International Railroad, chartered in August 1870, was originally planned to enter the State near Fulton, Arkansas, and extend to Laredo, but with the approach of the Texas and Pacific to Longview the plan was changed. Construction began in 1872 simultaneously at Longview and Hearne. The Hearne section reached Palestine July 12, 1872, and the Longview sector reached the same town January 31, 1873. The Houston and Great Northern reached Palestine from Houston in May 1873. Construction on the International from Hearne westward toward Austin began in 1874, reaching Rockdale that year, and Austin in 1876. S. G. Reed, *A History of the Texas Railroads and of Trans-*

The Bishop paid his first visit to Hearne in February 1872, accompanied by Phillips and Waddill; Phillips, reporting for the mission again that year, stated that many of the contributing members had moved to follow the extension of the International Railroad. He was furnishing a monthly Sunday service at that time.[50]

Waddill took charge of the Hearne congregation in January 1873, and reported to the Council that the prospects were good for the erection of a church building.[51] By the following February it was up, and nearly enough complete to allow the Bishop to officiate in it, but because of a blunder on the part of someone, some of the work was improperly done, and had to be torn out and done over. The consecration of the building had to be delayed for this reason. By Council time the work was nearly finished, and the additional cost almost paid for. Monthly services were still being conducted by Waddill.[52]

Another point in the Brazos Valley along the rail line at which services were conducted during the decade was Courtney, which the Bishop visited from time to time, and for which Rucker filed a report as missionary in 1870. That was the first and last report, however; Rucker simply could not spare the time to go thus far, with all the other congregations to which he was ministering.[53]

The further development of this railroad mission north of what became the limits of the Diocese has been indicated in the account of the congregations which were to be incorporated into the Missionary Jurisdiction of Northern Texas. There were other railroads under construction in Texas during the decade following the war, and the Church directed its mission toward the people involved in some of these efforts, too. But this first mission furnishes an excellent example for study, because of the length of the line in territory almost unoccupied by the Church, it was extended over a period coincidental with that under study, and its strategy was described so clearly by the Bishop and other persons involved.

In evaluating the mission, one would have to recognize both success and failure. To the degree that the influences of the Church was brought to the people who were moving along with the railheads,

portation Conditions in Texas under Spain, Mexico and the Republic of Texas (Houston, 1941), pp. 315ff. The Diocese had no active mission in connection with the construction of these roads before 1874, but actively ministered in Palestine shortly after their junction there.

[50] Texas Journal, 1872, pp. 30, 68-9.

[51] Ibid., 1873, p. 68.   [52] Ibid., 1874, pp. 44, 79.

[53] Ibid., 1870, p. 25; Bishop's visits, ibid., 1867, p. 24; Gregg, manuscript Journal, 31 Dec. 1869.

the Church succeeded in its primary mission in presenting the Gospel and the sacraments to people, wherever they were. The work, though much too part-time because of lack of clergy and money, was performed reasonably well. For the Church's responsibility to the people who remained in the railroad towns after the construction forces had moved along, one would have to recognize that, for all the construction of church buildings and the organization of parishes, the influence of these parishes upon the local communities was weakened by the necessity for assigning to many congregations to one or two men for so long a time. This was, of course, unavoidable, with the limited resources at hand. The deep roots which some of the congregations took in their communities testifies to the consecration and wisdom of their leaders, clerical and lay. Overall, there is interesting testimony to the flexibility of the Texas Church in the story of this mission.

East of the Central railroad the work of the Church was varied and interesting.

XXI.   Eastern Texas

IN THE rather large remaining region of the Diocese the work of the Church was widely scattered. Two pieces of work close to the east of the Central railroad, really in Central rather than East Texas, are considered here because their rural character makes them unlike what was being done in the railroad mission.

OWENSVILLE AND ANDERSON

The Church had been at work in a small way in Robertson County, just north of Brazos County (of which Bryan is the County Seat), long before the Railroad Mission arrived. In October 1866, the Reverend R. S. Seely had moved to the little community of Owensville, where he officiated two Sundays each month, giving the other Sundays alternately to Wheelock and Stirling. He reported:

> The congregations have been uniformly good, but the few Church families are scattered all over the county. We hope however to be enabled to concentrate our efforts at some point upon the railroad so soon as it penetrates to our region. There appears to be no very strong prejudice against the Church in this country, and we think the prospects here for building up the walls of Zion to be good.[1]

[1] *Texas Journal,* 1867, p. 36.

Seely's greatest handicaps arose from the difficulties of travel during wet weather, there being no roads worthy of the name, and from the lack of buildings available for worship in the communities he served. During the next year he found it impossible to hold services more than once a month at Owensville, and finally, due to circumstances beyond his control, had to give up the services at the other two places. He was able, however, to minister to another point, Mineral Creek, a small settlement six miles away from his home in Owensville.[2]

Bishop Gregg had held out good hopes for the work at Owensville on his visit in 1867. He was prevented by flood waters from making a visit the following year, and in the great rush of his Fall visitation in 1869, after may delays along the road made him telescope engagements, passed Owensville by to visit the new Calvert mission.[3] Seely rendered no report for that year, and in 1870 related that he was still confined to one Sunday a month services at Owensville, and weekday nights at other points at which he could obtain the use of schoolhouses or private homes for services.[4] At the end of 1870 he removed to Woodville, Tyler County, to start again there, his stipend from the Domestic Committee being continued for the new post on the recommendation of Bishop Gregg.[5]

Seely's move was no doubt dictated by the shifting of population brought about by the arrival of the railroad in Robertson County. His principal occupation was teaching; he probably had followed some of his patrons to Owensville when the population of Washington would no longer support his school, and he saw an opening in the new location. The same must have been true of his move to Woodville. He did not long survive this move; he died on February 18, 1871. Of him Bishop Gregg said:

> He made the work of instruction his principal business here, doing missionary duty, however, as opportunity offered. He was of a retiring disposition, devoted chiefly to books, knew little of the world and its ways, and exhibited always a strong conviction of its principles, and a warm attachment for the Church. His life was one of much trial and privation—and doubtless for him rest—the last rest, was sweet.[6]

[2] *Ibid.*, p. 36.

[3] *Ibid.*, pp. 24, 36; 1868, p. 34; Gregg, manuscript Journal, 7 Jan., 1870.

[4] *Texas Journal,* 1870, p. 28.

[5] Gregg, manuscript Journal, List of Missionaries, 1871; Minutes, Domestic Committee, 1871, Minutes Book, p. 121.

[6] *Texas Journal,* 1871, p. 38.

At Anderson, only ten miles east of Navasota, the name of Redeemer Parish remained on the records of the Diocese throughout the decade. The town possessed a certain stability on account of retaining the County Seat. The Central Railroad had originally planned to pass through the town, but was rerouted through Navasota on account of the proximity of the latter place to the rich Brazos Valley plantation business, which could be more successfully attracted from that point.[7] In November of 1866 Bishop Gregg observed that the Anderson people continued their interest in the Church, evidenced by seven people being confirmed at his visitation. Mr. A. J. Yeater was appointed to care for the flock in conjunction with Navasota while preparing for Deacon's examinations.[8] But when Yeater was ordained at the close of the 1867 Convention in Brenham, he was appointed missionary to Millican, Bryan, and other points northward soon to be reached by the Central Railroad. This left Anderson without regular services; yet the Bishop, visiting in March 1868, said that in spite of the lack of a building or regular services, the Parish seemed to have a hopeful future.[9] The Bishop did the best he could for the Anderson members; he visited in May and December 1869, and again in June 1870.[10]

The provision of quarterly services by the Reverend V. O. Gee in 1873, however meagre this might seem on the surface, was better than the people had been getting; the Bishop, who had continued to visit at least annually, confirmed six more persons in 1873,[11] no doubt prepared by Mr. Gee.

HUNTSVILLE

The first Parish east of Anderson was St. Stephen's, Huntsville, which at the end of the war was under the care of the Reverend W. R. Richardson, whose zeal insured that it should be both lively and generous. On the Bishop's Fall visitation in 1866 services were held in which the Bishop was assisted by the Reverend Messrs. Rottenstein, Shepherd, Davenport and Richardson, an occasion which must have been both memorable and encouraging to the little flock in so small a town. Lively though the congregation was, it could not surmount the financial hardships of the post-war depression sufficiently to achieve its dearest hope, the building of a proper

---

[7]Various articles in Centennial Edition, *Navasota Examiner*, July 1, 1954.

[8]*Texas Journal*, 1867, pp. 19, 24-5.   [9]*Ibid.*, p. 3; 1868, pp. 20-1.

[10]*Ibid.*, 1869, p. 24; Gregg, manuscript Journal, 22-23 May, 29-30 Dec., 1869, 1 June 1870.

[11]*Texas Journal*, 1873, p. 36.

church. The members had to be content for the time with the use of an upper room.[12] By the following Fall, however, the Bishop found them struggling manfully for sufficient funds to begin construction; it was his opinion that a really strong parish would develop should the building be erected.[13] Within that year a yellow fever epidemic struck the congregation a hard blow; though only two communicants of the Church were taken in an outbreak that severely reduced the population of the town, those members were the active if elderly senior warden and a zealous young man who died while ministering to the sick. Two candidates for confirmation were also lost.

The town was so hard hit that business fell off, and no money could be depended on to continue the program of the Parish; in addition, the satellite mission at Danville was completely broken up by deaths and removals. There seemed little else for Richardson to do than accept the call which St. Mark's Church in San Antonio had extended to him; he left to assume his new duties there after the 1868 Convention.[14]

The loss of their beloved Rector did not stop the Huntsville flock in their determination to maintain their Parish and build a church; when the Bishop visited them in November 1868, they had cleared ground, and arranged to lay the cornerstone shortly afterward.[15] Nor were they interested exclusively in their parochial affairs; like many people in the Diocese, no doubt, they were distressed that Bishop Gregg and his family had given up their home in San Antonio and moved into a boarding house in Galveston. But they were very likely the first group in the Diocese to try to do anything about it, as the following news item would indicate:

> The ladies of St. Stephen's parish, Huntsville, Texas, have formed themselves into a society for the purpose of soliciting the means to purchase a homestead for their chief pastor.[16]

Bishop Gregg spent the Christmas of 1869 in Huntsville. Evidently the Sunday School had been kept up, for he catechized the children, but there was apparently no one whom the Bishop felt he could license as layreader. Mr. I. P. Nixon, reporting to the 1870 Council as senior warden, said that there had been no services except

[12]*Ibid.*, 1866, pp. 19, 34.   [13]*Ibid.*, 1867, pp. 19, 34.
[14]*Ibid.*, 1868, pp. 21, 31-2.   [15]*Ibid.*, 1869, p. 19.
[16]*The Churchman*, August 21, 1869, p. 270. It was eleven years later that the residence in Austin was secured for the Greggs, partly paid for by the funds raised by the ladies of the Diocese. *St. David's*, p. 53; Gregg, manuscript Journal, has several account sheets listing these contributions.

for those conducted during the Bishop's visitation. The church building was not yet complete, but was in use (evidently for Sunday School).[17] In January 1871, the Bishop officiated for the first time in this church, which he described as "neat and roomy," and seemed well pleased with it, even though it was not yet ready for consecration.[18]

No clergyman was as yet available for Huntsville, but the Bishop was able to license a layreader, whom he described as "young and earnest." This was Mr. A. L. McDonald, who also signed the 1871 parochial report as senior warden. The vacancy in the rectorship lasted for only a year longer; in January 1872, the Bishop arranged to settle in Huntsville as Deacon in charge the Reverend Jeremiah Ward, who was accompanying him on visitation.[19]

The Parish set to work with a will to complete their church building, clear it of debt, and ready it for consecration; they succeeded, and the building was consecrated by Bishop Gregg on March 23, 1873.[20] Ward was ordained to the Priesthood May 26, 1872, in St. David's, Austin, and continued to serve Huntsville as Rector until November 1874, when he was compelled to resign, much to the regret of his parishioners, who were no longer able to support a married clergyman. There were but twenty-four communicants at that time. Ward did not revive the work at Danville or Waverly but did conduct monthly services at Willis, where he reported that he had large and attentive congregations.[21]

CROCKETT, PALESTINE AND RUSK

If the career of the Huntsville congregation seemed to have more discouragement than cheer about it during the decade, it was full of joy as compared to that of its nearest neighboring Parish on the East, All Saints', Crockett. Here the day of great things, centering in an exemplary Negro missionary enterprise, ended when Mrs. Dorsey returned to her home in Louisiana.[22] Nothing more was heard of the building for which materials had been accumulated. No confirmation candidates awaited the Bishop on his visit in November 1865, though he confirmed four in November of the following year. Unable to reach Crockett in 1867, he visited again in December 1868, but did not have a confirmation. Mr. E. A. Gause was licensed

17Gregg, manuscript Journal, 25-27 Dec. 1869; *Texas Journal*, 1870, p. 26.

18*Ibid.*, 1871, p. 22.

19*Ibid.*, 1871, pp. 22, 29, 43; 1872, pp. 28-9.   20*Ibid.*, 1873, p. 37.

21*Diocese of Texas*, Nov. 1874, p. 3; *Texas Journal*, 1874, p. 80. Willis was on the Houston and Great Northern Railway.

22*Texas Journal*, 1866, p. 19; see above, p. 111.

as layreader in 1867. A year later Gregg spent four days in the town, and called all around the Parish; there was one confirmation.[23] At the Council of 1870 the senior warden, William M. Taylor filed a report which reflected the discouragement of the people:

> This Parish has never had a Rector; there has been no meeting of the Vestry for over twelve months; we have now no layreading, and have had no service since the Bishop visited us December last. But few of the citizens of our County know anything about our Church, yet if we had a Minister with us I think we could soon build up a good Church in our midst, this, however, cannot be done by Lay Reading.[24]

This need was more than could be filled; there was nothing close enough to Crockett to link up with it, and the slender resources of diocesan missionary funds and Domestic Committee grants had to be used where the maximum number of people could be reached. The Bishop continued annual visitations, confirming one or more people each time but one, but unable to do more than this. He repeatedly failed in his efforts to enlist a clergyman to give Crockett some attention.[25]

St. Philip's Parish, Palestine, received even less attention; because of his illness on the road, the Bishop had to cancel his appointment in 1865; he did not visit the place until 1869, and then not again until the two successive visits of 1873 and 1874. Mr. Louis Cormick was licensed layreader in 1869. The Parish had not gone completely dormant during the period, but its real revival had to await the division of the Diocese.[26] Mr. John Word reported for his father who was absent in 1873:

Baptisms   1
Confirmations 1
Communicants   6
Families   4
. . . The Church here is not in a flourishing condition; we have no minister, and only occasional services.[27]

This is the only report for Palestine appearing in the *Journal* for the entire decade. It will be recalled that the Reverend Caleb Dow had resided in Palestine and officiated during the war. But he

[23] *Texas Journal*, 1866, p. 19; 1867, pp. 19, 25; 1869, p. 19; Gregg, manuscript Journal, 20-33 Dec., 1869.

[24] *Texas Journal*, 1870, p. 25.

[25] *Ibid.*, 1871, p. 22; 1872, p. 28; 1873, p. 33; 1874, p. 41.

[26] *Ibid.*, 1866, p. 19; Gregg, manuscript Journal, 18 Dec. 1869; *Texas Journal*, 1869, p. 24; 1873, p. 33; 1874, p. 41.

[27] *Ibid.*, 1873, p. 74.

was not canonically connected with the Diocese, and thus could not be Rector.

The Bishop visited Rusk only twice during the decade; but there had been no organization here, and apparently no hopes for forming a parish for the present. One person was confirmed during the visitation of 1865, but no one at that of 1869, though the Bishop called extensively through the community on this visit.[28]

SAN AUGUSTINE AND NACOGDOCHES

The two charter Parishes of far East Texas, San Augustine and Nacogdoches, had their severe hardships during the decade following the war, but they received all the aid and attention it was possible to give them. At the war's end the Church in San Augustine was still benefiting from the work which the Reverend T. R. B. Trader had done there while a refugee from the federal occupation of Louisiana. Bishop Gregg said that he had "stirred up afresh the ground which had been faithfully worked before." Only a resident clergyman was wanting to make the work succeed.[29] The original scheme to send the Reverend A. F. Dobb to San Augustine and Nacogdoches was not carried out even though an appropriation of $400 per year from the Domestic Committee had been granted for it.[30] Instead, the Reverend Robert D. Shindler of the Diocese of Tennessee was called for San Augustine alone, and reported to the Convention of 1866 that he had arrived only a few days before the meeting, and could furnish no details of the state of the Parish. Shindler was granted a stipend by the Domestic Committee.[31]

Shindler received a hearty welcome in San Augustine, for he was, according to Crocket, "a man of deep learning, an advanced mathematician and classical scholar, and, amongst other accomplishments, an excellent Shakesperian." He added the teaching chores of the public school to his work as Rector.[32] The Parish did well under his ministration, Bishop Gregg recorded when he visited in 1866.[33] However, something arose to cause his resignation as Rector on February 25, 1867; after his resignation he continued to serve as "Minister in Charge" until a short time after Bishop Gregg's visitation in

---

[28]*Ibid.*, 1866, p. 19; Gregg, manuscript Journal, 15 Dec. 1869.

[29]*Texas Journal*, 1866, p. 19.

[30]Minutes, Domestic Committee, 6 Feb. 1866; Minutes Book, p. 362.

[31]*Texas Journal*, 1866, p. 38; Minutes, Domestic Committee, 6 Feb. 1867, Minutes Book, p. 7. The amount was $300 per year, to date from Feb. 1, 1866.

[32]Crocket, *Two Centuries*, p. 293.

[33]*Texas Journal*, 1867, pp. 18-19.

November 1868, at which time he accepted the call of Christ Church, Nacogdoches, to become its Rector.[34]

Left thus without a rector, the Church folk of San Augustine were not disposed to allow their Parish to become dormant. Mr. George F. Crocket, Sr., was appointed layreader, and functioned as such during the rest of the decade.[35] The Bishop spent an entire week in the town in December 1869, during which he met with the men of the Parish to plan for building a church; then spent two days calling to secure subscriptions for the purpose.[36] The Reverend W. R. Richardson drew the plans and wrote the specifications. A year later the Bishop officiated in the new building, which, though nearly complete, lacked doors and windows; the congregation was so enthusiastic about their new structure that they were not kept away by the most intense cold spell for some years, which caused considerable discomfort. The new lot had been given by Mr. Crocket, the lumber by Colonel S. W. Blount, and Mrs. J. P. Henderson, the donor of the first church building and continuing benefactor of the Church in Texas, sent $150 toward the cost of erection.[37] Impressed with the zeal and the hard work put forth in just a year by ladies and gentlemen alike, the Bishop expressed his faith in the future of the Parish.[38] The following December came the joyful occasion of the consecration of the new church.[39] Christ Church, San Augustine, again had a house of worship of its own, and was doing the best it could without a rector to meet the needs of that part of the community which looked to it for ministrations. Layreading continued faithfully, and the Bishop spent as much time as he could with the flock each year on his visitation; it was not found possible to place a clergyman in the town for some years to come. Meanwhile the son of the faithful layreader, George F. Crocket, Jr., a boy old enough to remember in years to come how cold it was in the church the first day it was opened for services, was receiving his early schooling in the community where he was to serve as Rector of Christ Church for many years, and whose history he was to write so effectively toward the close of his devoted career.[40]

---

[34]*Ibid.*, 1867, p. 37; 1868, p. 34; 1869, p. 18.

[35]Crocket, *op. cit.*, p. 294. The elder Mr. Crocket was a merchant.

[36]Gregg, manuscript Journal, 2-8 Dec. 1869.

[37]Crocket, *op. cit.*, p. 294.

[38]*Texas Journal*, 1871, p. 22.

[39]*Ibid.*, 1872, p. 28. This is the present Church building, modified only slightly.

[40]Dr. Crocket, whom I remember as a dear elder brother in the Ministry after my own ordination, was my predecessor as Registrar of the Diocese, and did much to gather and preserve the records and documents upon which I have heavily

The history of Christ Church, Nacogdoches, similar in many ways to that of its sister Parish during the decade, did not begin the period in such an encouraging manner. Though the Bishop said upon his visitation in November of 1865, "This Parish continues to present an encouraging prospect for steady increase,"[41] it was without clerical ministrations except for those provided by the Bishop's visitation until Shindler became its Rector around the first of 1869. Mr. William Voight signed the 1866 report as secretary of the vestry; Mr. Aldrich A. Nelson was licensed as layreader; this gentleman, for some years a Candidate for Deacon's orders,[42] was no doubt effective as a reader. The congregation had the advantage of owning their own church building, however, which gave some feeling of stability to the members.

The communicant strength of the Nacogdoches Parish increased from twenty to thirty in the first year of Shindler's tenure,[43] and all seemed to go well for a while; in January 1871 Bishop Gregg found Shindler too ill to officiate, but he was still Rector. No parochial report, even statistical, was rendered to the Council of that year from Nacogdoches, and Shindler was not present at its meeting,[44] and the same was true the following year. In December 1872 Bishop Gregg noted about Nacogdoches: "Rev. Mr. Shindler has resumed service here, and though the town has declined, it is hoped, with God's blessing, the church may maintain its ground."[45] Shindler, in submitting a report to the 1873 Council, said: "These services [listed in the report] were all performed within the parish limits, at Christ Church, which Church is still vacant, and where I still officiate." In the statistical table, the communicant strength is listed as ten.[46] It looks very much as though Shindler had resigned, either for his health, or because the Parish was unable to pay his salary; probably teaching for a living, he began officiating again when it became evident that the Parish was not going to call another rector. There was no report for 1874; seemingly the day of better things for the old Parish was in the future.

Bishop Gregg held services at Shelbyville, Shelby County, in December 1871, and at Cherino, Nacogdoches County, in November

depended in this study. Crocket also did the marvelous woodcarving in the churches in San Augustine and Nacogdoches.

[41] *Texas Journal*, 1868, p. 19.

[42] *Ibid.*, 1866, pp. 25, 37; 1869, p. 24, and subsequent ones up to 1873; Nelson was dropped at his own request in that year; *ibid.*, 1873, p. 43.

[43] Statistical tables, *Texas Journal*, 1869, 1870.

[44] *Texas Journal*, 1871, p. 22.

[45] *Ibid.*, 1873, p. 33.   [46] *Ibid.*, p. 72, Statistical table.

1873. At the latter place he found a lively interest in the Church, such as would promise good results could a missionary be found to work there.[47]

On the way between Jefferson and San Augustine Bishop Gregg habitually visited in De Soto Parish, Louisiana, among former South Carolinians who were friends of his, and some his relatives. He baptized, celebrated the Holy Communion, and even confirmed persons there so frequently as to suggest that "Trinity Church, De Soto Parish, Louisiana," was part of his jurisdiction. The truth is that this settlement in which he was so well acquainted was at that time rather isolated from either Shreveport or Mansfield, and a trip there represented a time-consuming detour for the Bishop of Louisiana. With Bishop Polk's consent and encouragement Gregg officiated there in the first place, since this route between Jefferson and San Augustine was at least as good as any other for him. The Bishop used to stay at the Witherspoon plantation home, in which a room was fitted out for the church. When Polk went into the army, Gregg cared for the Parishes in Shreveport and Mansfield as well, by Polk's request, and after Polk's death continued to do so until the consecration of Bishop Wilmer. Even after this, for many years, Gregg continued to visit in De Soto Parish, and, while there, minister to the congregation.[48]

JEFFERSON

The joy and strength of the Church in Northeast Texas was Jefferson. The town was the head of navigation for the Red River waterway from New Orleans, by way of Caddo Lake and Cypress Creek, and was thus the port of entry for all of North Texas before railway transportation brought an end to the river traffic. A port of importance before and during the Civil War, Jefferson boomed with the great increase in traffic brought on by the rapid settlement of North Texas following the war.[49]

Christ Church Parish benefited by the increase in population and prosperity. Up to May 1865 the congregation was served by the

[47]*Ibid.*, 1872, p. 28; 1874, p. 41.

[48]Bishop's Address, *Texas Journal*, 1861, 1867, 1869, 1871, 1872, 1887. In the last reference, Bishop Gregg referred to "relatives" there. Mr. F. M. Witherspoon, Jr., of Trinity Church, Longview, has taken me to view his family plantation home, where we saw the "chapel" room, and the organ used for services. The lovely little All Saints' Church, Stonewall, located in the neighborhood, is the descendant of this congregation.

[49]Mrs. Arch McKay and Mrs. H. A. Spellings, *A History of Jefferson, Marion County, Texas* (Jefferson, 1936), *passim*.

Reverend G. W. E. Fisse, Deacon, of the Diocese of Maryland, who came over from Marshall two Sundays a month, but resigned when the Parish called the Reverend J. M. Curtis; this left Jefferson without a minister since Curtis went instead to Houston.[50] In October of that year the Reverend S. D. Davenport accompanied the Bishop on his visitation to Jefferson and Marshall; by Epiphany-tide he had become Rector of the two Churches, dividing Sundays equally. With $240 already in the building fund, prospects for a church building in the near future were good.[51] By October, when the Bishop was present, definite steps were taken to begin the project; by the 1867 Convention Davenport could report:

> . . . the frame for a church building is now ready to be put together. The lumber is of an excellent quality, and well dressed. In a few weeks brick will be obtained for a foundation, and then in a short time it will be far enough completed for us to hold services in.[52]

Bishop Gregg requested Davenport to accompany him on his Spring visitation in 1868, and to do some general missionary work in the Diocese. As a consequence, he was absent during most of the year; Mr. E. G. Benners, the senior warden and layreader, reported to the Convention of that year that the church was almost complete, and soon ready to be occupied. Lay services had been kept up in private homes during the Rector's absence.[53]

Somewhere around this time Benners became a Candidate for Holy Orders; when the Bishop came again to Jefferson, in November 1869, the visitation was really a memorable one for the members of Christ Church. After successfully passing his examinations before the examiners, (who were, in addition to the Bishop, the Reverend W. T. Dickinson Dalzell, by then Rector of St. Mark's, Shreveport, Louisiana, and the Reverend F. R. Starr), Benners was ordained to the Diaconate, and took charge of the Parish. On the same visitation the church building was consecrated, and twenty persons were confirmed. Just to round it out, a new layreader and Candidate for Orders was secured in the person of Captain James G. Tansill. Large congregations, widespread interest in the Church, and the vigor of the Parish gave Bishop Gregg great courage.[54]

---

[50] *Texas Journal*, 1864, p. 19; 1865, pp. 16-17.

[51] *Ibid.*, 1866, pp. 19, 35.   [52] *Ibid.*, 1867, pp. 18, 34-5.

[53] *Ibid.*, 1868, p. 33. Benners was junior warden of Trinity, Marshall, in 1851. Lale, *As It Was in the Beginning*, p. 3.

[54] Gregg, manuscript Journal, 11-14 Nov. 1869. Benners had also assumed charge of Trinity Church, Marshall, and Captain Tansill read services in his absence.

Benners was ordained to the Priesthood at the Council of 1870.[55] He reported there that Christ Church had eighty-five communicants. The church had been embellished with a new organ and a bell, and given finishing touches at a cost of $1500. Contributions for outside purposes were not neglected in the meantime.[56] A feature of the life of the Jefferson flock was its work among Negroes; only one Sunday School was reported, but negro as well as white scholars were counted in it. Two more Negroes were confirmed, along with twenty more white people in the following November. Bishop Gregg reported that the unity of the congregation was notable.[57]

The Council year 1871-72 was the high point for the life of Christ Church; in December 1871 Bishop Gregg confirmed twenty-four persons, and remarked that the new church building was becoming too small for the growing congregation. A total communicant strength of 124 was listed in the 1872 report.[58] Then the inevitable result of the new railroads upon the business of an inland river port began to appear; business stagnated and people moved away. In two years the communicant list had dwindled to 86, in spite of the fact that the harmonious and active life of the Parish under its excellent Rector continuing in its faithful course.[59]

In spite of its loss of strength, the Jefferson Parish was host to the last Diocesan Council of the undivided Diocese in May 1874, dispensing to the members of the Council its outstanding kind of hospitality, and receiving the benefit of the widespread interest which the meeting of the Council aroused in the town.[60] The day of great things was over for the Church in Jefferson, but its faithful ministration to the people who remained there continued. It is patent that this was largely due to the unselfish devotion of Benners, who seemed to have taken Holy Orders with no thought of serving elsewhere than in his home Parish.

MARSHALL

Trinity Parish, Marshall, had been fortunate in enjoying the ministrations of a resident minister during much of the war even though he was but a refugee for conscience's sake from Maryland, and only in Deacon's orders. Before the war's end the Reverend Mr. Fisse returned to Maryland, leaving on record the comment, "Through observation and experience, both in Texas and at home,

[55] Texas Journal, 1870, p. 7.   [56] Ibid., p. 27.
[57] Ibid., 1871, pp. 21, 44.   [58] Ibid., 1872, pp. 27, 70.
[59] Ibid., 1873, pp. 32, 69; 1874, pp. 80-1.   [60] Ibid., 1874, p. 29.

I am forced to say, that I believe a Deacon should never be sent to occupy a position like this."[61]

The Reverend S. D. Davenport took charge of Marshall in early January, 1866, making his residence there, and giving equal time to Jefferson. He was for a while able to afford the people of Trinity Church services every Sunday, due to the temporary residence in town of the Reverend E. A. Wagner, who held services on the Sundays on which Davenport was in Jefferson.[62] Marshall seemed to Davenport the more hopeful of the two fields, first because there was a church building there, while Jefferson had only a lot, second because it was a quieter and more stable sort of community, with less of the boom atmosphere which characterized the great river port of Jefferson, and third (and this quite accurately) the impending completion of a railroad to Marshall from Vicksburg by way of Shreveport would afford a more reliable base for a prosperous economy than the waterway-freight wagon commerce which afforded Jefferson its precocious wealth and excitement. Yet the advantage which Marshall had enjoyed in having had three missionaries resident at different times during its life was really something of a mixed blessing; their tenures had been so short that now no one in the town was disposed to believe that the new Rector would stay any longer. Though there was some background of Church knowledge among the parishioners, there was much to overcome and much yet to be done.[63]

There was much that was reasonable in the estimate of his two fields, yet the almost exact reverse of Davenport's prophesy came about during the decade after the war. By the 1867 Convention a slight decline in communicant strength was reported for Marshall; there was no report at all filed for the 1868 Convention, at which Davenport had reported having been absent from his Jefferson cure for most of the year. Wagner, then resident as diocesan missionary at Marshall, had presumably conducted some services, but Davenport was still listed as Rector of Trinity Church. By the Fall of 1869 Davenport had moved to Dallas, and Wagner had again become Rector at Marshall.[64] Bishop Gregg, on his visitation in November

[61]*Texas Journal,* 1864, p. 19.

[62]*Ibid.,* 1868, p. 36. Davenport removed from Waco to Marshall; see above, p. 208. Wagner evidently spent some time without a cure between the war's end and his assumption to the rectorship of St. Mark's, San Antonio. As will be seen below, his ties in Marshall, formed during his earlier tenure, were quite deep.

[63]Letter of Davenport to the Domestic Committee, *Spirit of Missions,* 1866, p. 312. He evidently missed one missionary, unless he intended not reckoning Fisse; Sansom and Albert had preceded Wagner.

[64]*Texas Journal,* 1867, p. 35; 1868, pp. 3, 33, 36; 1869, p. 3.

of that year, found Wagner gravely ill, and reported that he continued so for some time afterward. By council time in 1869 he had been transferred to South Carolina.[65]

Marshall was without a Rector during 1869; Bishop Gregg, on his visitation in November, prepared the candidates for Confirmation himself, and visited very thoroughly through the Parish. He must have judged its life at rather low ebb, for he reported "signs of life" amongst the ladies, and met with the men of the Parish to attempt a quickening of activity.[66] Possibly as a result of this meeting the Reverend E. G. Benners came over from Jefferson for two services before the Council of 1870, and rendered this report to that meeting:

> . . . The present number of Communicants is 17. The Sunday School is kept up under the faithful supervision of Dr. A. T. Smith. A large portion of the Church building has fallen, and the attempt to repair it is not deemed advisable. The ladies have realized about $850 by means of a Fair, in aid of a new building. . . .[67]

By December Bishop Gregg found the building fund well enough advanced that he could hope for an early start toward a new church, in view of the continuing energy and devotion of the ladies, [68] but in December of the following year it was still not begun. On this visitation, however, the Bishop reported, "Steps were again taken for the erection of a church building. The zeal of the ladies has not abated, and better hopes were excited for the future."[69]

From this point the tempo of congregational life increased; the building was still not begun, but there were stirrings which bore fruit at the Bishop's next visitation. At this time Gregg met with the vestry and the congregation together, with the result that Wagner was issued a call to return as Rector, and he accepted.[70] By February 1873 he was back in Marshall, and hard at work. By Council time he was able to report that contract had been let for the new building, which he had himself designed. The prospects for the Parish, Wagner felt, were encouraging.[71] The Bishop found the building progressing in December 1873, and though the town had received a severe setback from an epidemic, Wagner's work was showing good

[65]Ibid., 1869, pp. 17, 25.

[66]Gregg, manuscript Journal, 19-21 Nov. 1869.

[67]Texas Journal, 1870, p. 27.　　[68]Ibid., 1871, p. 22.

[69]Ibid., 1872, p. 28.　　[70]Ibid., 1873, p. 33.

[71]Diocese of Texas, Feb. 1873, p. 7; Texas Journal, 1873, pp. 43, 71; Diocese of Texas, Aug. 1873, p. 5.

results; Gregg believed once the new church was open and a rectory built, the Parish could become self-supporting.[72]

Wagner had returned without his family when he left Tennessee to return to Marshall; his circumstances evidently did not permit the expense of moving them. His self-sacrifice and devotion were rewarded in a way he told about touchingly:

> To Miss Amory, Mrs. Neilson and Miss Dunlap, as representative agents of a great company of loving and generous friends, is due the grateful acknowledgment of efficient aid. In the fund which they provided to defray the travelling expenses of the Rector's family, the supply of clothing, and valuable additions to the Parish Library.
>
> Thus are the members of this Parish and of the Church, everywhere taught the Divine command by the example of its living saints. May it be perpetuated by us, and our children's children, and ever down the stream of time flow the current of charity, which remembers that having *freely received,* they must *freely give.* We have not gone abroad to ask aid in our work, but God, who seeth in secret, has rewarded us openly, and raised up for us those who *helped* us in our hour of need.[73]

Trinity Church grew again under Wagner's care. By 1874 it was back up to fifty communicants, partly due to the removal of the Texas and Pacific shops from Hallville to Marshall, but also to the love and respect which the veteran Priest commanded in the town to which he had ministered so faithfully during his previous residences.[74]

HALLVILLE, LONGVIEW AND TYLER

Only a few miles west of Marshall a mission was started at the town of Hallville (the present Hallsville) when the Reverend John Portmess, received from the Diocese of Iowa, moved there to take charge of the Masonic Institute. It was arranged that he would do missionary work along the line of the advancing Texas and Pacific Railroad as well as at his home base.[75] On December 23, 1873, Bishop Gregg confirmed a class at Hallville, and remarked on the hopeful prospect for the mission, giving praise to "the faithful Missionary."[76] However, the work there, like that of many of the railroad missions,

[72]*Texas Journal,* 1874, p. 42.

[73]*Ibid.,* 1874, p. 82. Wagner, having removed to South Carolina and then shortly afterward to Tennessee, must have been in considerable financial distress.

[74]*Ibid.,* 1874, pp. 79, 82.

[75]*Diocese of Texas,* Jan. 1873, p. 5; *Texas Journal,* 1874, p. 79.

[76]*Ibid.,* p. 42.

was a useful temporary measure designed to minister to the needs of transient people; at the Council in Jefferson in May 1874, Portmess reported that the railroad shops had been moved to Marshall, taking with them almost all of the communicants of the mission.[77] The work was closed with the removal of Portmess to Terrell, in the new Missionary Jurisdiction of Northern Texas, at the year's end.

But Portmess had meanwhile spied out the land in the next town along the line to the westward, Longview. Bishop Gregg had indeed been there before him, having baptized a child there in December 1871, but had conducted no other service. Portmess after scouting for Church members, found quite a number of them in Longview, and on Easter, 1874, officiated for a large congregation.[78] Though several years were to pass before the organization of Trinity Church there, this beginning was made in the days of the railroad boom.

The new mission with the real success story in its early days was Tyler, a fairly ancient place, as East Texas towns go. Populated in the days of the Republic, and incorporated in 1846,[79] it was unknown to the records of the Episcopal Church until Bishop Gregg spent three days there in November 1870, doubtless following up news of the arrival of Church people in the town. The Bishop wrote about his visit:

> An earnest desire was expressed here for the Church, and liberal provision made for the support of a clergyman, who had promised but failed afterward to come. This is a point of much importance, and will be provided for as soon as possible.[80]

Many months elapsed before the Bishop could make good his promise; visiting on December 14, 1871, he reported "The prospect for the Church is improving here, and a Clergyman will soon be provided."[81] The man who was eventually sent was worth waiting for; he was that intriguing character, Emir Hamvasy.

Described by the authors of *St. David's Through the Years* as an "exiled Hungarian nobleman," Hamvasy was a musician of note. Once in his childhood, according to the same source, he had played in a concert with Franz Liszt. While serving as Lord Mayor of Budapest Hamvasy had become involved in the 1848 Revolution in his homeland, and upon its collapse had to escape Hungary. After a varied career in other parts of America, he had established himself as a music professor in R. J. Swancoat's school in Austin, occupying

---

[77]*Ibid.*, p. 79.   [78]*Ibid.*, 1872, p. 27; 1874, p. 79.
[79]*Handbook of Texas*, "Tyler, Texas," *en. loc.*
[80]*Texas Journal*, 1871, p. 21.   [81]*Ibid.*, 1872, p. 27.

on the side the position of choir director for St. David's Church.[82]
Here Professor Hamvasy begun to be interested in the Ministry;
he was licensed as layreader in 1870 and became a Candidate for
Orders in February 1871. Ordained to the Diaconate in St. David's
on March 10, 1872, Hamvasy finished the school year in Austin.
He was ordained Priest at the close of the 1872 Council, May 26,
1872, and apparently remained through the Summer, taking charge
of the Tyler mission some time in the Fall of 1872.[83]

When Bishop Gregg was again in Tyler on November 21, he
reported:

> Rev. Mr. Hamvasy has begun well here. Eligible lots have been se-
> cured and steps taken for the erection of a church building.
> A vigorous parish, a few years hence will doubtless, under God,
> be the result of the faith and devotion of those who have
> begun the work.[84]

The good beginning was not allowed to waste away. Aided by generous contributions of some Galveston Churchmen, the building fund
began to grow. Major and Mrs. J. S. Grinnan of Galveston, owners
of considerable property in Tyler, allowed the congregation to select
the lots they thought most suitable. By August 1873 funds were in
hand to get a building up, if not completed.[85]

The more important work of the mission was not meanwhile
neglected; in his 1873 council report Hamvasy related there was a
Sunday School of thirty-six pupils, with the remarkable number of
fourteen teachers for them. He had a Bible Class of thirty-one, and
reported eleven catechumens.[86] This was only the beginning of an
impressive evangelistic and educational drive. Bishop Gregg confirmed a class of ten persons on November 9, 1873, which would
have been a good average class for most smaller parishes, and was
an amazingly large one for a mission that had listed only ten communicants the previous May. But the Bishop was asked back to
Tyler twice before the next Council, and confirmed twenty-eight in
all in the three classes, a total third highest in the Diocese for that
council year. The church building was nearly ready for consecration
at the time of the 1875 council.[87]

With the establishment of the work in Tyler the advance of the

[82]*St. David's*, pp. 44-5.
[83]*Texas Journal*, 1871, pp. 12, 29; 1872, p. 32; 1873, pp. 29, 77.
[84]*Ibid.*, 1873, pp. 32-3.
[85]*Diocese of Texas*, Jan. 1873, p. 5; Aug. 1873, p. 6.
[86]*Texas Journal*, 1873, p. 77.
[87]*Ibid.*, 1874, pp. 40, 41, 51; 1875, p. 22.

Church in what was to become the northeast corner of the reduced Diocese of Texas began; in the years ahead Christ Church, Tyler, was to assume importance as it gained strength; Marshall, Palestine and Longview became important because of their strategic locations as railroad junctions. Work was to be opened in the Southeast, not only at Orange, but at Woodville, Beaumont and other places as improved transportation opened up the large scale exploitation of the pine forests of East Texas. As with the rest of the State, East Texas stood on the threshold of new opportunities as the Reconstruction Decade ended. The Episcopal Church was to attempt to meet the needs of this new order in the years ahead.

XXII. Conclusion

A NATURAL PERIOD is set to this history by the division of the Diocese of Texas, for after that event there followed what the late Dr. DuBose Murphy called the period of intensive cultivation.[1] There were large areas within the territory remaining in the Diocese where the Church had not taken root. Bishop Gregg was to be spared to lead the intensified campaign for another eighteen years after the division. Following him as bishops of Texas, George Herbert Kinsolving, Clinton Simon Quin and John Elbridge Hines have in succession shouldered the burden. The achievements of the Church in the remaining years of Gregg's episcopate and in the times of his successors forms a story that must be told in time to come; it is no dull or uninspiring one, either. Yet the partition of the Diocese— just at the end of Reconstruction, and at the time when the railroads attracted a larger population and changed the character of the work— forms a boundary that sets apart the period of the undivided Diocese as something heroic. It is reminiscent of vast distances, of dusty wagon roads, of the hospitality of plantations, farms and villages, of strenuous travels broken by unhurried visitations of the Chief Pastor; these reminiscences serve to display the nature of the Church by its very triumph over difficulties.

From the span of about forty years in the life of the Episcopal Church in Texas studied in this work, there emerge several constant factors pointing to general conclusions. The first of these is the unfaltering belief of the three bishops that the Episcopal Church had a calling to minister in Texas, that it was sorely needed in the State.

[1]*History of the Protestant Episcopal Church in Texas*, p. 65.

This belief was shared by all of the clergy who expressed themselves in their reports, and by laymen whose words have come down to us in one way or another. The common conviction of these men was that the Episcopal Church offered the people of Texas certain values which no other institution could offer as well. Generally, this conviction did not involve exclusive or sectarian claims. Theirs was not the *whole* Church, or *the Church,* in a sense that unchurched other Christians, but it was by all means the best, in the sense that it most faithfully presented the Gospel and the corporate life of the Christian fellowship in their fulness. All three bishops warned against condemning others, but all three exhorted the clergy to speak out positively about the Church's message and meaning.

The conviction that the Church was appropriate to Texas life was held in full knowledge of the roughness and hardness of the frontier conditions typical of much of Texas through most of the period. Precisely because these conditions existed, these men felt that the Episcopal Church would be welcomed particularly wherever its message could be heard before prejudice was inculcated against it. They believed the Church spoke to the needs of people.

Moreover, the Episcopal Church gained from the influence Texas exerted upon it. An impatience with dawdling and with endless technicalities in synodical action showed itself in Texas Church life, and spurred the General Convention and the Missionary Society to a quicker pace. Texas Episcopalians cut red tape and compromised theoretical quarrels; not always unsuccessfully they asked the same of the parent body.

The life of the Church, with its orderly round of daily and Sunday devotion, its regular presentation of the whole of the Scripture and the whole of the Creeds, and its objective worship of God without excessive emotional excitement, offered a refuge from the distortions of the Gospel that were common on the American frontier. The Church's ideals of growth through learning and of spiritual development through faithful devotion furnished a haven for those repelled by the more sensational presentations of the Christian religion. These ideals were as much needed by the simple of little literacy as by the well-lettered, and they spoke to slave or free, poor or wealthy.

The Church was a reconciling influence in the midst of Texas society. Political and economic affairs in the troubled times of Texas' infancy furnished opportunities in plenty to set men against one another, opportunities exacerbated by the severe and inescapable issues of the War between the States. Conflicting loyalties were common in the breasts of many individuals as they faced the issues of their times with the unseen influence of intermingled traditions tearing their thoughts and feelings. Hostile associations of neighbors against neighbors were all too easy and prevalent, from colonial times to the end of Reconstruction. Only a common, enduring and higher loyalty could reconcile. The Episcopal Church believed that it preached and lived the wholesome, reconciling Gospel of Christ faithfully enough—though it was rightly penitent for its many failures—to offer people a reconciliation that enabled those who received it to forbear one another and forgive one another for the sake of their common loyalty to Christ, a loyalty whose relevance to issues upon which people differed was made evident in the Gospel as the Church presented it.

The Episcopal Church exemplified this reconciling influence to a remarkable degree throughout the period. The fact of secession caused most severe pain to the leaders of the Church as they contemplated the severance of associations with leaders of the Church in the North, precisely because the reconciling influences of the Church had kept them together up to that time. When the parting came, it caused most sincere sorrow. As soon as the conflict between the States was over, the Church came back together, not in superficial reconciliation, but with heartfelt relief. Within the fellowship of the Diocese of Texas controversy over action forced by secession was perhaps inevitable, yet when the war was over, Gillette was elected a Deputy to General Convention by a Diocesan Convention that forfeited not one whit of its affection and loyalty to the Bishop. In the decade of Reconstruction, amidst the passions engendered by military occupation, disenfranchisement, and repressive policies of the Reconstruction regime of Governor Davis,[2] Union Army Officers and Republican politicians worshipped with ex-Confederates and Democrats, and all took counsel together for the Church and its work, even in the intimacy of the small group which then made up the Diocesan Council. Union General Augur was as highly valued a member as was Confederate General Nichols. Northern clergy like Benjamin Rogers and J. Wilkins Tays ministered happily in the Diocese, and won the affection of their parishioners.

Finally, the Church was an anchor in the midst of uncertainty. Purpose was hard to achieve in frontier life, defeat and discouragement the common lot. The form of society was forever changing, hopes all too often dashed. The ministrations of the Church brought

[2]See above, p. 204.

faith in the unchanging, good God, and a hope for meaning in life that would not change. In the midst of raw ugliness on the scene of men's frantic frontier assaults upon nature, and in the crude improvisations of frontier society, calm faith and assurance issued from the beautiful liturgy that had spoken to so many generations in so many places of God's watchful providence over all man's need. The Church brought healing reminders of more orderly and gentler societies left behind; it nourished hope for man's true destiny in the Society of God; it engendered faith in man's divine origin and destiny. In the regular and unhurried way of liturgical rhythm, the sense of rootedness was imparted, bringing peace, courage, and vision to Churchmen.

The Church carried out its mission in enough places in Texas to indicate that the faith of men who believed in that mission was not false. They were pitifully few, for there were never men enough, nor money enough, to send all who would go. In too many places the mission arrived late, sometimes too late; prejudices inherited from controversies of bygone days sometimes made ears deaf to the Church's message. But the Church took root where planted, and in turn it fruited, and spread its own seed abroad elsewhere in Texas. Within twenty years of its erection as a Missionary Jurisdiction, Northern Texas became the Diocese of Dallas; and ten years later, the Diocese of West Texas emerged from the other Missionary Jurisdiction. These Dioceses in turn gave up territory in which the Diocese of Northwest Texas has recently joined the family of self-supporting Episcopal jurisdictions, and the Diocese of New Mexico and Southwest Texas has incorporated Texas west of the Pecos River. The Mother Diocese, though it suffered severe financial loss by its self-sacrificing surrender of strong congregations at the partition, has gone from strength to strength, and stands high among the Dioceses of the National Church, not only in numbers, but in leadership and in support of the mission of the whole Church. The zeal and devotion of the founders has not been lost in any of the branches which have sprung from their planting.

APPENDIX A

CLERGY OF THE DIOCESE, 1850-1874

(As listed in the *Journals of the Diocese of Texas;* Clergy for 1849 listed in text.)

1850: Rt. Rev. Geo. Washington Freeman, D.D., Provisional Bishop; Benjamin Eaton, *Galveston;* Charles Gillette, *Houston;* J. F. Young, *Brazoria Co.;* H. N. Pierce, *Washington Co.;* Henry Sansom, *San Augustine & Nacogdoches;* J. F. Fish, Chaplain, U.S.A. (Diocese of New York), *San Antonio;* S. D. Dennison (Diocese of Massachusetts), *Matagorda;* L. P. Rucker, Deacon, *Washington Co.*

1851: Rt. Rev. G. W. Freeman, D.D., Provisional Bishop; B. Eaton, *Galveston;* C. Gillette, *Houston;* H. N. Pierce, *Washington Co.;* H. Sansom, *Marshall;* L. P. Rucker, *Chappell Hill;* E. Fontaine, *Austin;* J. F. Fish (Diocese of N. Y.), Chaplain, U.S.A., *San Antonio;* D. D. Flowers, *Matagorda.*

1852: Rt. Rev. G. W. Freeman, D.D., Provisional Bishop; B. Eaton, *Galveston;* C. Gillette, *Anderson;* H. N. Pierce, *Matagorda;* H. Sansom, *Houston;* L. P. Rucker, *Washington & Chappell Hill;* E. Fontaine, *Austin;* W. Passmore, *Brownsville;* E. H. Downing, *San Augustine & Nacogdoches;* C. F. Rottenstein, Deacon, *Washington Co.;* J. F. Fish (Diocese of N. Y.), Chaplain, U.S.A., *Ft. McKavitt.*

1853: Rt. Rev. G. W. Freeman, D.D., Provisional Bishop; B. Eaton, *Galveston;* C. Gillette, *Anderson;* H. N. Pierce, *Matagorda;* L. P. Rucker, *Washington Co.;* E. Fontaine, *Austin;* W. Passmore, *Brownsville;* E. H. Downing, *San Augustine & Nacogdoches;* C. F. Rottenstein, *San Antonio;* J. F. Fish (Diocese of N. Y.), Chaplain, U.S.A., *Ft. McKavitt.*

1854: Rt. Rev. G. W. Freeman, D.D., Provisional Bishop; B. Eaton, *Galveston;* C. Gillette, *Anderson;* L. P. Rucker, *Washington;* E. Fontaine, *Austin;* W. Passmore, *Brownsville;* E. H. Downing, *San Augustine & Nacogdoches;* C. F. Rottenstein, *San Antonio;* J. W. Dunn, *Lockhart & Seguin;* C. S. Hedges, *Lavaca & Indianola;* J. J. Nicholson, *Houston;* H. Pratt, *Anderson;* Geo. Rottenstein, Missionary to Germans, *San Antonio.*

1855: Rt. Rev. G. W. Freeman, D.D., Provisional Bishop; B. Eaton, *Galveston;* C. Gillette, St. Paul's College, *Anderson;* S. R. Wright, *Matagorda;* J. J. Nicholson, *Houston;* L. P. Rucker, *Washington Co.;* E. Fontaine, *Austin;* W. Passmore, *Brownsville;* E. H. Downing, *Brenham & Chappell Hill;* C. S. Hedges, *Lavaca & Indianola;* J. W. Dunn, *Lockhart, Seguin & Gonzales;* J. B. F. Smith, *Anderson;* H. Pratt, Ass't., *Anderson;* C. F. Rottenstein (removed but not transferred); Geo. Rottenstein, *San Antonio;* C. H. Albert, *San Augustine & Nacogdoches;* Ballard S. Dunn, Deacon, *Lockhart.*

1856: Rt. Rev. G. W. Freeman, D.D., Provisional Bishop; B. Eaton, *Galveston;* S. R. Wright, *Matagorda;* E. Fontaine, *Austin;* W. Passmore, *Brownsville;* E. H. Downing, *Brenham & Chappell Hill;* L. P. Rucker, *Washington & Independence;* C. H. Albert, *San Augustine & Nacogdoches;* J. B. T. Smith, *Anderson;* J. W. Dunn, *Lockhart & Seguin;* B. S. Dunn, *Gonzales;* H. Pratt, *Columbus & La Grange;* Geo. Rottenstein, *Corsicana;* C. Gillette, Agent, St. Paul's College.

1857: Rt. Rev. G. W. Freeman, D.D., Provisional Bishop; C. H. Albert, *Marshall & Jefferson;* W. T. D. Dalzell, *Houston;* J. W. Dunn, *Lockhart;* B. S. Dunn, *Gon-*

zales; B. Eaton, *Galveston;* E. Fontaine, Epiphany, *Austin;* C. Gillette, Christ Church, *Austin;* L. H. Jones, Deacon, *Seguin;* Tobias H. Mitchell, Chaplain, U.S.A. *Ft. Chadbourne;* W. Passmore, Chaplain, U.S.A., *Brownsville;* R. H. Ranney, residing near *Seguin;* G. Rottenstein, *Dallas.*

1858: (Bishopric vacant); C. H. Albert, *Matagorda;* W. T. D. Dalzell, *Houston;* B. Eaton, *Galveston;* E. Fontaine, Epiphany, *Austin;* C. Gillette, Christ Church, *Austin;* T. H. Mitchell, U.S.A., *Ft. Chadbourne;* John Owen, *San Augustine & Nacogdoches;* W. Passmore, U.S.A., *Brownsville;* R. H. Ranney, residing near *Seguin;* L. P. Rucker, residing in *Burleson Co.;* Nathaniel P. Charlot, Deacon, *Cold Spring & Huntsville;* L. H. Jones, Deacon, *Seguin.*

1859: (Bishopric vacant); C. H. Albert, *Matagorda;* N. P. Charlot, *Cold Spring & Huntsville;* W. T. D. Dalzell, *Houston;* B. Eaton, *Galveston;* E. Fontaine, Epiphany, *Austin;* C. Gillette, Christ Church, *Austin;* J. M. Goshorn, *Gonzales;* L. H. Jones, St. Mark's, *San Antonio;* T. H. Mitchell, U.S.A., *Ft. Chadbourne;* J. Owen, *San Augustine & Nacogdoches;* R. H. Ranney, residing near *Seguin;* L. P. Rucker, residing in *Burleson Co.;* J. W. Godfrey, Deacon, *Richmond.*

1860: Rt. Rev. Alexander Gregg, D.D., Bishop, *Austin;* C. H. Albert, non-parochial; N. P. Charlot, *Richmond;* W. T. D. Dalzell, *Houston;* B. Eaton, *Galveston;* C. Gillette, St. David's, *Austin;* J. M. Goshorn, *Gonzales;* L. H. Jones, *San Antonio;* T. H. Mitchell, U.S.A., *Ft. Chadbourne;* J. Owen, *San Augustine & Nacogdoches;* J. Hamilton Quinby, Gen'l Missionary; R. H. Ranney & L. P. Rucker, non-parochial; R. S. Seely, *Washington;* E. A. Wagner, *Marshall & Jefferson.*

1861: Rt. Rev. Alexander Gregg, D.D., Bishop, *Austin;* W. T. D. Dalzell, *Houston;* Silas D. Davenport, *Corpus Christi;* B. Eaton, *Galveston;* C. Gillette, *Austin;* J. M. Goshorn, *Columbus;* L. H. Jones, *San Antonio;* T. H. Mitchell, U.S.A.; J. Owen, *San Augustine & Nacogdoches;* R. H. Ranney, non-parochial; L. P. Rucker, Missionary, *Milam & Burleson Cos.;* R. S. Seely, *Washington;* Daniel Shaver, *Brenham;* E. A. Wagner, *Marshall & Jefferson;* F. R. Brown, Deacon, Gen'l Missionary, *Austin;* H. B. Monges, Deacon, *Seguin.*

1862: Rt. Rev. Alexander Gregg, D.D., Bishop, *Austin;* B. Eaton, *Galveston;* C. Gillette, *Austin;* L. P. Rucker, *Burleson & Milam Cos.;* W. T. D. Dalzell, *San Antonio;* L. H. Jones, Chaplain, C.S.A.; T. H. Mitchell, in the North, R. H. Ranney, non-parochial; J. Owen, *Matagorda;* J. M. Goshorn, *Columbus;* R. S. Seely, *Washington;* E. A. Wagner, *Houston;* D. Shaver, *Brenham;* S. D. Davenport, *Corpus Christi;* F. R. Brown, Deacon, *Austin;* H. B. Monges, Deacon, *Seguin;* H. G. Batterson, Deacon, in the North; W. R. Richardson, Deacon, *Victoria;* C. W. Stone, Deacon, *Burleson Co.*

1863: Rt. Rev. Alexander Gregg, D.D., Bishop, *Austin;* B. Eaton, *Galveston;* C. Gillette, *Austin;* L. P. Rucker, *Caldwell;* W. T. D. Dalzell, *San Antonio;* L. H. Jones, Chaplain, C.S.A.; T. H. Mitchell, in the North; R. H. Raney, *Seguin;* J. Owen, *Matagorda;* J. M. Goshorn, *Columbus;* R. S. Seely, *Washington;* E. A. Wagner, *Houston;* D. Shaver, *Brownsville;* S. D. Davenport, *Waco;* F. R. Brown, Deacon, *Austin;* H. B. Monges, Deacon, *Seguin;* H. G. Batterson, Deacon, in the North; W. R. Richardson, Deacon, *Victoria;* C. W. Stone, Deacon, *Caldwell;* G. W. E. Fisse (Diocese of Maryland), Deacon, *Marshall & Jefferson.*

1864: Rt. Rev. Alexander Gregg, D.D., Bishop, *Austin;* B. Eaton, *Galveston* (in England); C. Gillette, *Austin;* L. P. Rucker, *Caldwell;* W. T. D. Dalzell, *San Antonio;* R. H. Ranney, Missionary near *Seguin;* J. Owen, *Matagorda;* J. M. Goshorn, Rector pro tem, *Houston;* R. S. Seely, *Washington;* E. A. Wagner (in South Carolina); S. D. Davenport, *Waco;* W. R. Richardson, *Huntsville;* H. B.

Monges, Deacon, C.S.A.; C. W. Stone, Deacon, Missionary, *Milam & Burleson Cos.;* S. Kay, D.D., Deacon, Missionary, *Richmond;* G. W. E. Fisse, Deacon (Diocese of Maryland), *Marshall.* Absent in the North: T. H. Mitchell, Daniel Shaver, H. G. Batterson, Deacon.

1865: Rt. Rev. Alexander Gregg, D.D., Bishop, *Austin;* B. Eaton, *Galveston* (in England); C. Gillette, *Austin;* L. P. Rucker, *Caldwell;* W. T. D. Dalzell, *San Antonio* (in England); R. H. Ranney, near *Seguin;* J. Owen, *Matagorda;* R. S. Seely, *Washington;* E. A. Wagner (in S. Carolina); S. D. Davenport, *Waco;* W. R. Richardson, *Huntsville;* S. Kay, D.D., *Richmond;* J. M. Curtis (Diocese of Arkansas), elect of Christ Church, *Houston;* T. R. B. Trader (Diocese of Louisiana), *Nacogdoches;* C. Dow (Louisiana), *Palestine;* R. H. Murphy (Arkansas), pro tem at *San Antonio;* H. B. Monges, Deacon, *Seguin;* C. W. Stone, Deacon, *Milam & Burleson Cos.;* G. W. E. Fisse (Maryland), *Marshall.*

1866: Rt. Rev. Alexander Gregg, D.D., Bishop, *San Antonio;* B. Eaton, *Galveston;* L. P. Rucker, *Caldwell;* R. H. Ranney, non-parochial; J. Owen, *Matagorda;* R. S. Seely, *Washington;* E. A. Wagner, *San Antonio;* D. Shaver, *Brownsville;* S. D. Davenport, *Marshall & Jefferson;* W. R. Richardson, *Huntsville;* J. M. Curtis, *Houston;* A. F. Dobb, non-parochial; Geo. Rottenstein, *Dallas;* Gideon B. Perry, D.D., L.L.D., non-parochial; H. B. Monges, Deacon, *Seguin;* C. W. Stone, Deacon, *Lexington;* D. W. Chase, Deacon, *Brenham & Independence;* J. W. Tays, Deacon, *Columbus, Richmond & La Grange;* R. D. Shindler, *San Augustine;* Benj. A. Rogers, *Austin.*

1867: Rt. Rev. Alexander Gregg, D.D., Bishop, *San Antonio;* B. Eaton, *Galveston;* L. P. Rucker, *Caldwell;* R. H. Ranney, *Seguin;* J. Owen, *Matagorda;* R. S. Seely, *Owensville;* E. A. Wagner, *San Antonio;* D. Shaver, *Brownsville;* S. D. Davenport, *Marshall & Jefferson;* W. R. Richardson, *Huntsville;* A. F. Dobb, *Brenham;* G. Rottenstein, *Dallas;* J. W. Tays, *Indianola;* B. A. Rogers, *Austin;* Joseph Cross, D.D., *Houston;* R. D. Shindler, *San Augustine;* G. B. Perry, non-parochial; W. W. Patrick, *Waco;* H. B. Monges, Deacon, *Bellville;* D. W. Chase, Deacon, *Independence;* A. J. Yeater, Deacon, *Millican, Bryan & Railroad Mission.*

1868: Rt. Rev. Alexander Gregg, D.D., Bishop, *San Antonio;* B. Eaton, *Galveston;* L. P. Rucker, *Brenham;* R. H. Ranney, *New Braunfels;* R. S. Seely, *Owensville;* E. A. Wagner, Gen'l Missionary, *Marshall;* D. Shaver, non-parochial; S. D. Davenport, *Marshall & Jefferson;* W. R. Richardson, *San Antonio;* R. D. Shindler, *San Augustine;* B. A. Rogers, *Austin;* J. Cross, *Houston;* Robert Jope, *Bryan;* J. W. Tays, *Indianola;* W. W. Patrick, *Waco;* H. B. Monges, Deacon, *Bellville;* D. W. Chase, Deacon, *Independence;* A. J. Yeater, Deacon, *Millican;* Elijah Guion, D.D., Chaplain, U.S.A.; Melville C. Keith, M.D., Deacon (Diocese of New York).

1869: Rt. Rev. Alexander Gregg, D.D., Bishop, *San Antonio;* B. Eaton, *Galveston;* L. P. Rucker, *Brenham & Hempstead;* S. D. Davenport, *Dallas;* W. R. Richardson, *San Antonio;* J. W. Tays, *Bryan;* R. D. Shindler, *Nacogdoches;* B. A. Rogers, *Austin;* W. W. Patrick, *Waco;* R. Jope, *Lavaca;* R. H. Ranney, *New Braunfels;* R. S. Seely, *Owensville;* D. Shaver, non-parochial; E. Guion, U.S.A., *Ft. Clark;* H. B. Monges, Deacon, *Bellville;* D. W. Chase, Deacon, *Independence;* John Rosenberg, Deacon, *La Grange;* R. J. Swancoat, Deacon, *Bastrop,* residing in *Austin.*

1870: Rt. Rev. Alexander Gregg, D.D., Bishop, *Galveston;* B. Eaton, D.D., *Galveston;* L. P. Rucker, *Brenham;* S. D. Davenport, *Dallas;* W. R. Richardson, *San Antonio;* R. D. Shindler, *Nacogdoches;* B. A. Rogers, *Austin;* W. W. Patrick, *Waco;* R. Jope, *Indianola;* J. W. Tays, Chaplain, Texas Senate, *Austin;* R. H. Ranney, *Galveston;* R. S. Seely, *Owensville;* Daniel Shaver, non-parochial; E. Guion, U.S.A., *San Antonio;* F. R. Starr, *Paris;* T. R. B. Trader, *Houston;* E. G. Benners, *Jefferson;*

S. H. S. Gallaudet, non-parochial; J. W. Phillips, *Bryan & Navasota;* H. B. Monges, Deacon, *Bellville;* D. W. Chase, Deacon, *Independence;* J. Rosenberg, Deacon, non-parochial; R. J. Swancoat, Deacon, Principal of School, *Austin;* R. S. Nash, Deacon, *Waco;* N. E. Carrington, Deacon, *Chocolate.*

1871: Rt. Rev. Alexander Gregg, D.D., Bishop, *Galveston;* L. P. Rucker, *Brenham;* R. H. Ranney, pro tem of Trinity, *Galveston;* S. D. Davenport, *Dallas;* W. R. Richardson, *San Antonio;* R. D. Shindler, *Nacogdoches;* B. A. Rogers, *Austin;* J. W. Tays, *El Paso;* R. Jope, *Indianola;* E. G. Benners, *Jefferson;* T. R. B. Trader, *Houston;* F. R. Starr, *Paris;* W. W. Patrick, *Gatesville;* J. W. Phillips, *Navasota & Bryan;* J. Cooper Waddill, *Calvert;* E. Guion, U.S.A., *Ft. Sill, Ind. Ter.;* D. Eglinton Barr, U.S.A., *Ft. Clark;* E. B. Tuttle, U.S.A., *Ft. Duncan;* Norman Badger, U.S.A., *Ft. Concho;* H. B. Monges, Deacon, *Bellville;* D. W. Chase, Deacon, *Independence;* R. J. Swancoat, Deacon, *Austin;* R. S. Nash, Deacon, *Waco;* N. E. Carrington, Deacon, *Chocolate;* Robt. Carley, Deacon, *Seguin.*

1872: Rt. Rev. Alexander Gregg, D.D., Bishop, *Galveston;* L. P. Rucker, *Brenham;* R. H. Ranney, non-parochial, *Galveston;* S. D. Davenport, *Dallas;* W. R. Richardson, *San Antonio;* R. D. Shindler, *Nacogdoches;* B. A. Rogers, *Austin;* J. W. Tays, *El Paso;* R. Jope, *Indianola;* E. G. Benners, *Jefferson;* T. R. B. Trader, *Houston;* F. R. Starr, *Paris;* W. W. Patrick, Missionary, residing in *Waco;* J. W. Phillips, *Bryan;* J. C. Waddill, *Calvert;* E. Guion, U.S.A., *San Antonio;* D. E. Barr, U.S.A., *Ft. Clark;* H. B. Monges, Deacon, *Bellville;* D. W. Chase, Deacon, *Independence;* R. S. Nash, Deacon, *Cleburne;* N. E. Carrington, Deacon, *Victoria;* Robt. Carley, *Seguin;* Wm. Brittain, *Corpus Christi;* Albert Lyon, *New Braunfels;* J. T. Hutcheson, *Hempstead;* Virginius O. Gee, *Corsicana;* Jeremiah Ward, *Huntsville;* Otis Hackett, *Waco;* Emir Hamvasy, non-parochial, *Austin;* Stephen Moylan Bird, Sr., *Galveston.*

1873: Rt. Rev. Alexander Gregg, D.D., Bishop, *Galveston;* L. P. Rucker, *Brenham;* R. H. Ranney, non-parochial; S. D. Davenport, *Dallas;* W. R. Richardson, *San Antonio;* R. D. Shindler, *Nacogdoches;* B. A. Rogers, *Austin;* J. W. Tays, *El Paso;* R. Jope, *Indianola;* E. G. Benners, *Jefferson;* T. R. B. Trader, *Houston;* F. R. Starr, *Paris;* W. W. Patrick, Missionary, residing in *Waco;* J. W. Phillips, Missionary, residing in *Austin;* J. C. Waddill, *Calvert;* E. Guion, U.S.A., *Ind. Ter.;* D. W. Chase, Deacon, *Independence;* R. S. Nash, Deacon, *Cleburne;* N. E. Carrington, Deacon, *Calhoun Co.;* A. Lyon, *New Braunfels;* J. T. Hutcheson, *Seguin;* V. O. Gee, *Navasota;* J. Ward, *Huntsville;* O. Hackett, *Waco;* E. Hamvasy, *Tyler;* S. M. Bird, *Galveston;* John Portmess, Missionary, *Hallville;* Nelson Ayres, *Bryan;* E. A. Wagner, *Marshall;* Edwin Wickins, Missionary on visitation with Bishop.

1874:Rt. Rev. Alexander Gregg, D.D., Bishop, *Galveston;* L. P. Rucker, *Brenham;* R H. Ranney, non-parochial; S. D. Davenport, *Dallas;* W. R. Richardson, *San Antonio;* R. D. Shindler, *Nacogdoches;* B. A. Rogers, *Austin;* J. W. Tays, *El Paso;* R. Jope, *Indianola;* E. G. Benners, *Jefferson;* T. R. B. Trader, non-parochial; F. R. Starr, *Paris;* W. W. Patrick, *Belton;* J. W. Phillips, Missionary, *Austin;* J. C. Waddill, *Calvert;* J. T. Hutcheson, *Seguin;* V. O. Gee, *Bryan;* J. Ward, *Huntsville;* O. Hackett, *Waco;* S. M. Bird, *Galveston;* E. A. Wagner, *Marshall;* N. Ayers, *Corpus Christi;* E. Hamvasy, *Tyler;* A. Lyon, Master, Trinity Parish School & Missionary, *Galveston;* J. Portmess, *Hallville;* E. W. Gilliam, *Sherman;* Wallace Carnahan, *San Marcos;* R. J. Swancoat, Missionary residing in *Austin;* E. Guion, U.S.A., *Ft. Gibson, Ind. Ter.;* E. Wickins, Deacon, *Matagorda Co.;* D. W. Chase, Deacon, *Independence;* R. S. Nash, Deacon, *Cleburne;* N. E. Carrington, Deacon, *Victoria;* Thos. J. Morris, Deacon, *Brazos and Colorado Railroad Mission.*

APPENDIX B

LAY DELEGATES TO DIOCESAN COUNCILS

(As listed in the *Journals of the Diocese of Texas;* delegates to the 1849 Convention are listed in the text.)

1850: *Galveston,* Trinity: P. G. Merritt, A. Lynn. *Matagorda,* Christ: S. G. Powell, J. C. McGonigal. *Houston,* Christ: A. S. Ruthven, P. W. Gray, Dr. F. Moore, Jr., E. W. Taylor. *Brazoria County,* St. John's: Dr. P. A. Davenport, R. J. Townes, J. Adriance, S. S. Perry.

1851: *Matagorda,* Christ: None. *Galveston,* Trinity: P. G. Merritt, Geo. Butler, E. O. Lynch, L. Frosh. *Houston,* Christ: A. S. Ruthven, P. W. Gray, Dr. F. Moore, Jr., E. B. Nichols. *Brazoria,* St. John's: None. *San Augustin,* Christ: None. *Nacogdoches,* Christ: None. *San Antonio,* Trinity, None. *Brenham,* St. Peter's: None. *Washington,* St. Paul's: Henry Bailey, Dr. A. Jones, Wm. T. Austin, C. M. Lockhart. *Fireman's Hill,* St. Paul's: A. Middleton. *Brownsville,* Advent: Jos. P. Couthouy, John S. Rhea. *Chappell Hill,* St. Luke's: W. L. Tunstall, Wm. H. Sherman, John C. Wallis.

1852: *Matagorda,* Christ: None. *Galveston,* Trinity: C. Ennis. *Houston,* Christ: Dr. F. Moore, Jr., *W. M. Rice, W. W. Stiles. *Brazoria,* St. John's: None. *San Augustine,* Christ: None. *Nacogdoches,* Christ: None. *San Antonio,* Trinity: None. *Brenham,* St. Peter's: A. C. Compton, A. M. Lewis, H. A. Robertson, G. Cooke. *Washington,* St. Paul's: Dr. Anson Jones, *W. T. Austin, H. Baily, O. S. Sheldon. *Fireman's Hill,* St. Paul's: *J. D. Turner, *G. B. Middleton, *W. S. Maxcey, H. F. Gillette. *Brownsville,* Advent: None. *Chappell Hill,* St. Luke's: A. M. Upsher, W. L. Tunstall, F. J. Cooke. *Austin,* Epiphany: *S. G. Haynie, *E. Ten Eyck, *J. M. Swisher, M. Evans. *Marshall,* Trinity: None. *Anderson,* Redeemer: C. B. Oney, *J. Lawrence, *B. B. Goodrich, J. B. Harris. *Liberty,* All Faith: H. E. Perkins. (*Not present at the Convention.)

1853: *Matagorda,* Christ: None. *Houston,* Christ: Col. James Reily, Dr. Fran. Moore, Jr., Col. C. D. Andrews, Peter W. Gray. *Galveston,* Trinity: None. *Brazoria,* St. John's: None. *San Augustine,* Christ: Gen. J. P. Henderson, Charles Stewart, J. D. Thomas, Jas. B. Thornton. *Nacogdoches,* Christ: Col. Frost Thorn, Gen. H. H. Edwards, R. S. Walker, W. C. Pollock. *San Antonio,* Trinity: None. *Brenham,* St. Peter's: A. G. Compton, G. B. Cooke. *Washington,* St. Paul's: Dr. Anson Jones, Col. J. H. Dawson, John R. Bertrand, Henry Bailey. *Fireman's Hill,* St. Paul's: G. B. Middleton, W. S. Maxcy, A. Middleton, H. F. Gillette. *Brownsville,* Advent: None. *Chappell Hill,* St. Luke's: Col. A. M. Upshaw, F. J. Cooke, Alex. Cooke, Dr. W. L. Tunstall. *Austin,* Epiphany: M. Evans, S. G. Haynie, W. S. Oldham, John M. Swisher. *Marshall,* Trinity: None. *Anderson,* Redeemer: Dr. D. C. Dickson, C. B. Oney, James Lawrence, B. H. McDaniel. *Liberty,* All Faith: None.

1854 (places not indicated): James Reily, J. D. Andrews, W. W. Stiles, P. W. Gray, E. B. Nichols, J. Manly, Oscar Farish, H. Jenkins, *A. M. Lewis, A. G. Compton, G. B. Cooke, J. G. Knapp, *W. T. Austin, Anson Jones, Thos. G. Heard, Chas. M. Lockhart, *H. F. Gillette, *J. D. Turner, W. S. Maxey, *A. M. M. Upshaw, F. J. Cooke, J. M. McDade, W. L. Tunstall, *J. M. Swisher, R. M. Elgin, W. H. Henderson, S. G. Haynie, *B. B. Goodrich, *C. B. Oney, *A. S. Richardson, *J. G.

Chatham, *C. G. Keenan, G. M. Baker, J. M. Roundtree, R. C. Smith, W. R. Cowan, F. F. Hooper, T. J. Potts, L. A. Perryman, H. T. Burke. (*IN ATTENDANCE.)

1855: *Matagorda*, Christ: None. *Galveston*, Trinity: S. Southwick, J. H. Hutchins, *W. Wakelee, Jr. *Houston*, Christ: J. D. Andrews, James Reily, C. Ennis, *H. E. Perkins. *Brazoria*, St. John's: None. *San Augustine*, Christ: None. *Nacogdoches*, Christ: None. *San Antonio*, Trinity: F. T. Pryor, Henry Lewis, James Dennison, *E. F. Buckner. *Brenham*, St. Peter's: A. M. Lewis, J. H. Dawson, *G. B. Cooke, J. T. Norris. *Washington*, St. Paul's: *Dr. Anson Jones, H. Bailey, H. E. Lockett, Robert F. Wood. *Fireman's Hill*, St. Paul's: None. *Brownsville*, Advent: None. *Chappell Hill*, St. Luke's; *A. M. M. Upshaw, F. J. Cooke, Alexander Cooke, J. Applewhite. *Austin*, Epiphany: S. G. Haynie, R. Elgin, W. H. Henderson, *A. G. Compton. *Marshall*, Trinity: None. *Anderson*, Redeemer: B. B. Goodrich, Thos. H. Pointer, Dr. D. C. Dickson. *Liberty*, All Faith: None. *Seguin*, Redeemer: *E. Root, *Wm. M. Rust. *Lockhart*, Immanuel: *Gen. J. L. Hunter, C. E. Metcalf. *Gonzales*, Messiah: *C. D. Bennett, A. N. Mills, T. Shepherd. *Indianola*, St. John's: None. *Lavaca*, Grace: None. *Huntsville*, St. Stephen's: None. (*DELEGATES IN ATTENDANCE.)

1856: *Galveston*, Trinity: *E. B. Nichols, *S. Southwick, *Oscar Farish, *J. S. Rhea. *Houston*, Christ: *J. D. Andrews, Peter W. Gray, Wm. M. Rice, *H. E. Perkins; ALTERNATE: C. Ennis. *Matagorda*, Christ, *W. L. Sartwell, *James H. Cutler. *Cold Spring*, St. Paul's: *J. D. Turner, *F. R. Gillette. *Huntsville*, St. Stephens: A. M. Branch, A. Middleton, J. R. Smither, *C. G. Keenan. *Anderson*, Redeemer: *A. S. Richardson, B. B. Goodrich, Thomas H. Pointer, J. G. Chatham. *Brenham*, St. Peter's: A. M. Lewis, James Byars, Daniel B. Anderson, T. W. Morriss. *Chappell Hill*, St. Luke's: A. M. M. Upshaw, F. J. Cooke, W. H. Sherman, George T. Chappell. *Austin*, Epiphany: W. S. Oldham, T. J. Green, John Bremond, W. S. Robarts. (*DELEGATES IN ATTENDANCE.)

1857: *Houston*, Christ: J. D. Andrews, W. H. Elliott, James Reily, *Walter R. Richardson. *Matagorda*, Christ: Wm. Sartwell, *Jas. H. Cutler. *Austin*, Epiphany: *R. M. Elgin, W. S. Oldham, Wm. Byrd; ALTERNATES: *W. L. Robarts, Wm. M. Bryce, W. C. Perry. *Lockhart*, Immanuel: *Wm. R. Cowan, E. R. Hepenstall, J. L. Hunter; ALTERNATES: *F. P. Nichols, *L. S. Miller. *Seguin*, Redeemer: D. McKnight, *G. H. Sherwood, J. P. White; ALTERNATES: *N. Henderson, *C. Reich. *Brenham*, St. Peter's: A. M. Lewis, T. W. Morriss. *La Grange*, St. Jame's: G. W. Sinks, J. R. Casselman, B. Shropshire. *Cold Springs*, St. Paul's: *H. F. Gillette, D. L. Jagers, F. R. Gillette, John Ellis. *Columbus*, St. John's: Robert Robson, W. J. Darden, J. S. Shropshire, Wm. G. Banks. *Austin*, Christ: *E. M. Pease, *J. M. Swisher, *S. G. Haynie, *A. G. Compton. *Dallas*, St. Matthew's: E. H. Tarrant, N. H. Darnell, C. R. Pryor, J. C. McCoy. (*IN ATTENDANCE.)

1858: *Matagorda*, Christ: *A. DePelchin. *Houston*, Christ: *J. D. Andrews, *P. W. Gray, *W. J. Hutchins, *A. S. Richardson; SUPPLEMENTAL: W. H. Eliot, E. W. Taylor. *Galveston*, Trinity: *E. B. Nichols, *O. Farish, *S. Southwick, *G. Butler. *Cold Spring*, St. Paul's: J. D. Turner, W. S. Maxcy, *H. F. Gillette. *Austin*, Epiphany: G. T. Boardman, J. C. Perry, W. L. Roberts, F. W. Moore; SUPPLEMENTAL: Wm. Bird, G. Hancock, R. Fisher, W. S. Oldham. *Huntsville*, St. Stephen's: S. R. Smith, *F. D. Thornton, S. Leigh, C. Robinson. *Seguin*, St. Andrew's: J. P. White, C. Reich, D. McKnight, *H. B. Monges. *La Grange*, St. James: *B. Shropshire. *Columbus*, St. John's: L. M. Newsom, W. J. Darden, A. Jones, J. S. Shropshire. *Austin*, Christ: J. M. Swisher, E. M. Pease, S. G. Haynie, J. H. Raymond; SUPPLEMENTAL: S. M. Swenson, C. G. Keenan, *W. R. Richardson, —Van Nostrand. (*DELEGATES IN ATTENDANCE.)

1859: *Matagorda*, Christ: Wm. L. Sartwelle, *A. DePelchin, J. B. Hawkins, *Jas. H. Cutler. *Houston*, Christ: J. D. Andrews, *P. W. Gray, W. J. Hutchins, *J. Reily.

Galveston, Trinity: *E. B. Nichols, O. Farish, *S. Southwick, *P. C. Tucker, Jr. *Austin,* Epiphany: *Chas. S. West, W. S. Oldham, Wm. Byrd, *W. L. Robarts; SUPPLEMENTAL: Wm. M. Bryce, Wesley Johnson, W. H. Brown, R. F. Brownrig. *Huntsville,* St. Stephen's: *James C. Rome. *Seguin,* St. Andrew's: *D. McKnight, P. T. McDowell, *M. S. Dunn. *Gonzales,* Messiah: *I. E. Nicholson, A. N. Mills, J. F. Gay. *Austin,* Christ: Amos Morrell, *A. G. Compton, J. H. Raymond, C. G. Keenan. *San Antonio,* St. Mark's: Wm. J. Clarke, J. H. Beck, J. Waelder, J. J. Allen; SUPPLEMENTAL: R. H. Chilton, H. B. Monges. *Richmond,* Calvary: *J. R. Pettus, *Wm. E. Kendall, H. C. Deshields, W. D. Mitchell. (*DELEGATES IN ATTENDANCE.)

1860: *Matagorda,* Christ: *J. H. Selkirk, *J. H. Cutler, *J. B. Hawkins, John Rugeley. *Houston,* Christ: *Wm. J. Hutchins, E. W. Taylor, W. B. Botts, Joseph Evans. *Galveston,* Trinity: *Marcus F. Mott, *Wm. H. Williams, S. Southwick, A. T. Lynn. *Seguin,* St. Andrew's: J. R. Jefferson, R. J. Coorpender, T. P. McDowell, Alex. Henderson. *Gonzales,* Messiah: D. W. Brodnax, R. A. Atkinson. *San Antonio,* St. Mark's: Col. W. Seawell, J. H. Beck, E. E. McLean, Wm. J. Clarke. *Richmond,* Calvary: *Joel T. Weston. *Austin,* St. David's: *E. M. Pease, *J. T. Graves, W. C. Philips, S. Harris; SUPPLEMENTAL: James Cole, R. J. Towns, D. W. C. Baker, B. F. Townsend. (*DELEGATES IN ATTENDANCE.)

1861: *Houston,* Christ: W. J. Hutchins, A. S. Richardson, W. H. Elliott, E. W. Taylor; SUBSTITUTE, appointed by the Rector: *A. M. Gentry. *Galveston,* Trinity: C. R. Hughes, M. M. Potter, W. Richardson, W. H. Williams. *Brenham,* St. Peter's: *A. M. Lewis, A. M. M. Upshaw, A. G. Compton, T. W. Morriss. *Seguin,* St. Andrew's: *H. G. Batterson, *W. P. H. Douglas, *J. W. Clemons, G. H. Sherwood. *Columbus,* St. John's: Robert Robson, W. J. Hunt. *San Antonio,* St. Mark's: *Samuel A. Maverick, Jacob Waelder, Henry M. Smyth, Ira L. Hewlitt; ALTERNATES: John James, Samuel Newton, J. R. Sweet, W. H. Mechling. *Austin,* St. David's: *S. M. Swenson, *John M. Swisher, *W. L. Robarts, *R. M. Elgin; ALTERNATES: Amos Morrill, John A. Greene, Thos. Freeman, F. T. Duffau. (*DELEGATES IN ATTENDANCE.)

1862: *Houston,* Christ: *Wm. J. Hutchins, *E. S. Perkins, W. H. Eliot, *Col. J. D. Andrews; ALTERNATES: A. C. Gray, H. W. Benchley, A. S. Richardson. *Galveston,* Trinity: *J. H. Hutchings, George Ball, T. M. League, O. Farish. *San Antonio,* St. Mark's: *Major S. Maclin, Col. J. Y. Dashiel; ALTERNATE: *Gen. H. P. Bee. *Washington,* St. Paul's: *Maj. B. F. Rucker, Col. H. E. Lockett, John Allen, T. J. Lockett. *Brenham,* St. Peter's: *Col. A. M. Lewis, Col. A. M. M. Upshaw, B. H. Bassett, J. H. Dawkins. *Matagorda,* Christ Church: *Col. J. B. Hawkins, M. Talbot, J. H. Selkirk, *J. H. Cutler. *Austin,* St. David's: F. T. Duffau, S. M. Swenson, R. M. Elgin, *J. Bremond. *Corpus Christi,* Good Shepherd: Charles Collins, W. P. Crafts, James A. Ware; ALTERNATES: Walter Merriman, J. P. Harrison, R. J. Denny. *Jefferson,* Christ: E. G. Benners, Orville Yerger. *Bellville,* St. Mary's: Wm. Thompson, S. R. Blake, R. T. Paine, N. Holland. (*DELEGATES IN ATTENDANCE.)

1863: *Matagorda,* Christ: *Col. J. B. Hawkins, Judge M. Talbot, Dr. R. H. Chinn, J H. Cutler. *Houston,* Christ: *Hon. P. W. Gray, Dr. W. H. Eliot, E. S. Perkins, A. S. Richardson. *Galveston,* Trinity: *Dr. Wm. R. Smith, Stephen Southwick, Oscar Farish, Marcus F. Mott. *Brenham,* St. Peter's: Col. J. H. Dawson, *Col. A. M. Lewis, *Col. A. M. M. Upshaw, *Dr. Lewis Polk. *Brownsville,* Advent: *Gen. H. P. Bee, *Major A. M. Lea, *F. Cummings, *Jos. Hopkins. *Marshall,* Trinity: Dr. A. T. Smith. *Huntsville,* St. Stephen's: J. C. Rome. *San Antonio,* St. Mark's: *Major S. Macklin, Col. Geo. W. Baylor, *G. H. Giddings, *S. Maverick. *Jefferson,* Christ: E G. Benners, *Sam'l. Woodall, *H. Witherspoon, *A. M. Walker. *Bellville,* St. Mary's: N. Holland, W. Thompson, *S. R. Blake. (*NOT IN ATTENDANCE.)

1864: *Matagorda*, Christ: Col. J. B. Hawkins, Judge M. Talbot, *Dr. R. H. Chinn, J. H. Cutler. *Houston*, Christ: Hon. P. W. Gray, W. B. Botts, E. S. Perkins, A. S. Richardson. *Galveston*, Trinity: S. Southwick, *J. H. Hutchings, P. C. Tucker, C. R. Hughes. *Brenham*, St. Peter's: *Col. A. M. M. Upshaw, *Benj. Bassett, *E. A. Gause, D. C. Stone; ALTERNATE: Col. J. H. Dawson. *Washington*, St. Paul's: *Maj. B. F. Rucker, *Henry N. Jones, Geo. D. Haswell, Dr. Thomas Heard. *Huntsville*, St. Stephen's: J. C. Rome, *Emory Hall, *Judge R. C. Campbell, *Col. Thos. C. Carothers. *San Antonio*, St. Mark's: Maj. S. Maclin, *Col. J. Y. Dashiel, *Capt. J. Waelder, *Mr. S. A. Maverick. *Richmond*, Calvary: Hon. C. W. Buckley, *Dr. J. R. Pettus, Col. J. H. Herndon. *Jefferson*, Christ: *E. G. Benners, *W. H. Sutton, *A. M. Walker. *Independence*, Grace: *Col. J. R. Lewis, *J. W. Harris, *Dr. Lewis Polk, D. W. Chase. (*NOT IN ATTENDANCE.)

1865: *Austin*, St. David's: *R. M. Elgin. *Brenham*, St. Peter's: A. M. M. Upshaw, D. C. Stone, J. H. Dawson, E. A. Gause. *Crockett*, All Saints': *Wm. M. Taylor, J. R. Burnett, A. T. Monroe, D. M. Coleman. *Galveston*, Trinity: *S. Southwick, *M. F. Mott, *P. C. Tucker, *C. R. Hughes. *Gonzales*, Messiah: *A. M. Lea, A. V. Mills. *Houston*, Christ: *W. B. Botts, *H. E. Perkins, *E. S. Perkins, *A. S. Richardson. *Huntsville*, St. Stephen's: F. D. Thornton, C. G. Keenan, J. C. Rome, *Emory Hall. *Independence*, Grace: T. T. Clay, Benj. Polk, Louis Polk. *Marshall*, Trinity: *P. W. Gray. *Matagorda*, Christ: *W. B. Grimes, J. H. Cutler, J. B. Hawkins, R. H. Chinn. *Richmond*, Calvary: *John H. Herndon, *C. W. Buckley. *Washington*, St. Paul's: *H. N. Jones, *D. W. Shannon, *J. R. Thomas, B. F. Rucker, T. J. Heard, Geo. D. Haswell. (*DELEGATES IN ATTENDANCE.)

1866: *Austin*, St. David's: L. B. Collins. *Brenham*, St. Peter's: *A. M. M. Upshaw, W. S. Millett, J. F. Norris, *Emil Neumann. *Galveston*, Trinity, *S. Southwick, *C. R. Hughes, W. R. Smith, *W. S. Davis. *Gonzales*, Messiah: Albert M. Lea, A. J. McKean. *Houston*, Christ: *Peter W. Gray, *E. S. Perkins, *A. S. Richardson, *W. B. Botts. *Huntsville*, St. Stephen's: C. G. Keenan, John Riley. *Independence*, Grace: *S. A. Bryant, T. W. Morris, Ira R. Lewis, T. T. Clay. *Jefferson*, Christ: E. G. Benners, J. H. Pratt, A. M. Walker. *La Grange*, St. James': *James W. Mathews. *Marshall*, Trinity: A. T. Smith, Frederick Smith, Albert Martin, Henry Rawson. *Matagorda*, Christ: J. B. Hawkins, R. H. Chinn, W. B. Grimes. *Nacogdoches*, Christ: William Voigt. *Navasota*, Holy Comforter: *J. H. Kerr, *R. H. Toms, H. N. Jones, *J. T. Eppinger. *Richmond*, Calvary: J. R. Pettus, W. E. Kendall, B. F. Atkins, *H. DeVieuve. *San Antonio*, St. Mark's: S. Maclin, John James, Marcellus French, W. T. Mechlin. *Washington*, St. Paul's: D. W. Shannon, Geo. D. Haswell, *B. F. Rucker, *A. Johnstone. (*PRESENT IN CONVENTION.)

1867: *Austin*, St. David's: Eugene Bremond, W. L. Robarts, John A. Green, D. W. C. Baker; ALTERNATES: George F. Moore, Geo. Hancock, *J. H. Herndon, L. C. Bootes. *Bellville*, St. Mary's: *W. Holland, B. F. Harris, Z. Hunt, W. J. Cocke. *Brenham*, St. Peter's: *J. H. Dawson, A. M. M. Upshaw, *W. W. Wheeler, *John Dunning. *Dallas*, St. Matthew's: J. M. Crockett, J. M. Patterson, T. C. Jordan, J. W. Haynes. *Galveston*, Trinity: *C. R. Hughes, *Walter L. Mann. *Hempstead*, St. Bartholomew's: *D. W. Brodnax, J. C. Grace, J. L. Hollowell, J. C. Rome; ALTERNATES: *J. W. McDade, *F. J. Cooke. *Houston*, Christ: Peter W. Gray, J. T. Harrison, *Henry E. Perkins, *A. S. Richardson. *Huntsville*, St. Stephen's: F. D. Thornton, J. P. Nixon, C. G. Keenan; ALTERNATES: J. F. Gay, J. L. Smither, J. A. Moore, Geo. V. Perrie. *Independence*, Grace: T. T. Clay, Archibald Hughes, G. W. Morris, *Lewis Polk. *Indianola*, Ascension: W. P. Milby, J. McCoppin. *Jefferson*, Christ: J. C. Hynson, J. H. Pratt, A. M. Walker, E. G. Benners. *La Grange*, St. James': *James W. Matthews. *Lavaca*, Grace: L. H. Jacobs, E. L. Beaumont, R. H. Forbes. *Marshall*, Trinity: A. C. Martin, Archibald Hotchkiss, F. M. McIvor, H. Rawson; ALTERNATE: A. T. Smith. *Matagorda*, Christ: J. B. Hawkins, *J. H. Cutler,

W. B. Grimes, *J. Burkhart. *Navasota*, Holy Comforter: J. H. Kerr, H. N. Jones. *Washington*, St. Paul's: *T. J. Lockett, B. F. Rucker, Andrew Johnstone, Dr. Neal. (*PRESENT IN CONVENTION.)

1868: *Austin*, St. David's: *S. G. Haynie, *J. H. Raymond, *Jno. Hancock, Gen. J. J. Reynolds. *Bryan*, St. Andrew's: Geo. D. Haswell, George Johnson, Frank Clark, R. S. McKeen. *Dallas*, St. Matthew's: *J. M. Crockett. *Galveston*, Trinity: *S. Maclin. *Houston*, Christ: *Robert M. Elgin, E. S. Perkins, W. J. Hutchins, Peter W. Gray. *Huntsville*, St. Stephen's: *Geo. W. Sinks, Jo. Bates, Jr., Geo. V. Perrie, T. W. Markham. *Independence*, Grace: T. W. Morris, M. A. Bryan, Wm. Dever, Louis Polk. *Jefferson*, Christ: E. G. Benners, H. C. Hynson, L. S. Rayfield, J. H. Pratt. *La Grange*, St. Jame's: *L. Lindsay. *Waco*, St. Paul's: *F. S. Hawley, *Fred Quarles. (*PRESENT IN CONVENTION.)

1869: *Austin*, St. David's: J. H. Raymond, J. W. Phillips, Thos. Freeman; ALTERNATES: T. P. Hunt, M. S. Miller, L. B. Collins, E. Z. Eggleston. *Brenham*, St. Peter's: J. J. Stockbridge, J. D. McAdoo, J. C. Moore, *Peter Rucker. *Bryan*, St. Andrew's: Dr. Conger, Maj. Clarke, Emmet Mix, Thos. Wright; ALTERNATE: *Geo. D. Haswell. *Corpus Christi*, Good Shepherd: *R. I. Denny. *Dallas*, St. Matthew's: J. M. Crockett, T. C. Jordan, J. W. Swindells, John J. Word. *Galveston*, Trinity: O. Farish, *S. Southwick, *J. H. Hutchings, *E. B. Nichols. *Hempstead*, St. Bartholomew's: A. B. Coggeshall, *Geo. F. Lester, J. W. Nooner, P. S. Clarke. *Houston*, Christ: Peter W. Gray, *W. J. Hutchins, W. D. Cleveland, *R. M. Elgin. *Huntsville*, St. Stephen's: *J. P. Nixon, F. D. Thornton, T. S. Caswell. *Indianola*, Ascension: F. S. Stockdale, W. P. Milby, Jas. McCoppin, Geo. Vincent. *Jefferson*, Christ: *E. G. Benners, H. C. Hynson, J. W. Sims, L. S. Rayfield. *Lavaca*, Grace: E. L. Beaumont, T. S. Burke, Geo. P. Finley, C. S. Kibbie. *Matagorda*, Christ: *J. H. Cutler. *Navasota*, Holy Comforter: *Edgar Demaret, *E. L. Bridges. *Richmond*, Calvary: Wm. E. Kendall. *Victoria*, Trinity: Prhidam J. H. Allen, W. J. Neally, N. A. Thompson. (*PRESENT.)

1870: *Austin*, St. David's: *Emir Hamvasy, *T. F. Mitchell, T. B. Hunt, Dr. Middleton. *Bellville*, St. Mary's: *N. Holland, Z. Hunt, A. Chesley, Benj. T. Harris. *Brenham*, St. Peter's: *J. E. Shepard, T. W. Morris, H. L. Allen, C. L. Lowday; ALTERNATES: A. M. M. Upshaw, Robt. Bassett. *Bryan*, St. Andrew's: *Frank Clark, *Geo. D. Haswell; ALTERNATES: R. R. Gilbert, *Geo. Johnston. *Calvert*, Epiphany: *B. E. Roper, Thos. B. Wright, J. W. Beard, Emmit S. Mix. *Dallas*, St. Matthew's: N. M. Burford, T. C. Jordan, John W. Swindells, T. Walker. *Galveston*, Trinity: *L. Cannon, *A. Thurlow, *S. B. Southwick. *Houston*, Christ: E. S. Perkins, *Peter W. Gray, *Wm. J. Hutchins, *R. M. Elgin. *Huntsville*, St. Stephen's: I. P. Nixon, T. W. Markham, Joe Bates, Jr., Minor D. Wynne. *Independence*, Grace: Louis Polk, M. Austin Bryan, Thomas M. Clay. *Jefferson*, Christ: L. S. Rayfield, James Arbuckle, H. C. Hynson, John A. Wayland. *Navasota*, St. Paul's: *Edgar Demaret. *San Antonio*, St. Mark's: Wm. H. Young, *J. Y. Dashiell, Geo. B. Torrey, D. W. Porter. *San Augustine*, Christ: *Rufus Price, G. F. Crockett. *Waco*, St. Paul's: Geo. W. Jackson, G. B. Gerald. (*PRESENT.)

1871: *Austin*, St. David's: John W. Glenn, *Jas. H. Raymond, J. C. Raymond, *E. Hamvasy. *Bryan*, St. Andrew's: *B. F. Leman, J. J. Harrison, P. W. Hinton, *S. D. Conger; ALTERNATES: O. P. Bowles, *H. A. Moore. *Calvert*, Epiphany: J. H. Littlefield, *J. W. Beard, Tyler D. Harn. *Crockett*, All Saints': *Wm. M. Taylor. *Dallas*, St. Matthew's: *John W. Swindells, T. C. Jordan, N. M. Burford, W. L. Murphy. *El Paso*, St. Clement's: A. J. Fountain, J. A. Zabriskie, A. H. French, Henry S. Gillett. *Galveston*, Trinity: *E. B. Nichols, Geo. E. Mann, H. B. Yard, J. H. Hutchings; ALTERNATES: Geo. Butler, C. R. Hughes, Oliver Steele, Leander Cannon. *Hempstead*, St. Bartholomew's: John Thatcher, *Geo. G. Lester. *Houston*,

Christ: *Wm. J. Hutchins, Peter W. Gray, Henry E. Perkins, R. M. Elgin; ALTERNATES: A. Ewing, *Adam Bentley, Samuel Williams, James Blake. *Huntsville,* St. Stephen's: *A. L. McDonald, I. P. Nixon; ALTERNATES: *J. R. Burnett, J. C. Rome. *Independence,* Grace: *Louis Polk, M. Austin Bryan, T. M. Clay, Harry Love; ALTERNATE: John Seward. *Jefferson,* Christ: Thos. G. Anderson, W. P. Woodroof, Amos Morrill, James G. Tansill. *Matagorda,* Christ: Wm. B. Grimes, Jas. H. Cutler, John Ives. *Navasota,* St. Paul's: *E. Demaret, *B. F. Rucker, *J. C. Easton, *E. L. Bridges. *San Antonio,* St. Mark's: J. Y. Dashiell, Arthur H. Edey, Robert Eagar, George Maverick. *Victoria,* Trinity: W. J. Neely, S. Wilkins, W. J. Whitehead, F. R. Pridham. *Waco,* St. Paul's: Geo. W. Jackson, Edward G. Hanrick, J. W. Golledge; ALTERNATE: G. B. Gerald. (*PRESENT.)

1872: *Austin,* St. David's: *S. Mussina, *Geo. F. Moore, M. W. Glenn, D. W. C. Baker; ALTERNATES: Geo. Hancock, *Jas. H. Raymond, *T. S. Denny, S. G. Haynie. *Bastrop,* Calvary: D. W. Jones, *J. C. Higgins, J. H. Mathison, J. R. Nicholson. *Bryan,* St. Andrew's: *Dr. W. R. Johnston, Frank Clark, S. D. Conger, Mr. McCarty. *Brenham,* St. Peter's: J. E. Shephard, *J. T. McAdams, *P. G. Rucker, *A. M. Hughes; ALTERNATES: *J. T. Norris, H. McClurg, Wm. Thompson, P. Diller. *Corpus Christi,* Good Shepherd: Joseph Almond. *Calvert,* Epiphany: Mason Washington. *Dallas,* St. Matthew's: T. C. Jordan, W. L. Murphy, John W. Swindells, Thos. G. Walker. *El Paso,* St. Clements: A. J. Fountain, S. B. Newcomb, Sherman E. Slade, J. A. Tays. *Galveston,* Trinity: *Geo. E. Mann, C. R. Hughes, J. H. Hutchings, H. Rosenberg. *Houston,* Christ: *Wm. H. Elliot, *A. Ewing, W. D. Cleveland, Robt. Elgin. *Hempstead,* St. Bartholomew's: J. M. Coggin, John Thatcher. *Jefferson,* Christ: L. S. Rayfield, Thos. S. Maxey, James S. Grinnan, James Arbuckle. *La Grange,* St. James': L. Lindsay, *J. P. Ledbetter, W. H. Gayley, *B. Timmons. *Matagorda,* Christ: *W. B. Grimes, J. H. Cutler. *Navasota,* St. Paul's: *Edgar Demaret. *San Antonio,* St. Mark's: Hugh F. Young, T. B. Hunt, G. Maverick, J. Y. Dashiel; ALTERNATES: W. H. Young, J. F. Minter, Major Glenn, Mr. Parker. *Victoria,* Trinity: W. J. Neeley, F. R. Pridham, N. A. Thompson, F. E. Sibley. *Waco,* St. Paul's: *Geo. W. Jackson, *C. C. McCulloch, *A. Swartzwelder, *James W. Golledge. (*PRESENT.)

1873: *Austin,* St. David's: James H. Raymond, Edward Wise, *S. Mussina. *Bastrop,* Calvary: *James Nicholson. *Brenham,* St. Peter's: A. M. Hughes, T. W. Morris, William Thompson, J. T. Norris; ALTERNATES: J. E. Shepherd, T. G. Griffin, *L. P. Rucker, Jr., H. C. McClung. *Bryan,* St. Andrew's: *S. D. Conger, P. D. Page, *Frank Clarke, *B. F. Leman. *Calvert,* Epiphany: *J. W. Beard, Frank Maddox, M. D. Wynne. *Dallas,* St. Matthew's: W. C. Murphy, G. K. Merriweather, G. W. Baylor, *E. W. Baylor. *Galveston,* Trinity: *G. E. Mann, J. S. Grinnon, *A. H. Belo, Oliver Steele. *Hempstead,* St. Bartholomew's: John Thatcher, A. B. Coggshall, *C. L. Riddell. *Houston,* Christ: *W. J. Hutchins, R. M. Elgin, A. S. Richardson, Peter W. Gray. *Huntsville,* St. Stephen's: J. R. Burnett, F. D. Thornton; ALTERNATES: T. W. Markham, J. M. Smither. *Independence,* Grace: Louis Polk, C. W. Chase, M. A. Bryan, T. C. Clay; ALTERNATE: Felix Robertson. *Jefferson,* Christ: John A. Wayland, John W. Chambers, Frank M. Benson, *Henry D. Burrows; ALTERNATES: H. C. Hynson, Edward Thomas, W. L. Collins, George A. Wheatley. *Marshall,* Trinity: *Charles Brooke. *Matagorda,* Christ: *Jno. T. Ives, D. E. E. Braman. *Navasota,* St. Paul's: Edgar Demaret, Sr., E. L. Bridges, *S. B. Rucker, *Edward Hope; ALTERNATES: P. B. Perry, Edgar Demaret, Jr., William Goodrich, Clarence Bradley. *Paris,* Holy Cross: D. S. Hammond. *San Antonio,* St. Mark's: J. Y. Dashiell, C. C. Augur, Wm. H. Young, James Parker; ALTERNATES: Clifton Comley, J. F. Minter, J. Waelder, Joseph M. Bell. *Waco,* St. Paul's: *Geo. W. Jackson, *G. B. Gerald, *A. C. Swartzwelder, *E. A. Jones; ALTERNATES: C. C. McCullough, Joseph Hopkins, E. L. Herriott, E. G. Hanrick. (*PRESENT.)

1874: *Austin,* St. David's: *S. G. Haynie, D. W. C. Baker, Geo. Hancock, B. C. Ludlow; ALTERNATES: Eugene Bremond, M. D. Mather, A. G. McCrary, Jas. H. Raymond. *Bastrop,* Calvary: C. G. Garwood, W. M. Gibson, R. W. Miller, C. S. Millett. *Bellville,* St. Mary's: A. Chesley, N. Holland, Z. Hunt, E. R. Thomas. *Brazoria,* St. John's: John Adriance, Jas. L. Bates. *Brenham,* St. Peter's: H. L. McClung, T. W. Morris, J. T. Norris; ALTERNATE: *L. P. Rucker, Jr. *Bryan,* St. Andrew's: P. D. Page, Frank Clark, Wm. H. Flippen, B. F. Leman. *Dallas,* St. Matthew's: Geo. W. Baylor, G. K. Merriweather, *W. L. Murphy, Geo. W. Swindells. *Galveston,* Trinity: C. R. Hughes, *J. S. Grinnan, *Geo. E. Mann, H. Rosenberg. *Houston,* Christ: R. M. Elgin, Peter W. Gray, Wm. G. Hutchins, A. S. Richardson; ALTERNATES: *Leigh Hutchins, Wm. D. Cleveland, T. Robinson, S. C. Timpson. *Independence,* Grace: Charles Chase, Thos. C. Clay, Louis Polk, Felix Robertson; ALTERNATE: Louis Polk, Jr. *Jefferson,* Christ: *Thos. G. Anderson, *F. M. Burrows, *James Arbuckle, *Thos. S. Maxey. *Marshall,* Trinity: *Edw. Boyle, *Charles Brooke, *F. B. Sexton, A. T. Smith; ALTERNATES: E. J. Fry, Daniel Hawley. *Matagorda,* Christ: Wm. B. Grimes, Jas. H. Selkirk, Jno. F. Holt. *Navasota,* St. Paul's: E. L. Bridges, Wm. Goodrich, Edgar Demaret, Sr., S. B. Rucker; ALTERNATES: S. M. Jack, Edgar Demaret, Jr., B. F. Rucker. *Paris,* Holy Cross: F. W. Bassino; J. T. Berry, Jno. C. Easton. *San Antonio,* St. Mark's: *C. C. Augur, H. B. Adams, E. L. Beaumont, *J. Y. Dashiell; ALTERNATES: Elias Edmonds, *Geo. E. Glenn, C. Upson, W. H. Young. *Sherman,* St. Stephen's: *Emile Jouvenat, *C. P. Field, Robt. Kirkpatrick. *Tyler,* Christ: *J. H. Bowen, W. W. Grinnan, A. Kayser, H. M. Whitaker; ALTERNATES: Archibald F. Brown, Alfred Davis, W. C. Robards, W. A. Woldert. *Waco,* St. Paul: G. B. Gerald, E. L. Heriott, *Geo. W. Jackson, A. C. Swartzwelder; ALTERNATES: *J. W. Golledge, *E. G. Hanrick, E. A. Jones, C. C. McCulloch. (*PRESENT.)

INDEX

(Does not include names and places listed in the Appendices)